CLOSE VIEWINGS

CLOSE

An Anthology of New Film Criticism

VIEWINGS

Edited by Peter Lehman

The Florida State University Press / Tallahassee

An earlier version of chapter 3, "Visual Motifs in Rossellini's *Voyage to Italy*," appeared in *Roberto Rossellini*, by Peter Brunette (New York: Oxford University Press, 1987); copyright by Peter Brunette. An earlier version of chapter 18, "Fassbinder's *Ali: Fear Eats the Soul* and Spectatorship," by Judith Mayne, appeared in *New German Critique* 12 (1977). Both are reprinted by permission of the publishers.

Library of Congress Cataloging-in-Publication Data

Close viewings : an anthology of new film criticism / edited by Peter Lehman. p. cm.
ISBN 0-8130-0967-7 (alk. paper).—ISBN 0-8130-0991-X (pbk.: alk. paper)
1. Motion picture plays—History and criticism. 2. Motion pictures. I. Lehman, Peter.
PN1995.C543 1990 791.43'75—dc20 89-29034

UNIVERSITY PRESSES OF FLORIDA is the central agency for scholarly publishing of the State of Florida's university system, producing books selected for publication by the faculty editorial committees of Florida's nine public universities: Florida A&M University (Tallahassee), Florida Atlantic University (Boca Raton), Florida International University (Miami), Florida State University (Tallahassee), University of Central Florida (Orlando), University of Florida (Gainesville), University of North Florida (Jacksonville), University of South Florida (Tampa), University of West Florida (Pensacola).

ORDERS for books published by all member presses should be addressed to University Presses of Florida, 15 NW 15th Street, Gainesville, Florida 32603.

Printed in the U.S.A. on acid-free paper

In Memory of Beverle Houston

ACKNOWLEDGMENTS

This book owes its inception to a suggestion made by Evelyn Ehrlich, and I am grateful to her for it. Melanie Magisos made valuable comments about my contributions and, as always, I am indebted to her insight and her personal support. I would also like to thank Susan Hunt for preparing the index. Beverle Houston was to be one of the contributors to this book. She is deeply missed both as a treasured colleague and a contributor to this volume, and I hope that her rare spirit of breadth, support, and enthusiasm for people of varying interests can be felt throughout this anthology.

CONTRIBUTORS

CHARLES AFFRON is a professor of French at New York University. Among his publications are *Star Acting: Gish, Garbo, Davis, Cinema and Sentiment*, and *Fellini's "8 1/2."*

EDWARD BRANIGAN is associate professor and chair of the Film Studies Program at the University of California, Santa Barbara. He is the author of *Point of View in the Cinema* (1984) and is presently completing *Narrative Comprehension in Film*.

MIKE BUDD teaches film, television, cultural theory and cultural studies in the Department of Communication, Florida Atlantic University, Boca Raton.

DOLORES BURDICK is an Emerita Professor of French at Oakland University (Rochester, Michigan), where she taught French language and literature, women's studies, and film. She has published poetry and translations as well as scholarly articles on film and literature; she is presently working on a novel.

NOËL CARROLL is an associate professor in the Department of Philosophy and the Department of Theatre Arts at Cornell University. He is the author of *Philosophical Problems of Classical Film Theory* and *Mystifying Movies: Fads and Fallacies in Contemporary Film Theory*.

THOMAS CRIPPS, a professor of history at Morgan State University, has written *Slow Fade to Black: The Negro in American Film* and *Black Film as Genre*; the script for the prizewinning film *Black Shadows on a Silver Screen* (Post-Newsweek TV); many articles, among them winners of the Hammond Prize (1962) and the Charles Thomson Prize (1982); and *A Matter of Pride*, a 35-show series (Group W, 1971).

ROBERT EBERWEIN is chair of the English Department at Oakland University, where he teaches film theory, history and appreciation. His publications include *Film and the Dream Screen* (1984), *A Viewer's Guide to Film Theory and Criticism* (1979), and various articles. He is currently at work on a book about adaptations, remakes, and sequels.

LUCY FISCHER is director of the Film Studies Program at the University of Pittsburgh, where she is a professor of film and English. She is the author of *Shot/Countershot: Film Tradition and Women's Cinema* (1989) and *Jacques Tati: A Guide to References and Resources* (1983). She has published widely on film in such journals as *Cinema Journal, Quarterly Review of Film Studies, Film Quarterly, Wide Angle, Screen, Journal of Film and Video, Millennium Film Journal,* and *American Film*.

DONALD KIRIHARA is a lecturer in media arts at the University of Arizona. His essays on film history and criticism have appeared in *Journal of Film and Video, Film Reader,* and *Wide Angle*.

DOUGLAS GOMERY, author of *The Hollywood Studio System*, lives in Washington, D.C., and teaches at the University of Maryland. His late friend Cassie Moon provided invaluable help with the research for this essay.

MARY BETH HARALOVICH teaches film history in the Department of Media Arts at the University of Arizona. Her recent publications include a social historical analysis of *Father Knows Best* and *Leave It to Beaver* in *Quarterly Review of Film and Video* and "The Sexual Politics of *The Marriage of Maria Braun*" in *Wide Angle*.

PETER LEHMAN is a professor of film in the Department of Media Arts at the University of Arizona and coauthor (with William Luhr) of *Returning to the Scene: Blake Edwards*, vol. 2; *Blake Edwards*; and *Authorship and Narrative in the Cinema: Issues in Contemporary Aesthetics and Criticism* (with William Luhr). He is the president of the Society for Cinema Studies and was the founding editor of *Wide Angle*. His articles have appeared in *Journal of Film and Video, Genders, Wide Angle* and *Film Reader*.

WILLIAM LUHR is a professor of English at Saint Peter's College in Jersey City, New Jersey. His most recent book is *Returning to the Scene: Blake Ed-*

wards, vol. 2 (1989, with Peter Lehman). He is also the author of *Raymond Chandler and Film* (1982), *Blake Edwards* (1981, with Peter Lehman), and *Authorship and Narrative in the Cinema: Issues in Contemporary Aesthetics and Criticism* (1977, with Peter Lehman), and the editor of *World Cinema Since 1945* (1987). He is currently working on a biography of Blake Edwards.

JUDITH MAYNE teaches in the Department of French and Italian and the Center for Women's Studies at Ohio State University. She is the author of *Private Novels, Public Films* (1988), *Kino and the Woman Question: Feminism and Soviet Silent Film* (1989), and *The Woman at the Keyhole* (forthcoming).

PATRICIA MELLENCAMP is an associate professor in the Department of Art History at the University of Wisconsin, Milwaukee. She has published many essays on film and video in *Screen, Afterimage,* and *Discourse*. She is the author of *Indiscretions: Avant-Garde Film, Video, and Feminism* and the editor of *Logics of Television: Essays in Cultural Criticism*.

RUSSELL MERRITT has taught at the University of California–Berkeley and the University of Wisconsin–Madison. His articles have appeared in *Film, Comment, Wide Angle,* and *Cinema Journal.*

ROBERT T. SELF is a professor of English and the director of Freshman English at Northern Illinois University. He has published research on American literature and film in *American Quarterly, Film Criticism, Literature/Film Quarterly, Wide Angle,* and *Cinema Journal*. He is the author of *Barrett Wendell* and the editor of *Literature, Society, and Politics: Collected Essays of Barrett Wendell*. His current project focuses on the narrative dimensions of the films of Robert Altman.

DIANE WALDMAN is an associate professor in the Department of Mass Communications at the University of Denver, where she also teaches in the Women's Studies Program. She has published numerous articles on film and social history and feminist analysis in such journals as *New German Critique, Camera Obscura, Wide Angle,* and *Cinema Journal*. She has also written on the popularization of psychoanalysis in Hollywood films of the 1940s.

JANET WALKER is a visiting assistant professor of film studies at the University of California, Santa Barbara. She has published in such journals as *Wide Angle* and *Camera Obscura*, and is currently revising her study of the sociocultural relations between women and psychiatry and their representation in Hollywood films.

CHARLES WOLFE teaches in the Film Studies Program at the University of California, Santa Barbara. He is the author of *Frank Capra: A Guide to References and Resources* (1987) and the editor of *Meet John Doe* (1989).

CONTENTS

Part 1

FORMAL ANALYSIS

INTRODUCTION

Peter Lehman

A cynic once remarked that the term "close reading" implies that there is a proper critical distance from which to interpret a film—one can, as it were, be too close to it or too far away from it. This idea is reminiscent of the notorious claim that there is an ideal position in an auditorium from which to view a movie; one can literally sit too close or too far away from the screen. The term "close" has a more positive and productive sense, however, which is not prescriptive, restrictive, or normative. That is the sense in which the word is used in this book's title and in which it is demonstrated by these essays. Regardless of what interests us in a film, we should be careful to support the significance we attribute to it with a grasp of the film and not to generalize too quickly. This does not mean that there is a proper amount of textual detail that we should cite or that we should stop asking extratextual questions or even that the two activities are distinct. Rather, it implies that all critical activities will be well served by careful attention to textual features. We should not, in other words, talk about films as if they were simple and obvious things to which we need give only a general response.

Nearly all of the essays in this book appear for the first time, although a few are revisions of previously published material. The book is divided into two sections: the first emphasizes formal analysis and the second, cultural analysis. The division is pedagogical and does not imply either a separation or a hierarchy. An analysis of space, for example, can be related both to the economic system that governs the production of texts that adhere to a given system of spatial representation and to the consequences of representing men and women differently within such a system. Either enterprise will be doomed, however, if we do not first understand how space is represented in cinema. For this reason the essays on formal analysis in this book are presented first.

In part one the essayists analyze narrative structure and character, visual motifs, space, color, and sound. William Luhr discusses narrative structure and characterization in *The Maltese Falcon*, a classical Hollywood text that unambiguously resolves both a crime plot in the public sphere and a romantic plot in the private sphere. Dolores Burdick analyzes *Persona*, a modern European art cinema text fraught with ambiguity that cannot be simply clarified and that makes different demands upon its audience than the Hollywood film does. The two analyses indicate the vastly differing assumptions about the nature of character, plot, and theme at work within the two styles of filmmaking. In a related way, Peter Brunette shows how carefully structured, recurring images of cars, landscapes, and buildings contribute to the thematic development of *Voyage to Italy*, a film that does not explain much of its visual imagery. Mary Beth Haralovich describes some of the assumptions about color operative in traditional Hollywood films and shows how those assumptions can be challenged by a melodrama like *All That Heaven Allows* that departs from realist color convention. Edward Branigan details Ozu's representation of space in *Equinox Flower*, sharply contrasting that Japanese film's use of shot scale (i.e., establishing shots, long shots, medium shots, etc.), editing, and space with the Hollywood classical paradigm, which he also clearly illustrates. Cutting patterns and camera positions are the subjects of Charles Affron's essay on *8 1/2*, a film in which space is structured by the central character's dilemma. In his essay on *The General*, Noël Carroll examines the rationale behind Buster Keaton's extensive use of long shots in the film and finds inadequate such common explanations as the argument that the shots lend authenticity to the gags. Robert Self discusses sound in *MASH*, a film that breaks the usual unified relationship between image and sound and calls attention to the sound track as a separate component. Donald Kirihara treats the use of sound in *Les Vacances de Monsieur Hulot* and shows how the film's rich sound track challenges viewers used to the dominance of informational dialogue and plausible sounds. Although Altman's film was made in Hollywood and Tati's in France, both depart significantly from the common practices of Hollywood and the European art cinema.

I hope that the diversity of films represented illustrates the various ways in which the formal components of film can be constructed. Obviously, no limited selection can be comprehensive. All the contributors have therefore supplied additional bibliographies on both their method of analysis and further readings not cited in the text. These bibliographies are presented separately in the belief that this will help readers pursue specific interests arising from the individual chapters.

1

TRACKING *THE MALTESE FALCON*: CLASSICAL HOLLYWOOD NARRATION AND SAM SPADE

William Luhr

The Maltese Falcon is often cited as a milestone film. Its unexpected success not only solidly launched John Huston's career as a director and provided a major stepping stone in Humphrey Bogart's climb from contract player to major star but it also, with *Citizen Kane* in the same year (1941), became a progenitor of *film noir*. It is frequently shown in revival houses and on television but despite its popularity has seldom attracted detailed scholarly attention. As a partial corrective, this essay explores aspects of the film's narrative organization and indicates useful areas for further investigation.

The Maltese Falcon was made by Warner Brothers during the peak period of the production mode known as the studio system. That system used the narrative paradigm within which this film operates, and since that paradigm is the dominant one in fiction film production, it is useful here to outline some of its presumptions and techniques.

Classical Hollywood narration became regularized around the time of World War I, is still operative, and functions in distinctly different ways from other narrative modes, such as the international art cinema and many avant-garde cinemas.[1] It focuses upon an individual or small group of individuals who early on encounter discrete and specific goals that are either clearly attained or clearly unattained by the film's end. The goals tend to exist in two spheres, and their pursuit is developed along parallel and often interdependent plot lines. One sphere is private, generally a heterosexual romance; the second is public—a career advance, the obliteration of an enemy, a mission, a discovery, and the like. In *The Maltese Falcon*, for example, Samuel Spade explores a romance with Brigid O'Shaughnessy as well as the case of the Maltese Falcon, and the two are interrelated. He resolves both in separate scenes at the film's end.

Causality provides the prime unifying principle in classical narration. Plot construction tends to be linear, one scene clearly leading to the next. The major hermeneutics raised near the beginning of the film (Will Shane, in *Shane*, bring peace to the valley? Will Marty, in *Marty*, find true love?) are developed, complicated, and then neatly resolved by the film's ending. This does not mean that classical narration requires a happy ending; a definitive failure to attain a goal is as clear a resolution as a success, but the spectator should know the outcome one way or the other.

A distinction between the notions of story and plot is useful here. Plot is the sequence of events as presented in the film whereas story is the causal/chronological sequence of events as they theoretically would have occurred in actuality. The plot may begin near the end of the story sequence as a main character nears death and then backtrack to reveal the events that led up to this point, as in *Double Indemnity* or *Citizen Kane*. A story sequence for a film that runs 1–2–3–4–5 may be presented to the viewer as plot sequence 4–1–3–2–5, with the reshuffled event structure indicating part of the film's strategy for evoking spectator response. Classical narration often uses its plot to generate confusion, but it invariably clears up all such confusion by the end. It seldom allows for ambiguous presentation of story elements, something that commonly occurs in the international art cinema in films such as *Persona*.

The spatial, temporal, and sonic techniques of classical narration reinforce this story clarity. The spaces that are shown and the sounds that are heard are

1. Much of the best work on classical Hollywood narration appears in David Bordwell, *Narration in the Fiction Film* (Madison: University of Wisconsin Press, 1985) and David Bordwell, Janet Staiger, and Kristin Thompson, *The Classical Hollywood Cinema: Film Style and Mode of Production to 1960* (New York: Columbia University Press, 1985). My summary here draws significantly upon the first book, particularly chapters 4, 5, and 9.

subordinated to the logic of the narrative. We seldom see space, for example, that we cannot situate in relation to the film's characters. A character may be seen in the space or may be looking at it, and the linkage is generally quite clear. Objects are similarly subordinated to narrative causality. In differentiating the narrative strategies of Ozu from those of the classical paradigm, Kristin Thompson and David Bordwell use *The Maltese Falcon* to underline precisely this point: "John Huston wouldn't think of cutting away from Sam Spade and Brigid O'Shaughnessey [*sic*] to a shot of the coat-rack in the corner of the office unless the hats on it had some significance (e.g., in the unravelling of the enigma). Yet in *There Was a Father*, Ozu does cut to a coatrack to begin a sequence in a *go*-parlor, without ever drawing the hats or the space of the rack into the narrative action" (1976, 46).

In classical narration the camera pretends to be an invisible and ideal observer of preexistent events. We get the best views, cued by codes of lighting, framing, and movement, of the most significant actions necessary to further the plot. We see punches thrown and, from a different perspective, received; dialogue spoken and responded to; rockets fired and, miles away but seconds later, hitting their target. The events are presented as having their own integrity and not, as in some Godard films, as being developed with an intimate and formative relationship to the filmmaking apparatus. We do not see camera equipment in the rear of the shot or reflected in mirrors, and actors do not acknowledge the camera's presence. The process of production is concealed; the camera is omnipresent. The individual shots are stitched together according to the highly coded principles of classic continuity editing that emphasize clarity of action and story continuity according to realist norms.

Classical narration has not only changed over time but it also incorporates a wide range of options. It includes a number of genres whose norms of realism vary. A character in a comedy or musical may much more directly acknowledge the camera's presence or defy gravity than one in an historical epic; character options and motivations may be much different in a western than in a detective film.

As a mystery, *The Maltese Falcon* works to confuse the viewer in ways that films in other genres, such as war films or romances, do not. Virtually all classical narrative tries to keep the viewer guessing as to what will happen next, but the mystery foregrounds this and also makes the viewer wonder what has happened in the past and even question the significance of what is happening right now. The project of the film's plot, as well as of the detective, is to uncover its story, and the plot reveals story information in often confusing and apparently contradictory ways. Little can be taken at face value when it appears, although all major story and plot elements become retrospectively consistent at the film's end.

The plot of *The Maltese Falcon* is linear and follows the involvement of the private detective Samuel Spade (Humphrey Bogart) with Brigid O'Shaughnessy (Mary Astor) and the case of the Maltese Falcon. It limits itself primarily to his point of view; with minor exceptions, new information appears as he learns it and events progress according to his participation in them. The film begins when O'Shaughnessy enters his office, moves chronologically forward as he becomes more deeply involved with her and with the complexities of the case (fig. 1–1), and ends when he turns her over to the police.

Spade must constantly process, question, and reformulate the often deceptive information he receives, and the sinister characters he encounters are developed with reference to deviations from cultural norms only hinted at in

Figure 1-1. (Figures 1-1 through 1-11, copyright 1941 by Warner Brothers Pictures, Inc.; renewed 1969 by United Artists Television, Inc.)

the dialogue. His triumph over mystery and danger lies at the center of the film. The ways in which the director, John Huston, organizes formal motifs, explores narrative alternatives and manipulations, and develops subtextual implications of foreignness and deviant sexuality to give that mystery and danger its specificity demonstrate the complexity and aesthetic value of *The Maltese Falcon.*

Early in the film we see a night shot of a half-open window with a slowly fluttering curtain before it. A telephone and a clock sit on a night table in the front of the frame. The phone rings. A hand reaches in from the right and pulls the telephone out of frame. The camera does not move. On the sound track, Spade's voice responds as he learns that his partner, Miles Archer (Jerome Cowan), has been killed. His hand returns the telephone into the frame. Only when the room light goes on do we see Spade's head, in silhouette, enter the frame as the camera moves slightly back. The curtain still flutters (fig. 1–2).

Spade leaves the apartment to view the scene of Archer's murder. When he returns, two police detectives arrive to tell him of another murder, that of Floyd Thursby, the man Archer had been following. When Detective Polhaus (Ward Bond) describes how Thursby was killed ("He was shot in the back four times with a .44 or .45 from across the street") Polhaus is framed by the same window, with the same fluttering curtain. That window and curtain become visual motifs increasingly associated with sinister events in and influences upon Spade's life.

Although Brigid O'Shaughnessy had first approached Spade concerning Thursby, Archer took the case because he was attracted to her. This leads to

Figure 1-2.

his death, which provides the film's first victim of O'Shaughnessy's relentless duplicity. She had originally given her name as "Wonderly" along with a false story designed to get Spade to take the case. When she contacts him after the two killings, she is living under the name "Leblanc." Her names have changed, and her stories have changed, each change giving Spade a different perception of the situation. Although she has not told him the truth and repeatedly endangers him, she throws herself on his mercy, saying she has no one to turn to. She says she has no money and coyly asks, "What can I buy you with?" He kisses her.

When Spade first brings her to his apartment, she continues to deceive and coyly tantalize him. He catches her in her lies and she reclines on his sofa, saying she is tired of lying, of not knowing what is the truth and what is not. Clearly, part of Spade's attraction to her lies in the very blatancy of her evil, in the seductive danger she embodies. When she reclines, Spade's fluttering curtains are directly behind her, and he bends over to kiss her. Huston cuts to a close shot of her (fig. 1–3), then Spade's head descends into the frame (fig. 1–4). Suddenly he stops and looks at the curtains (fig. 1–5). The camera moves toward and into them (fig. 1–6), and we see through an opening at the center a sinister-looking man in the street below, watching (fig. 1–7).

This shot encapsulates major motifs in the film. The curtains have become associated with the dangers that surround Spade's involvement in the case; they evoke the often malignant world that so often intrudes upon him. He is in this scene physically closer to the curtains than at any other time in the film. The man outside is a murderer who has already killed at least one character and will kill more. At this point Spade does not know who this man is or why he is there, but he knows he is dangerous. Furthermore, at this point the danger comes not only from outside the curtains, as it did in the earlier instances, but also from inside them. O'Shaughnessy is within the apartment. She is sexually desirable and available to Spade. As with the man outside, Spade knows little about her, but he knows that she too is dangerous.

The narrative progression of this film is developed largely around befuddlement, around the trying out and discarding of one potential narrative linkage for another. Brigid O'Shaughnessy first came to Spade with a story about how Floyd Thursby ran off with her sister. She asked Archer to follow Thursby. Archer was killed and Thursby was killed and there was no sister. Spade had to return to square one. A bizarre, dandified foreigner, Joel Cairo (Peter Lorre), came to Spade's office and demanded the "black bird." Soon, both Cairo and O'Shaughnessy are terrified to learn that Gutman, "The Fat Man" (Sidney Greenstreet), is in town, and Spade learns that all seek the

Figure 1-3.

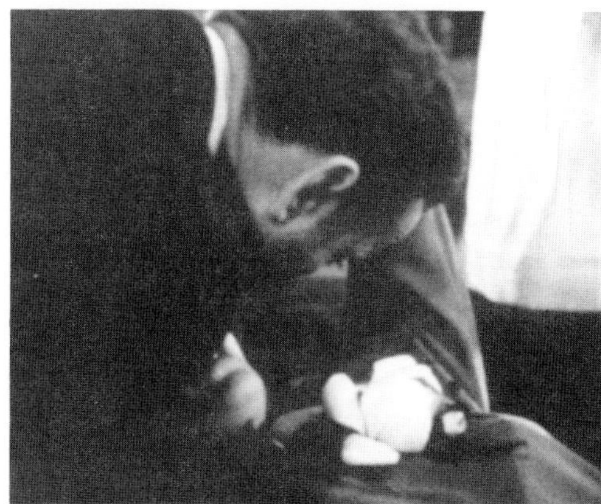
Figure 1-4.

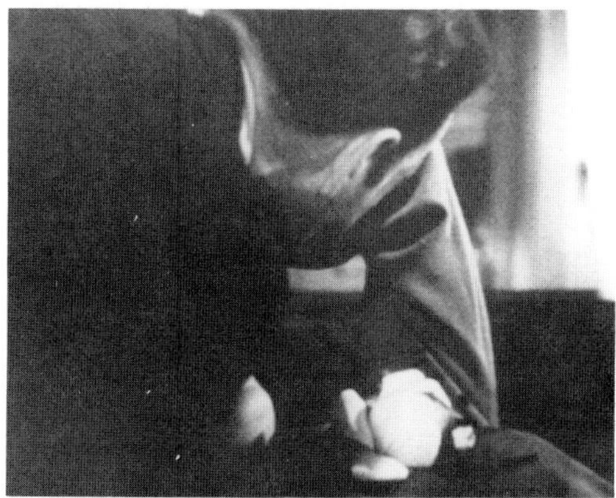
Figure 1-5.

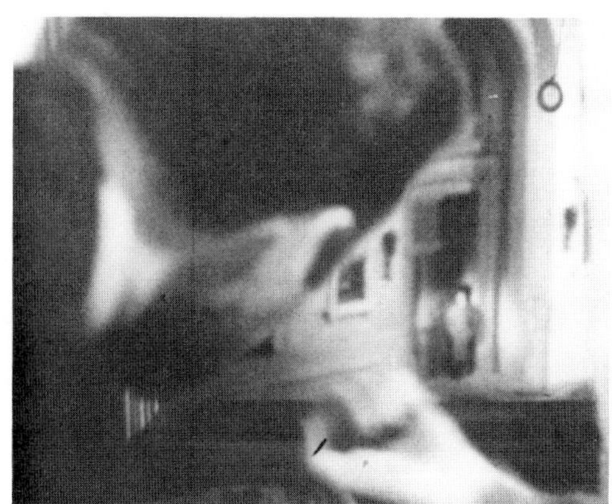
Figure 1-6.

Figure 1-7.

"bird," the fabled Maltese Falcon. From Brigid O'Shaughnessy's first story, apparent truths and continuities are replaced by other apparent truths and continuities: nothing is certain.

At the center of all of this is Samuel Spade, who is particularly suited to function in such an environment. One of his basic characteristics is a remarkable analytical intelligence. When O'Shaughnessy first comes to him, she gives him a complicated story. He says little; he watches. When Archer arrives, however, Spade fires off an elaborate and detailed summary of what has been said, showing that he had missed nothing, retained everything, and plotted out a course of action. When he visits the scene of Archer's death he says little, simply looking around for a few moments; but then he quickly tells the police precisely how the murder took place. Many shots in the film simply show him watching, taking it all in, with little indication of his response. The film carefully develops in the viewer the sense that Spade understands virtually everything in complex ways (fig. 1–8).

A reinforcing instance occurs the day after the first two killings when Spade goes to O'Shaughnessy's rooms. She admits that her initial story was false. He shows neither surprise nor annoyance but tells her that neither he

Figure 1-8.

nor Archer believed her story; what they did believe was the two hundred dollars she paid them. He says that they knew the money was more than she would have given had she been telling the truth, and they considered it "enough more" to make her lie all right with them. In going over whether or not she bears responsibility for Archer's death, he tells her no—"Of course you lied to us about your sister and all that, but that didn't count. We didn't believe you." This gives a further insight into what he knew but did not reveal the day before and indicates very untraditional notions of truth, truthfulness, and moral responsibility.

She throws herself on his mercy. She admits that she has been "bad," says she is all alone and in danger, and begs to be allowed to rely on his strength. Utterly abject, she pleads, "Help me." She is appalled to find him not melting with compassion but smirking at her. He responds not to the abject situation she has described but rather critiques her performance in creating it. He says, "You won't need much of anybody's help. You're good. It's chiefly your eyes, I think, and that throb you get in your voice when you say things like, 'Be generous, Mr. Spade.' " In another scene in her room, after asking her a difficult question, he smiles and says, "You're not going to go around the room straightening things and poking the fire again, are you?", indicating his awareness of her ploys of nervous agitation, of diverting attention, of clever deception.

Spade is himself continually performing. In Gutman's rooms, dissatisfied at the slow pace of the negotiations, he loses control of himself, explodes, demands a deadline for a deal, and smashes a glass as he rages out of the room. Huston cuts to a long shot of him walking down a hallway toward the camera. He first appears to be storming, in a rage, but as he gets closer to the camera it is obvious that he is smiling. It has all been an act.

When summoned before the district attorney, he apparently becomes enraged at the infringement on his rights and launches into a seemingly deeply felt tirade against the D.A.'s methods. He suddenly stops, looks at the stenographer, and asks, "You getting all this right, son, or am I going too fast for you?" When the stenographer says he is getting it, Spade says, "Good work," switches back to his tone of outrage, and continues the tirade. Once more he shows himself to be in command of and carefully orchestrating what initially appears to be a spontaneous emotional outburst.

Much of the film's forward narrative drive revolves around Spade's aggressive search for the truth and his processing of and acting upon each new piece of information he receives. He shows a strong awareness of impediments in his way, of people's ability to lie, both in the information they give and in their manner. Not only can he see through many of the deceptions of others but he is also himself able to link and interpret information so as to give the appearance of truth. When he gathers O'Shaughnessy and Cairo in his apartment for the first time, the police arrive and demand entrance. Spade refuses. Suddenly they hear a scream and a crash, and they enter. Cairo's face is bloodied and O'Shaughnessy is holding a gun on him. As the police prepare to arrest them all, Spade smiles and says, "Oh don't be in a hurry, boys, everything can be explained." He then proceeds to concoct a story to "explain" the situation in a way that will divert the police from arresting them and also mollify the terrified Cairo. But no sooner has he finished with this story than he tells the police that both the violent incident and the story were jokes played upon them. He proceeds to tell an entirely different story using the same basic information but giving an entirely different narrative interpretation to the events. At the end of the second story, he provokes one of the police into hitting him, making the detective vulnerable to brutality charges should the incident become public. Finally the police leave and no one is arrested. O'Shaughnessy looks at Spade in astonishment and admiration and says, "You're absolutely the wildest, most unpredictable person I've ever known." He has, reflecting the narrative tactics of the film, given two entirely different and reasonably logical versions, both false, of a simple event. The next day he encounters the exhausted and suspicious Cairo, who tries to break off contact with Spade after telling him that he always has a smooth explanation for everything. Spade defends himself by saying that it worked and arrogantly asks, "What do you want me to do, learn to stutter?"

When the Falcon is delivered to his office by a dying man, Spade leaves with the statuette and advises his secretary to tell the police everything as it happened, only to leave out the arrival of the statuette and to say that he, and not she, received a call from O'Shaughnessy. We see him making very slight alterations in the truth to create a new truth—not true, but coherent enough to convince. The film is comprised of dozens of these small narratives and narrative adjustments.

One of Spade's prime antagonists is Gutman (fig. 1–9), whose activities also point to the existence of different realms of truth. When he first appears, approximately halfway through the film, he does not lie about his goals. He quickly clears up a number of cryptic references to the "black bird" by telling Spade the history of the coveted Maltese Falcon. He tells Spade, "These are facts, historical facts. Not schoolbook history, not Mr. Wells's history, but history nevertheless." He then gives the story, largely one of piracy and murder, of the Falcon. Here he provides not a false reorganization of present information, but facts not recorded in traditional histories. He

Figure 1-9.

gives an alternate truth—not a false one as those presented by O'Shaughnessy and Spade—but a repressed one associated with evil. He has devoted his life to it.

The trail of evil that the film explores comes mainly from the search for the Maltese Falcon—originally gold and bedecked with jewels but later covered with black enamel for concealment. The one that ultimately appears turns out to be a copy—an enamel-coated, lead statuette. Like most of the "truths" in the film, this is also a chimera; it is constructed to convince but is not real.

It is important that the statue is Maltese—foreign—because the notion of foreignness is central to the presentation of evil in the film. The film is set entirely in San Francisco and carefully associates things evil with things different from the position that Spade occupies—that of an American, heterosexual, Anglo-Saxon male. The notion of foreignness is introduced early on. O'Shaughnessy first claims Thursby had a wife and three children "in England." Spade instantly recognizes the gun that killed Archer as British. O'Shaughnessy later admits that she met Thursby, a killer, in "the Orient," and her clothes come from Hong Kong.

Before we even see Joel Cairo, Effie (Spade's secretary, played by Lee Patrick) hands Spade Cairo's scented card and with a knowing smirk says, "Gardenia," implying effeminacy. This introduces another aspect of foreignness, that of deviant sexuality. Cairo (fig. 1–10) is of unspecified origin, although he has at least three passports, and his name, if it is his, might suggest that he is Egyptian. But he is clearly coded as foreign, not American. The film also strongly implies that he is homosexual as perceived by codes of the 1940s: his effeminacy, dandification, "feminine" hysteria, at times mothering affection for Wilmer (Elisha Cook, Jr.), and apparent sexual rivalry with O'Shaughnessy over "that boy in Istanbul" all point to deviations from contemporary norms.

Associations of homosexuality are also given to Wilmer, Gutman's bodyguard and hired killer. While he shares none of Cairo's effeminate qualities and is in fact morosely pugnacious, he is constantly referred to as the "boy," and Spade refers to him as a "gunsel"—a term meaning gunman, but also meaning a boy used in pederasty. When Spade knocks him out near the end of the film, we see him unconscious on a sofa in a very curious shot that em-

Figure 1-10.

phasizes his groin (fig. 1–11). Nothing is overt, but associations of homosexuality, of sexual otherness, are implied.

Gutman's nationality is not given, but he sounds and appears British. He shows a profound attraction to the Falcon, whose history is one of evil and betrayal in foreign places. His most recent encounter with it took place in Istanbul, where he also dealt with Cairo and O'Shaughnessy. When the false Falcon arrives, it has come from Hong Kong. When Gutman learns it is false, he prepares to return to Istanbul.

Gutman's sexuality is questionable. He shows no interest in women. Wilmer and Cairo seem fiercely devoted to him. But his real obsession appears to be a fetishistic one with the Maltese Falcon. When Spade demands he betray Wilmer in order to get the Falcon, Gutman does so. By way of apology he tells Wilmer, "I couldn't be fonder of you if you were my own son but, well, if you lose a son, it's possible to get another. There's only one Maltese Falcon. When you're young you simply don't understand these things." When what he thinks is the Falcon arrives, he unwraps it in an almost orgiastic ecstasy.

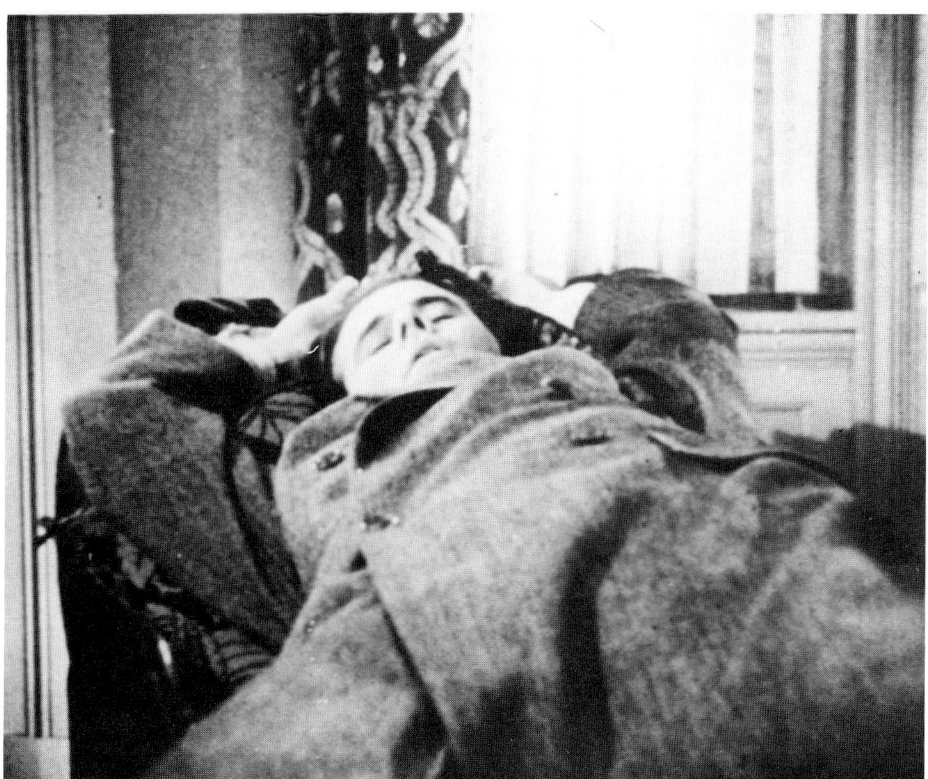

Figure 1-11.

The film opens with a number of shots of San Francisco. It and Spade become established as norms against which all else is measured. Virtually all danger and evil come from "somewhere else." The most immoral thing we see Spade involved in is heterosexual excess; he has been sleeping with Archer's wife. And Archer is killed largely as a result of his heterosexual lust for O'Shaughnessy. The film ends as Spade sends O'Shaughnessy off to jail for Archer's murder, a decision influenced by her sexual promiscuity. He knows she was Thursby's mistress and says, "I won't walk in Thursby's and I don't know how many other footsteps."

In many ways the film has two endings and two narratives cleverly blended. It seems to end after the Falcon is discovered to be false and Gutman and Cairo prepare to return to Istanbul to continue the hunt. Spade calls the police and reports them. All seems tied up. He has dealt definitively with the business of the Falcon, and he has saved O'Shaughnessy from the sinister crew, so the public and private spheres of the story seem resolved; but suddenly he turns on O'Shaughnessy and accuses her of Archer's murder. To this point it has seemed apparent that Thursby killed Archer, and all seem to accept this. Archer was following Thursby and was killed with Thursby's gun. Spade now shows O'Shaughnessy why this could not have happened, and she admits her guilt.

Now it is clear that what had first appeared to be the film's resolution was only a partial resolution. It is also apparent here that the story of O'Shaughnessy has very little to do with the story of the Maltese Falcon. It frames that story. That story really begins when Cairo enters Spade's office and ends when the statuette is found to be false. Within that story, O'Shaughnessy is little more than a pawn, an ally of Thursby, whom we never see. Even her intense sexual desirability serves her little in that story, since that is the story of deviant sexuality, of Gutman's fetishistic obsession and his possibly homosexual acolytes in exotic, foreign places.

In San Francisco, however, her sexuality serves her much better, and the framing story, the one opening and closing the film, is of her and Spade. It is also one of heterosexual excess in which Spade is complicit. Spade desires her; so does Archer. She kills Archer to implicate her lover, Thursby. Spade is implicated in the killing because the police know he has been sleeping with Archer's wife, who was also suspiciously absent from her home on the night her husband was killed. Archer's wife at times implicates Spade, perhaps because Spade has lost interest in her after he has met O'Shaughnessy.

When Spade tells O'Shaughnessy he is going to turn her in to the police, he sits in his apartment with a sickened, dazed look on his face. It is the only time in the film that he appears to be genuinely speaking from his heart. He explains his confusion and his vestigial morality and the reasons he must turn her in. It is part of the only daylight sequence in his apartment, and he sits not in front of the curtains in the window but in front of their prominent shadow on the wall.

At this point, the Maltese Falcon has become irrelevant to the story, which now concerns only Spade, O'Shaughnessy, Archer, and Thursby. The curtains had earlier been significant in shots related to scenes of O'Shaughnessy's evil—when Spade learned of Archer's death, when Polhaus described Thursby's death, and when Spade was about to kiss O'Shaughnessy and paused as he spotted Wilmer through the curtains. At that point it appeared that Wilmer was the danger; we now know that in fact O'Shaughnessy was more dangerous. Her desirability masked her evil and almost entrapped Spade. It is likely that that kiss we never saw was only interrupted, not prevented by the sight through the curtains. The next time we see the two together they are much less formal, more affectionate; they call each other "Darling" and "Angel," and O'Shaughnessy tells Spade her apartment had been searched that morning, indicating that she may have spent the night with Spade. Given the censorship codes of the time, these subtextual hints provide a strong indication that the two have slept together, thus making Spade more vulnerable to her machinations.

From that point to the final scene in Spade's apartment the curtains do not serve a significant formal function. Then, suddenly, when the Falcon story is cleared away, they again become central. O'Shaughnessy sits more or less in front of them, but most important, their shadow now frames Spade in daylight. Now that Spade understands everything they no longer appear ominous, but they serve as a muted reference to the dangers Spade encountered and tamed.

WORKS CITED

Thompson, Kristin, and David Bordwell. 1976. "Space and Narrative in the Films of Ozu." *Screen* 17 (Summer): 46.

BIBLIOGRAPHY

The Maltese Falcon

Anobile, Richard J., ed. *The Maltese Falcon*. New York: Universe, 1974.

Behlmer, Rudy. *America's Favorite Movies: Behind the Scenes*. New York: Frederick Ungar Publishing Co., 1982, 135–53.

Naremore, James. "John Huston and *The Maltese Falcon*." *Literature/Film Quarterly* (July 1973): 239–49.

Andrew, Dudley. *Concepts in Film Theory*. New York: Oxford University Press, 1984, 75–95.

Barthes, Roland. *S/Z: An Essay*. Translated by Richard Miller. New York: Hill and Wang, 1974.

Bordwell, David. *Narration in the Fiction Film*. Madison: University of Wisconsin Press, 1985.

Bordwell, David, Janet Staiger, and Kristin Thompson. *The Classical Hollywood Cinema: Film Style and Mode of Production to 1960*. New York: Columbia University Press, 1985.

Branigan, Edward. *Point of View in the Cinema: A Theory of Narration and Subjectivity in Classical Film*. New York: Mouton, 1984.

Browne, Nick. *The Rhetoric of Filmic Narration*. Ann Arbor: UMI Research Press, 1982.

Burch, Noël. *Theory of Film Practice*. New York: Praeger, 1973.

Chatman, Seymour. *Story and Discourse: Narrative Structure in Fiction and Film*. Ithaca: Cornell University Press, 1978.

Cohen, Keith. *Film and Fiction: The Dynamics of Exchange*. New Haven: Yale University Press, 1979.

Genette, Gerard. *Narrative Discourse: An Essay in Method*. Translated by Jane E. Lewin. Ithaca: Cornell University Press, 1980.

Heath, Stephen. *Questions of Cinema*. Bloomington: Indiana University Press, 1981.

Luhr, William, and Peter Lehman. *Authorship and Narrative in the Cinema*. New York: G. P. Putnam's Sons, 1977.

Metz, Christian. *Film Language*. Translated by Michael Taylor. New York: Oxford University Press, 1974.

Scholes, Robert, and Robert Kellogg. *The Nature of Narrative*. New York: Oxford University Press, 1966.

Special thanks to Bill Knapp of the Instructional Resources Center of St. Peter's College for help with the stills used in this chapter.

A film for me begins with something very vague. . . . a brightly colored thread sticking out of the dark sack of the unconscious. If I begin to wind up this thread, . . . a complete film will emerge.
—Ingmar Bergman[1]

2

PERSONA: FACING THE MIRROR TOGETHER

Dolores Burdick

By *reversing* Bergman's process—by *undoing* the skein of his film—one ends up with any number of glowing threads leading back to cast light on the psyche of the reader. To anatomize the film's structure is already to interpret; different readers will define the structure in different ways, depending upon where they see a center, where they perceive a break.[2]

Persona begins without a moment of "warm-up": there is no time to get settled in your seat and relax into the credits. The first several minutes are taken up with a strange series of images, which on a first viewing seem to have an almost random order. The very first images have to do with the facts and history of cinema itself. The first frames, in fact, show the arc light of a projector like the one that is projecting the film we are actually seeing; then

1. Quoted in the introduction to *Four Screenplays of Ingmar Bergman*, trans. Lars Malmstrom and David Kushner (New York, 1960), xv.

2. This problem of segmentation has been theorized most fully by Christian Metz in books such as *Film Language: A Semiotics of the Cinema* (New York, 1974) and *Language and Cinema* (The Hague, 1974).

there are shots of film going through that projector, as well as countdown numbers such as we are used to seeing on a reel of film. For a few moments we may not even be sure we are watching *Persona*; the opening shots refer to film-as-such rather than telling any story at all.

But after a minute we see ominous natural objects: a spider, a sheared and gutted animal, and then a nail being pounded through a hand. Some trees, the spikes of an iron fence. The landscape of an old man's face. At last—a place we can almost identify: this may be a morgue. An old woman's head is shot from its own plane while it hangs downward from one end of a table; suddenly the eyes fly open, looking directly at us. On the sound track water is dripping and footsteps pass; we see a young boy on a table like the ones the old people lie on; he is trying to go to sleep. Then, very unnervingly, he turns and faces us directly, as though trying to make us out as his viewers. This gesture reminds us of the old woman's eyes that looked at us a minute or so earlier, and it prepares us for other moments in the film when a character will "step over the proscenium" to address us in that direct, disquieting way.

When characters in a serious play suddenly turn to the audience, as in Brecht, Anouilh, or Pirandello, the entire fabric of illusion is called into question. Are we watching the play or are we part of it? When a novel like Camus' *The Fall* is written as a dialogue one voice of which is suppressed, we must imagine that we ourselves are furnishing the missing lines. Twentieth-century fiction and film often generate this kind of rupture in our security as onlookers, voyeurs, mere observers of what is going on. The work has broken out of profile; it is demanding to be seen in the round.

To look directly into the camera lens is to invade the space reserved for the film audience. If the little boy can look at us directly during this prologue, then the film itself may try to look at us directly rather than play itself out for our passive reception. Already, this early in the film, we have the embryo of a theme: look at me; look at yourself looking at me.

But the little boy does something even more startling: not only does he look out at us, but he actually tries to touch us. His hand goes toward the camera lens. Then we are given a reverse shot from behind the child, and we see him trying to touch the screen on which we are seeing him and through which he just tried to touch us. His hand makes wide, tentative circles on the screen as though he were conjuring, summoning, *and* trying to make contact with the two women's faces that gradually appear and disappear, melting into each other, fading, the eyes both open and closed. For me, this is one of the most important images in the prologue. This is Bergman's cinematic poetry at its best, and if the rest of the prologue works by way of montage (i.e., emerging through juxtaposition of shots), this is the one place where it works by way of *mise en scène* (i.e., movement within the frame, composition). The little boy can be seen as Bergman's image of the child *and* the artist in him; groping to both find *and* create the mother; and by extension as an image of the male yearning to touch, to know, to magnify, to "create" Woman, the obscure object of male desire, the "soul," as Bergman says, the very core of the Romantic paradox of mystery and refuge.

This image of child/man/artist reaching out for mother and woman from the morgue, a place of death, immediately triggers a violent change of rhythm: the credits begin. They are very rapid, intercut with subliminal shots of the boy and the two women he has summoned to the screen. The ominous music and natural sounds of the prologue are replaced by an insistent drum beat that pulses in a shocking counterpoint to the more lyrical pace of the prologue.[3] This opening is a kind of overture that can serve as a map for the entire film to come.

Now the "fiction" begins, with the fade-in of a door and the entrance of Bibi Andersson, the actress who plays Alma the nurse, and one of the two faces we have seen on the boy's screen just before the credits. The psychiatrist is asking her to take over the case of Elisabet Vogler, a famous actress who has fallen silent after an attack of giggles during a performance of *Electra.*

The actress will not speak and begins to giggle when Alma turns on the radio—the way she giggled on the stage. We are hearing a radio drama with high-flown words about emotions and ideals. Elisabet (played by Liv Ullmann in her first screen role) suddenly seems enraged and turns the radio off. Alma gently finds her some Bach to listen to and leaves the room. In a remarkably long close-up of Elisabet we watch her face darken as the light fades; the only light is the reflection in her eyes. When that goes she is a silhouette, and when she turns her head away into profile, the composition is a direct echo of the facial landscape of the dead man we saw earlier in the morgue sequence. Slowly she puts one hand over her face, covering it the way the sheets cover up the dead; it can be read as a study of a person trying to "put herself out," literally extinguish herself. We have time to listen to the Bach along with her and experience along with her the contrast between silence, music, and the spoken word. What is she thinking? What are *we* think-

3. For an excellent and original segmentation and analysis of the opening passage—as well as of the rest of the film—see Robert T. Eberwein's chapter on *Persona* ("The Surface of Reality: Screen as Mirror in *Persona*") in his *Film and the Dream Screen: A Sleep and a Forgetting* (Princeton, N.J., 1984), 120–39.

ing? Why does "drama" make her laugh or go silent? Does the drama of my own life ever make me react like that? Bergman is giving me time to think this over.

This sequence has established the motif of contrast between speech, silence, and music; it will be repeated later, when the two women sit at a table sorting mushrooms. Again there will be the uncanny lengthening of time, almost requesting that we examine the textures of silence, music, and the unsaid.

An echoing sequence now shows Alma trying to go to bed; she is restless and tries to listen to the radio. She wonders about Elisabet, who has chosen silence rather than to "speak lines." (Is life nothing but an act?) Alma's curiosity about her patient is a space for our own; throughout the film we are being asked to wonder about these women just as they are wondering about each other, studying and dis/covering.

In her room Elisabet is faced with the television showing live coverage of the Vietnam War, including the real-life self-immolation of a Buddhist monk. Bergman counts on shocking us with the contrast between reality and fiction here, as he will later in the film when Elisabet finds the picture of the Warsaw ghetto. Now as later she retreats in horror; the pain of the world will not

Figure 2-1. Alma in bed, wondering about herself and about Elisabet—a fiction attempting to understand a fiction. What, then, is "real"? (Museum of Modern Art/Film Stills Archive.)

be forgotten, it "leaks in," as the doctor reminds her. (Does Bergman wonder how he dares make up fictions in a world so full of real suffering? Wouldn't any artist wonder?)

Elisabet receives a letter from her husband that Alma reads to her—in part; it contains a photograph of Elisabet's son, which the actress seizes and tears in half—almost. The music sounds a warning; it will be repeated later, when the theme of one human being destroying another reappears. The film proceeds by such themes and their recurring variations, particularly in *mise en scène* and sound track; there is a sense in which its structure is musical.

The doctor sends Elisabet and Alma to her own summer cottage by the sea. Here the two women take walks, lie on the beach, share meals. Throughout these lyrical passages it is Alma's voice alone that we hear; but their two bodies on the image track remind us that this is really a duet for one voice. One critic calls the film an essay on the number two (Sontag, 1975, 253ff.). We are constantly asked to compare their faces, bodies, clothes; the stark blacks and whites in hats and bathing suits, the positioning of arms and heads—all these draw us into the obsessive close-ups until we feel what this closeness does to two people, how a kind of merging can begin to take place. The social difference that distinguished them in the hospital (famous patient, humble nurse) gradually disappears in the natural setting of an isolated beach house where they are totally alone and thus, for the time being, totally interdependent.

What we usually take for a screen "character"—a fixed set of personality traits defined through unfolding action—becomes the real enigma here, for one speaks and the other is silent. "To be a person," says one critic, "is to be a performer. . . . Once there are two people, there is a show and an audience" (Braudy, 1983, 28). Cut off from the world, alone and away from their expected roles (or personae), Alma and Elisabet now become involved in a set of scenes where we learn how difficult if not impossible it is to define another person from the outside. Each seems to be creating a character for herself by way of the other, and the question we are constantly forced to ask is not only "Who is she now?" but also "*How can I be sure?*"

The close-up is one of cinema's most powerful techniques for giving us the truth about a character: since a film persona does not tell us his/her thought (as for example a character in a novel is able to do), we come to rely on the camera to tell us whether someone is telling the truth, by letting us examine—in close-up—the flicker of lashes or the turn of the mouth muscles. But in *Persona*, where the title refers not only to "personality" and "stage character" but also to "mask," we are never sure what the women are thinking. We can only speculate, and there is no one to ask for confirmation. "Is

Elisabet lying?" "Is Alma exaggerating?" Who can tell us? We are faced with faces, and we can know only by comparing with what we have learned to read on the faces of real people in real life. Presumably the film will teach us to read real faces better, since film and reality feed upon each other and use each other to test or confirm what feels credible. Gradually we come to see the inside of Bergman's questions: What does it mean to lie? And what do we even *mean* by "the truth"?

In the sequence where the women are picking over the mushrooms they are humming together and comparing their hands. Once again we are asked to compare the meaning of music with the meaning of speech. Elisabet broke down during a "performance"; she has chosen (according to the doctor) to avoid all lies in a lying world by resorting to silence. And yet she is willing to hum notes of music.

The women seem to be growing more intimate. Somewhat later Alma tells Elisabet about her ideals: the nursing profession gives her "something to believe in." They smoke cigarettes together, and Alma speaks of her first lover, "who smoked like a chimney"; they are costumed and positioned so

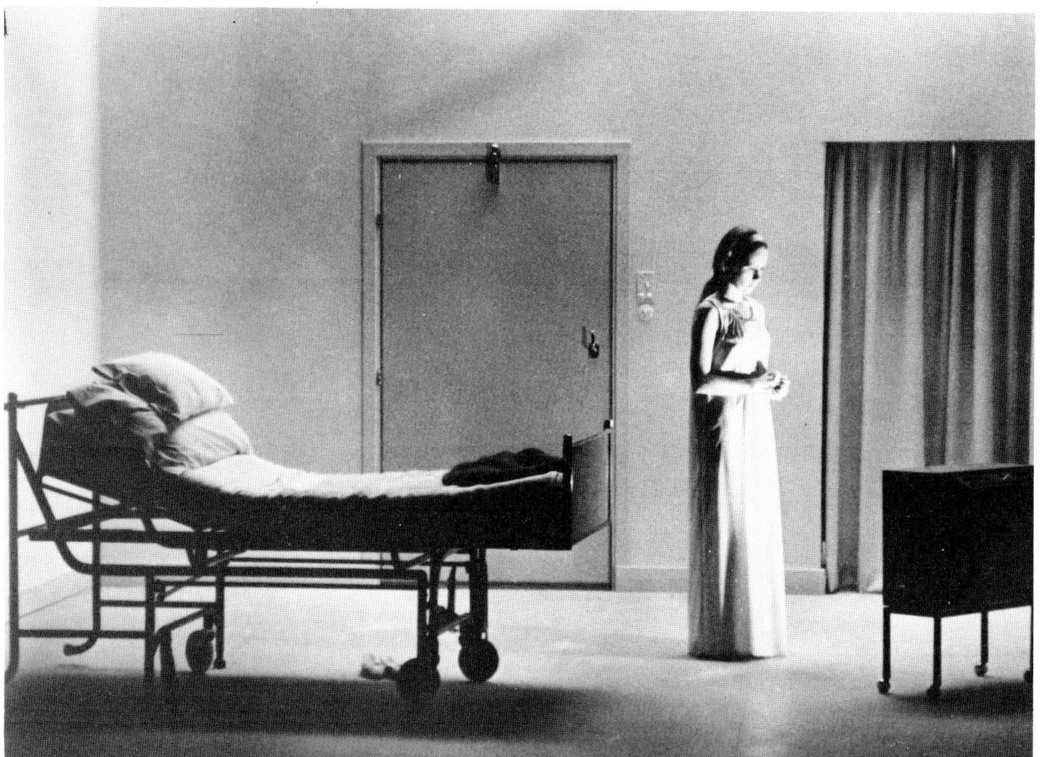

Figure 2-2. The pain of the world "leaks in." Elisabet (Bergman's fiction) faces the horror of the real. Will her silence vanquish its unspeakable betrayals? (Museum of Modern Art/Film Stills Archive.)

that Elisabet's arm could be Alma's. Alma delights in having someone listening to her at last. She who has always been known as a good listener is now the speaker! Exultant at being the object of attention, she finally gives a "performance" that caps this rising intimacy: the recital of an orgy at the beach, in which she and a girlfriend had sex with two young boys. The story is about her own sexual awakening, about betrayal, abortion, and guilt. But it is less a revelation of who she is than of her pleasure in having a chance to create a coherent image of herself with someone whose opinion and taste she values.

She established her respect for art and the artist in her first conversation with Elisabet. Now she is becoming a bit of an artist herself, putting on a show, as Braudy terms it, with a famous actress as the appreciative audience. The evening ends with a drunken Alma telling the actress that she could turn herself into Elisabet if she really tried, and that the actress could turn herself into Alma much more easily, because she has "a much bigger soul"; and then we hear the whispered words: "You must go to bed or you'll fall asleep at the table." Alma's head is on the table already. Are these words spoken by Elisabet or is Alma thinking them herself? We cannot tell, and neither can Alma. But she repeats the words aloud as though the idea had just come to her. How do ideas come to us? When people are relaxed and close, do thoughts cross boundaries between them? How do thoughts get transferred? taught? passed along? What *is* a person(a) if not the thoughts that inhabit him or her? The scene causes us to reflect on issues such as these.

We enter Alma's bedroom now, and once again we watch her trying to fall asleep, another echo motif. The room is composed, lit, and photographed as a study of mist and shadow, suggesting our own borderlines of dream and waking life. Is this Alma's dream? Elisabet enters by a door on screen right, approaches Alma, then moves out by way of another door at screen left. She seems to dissolve into white mist at the doorway, then turns and rejoins Alma. They study each other without speaking. The scene ends with their two faces facing us, after a slow ballet of hands, necks, cheeks. Elisabet's hand sweeps Alma's hair away from her brow; they pose as though to ask us to compare them to each other as they have been comparing themselves.

And to compare them to ourselves as well. For the next shot brings us into the next day; we are in sudden bright daylight on the beach—and Elisabet rises up over the bottom edge of the screen to look at us frontally, framing us directly in her camera as she snaps our picture. (What *else* could she be looking at?) This motif can be connected to the little boy who reached out to touch us through the screen, as well as to other frontal shots of faces and eyes. ("So what are you thinking now, Viewer? Hypocritical viewer, my fellowman, my brother.")[4]

Critic David Boyd makes much of this shot, since the thesis of his approach to *Persona* is that the film is a grid drawing our attention to two axes: one that connects the film characters to each other and a second connecting the characters to us (1983–84, 10–19). Indeed, Alma now asks the very questions the last scene aroused in me; she speaks for me in asking: "Did you speak to me last night? Did you come to my room?" Elisabet shakes her head no. And we viewers have been totally implicated in the asking, for there is no ironic distance from which we can observe, safely in on the secret. We are in on no secret at all; we must puzzle out the evidence along with Alma at this point. Do I trust Elisabet's answer? Her expression is warm and kind; but is she lying? She retreated into silence in order to escape from lies and lying. She could be lying now—*but how can I know?* We are absolutely chained now to the narrative focus—that is, the point of view—of Alma, whose ignorance we share. The fact that this scene began with Elisabet photographing us has helped draw us inside the situation; there we are, snapped, sealed in, and there is no way to keep the characters "in profile" anymore. We are on that island, confused and wondering, or else we are nowhere at all. We are both of those women now, alternately, and unable to judge anyone. This is about being, not seeming; it is painful to be without judging; and Bergman has robbed us of the outsider's stance that makes "judgment" possible.

It is the next day, perhaps. (Chronology itself is blurring now.) It is raining. Alma is taking their mail to town. In the car we are alone with her being alone. Alma (or Bibi Andersson?) is suddenly "off-camera," off-stage, isolated and private in one of the most private settings of modern life: the car. Through her eyes we see the mail lying on the passenger seat. We notice along with her that the top letter is not sealed. We want to look; we are along with her in this mystery now; she must do the looking for us; and she does.

She stops the car, opens the letter, puts on her glasses. We are forced to feel what she feels as she takes in the way Elisabet has described her to the doctor. Her "performance" (the recital of the orgy) has been reported; but it was a private show, and it was about that most private of matters—her own

4. The last line of the introductory poem "Au lecteur" ("To the Reader") of Charles Baudelaire's *Les Fleurs du mal* (1857) reads, "Hypocrite lecteur, mon semblable, mon frère." This line has been influential in twentieth-century arts and letters; it is one of the first self-conscious attempts of a modern writer to reach across to the reader in this direct I-You manner. (T.S. Eliot makes use of the quotation in "The Wasteland" [1922].)

"banal" little self. In spite of her insistence up to this point that she is somehow "littler" than Elisabet, here she sees her own "littleness" swallowed and disgorged to another *by way of* the real woman/actress she revealed herself *to* and *as* the actress/real woman she revealed herself to be—"half in love" with Elisabet Vogler. The doctor said that the actress wanted to be "seen through." Don't we all? And yet what danger to be seen through! That's why we need the masks. The yearning to drop the mask, to be listened to at last, to be given a chance to unbury one's "self," to hear one's own self in the telling, and yet one may so easily be betrayed.

There is a strange cut at this point from Alma in the car to Alma gazing at her own reflection in a pool. Whatever she is asking herself belongs to her; what I have just written is what this episode would make me think about. The silence of the film gives us the space to react, to fill the gaps, to see through our own masks, to drop them a little. The challenge continues.

We are back at the beach house. Is it still the same day? The weather has changed, and Alma is sitting in the sun in her bathing suit and beach hat. The camera, such a virtuoso at close-ups, is now stationed in long shot, spying like a voyeur. We see Alma get herself a drink, accidentally upset the glass, and sweep up the mess she's made. She leaves one piece of glass on the ground, a calculated afterthought. In medium shot now, we see Elisabet moving inside the house while Alma sits outside and smokes a cigarette, waiting. Elisabet comes out in her bathing suit. We see only her feet and legs, for we are in Alma's mind, and Alma is waiting for revenge. Elisabet's bare feet move back and forth on the stones. Alma rises and goes inside; there she parts the curtains and looks outside.[5] Elisabet cries out: she has stepped on the piece of glass. We see the face of each looking at the other—accusation, betrayal, counter-accusation. *And then the film breaks down.*

Or rather: one thinks one is witnessing a mechanical breakdown of the

5. The motif of curtains opening runs subtly throughout the film. Any object in cinema can be made into a powerful carrier of meaning through sheer repetition. The first time we see an object it may not impress us; the second time it becomes a reminder. The freight of meaning grows as the transformations multiply. One fine example of the cinematic transformation of objects is the treatment of a pair of earrings in Max Ophuls's *Madame de . . .* (1953). Another is the newel post on the staircase of George Bailey's home in Frank Capra's *It's a Wonderful Life* (1946). In *Persona* the curtains may recall many things, not the least of which are the "curtains" at the theater, which part to reveal . . . what? I think this is one of Bergman's driving "questions." What other objects take on meaning by accumulation and repetition in this film? And what elements beyond mere objects can be made meaningful by cinema's ability to repeat experience?

apparatus of projection. The film seems to burn and tear; we hear the feverish voices of technicians; and when the image returns it is out of focus. An extreme close-up of the human eye reminds us of the act of looking, which has been interrupted. It takes some time before the film—and our vision—clears again. We have a little time to think of what this expressionistic breakdown "means" in terms of the developing narrative.

The shock of this strange sequence underlines the theme of trust and betrayal. So far there have been two human "breakdowns" in this film—Elisabet's retreat from language (her breakdown on stage) and the rupture of Alma's faith in Elisabet as a human being (the letter), followed by her revenge and Elisabet's answering sense of betrayal. But in a larger sense the fragility of human relations has been the topic all along, as has the terrifying choice between trusting others or being alone.[6]

Now Alma is driven by panic; she asks Elisabet to forgive her as she runs after her along the beach. She voices her anguish at having her story told; she admits having read the letter. She pleads for Elisabet to talk to her and violently alternates between apologizing and attacking. She even calls attention to the theatrical nature of their relations, accusing herself of overacting, of sounding false, of dramatizing the orgy story because she enjoyed the limelight. At the same time she accuses Elisabet of using her as a model for a future role, studying her inflections, the way any artist must study life in order to give it shape in art. Their quarrel rises to a fever pitch: Elisabet's slap draws Alma's blood, and Alma threatens the actress with a pot of boiling water.

When Alma tries to scratch her face, Elisabet's expression of fear is quickly replaced by a smile. (Is she laughing again at the "false drama" of it?) When Alma flees to the bathroom we are given a chance to inspect the way despair looks in public as opposed to its private expression and to decide for ourselves what is going on. For in a sense this whole film has been a journey from the outside to the inside, from the public to the private, from the social to the soul.

That night Alma sulks on the beach alone, while Elisabet, lonely and bored in the house, lights a lamp and leafs through a book. A photograph falls out: it is one of the more famous pictures to come out of World War II, as historically real as the TV coverage of Vietnam we saw earlier. This is a

6. This either/or became a major subject of serious literature in post–World War II Europe; much of the dialogue in Bergman's earlier films is reminiscent of French existentialist authors like Jean-Paul Sartre and Albert Camus.

picture of women and children being rounded up by the Nazis in the Warsaw ghetto. A little boy has his hands raised; he is looking into the camera. We know this is a real child, not an actor, and we know (if we recognize it) that this is a picture of people who are no longer alive—because the picture records the very moment of their being sent away to be exterminated.

All this Bergman knows, and all this Elisabet knows too. She who tore the picture of her own son now looks with horror and pity at another woman's child who will soon be destroyed. The theme of human betrayal now reminds us, by way of the music, of the moment when she tore her son's photograph—and then we can also recall the nail that was pounded through a human hand and the young boy of the prologue who was so alone in the morgue, trying to touch the woman on the screen. Different echoes will be available to different viewers, depending upon their knowledge and experience.

The central breakdown of trust has already occurred with Alma's reading of Elisabet's letter to the doctor; the cinematic breakdown of the celluloid and apparatus has already offered its visual metaphor. For the rest of the film, Bergman will desert any pretense at further linear narrative. We are inside a set of variations on the themes of looking, lying, guilt, and failure, all rendered through motifs of doubling.

While Alma visits the bedside of the sleeping (?) Elisabet, meditating on this face without a mask, we hear a man's voice in the distance calling Elisabet's name. Elisabet's eyes open, and Alma—now outdoors in the night—is suddenly confronted by a man. All at once Elisabet is there too, and although Alma repeats several times, "Mr. Vogler, I am not your wife," he continues to address her as Elisabet, and Elisabet herself places Alma's hand on his cheek. The Voglers have surrounded Alma; she throws herself into the man's arms and returns his words of affection, even sending messages to "their" son. It is a performance worthy of a professional actress. Then, while Elisabet's face dominates the screen at the right, Alma and Mr. Vogler make love. Mr. Vogler asks her if she has enjoyed sex with him. First she says, "You know you are a wonderful lover." Then she breaks down and utters a hysterical disclaimer. The camera focuses on Elisabet, who is looking frontally right at us. There is an ominous chiming sound, and the screen goes white.

Let us look at this brief scene again. Alma makes love to a man who mistakes her identity and whom she does not enjoy. We do not know if it "really" happens or whether it is a dream or fantasy. If it is a dream, we are not sure to whom it belongs. I suggest that the scene functions as an expression of Alma's dawning comprehension of why Elisabet broke down, retreated into silence. Whoever is dreaming, Alma does make love to Mr. Vogler. And what is this lovemaking? It is a lie.

In the only moment of the film in which sexuality is depicted as an act rather than as discourse or subtext—in the act—Alma finds herself acting. And she is promptly revulsed by her own fraudulence, her own "performance." Unable to go on with the scene, the lie, she instantly disavows it in a cry of self-loathing. Her breakdown after the sex act is a distinct echo of Elisabet's earlier breakdown on the stage, which led to her withdrawal from speaking, lies, and performance—that is, from life.

> Give me something to stupefy my senses, or beat me to death, kill me, I can't do it any longer, I can't. You mustn't touch me, it's shame, a dishonor, it's all counterfeit, a lie. Just leave me alone, I'm poisonous, bad, cold, rotten. Why can't I be allowed just to die away, I haven't the courage.[7]

This strange lovemaking scene is followed immediately by the most famous sequence in the film: the redoubled recital of Elisabet's failure at motherhood, spoken twice—both times by Alma; the first time with the camera focused on Elisabet, the hearer, the second on Alma, the speaker. By the time the second recital is finished (both begin with the torn picture of Elisabet's son, which Alma is hiding under her hands), Alma knows something so well that she surprises herself with her own knowledge. "No! I am Alma! I am not Elisabet Vogler!" But her face changes suddenly; despite her protest she has fused with the Other, the silent one; half of the face we see is that of Elisabet.

Now there is a series of scenes as expressionistic, as divorced from narrative as the images of the prologue. At one point Alma seems to cut her arm with her fingernail, and then Elisabet appears to drink her blood. A scene in the hospital in which Alma enters in her nurse's uniform has a dreamlike unreality. She cradles Elisabet's head and coaxes her into saying the word "nothing." Their heads are posed together as we remember them from the two-shot of the first "dream."

Alma awakes with a start; have these last scenes been parts of a lengthy dream? And if so, how far back should we go in naming it dream material? (How often does this film force us to question the distinction between "dream" and "life"?) Alma sees Elisabet packing her suitcase. Alma herself is preparing to leave, bringing in the chairs, closing the house. She seems to be

7. Ingmar Bergman, *Persona and Shame* (screenplays) (New York, 1972), 88–89. There are a good many differences (relatively minor in the case of the scene under discussion) between this published screenplay and the subtitles of the film.

totally alone; Elisabet is no longer there. She looks at herself one last time in the mirror, and we see a dissolve of the beautiful two-shot we have seen twice before.

As she leaves the house for the last time, Alma is partly hidden behind an enormous wooden image of a woman in the foreground, the figurehead from a ship's prow. A sudden insert of Elisabet playing Electra; another brief cut showing Ingmar Bergman and his cameraman Sven Nykvist filming the movie we are watching. Images behind images on top of images. Meanwhile, Alma disappears into a bus that takes her away while the camera tilts down from the road to the stony earth. We cut to the young boy from the prologue, with his screen. The women's faces are fading, have faded. The film runs out. The arc light is extinguished. *Persona* is over.

Because the structure of *Persona* is poetic and implicative rather than causal and linear, we can only make it mean by connecting its echoes, and its echoes only exist in the eyes, ears, and minds that have been seduced into grasping them. *Persona* is a mirror, not a window; it will always reveal my own face to me even as I try to see through it. It is about wanting to be seen through; it is therefore about my own wanting to be seen through; and Elisabet's—and Bergman's—and Alma's—and yours. And so I close by choosing three focal scenes to connect, as an example of the many you may have found yourself or may find as you react to and link up the elements Bergman has juxtaposed with such economy and elegance.

I suggest, then, that three focal scenes are related: whether Elisabet and Alma are taken as silence and speech, Art and Life, truth and performance, or two halves of the same full psyche, the three scenes of greatest revelatory power touch upon the agony of female fraudulence. First, the orgy recital, in which Alma reveals *her* secret in a scene of blistering honesty that is staged like a performance and that she later tries to deny by calling it her "exhibitionism"; second, the surreal love scene with Mr. Vogler; and finally the doubled accusation of failed motherhood. In each of these scenes, different cinematic techniques insist upon the fusion of the two women: the silent Elisabet gobbling Alma's tale with erotic pleasure; the weird spatial relations in the sharing of the husband figure; and the recital of Elisabet's failure at motherhood where Bergman fuses the women's faces, thereby implicating womanhood entire in the pain and guilt of failed mothering that haunts so many of his films and characters.

There is also a *progression* underlying the *order* of these scenes within the film. Alma speaks for herself in the beach narrative, but Elisabet seems to be silently coaching her and participating in the guilty pleasures she recounts.

In the lovemaking scene Alma seems to be speaking for them both, but more actively, more awarely; besides, she has been mistaken for Elisabet and is acting the actress's role the better to lay bare her own enactment of this role. In reenacting Elisabet's casting off of sexual lying Alma connects to Elisabet through a series of "looks." In the doubled "motherhood" recital Alma speaks—not once but twice—with a masterful and convincing authority about events she never lived. Elisabet cowers; Alma is assured. At the end their faces fuse, because Alma has learned that the similarity between them is deeper than their differences and that she "is" now the actress and can speak most accurately of them both in speaking most confidently of herself.

Even though the "story" ends indecisively (Will Elisabet return to the stage? Will the women ever meet again?), the film's formal structure maintains a balance in its perfect circular return to its opening images. Life is unsure; but art supplies a little form at least. Is that, perhaps, the function of art and the meaning of this very film?

Figure 2-3. An essay on the number 2: theme and variations. The contrast and comparison of separate and merging selves invite us to study both similarity and difference. (Museum of Modern Art/Film Stills Archive.)

Boyd, David. 1983–84. "*Persona* and the Cinema of Interpretation." *Film Quarterly* 37, no. 2 (Winter): 10–19.

Braudy, Leo. 1983. "Framing the Innocent Eye: *42nd Street* and *Persona*." *Michigan Quarterly Review* 22, no. 1: 9–29.

Sontag, Susan. 1975. "*Persona*: The Film in Depth." In *Ingmar Bergman: Essays in Criticism*, edited by Stuart M. Kaminsky, 253–69. New York, 1975. Written in 1967, this remains one of the finest essays on this film.

BIBLIOGRAPHY

On Narrative Structure

Bordwell, David, and Kristin Thompson. *Film Art: An Introduction.* 2d ed. Madison, Wis., 1986. This book is especially useful on the nature of narrative structure in film.

Chatman, Seymour. *Story and Discourse: Narrative Structure in Fiction and Film.* Ithaca, N.Y., 1978.

Critical Inquiry, 7, no. 1 (Autumn 1980). An entire issue devoted to questions relating to narrative.

Martin, Wallace. *Recent Theories of Narrative.* Ithaca, N.Y., 1986. See esp. chaps. 4, 5, and 6.

Scholes, Robert. "Narration and Narrativity in Film." In *Film Theory and Criticism*, edited by Gerald Mast and Marshall Cohen, 417–33. 2d ed. New York, 1979.

On *Persona* and on Ingmar Bergman

Blackwell, Marilyn Johns. *Persona: The Transcendent Image.* Champaign, Ill., 1986. The only book-length study of this film.

Cowie, Peter. *Ingmar Bergman, A Critical Biography.* New York, 1982. Contains an excellent bibliography.

Eberwein, Robert T. *Film and the Dream Screen: A Sleep and a Forgetting.* New Jersey, 1984, 120–40. An extraordinary chapter on *Persona* in the light of an original theory of the screen and audience desire.

Kawin, Bruce. *Mindscreen: Bergman, Godard, and First-Person Film.* New Jersey, 1978, 91–132. A fine introduction to Bergman and a clear analysis of *Persona.*

Manley, James C. "Artist and Audience, Vampire and Victim: The Oral Matrix of Imagery in Bergman's *Persona*." *Psychocultural Review* (Spring 1979): 117–39. Takes up the theme of vampirism and interpsychic exchange.

Samuels, Charles Thomas. *Encountering Directors.* New York, 1972, 179–208. Interesting interview with Bergman.

Simon, John. *Ingmar Bergman Directs.* New York, 1972.

Steene, Birgitta. *Ingmar Bergman.* New York, 1968.

Wood, Robin. "*Persona.*" In *Ingmar Bergman: Essays in Criticism*, edited by Stuart M. Kaminsky, 55–67. New York, 1975.

In no country in the world is death so domestic and affable as it is there, between Vesuvius and the sea.
—Italian saying

3

VISUAL MOTIFS IN ROSSELLINI'S *VOYAGE TO ITALY*

Peter Brunette

Given that cinema is a visual medium, one obviously fruitful way of examining a film is in terms of its visual motifs. By "visual motif" I mean the recurrence of one or more specific visual images, most commonly objects of some sort, that gradually take on thematic weight as the film progresses. *Voyage to Italy* (1953; in Italian *Viaggio in Italia*), Roberto Rossellini's third film made with Ingrid Bergman, is especially rich in this kind of visual suggestion. Thought by many to be both his finest work and one of the greatest films ever made, it regularly makes the top ten listing of the prestigious French journal *Cahiers du cinéma* thirty years after its première.

Unlike most conventional films, which rely all too heavily on dialogue and overt narrative action to suggest their themes, *Voyage to Italy* depends far more on the many complex and moving visual images it continuously presents to the viewer. Often, in fact, the film's visual track works in complex counterpoint to a banal sound track in order to suggest gradations of human emotion that could not be as delicately articulated through dialogue alone. For Rossellini, *Voyage to Italy* "was a film which rested on something very subtle, the variations in a couple's relationship under the influence of a third person: the exterior world surrounding them" (Douchet interview 1959, 6). Both this central emotional relationship and the more fundamental themes of the film, as we shall see, are for the most part established visually.

Rossellini's original plan was to adapt a Colette novel called *Duo* (1934), which concerns a "happily married" couple whose marriage falls apart because the husband insists on upholding traditional views of marriage rather than responding to the specific sexual and emotional needs of his wife. When the wife refuses to apologize or feel guilty for an old love affair that the husband has discovered, he begins to moralize obsessively, finally losing control and taking his own life. In its concentration on the dynamic shifts of power within a sexual relationship, the novel is obviously related to the film. The focus of the novel, however, is very intensely on the couple, with no attention paid to their environment, and it is here that the film most strikingly departs from Colette's fiction.

The director's refusal to do things in the Hollywood manner extended, as usual, to his storytelling as well, and *Voyage to Italy* represents the perfecting of unconventional narrative, affective, and thematic strategies already present in his work from the very first. Thus the film's "dramatic" moments are consistently undercut. Nor is there much plot to speak of: a marriage is breaking up under the strains of a trip to Italy, and we watch; little else happens. Apparently superficial visual detail, however—the smallest, most fleeting facial expression, for example—assumes enormous proportions, as it does in the work of Dreyer, Mizoguchi, and Bresson. Episodic rather than linear in its development, the film emphasizes rhythm, suggestion, and nuance. *Longueurs* and dead time are left in the finished film rather than being edited out to produce a snappy montage that presumably would have moved things along better. (But what things? The minimal plot? Here, the surface of life *is* its depths.) It is a film composed of elements as tiny as barely perceivable emotional textures and as immense as the meaning of life and death. Unsurprisingly, given these departures from standard Hollywood narrative practice, Rossellini was led to rely more than ever on visual motifs to convey his themes.

As usual, however, when one defies Hollywood—even in Italy—one must pay the price, and initial critical reaction was swift and predictable. G.C. Castello, writing in the influential *Cinema*, brought to new heights of righteous indignation the campaign Italian critics had been waging against the director for some years: "By this time, we've given up on Rossellini. But what is beginning to get annoying is that he has managed not only to ruin himself, but he's also ruining the woman who would, not unworthily, have succeeded Greta Garbo one day" (1954, 738). This same critic objects that the film does not give enough information, especially psychological information, about the characters. He wants to know *why* their marriage is going bad. What Castello misses is that the film offers their situation as an existential given, purposely denying us a previous "psychological case history" (an essential component of the code of realism) that would reduce the characters' rich, impenetrable presence, which is so much like that of people we meet in everyday life. The brilliance of *Voyage to Italy* is precisely its refusal to specify a why, for that would be to recuperate human complexity and ambiguity into the knowable, making it, like most films, an illegitimate domestication of the troubling inconsistencies of life. In fact, explanations and answers *are* suggested in the film, but visually rather than discursively; a reductive psychological specificity is in the process quite properly sacrificed to subtlety of treatment.

In *Voyage to Italy* Rossellini's use of dead time reaches a new level of complexity and suggestiveness, and thus the film's visual motifs, now more starkly emphasized, become increasingly important. In the much remarked opening scene, for example, when we first see the Joyces driving along the highway toward Naples, the boredom is palpable. What is perhaps the film's most important visual motif, the Joyces' car, is established immediately. It powers its way through space, its engine humming soporifically; as we shall see, it becomes ever more symbolically significant. A train speeds in the opposite direction, the image linking up with the train whistle that appeared immediately following the credits, rending them. No one speaks. Guarner has described this sequence well: "This rather long-held image of reality . . . give[s] a curious feeling of continuance, as if the film had begun a lot earlier. We are not present at the opening of a story, merely coming in on something that was already going on, as we do in real life. *Viaggio in Italia* is also a film about time and duration" (1970, 57). Seven years after the film was first released, Pierre Marcabru wrote in *Arts* that in this film the characters exist for themselves, not for the cinema, and thus proclaim a new cinema of immobility: "In the immobile and the insignificant is the very power of life" (1961, 13). Similarly, Leprohon feels that this kind of film is preferable to "those which rivet us to our seats with suspense or the more elementary emotions. 'Spectator involvement' is really a shoddy aim, and for its victim a second-rate satisfaction. The greatest literature sets up a resonance extending far beyond the immediate illusion that it creates; and the best films are those that have us *accompany* the characters as their friends rather than step into their shoes" (1972, 138–39).

Detail is built slowly and visually, as when the couple is taken on a tour of the Neapolitan villa they have inherited from Uncle Homer. At first the time spent on the tour seems wasted. It is only later, when the stability and presence of the house is implicitly contrasted with the forever moving automobile in which the Joyces insulate themselves, that we realize the significance of this dead time that almost any other director would have summarized with a series of quick cuts. It is also clear that Rossellini knew just what he was doing. In the interview with Pio Baldelli and his students in 1971 he referred obliquely to this sequence, linking it in an unexpected and not entirely clear way to his later films:

> If I don't live in the context of things, of everything, I can't arrive at those key points. . . . But do you remember, for example, *Voyage to Italy*? Well, I had to do that long walk inside the house, seeing things, which everybody scolded me for. . . . Now, if this weren't there, if this milieu weren't there, how would you get to everything else? You wouldn't. If she [mistakenly "he" in the interview] hadn't gone through all those rooms, she wouldn't have gotten to the museum; if she hadn't gone to the museum, she wouldn't have gotten to the discovery of the bodies, she wouldn't have gotten to . . . she can't get there, because she could only have gotten there in that way, by means of . . . the improbable." (1972, 222–23; ellipses in original)

Few of the visual images and motifs that are put before us are overtly explained. For example, when Katherine goes out for her first drive alone in Naples, reactions to what she sees play across her face, but only occasionally, when it is thematically pertinent, does the director actually show us in a countershot what she is looking at. With this too he is breaking one of the cardinal rules of "good" filmmaking, but the effect is to enhance the sense of waiting and the ever-fluttering possibility of a sudden outbreak of the unexpected. In any case, her reaction is more important than what she reacts to. At the same time, however, Rossellini's documentary interest is strong, as in many of his other films, and he also wants to show the "reality" of Naples itself. He knows, however, that this "reality" is never available directly but only through the consciousnesses of the characters, who thus mimic the director's own necessary and unavoidable mediation between the world and the film. Bazin has described this dynamic well, because it fits so neatly into a phenomenological paradigm of intentionality. For him the reality of Naples as presented in the film is incomplete yet whole at the same time, for "it is a Naples as filtered through the consciousness of the heroine. If the landscape is bare and confined, it is because the consciousness of an ordinary *bourgeoise* itself suffers from great spiritual poverty. Nevertheless, the Naples of the film is not false. . . . It is rather a mental landscape at once as objective as a straight photograph and as subjective as pure personal consciousness" (1976, 98).[1]

This play of the objective and subjective also reappears at the level of character identification: As Leprohon has told us, we *accompany* the characters rather than "become" them and, as in *Stromboli* (1949), Rossellini refuses to allow us the luxury of facile moral judgments in favor of one character over another. Most critics have assumed that Katherine is the aggrieved party, the clear victim of Alex's callous devotion to work and making money, but this may be because what are considered typically "male" faults of cruelty and violence are expressed in more obviously obnoxious ways. Bergman's traditional association with "good girl" parts may also be a factor here. Most important, of course, is that the narrative and what is even *seen* unrolls, basically, from Katherine's point of view. And it is almost exclusively she who sees the things that we are shown. Yet somehow Rossellini successfully mounts a subtle balancing act in which now one has the moral and emotional power advantage, now the other.

What is perhaps the most perfectly balanced sequence, a marvel of suggestion, is handled almost solely through visual means in tight counterpoint to the studied banality of the sound track. This scene occurs at Alex's return from Capri. Katherine has been waiting up for him, playing solitaire, hoping that he would return that evening. But when she hears his car pull up, she must immediately turn out the light and pretend to be asleep so that she will not in any way put herself at an emotional disadvantage. What follows is a subtle but riveting series of intercuts on her immobile face in the shadows as she registers and absorbs every sound he makes, her eyes darting everywhere. The petty noises—his gargling, for example—seem abnormally loud and penetrating, at least partly because they have been foregrounded by the nearly static visual track. An elaborate choreography of lights being turned on and off follows, as each fears giving an inch. It is perhaps not over-reading to find the play of the lights more than visual choreography, for they can also be seen as parallel to the sun, with its multiple opportunities for rap-

1. Bergman also told Robin Wood in an interview that "in *Voyage to Italy*, [his purpose] was also to show Pompeii. He adored Pompeii. He knew everything about it. He was only looking for a story into which he could put Pompeii and the museums and Naples and all that Naples stands for, which he always was fascinated with, because the people in Naples are different from the people in Rome and Milan. He wanted to show all those grottoes with the relics and the bones and the museums and the laziness of all the statues" ("Ingrid Bergman on Rossellini," *Film Comment* 10, no. 4 [July–August 1974]: 14).

prochement, especially through its connection to the idea of Italy. When the lights are on, there is a chance they will begin to communicate, but for fear of exposing herself Bergman each time extinguishes the light and plunges herself and their relationship back into darkness. Again, this entire scene is almost totally visual; there is virtually no dialogue.

Far more is at stake between Katherine and Alex, however, than their own emotional problems, for they also represent opposing sets of abstractions. Both sets are incomplete, and both are frequently conveyed through visual motifs. (His focus on these abstractions is another reason why Rossellini does little or nothing to sketch in their past lives for us or to define them in terms of personal idiosyncrasy.) Neither is a complete human being; each is a part of a whole, and thus they exemplify the distortions of humanity decried by Nietzsche's Zarathustra. Alex clearly stands for a soulless materialism that was for Rossellini the chief evil of postwar European society. Alex is constantly thinking of his business affairs and worrying about the time he is "wasting" in Italy, a country he views as the epitome of laziness and lack of industry. Katherine, however, represents an equally untenable spiritualism that is reflected in her idealization of her romantic poet friend Charles Lewington. He had served in the British Army near Naples and had written her about it, and, as Alex taunts her, her visit to Italy has become a kind of spiritual pilgrimage to evoke his presence in the locations he had written her about. As the couple sits out in the hot Neapolitan sun, which visually and physically suggests the sensuality of Italy, she intones from Charles's poetry: "Temple of the spirit, no longer bodies, but ascetic images, compared to which mere thought seems flesh, heavy, dim." Alex, his jealousy aroused like that of Gabriel Conroy's in James Joyce's story "The Dead," from which

Figure 3-1. The light-switching sequence from *Voyage to Italy*. (National Film Archive, London.)

Rosselini has borrowed, says that he learned from Lewington that a man's cough can tell you more than the way he speaks.

KATHERINE: What did Charles' cough tell you?
ALEX: That he was a fool.
KATHERINE *(getting angry):* He was not a fool! He was a poet!
ALEX: What's the difference?[2]

As the film progresses, we realize that at least Katherine is learning from her contact with the Italian environment that is so foreign to both of them. She gradually becomes less romantically caught up in her poet's otherworldliness, for the forceful realities of her Neapolitan experiences begin to call her to the world. After being exposed to those things that Charles had written her about, she begins to realize that his aestheticism was a projection of his own personality rather than an accurate description of Italy. She admits to Alex: "Poor Charles, he had a way all his own of seeing things." This progression on her part also serves to bring us closer to her—there is no equivalent learning by her husband—but her recognition and overcoming of an excessive, crippling spirituality is only part of the process.

It is more than hinted that Katherine's problems are also sexual in nature; the penchant for spiritualizing her relationship with Charles is an obvious function of her presumed frigidity. But if we can fault Rossellini for having recourse to this sexist stereotype, it must also be said that this subject is only visually implied, with a kind of purposeful vagueness appropriate to a visual image, rather than overtly thematized. Thus when Katherine goes to a museum early in the film, she is overwhelmed; her guide's homely, banal chatter only serves to counterpoint the raw violence of these startling nude marble figures, which perform the additional function of visually symbolizing a presumably more healthy, innocent past of civilization, a motif that Godard will later borrow in *Contempt*. (To point up his various borrowings, Godard in fact has his characters at one point watch *Voyage to Italy*.) Katherine's encounter with the statues is turned into a series of profound, almost physical confrontations with them, and the obviously foregrounded movements of the camera—all fast crane shots that whirl as they move closer, worthy of the most choreographed moments in Max Ophuls—bring her into a forced proximity with the statues that is clearly threatening. As Michael Shedlin has

2. Lines quoted from the film are taken directly from the English sound track and from a transcription of the sound track of the Italian version published in *Filmcritica*, no. 156–57 (April–May 1965). At times, the dialogue differs markedly in the two versions.

Figure 3-2. Rossellini coaching Bergman in the light-switching scene. (Museum of Modern Art/Film Stills Archive.)

correctly pointed out, most of the crane shots in the museum include Katherine and the statues in the same shot, as opposed to all the previous point-of-view shots that have kept her visually and thus psychologically dissociated from what she is seeing and experiencing (1972, 46). Again, nothing is said directly; everything is handled through the visual track in counterpoint, as earlier in the solitaire scene, to the meaningless droning of the sound track. Deeply moved by this encounter with the overtly physical, sexual presence of the past, she later confesses to Alex: "What struck me was the complete lack of modesty with which everything is expressed. There was absolutely no attempt . . ." At this point she is interrupted by a knock at the door, and the subject is never brought up again.

Later, when she is touring the ancient site of the Cumaean Sybil, the old and presumably harmless guide demonstrates to her how marauders of the past would have tied up a "beautiful woman" like her. She huffs away, muttering "All men are alike," and the bewildered reaction of the guide indicates that at least in Italian (male) terms, her response was not appropriate. In another of her outings into Naples, she sees a constant stream of pregnant women and women with young children. She shakes her head, in an indistinct movement that seems closest to bemusement, and the film cuts immediately to a close-up of another striking visual particularity of Naples, the "Little Vesuvius" (a small, bubbling crater, popular as a tourist sight). The lava is then covered by two shadows that the camera a few moments later reveals as belonging to Katherine and yet another guide. Wordlessly, again, Rossellini is able to provide an efficient visual index to the emotions that are welling up inside Katherine. The place also shows the effects of ionization, as when cigarette smoke is blown into one of the many holes in the ground, and all of them suddenly emit smoke. The overall effect is of a kind of wasteland of the emotions and the spirit, a perfect visual analogue for Katherine's state. The last hint of the sexual theme, conveyed for once through dialogue, comes at the end of the film when she is trying to identify aloud the source of the animosity between her and Alex. She suggests that "perhaps the mistake in our marriage was not having a child," and Alex responds that she didn't want one and that now he thinks that she was right, because it would only have made their impending divorce more painful.

If sexual frigidity is only suggested in the film, however, the Joyces' childlessness is more overtly linked with the poverty of their lives, but as symptom rather than cause. Again, this suggestion is conveyed visually, without overt comment, by the pregnant women mentioned above. Superficial interpretations of the film have complained that these images—especially since the Joyces' friend Natalia is praying for a child—show that Rossellini is in effect suggesting that the couple's problems would be solved if only Katherine surrendered herself to her "proper" biological role (or fate). It is finally rather more complicated than that, but to understand how, we have to probe more deeply into the dynamics of conflict in the film.

What rules *Voyage to Italy* is environment. Like Thomas Hardy's fictional Wessex, it becomes a powerful third character whose name is Italy. Baldly stated, the film is about Katherine and Alex's confrontation with this otherness so utterly opposed to everything they know and understand. Where Alex is materialist and superrational and Katherine is at least initially overly aesthetic and otherworldly, Italy is sensual and earth-bound. It might be argued, of course, that Rossellini is merely glorifying and idealizing his native land: if all those cold foreigners could only experience the warmth and carefree joy of Italy (and have lots of babies), their problems would be solved. What is important to understand, however, is the precise way in which a Mediterranean system of values is being touted over the coldness the Northerners bring with them.

In many ways, especially in visual terms, the film could be included in the genre of "road films," given the massive, continued presence of the Joyces' car (which I want to explore in more detail later) and the theme of the hostile environment that makes one reassess one's most deeply held values and convictions. On the road one is vulnerable, and so are the Joyces. The undeniable physical and psychological presence of Italy constantly forces itself into their consciousnesses despite their desire to conduct their business as quickly as possible and escape back to England. They wrestle with their pasta; they worry about coming down with malaria; they don't know enough to take a siesta (and don't ask); they expect everyone to know English. After they eat, all the "garlic and onions" gives Alex a thirst that he can't quench. He complains about the driving, about the rampant laziness; at the party given by Uncle Homer's aristocratic friends the Joyces learn about "dolce far niente," how sweet it is to do nothing, a concept totally alien to their Protestant souls. Uncle Homer, unlike the Joyces, was fully inserted into Italian life and his friends miss him deeply. An even more important foil to the deadness and vicious advantage seeking of the Joyces is the couple with whom they have most contact, Tony Burton (a fellow Englishman) and his wife, Natalia. Here, North and South (which Rossellini always felt was the true division of the world, rather than East and West) are happily joined. Both husband and wife speak the other's language and their relationship appears rewarding. They seem to embody that harmony of body, mind, and spirit that the film visually locates in classical civilization and continues to offer as a cure for present-day ills.

"Italy," the enemy, intrudes upon the Joyces in nearly every frame in countless details. The Neapolitan singing that accompanies the opening credits is heard again and again, acting as the symbolic but palpable presence of Italy, occupying a sound track that constantly presses against a visual track concerned chiefly with the British couple. While they sit out on the roof of the villa drinking wine instead of taking a siesta like everyone else, we see the symbolically suggestive Vesuvius volcano in deep focus in the background of the same shot. Here the motif of the volcano, which forms the silent visual background to several of their discussions, offers the possibility of reconciliation, for it seems to operate on two levels at once, suggesting both the male principle—as it does in *Stromboli*, Rossellini's first film with Bergman—and at the same time the "femaleness" of its crater, which is negated in the earlier film by the crater's violent, threatening activity. The Joyces fight the power of the Italian sun, another constant visual presence: Katherine, who "shields" herself from it by wearing dark glasses—which none of the Italians in the film does—and Alex, who in one scene is startled awake by the sun coming through the window. Italy also intrudes in the form of sleep, and much is made of sleep in the film. Both Katherine and Alex exclaim at different moments, "How well one sleeps here!" Natalia tells Katherine at another moment that she should let Alex sleep because "sleep is always good for one." The laziness of Italy, anathema to the businesslike Joyces, has begun insidiously to affect them as well.

Probably the most important visual motif that furthers this conflict between Italy and the Joyces is their car, so obviously and continuously present. With its prominently displayed British license plates it represents that combination of mindset and ideology known as England, which naturally the Joyces bring with them to Italy. It is where we initially see them, in this little bit of England pushing through a foreign land, and we understand seconds later that the very first shots we see have been taken through the car's windshield and side window, suggesting the inevitable construction of reality through one's own culture. The car comfortably envelops them, and it protects them at least initially from the influence of this strange country. Appropriately, it offers a cold and mechanical contrast to everything organic

Figure 3-3. Katherine (Ingrid Bergman) and Alex (George Sanders), protected by their automobile. (National Film Archive, London.)

and living that we see throughout the film (in the very beginning, for example, they force their way through a lazy herd of cattle). Later, it sticks out blatantly among the ruins of Pompeii.

This thematic use of the automobile also explains, in retrospect, the earlier, lengthy tour of Uncle Homer's villa, for the villa functions as the symbolically static opposite of the Joyces' car, as an overt manifestation of Uncle Homer's organic participation in Italian life. Similarly, at various points throughout the film a slow (often panning) establishing shot on the villa begins a scene, reminding us subtly of its symbolic role, opposing the ceaseless, frenetic movement of the automobile. The villa always seems to be bathed in the intense warmth of the Italian sun or snugly enveloped in an unthreatening darkness. When Katherine makes her trips into Naples she can only grumble about how selfish and unfeeling Alex is, for as long as she is in the car she is isolated in her own miserable little existence and its multiple blind spots. But like Alex and Katherine themselves the automobile is not impervious to Italy's influence, and the environment continues to assault Katherine through the windshield. Yet it is only when she actually gets out of the car—at the "Little Vesuvius," the museum, the Cumaean Sybil, Pompeii, and at the end of the film—that she becomes truly affected by what she experiences. Similarly, when Alex improbably has the car after his return from Capri, he picks up a prostitute. Until this point he, unlike Katherine, has remained rather shielded, but when the woman invades his physical and psychological territory by entering the car, she brings with her the messiness of life in the tragic story she recounts.

But what exactly does this continual presence of Italy stand for? Clearly it is not to be taken as the fulfillment of some tourist brochure writer's fantasies about sun and fun. It does, of course, represent a greater openness to sensuality and emotion and a greater connection with what we might call the fecundity of life, but it stands just as closely to *death*. Italy in this film is a place where one is more consciously aware of life *and* death: because life is contingent and death holds final sway, life itself, as Heidegger claimed, is enhanced in value and intensity by an awareness of its opposite. What the Joyces need is not babies (or not *only* babies) but to be snapped out of the abstraction their lives have become, linked as they are only with the conventional signs of money and the other intangibles that modern life substitutes for directly lived experience. Thus while it is true that in one of her drives through Naples Katherine is overwhelmed by the number of babies and pregnant women she sees, her *first* visual experience of the city stresses a funeral carriage and numerous black-edged announcements of local deaths. In Naples, as the epigraph to this essay suggests, one is even closer to death

Figure 3-4. Alex is accosted by a prostitute as he gets into his car. (National Film Archive, London.)

than in the rest of Italy, and Rossellini delighted in telling interviewers, when discussing this film, how Neapolitan black-marketeers spend the first big money they make on elaborately decorated coffins rather than on food and clothing. Natalia takes Katherine to visit the catacombs; the English woman is shaken by this place drenched with mortality and overflowing with skulls and cannot understand why anyone would adopt a dead person to "take care of." Poor Alex cannot pick up a prostitute without her instantly beginning to tell him of a friend's recent suicide and her own temptations in that direction. In an interview, Rossellini insisted that "[Katherine] is always quoting a so-called poet who describes Italy as a country of death—imagine, Italy a country of death! Death doesn't exist here, because—it's so much a living thing that they put garlands on the heads of dead men. There is a different meaning to things here. To them death has an archeological meaning, to us it is a living reality. It's a different kind of civilisation" (Aprà and Ponzi interview 1973–74, 113).

The death theme reaches its dramatic and characteristically understated climax in the magnificent scene at Pompeii. Seconds after the Joyces' most bitter argument, which has ended in a decision to get a divorce, their host Tony comes to collect them and insists that they go with him to the digs. The archaeologists have come upon a hollow in the ground, which usually indicates a place where people were caught and instantly killed in the great eruption of Vesuvius in 79 A.D. Their emotions rubbed raw, the Joyces beg off the visit, but Tony insists that it is the chance of a lifetime and that they *must* come with him. Unable to refuse, the distraught couple accompanies Tony to the site, where the workers are to pour fresh plaster of Paris down into the hollow through small holes they have drilled. As the rather bizarre musical theme picks up (a theme we have already heard during Katherine's other wanderings through history and the strange spots of Naples) and then modulates into a tense tragic/bitter melody, dirt is scraped off the hardened plaster. One by one, body parts are revealed. The parts begin to form themselves into a man and a woman; death has caught them making love, or at least wrapped tightly in each other's arms.

Suddenly the statues in the museum, the catacombs, and the Cumaean Sybil all come together in this one startling visual image, which conveys the raw physicality of the ancient world, its irrevocable pastness, the ubiquity of death in life—and love, however inadequate and flawed, as the only possible solution. At the sight Katherine breaks down sobbing and rushes away, and Alex moves to help her; Rossellini offers no overt explanation for her reaction. Alex makes the standard excuses to the men on Katherine's behalf, and they prepare to leave. To get back to the symbolic protection of their car, they have to traverse what remains of the Roman town, and the effect on us is similar to what Katherine has experienced in the museum. In long shot we see them move across the barren ruins, once full of life and now so full of death. The tragic musical theme intensifies with truly moving effect. Finally, the emotional encounter seems to have had a positive effect on both of them. Alex ventures: "You know, I understand how you feel. I was pretty moved myself. But you must try to pull yourself together." Hopeful, she responds, "Oh, did it affect you the same way? . . . I've seen so many strange things today that I didn't have the time to tell you about. . . . There are many things I didn't tell you."

She begins to apologize for their earlier argument, but Alex, perhaps assuming that she is only trying to trap him, rebuffs her: "Why? Our situation is quite clear. We've made our decision. You don't have to make any excuses." She hardens herself, and when Alex taunts her once again about her dead poet, she shouts, "Oh, stop it! Must you continue to harp on it? I'm sick and tired of your sarcasm. We've decided to get a divorce and that settles it!" They continue picking their way through the ruins, and suddenly the musical theme turns black. At this point, Katherine stops and utters the most convincing, devastating line of the entire film: "Life is so short!" The realization of death's omnipotence has completely overwhelmed her, given the "many strange things" she has been seeing all day, but there seems no way out of their endless bickering and advantage seeking. Alex replies ambiguously, "That's why one should make the most of it." The camera follows them for a long time in an utterly desolate long shot, until they reach their car.

Immediately after we hear the joyful bounce of parade music and cut to Katherine and Alex, once again safely ensconced in the automobile as they fight their way out of Naples. This is the final scene, the most controversial

Figure 3-5. Katherine and Alex amid the ruins of Pompeii. (National Film Archive, London.)

of the film. As we initially located them moving toward the city in the car, we now see them moving away. The circle seems to be complete, and while the constant presence of Italy has forced them to confront the emptiness of their married lives together, it has yet to effect any internal changes, at least any that we can see. But one does not go through such intense emotional encounters and emerge unchanged. Subtle influences are working on them without their knowledge.

They have wandered into the middle of a huge religious procession in honor of San Gennaro, a saint from whom Neapolitans virtually demand a miracle each year during his festival, as Rossellini told François Truffaut and Eric Rohmer in 1954. Horns blow and confusion reigns as the couple picks over the remains of their marriage. Katherine, who has been more deeply affected, seems to seek a reconciliation, but Alex, suspicious, continues to reject her advances. When he says it's lucky they didn't have children because "it would make the divorce even more painful," she jumps on this: "Painful? Is it going to be painful for you?" "Well, more complicated" is his cold response. They continue to push their huge British car through the crowd (and the claustrophobic visual effect is enhanced by the complete avoidance of long shots), cold steel against human flesh and religious emotion, and ultimately they are forced to halt. The car is eaten up by the wave of humanity, the way water washes over a seemingly immovable obstacle and carries it away. Attention shifts to the parade, which we watch for a while until Alex, still seemingly unaffected by his Italian experience, says: "How can they believe in that? They're like a bunch of children!" She replies softly, "Children are happy." "Alex," she suddenly blurts out, "I don't want you to hate me. I don't want it to finish in this way." And Alex replies with lines that make his resistance more understandable and that again right the emotional balance between them: "Oh, Katherine, what are you driving at? What game are you trying to play? You've never understood me, you've never even tried. And now this nonsense. What is it you want?" "Nothing," she spits out at him. "I despise you."

Then the significant moment: they decide to get *out* of their car, out from the protection of their lifeless culture. Instantly the crowd begins shouting "Miracolo! Miracolo!", and though we can't actually see anything—perhaps appropriate for a modern-day "miracle"—the immense crowd rushes forward, taking Katherine along with them. The shot is visually brilliant: the crowd moves powerfully ahead, away from us, and Katherine is pulled with them, fighting the emotional wave of the Italians but turned back toward us and Alex, screaming wildly for help. For once the sheer violent press of life forces them out of the sealed intellectual and spiritual realm they have wanted to remain within and into the swirling world of emotion. She needs Alex suddenly on a brute existential level that is apparently new to them. Alex rescues her; we cut to a closer shot of them—the Northern giants surrounded by the Neapolitan pygmies—as they clasp each other in their arms (like the Pompeian lovers):

> KATHERINE: Oh, I don't want to lose you. *(They embrace.)*
> ALEX: Katherine, what's wrong with us? Why do we torture one another?
> KATHERINE: When you say things that hurt me, I try to hurt you back, don't you see, but I can't any longer, because I love you.
> ALEX: Perhaps we hurt too easily.
> KATHERINE: Tell me that you love me.
> ALEX: Well, if I do, will you promise not to take advantage of me?
> KATHERINE: Oh, yes, but I want to hear you say it.
> ALEX: All right, I love you.

The camera at last pans away from them, resting a long time on the anonymous faces in the crowd, transfixed by the "miracle" they have just seen; it finally moves to an enigmatic one-shot of a single member of the band. As we too struggle to reconcile ourselves to the "miracle" we have just witnessed, the film ends.

Some critics have been disappointed by the ending of *Voyage to Italy*, refusing to accept the couple's reconciliation at face value, while others have found it well prepared for and perfectly logical. In any case most have found the film as a whole to represent a remarkable shift in filmmaking practice. In its free style, which leads, in Gianni Rondolino's words, to a new "freedom of observation" (1974, 84), one can glimpse the films of Antonioni and Godard that were to come in the sixties. An important part of this new freedom of observation is accomplished through the use of visual motifs, whose meaning by their very nature can never be finally specified. It seems that Rossellini has finally fulfilled the hopes of André Bazin, not just on the level of the image or sequence, beyond which the French critic seemed unable to theorize, but on the more inclusive level of the film itself.

WORKS CITED

Aprà, Adriano, and Maurizio Ponzi. 1973–74. "An Interview with Roberto Rossellini." *Screen* 14, no. 4 (Winter): 113. (Interview originally appeared in Italian in 1965.)

Baldelli, Pio. 1972. *Roberto Rossellini*. Rome: Edizione Samona e Savelli.

Bazin, André. 1976. *What Is Cinema?* Vol. 2. Berkeley: University of California Press.

Castello, G.C. 1954. "Roberto Rossellini." *Cinema*, no. 146–47 (10 December).

Douchet, J. 1959. Interview with Rossellini. *Arts*, no. 739 (9 September).

Guarner, Jose. 1970. *Roberto Rossellini*. New York: Praeger.

Leprohon, Pierre. 1972. *The Italian Cinema*. New York: Praeger.

Marcabru, Pierre. 1961. "Les derniers feux du néo-réalisme." *Arts* (21 June).

Rondolino, Gianni. 1974. *Rossellini*. Florence: La nuova Italia.

Shedlin, Michael. 1972. "Love, Estrangement, and Coadunation in Rossellini's *Voyage to Italy*." *Women and Film* 2.

BIBLIOGRAPHY

Voyage to Italy

Bergman, Ingrid. *My Story*. New York: Delacorte Press, 1980.

Bohne, Luciana. "Rossellini's *Viaggio in Italia*: A Variation on a Theme by Joyce." *Film Criticism* 3, no. 2 (Winter 1979).

Braudy, Leo. "Rossellini: From 'Open City' to 'General della Rovere.' " In *Great Film*

Directors: A Critical Anthology, edited by Leo Braudy and Morris Dickstein. New York: Oxford University Press, 1978.

Collin, Philippe. "Voyage en Italie." *Télé-Ciné*, no. 50 (July–August 1955).

Wood, Robin. "Rossellini." *Film Comment* 10, no. 4 (July–August 1974).

Visual Motifs

Arnheim, Rudolf. *Art and Visual Perception: A Psychology of the Creative Eye*. Berkeley: University of California Press, 1954.

———. *Visual Thinking*. Berkeley: University of California Press, 1969.

Balazs, Bela. *Theory of the Film*. New York: Dover, 1970.

Bobker, Lee R. *Elements of Film*. 2d ed. New York: Harcourt Brace Jovanovich, 1974.

Clarke, Charles G. *Professional Cinematography*. Hollywood, Calif.: American Society of Cinematographers, 1964.

Gibson, James J. *The Perception of the Visual World*. Boston: Houghton Mifflin, 1950.

Kepes, Gyorgy. *Language of Vision*. Chicago: Theobald, 1944.

Malkiewicz, J. Kris. *Cinematography*. New York: Van Nostrand Reinhold, 1973.

Nichols, Bill. *Ideology and the Image*. Bloomington: Indiana University Press, 1981.

Nilsen, Vladimir. *The Cinema as a Graphic Art*. New York: Hill & Wang, 1973.

4

ALL THAT HEAVEN ALLOWS: COLOR, NARRATIVE SPACE, AND MELODRAMA

Mary Beth Haralovich

Both color and melodrama can challenge the conventions of Hollywood cinematic realism. In melodrama the ideological bases of social life are given material existence through narrative structure and through cinematic expression, especially in the details of *mise-en-scène*. Color can contribute to the "visibility" of these ideologies through realist *mise-en-scène*, yet color can also subvert the "invisible" realism of narrative space. In the following analysis of *All That Heaven Allows* (Douglas Sirk, 1954), I consider how the film participates in the potentially subversive goals of melodrama and in the realist conventions of cinematic expression through color.[1]

1. In their dialogue in *Cinema Journal*, Christine Gledhill and E. Ann Kaplan place the concepts of realism and melodrama not in opposition to each other but on a continuum of textual practices ranging from those that are relatively complicit in and those that are relatively resistant to patriarchal representations of social life. Gledhill suggests that melodrama is related to realism in that it foregrounds "struggles within the status quo" by giving material existence to the social formation. Kaplan argues for an understanding of the *degree* to which textual strategies such as melodrama can expose or comment on existing gender positions. Their discussion has

All That Heaven Allows centers on a woman who is in the process of redefining her social and sexual identity. Her struggle is positioned within her community and her family. Cary (Jane Wyman) is a widow with two grown children who are ready to leave their comfortable middle-class suburban home for lives of their own. Cary also desires to leave that suburban home, to exchange it for the bucolic old mill that her gardener, Ron (Rock Hudson), a somewhat younger service worker, offers her in marriage. Unlike the departures of her children, Cary's departure from the suburban lifestyle is the subject of controversy and resistance—from her children and from the suburban community—two forces that had contributed to the former security of her identity.

One can argue that *All That Heaven Allows* exposes contradictions in the stated social benefits of suburbia. The perceived value of community homogeneity and segregation by class, race, age, and ethnicity was explicit in post–World War II social policies on suburban housing. The film can therefore be read as positioning this woman's resistance against that dominant ideology. Yet Cary is also in the process of outgrowing the target group of suburban dwellers. Her family is no longer the nuclear family with growing children for whom suburban living promised its benefits. Families that fit more comfortably into this social formation are television's 1950s suburban families. Neither the Andersons of *Father Knows Best* nor the Cleavers of *Leave It to Beaver* have problematic relationships with the ideologies that inform their domestic and social environment.[2]

All That Heaven Allows therefore can be considered as one instance of contemporary resistance to patriarchal ideologies in that the film comments upon the material determinations of Cary's social identity. These ideologies are partially expressed through the verisimilitude of narrative space that underscores the film's structure of oppositions between suburban repressiveness and an alternative way of living. Color helps give expression to Cary's ideological struggle. A primary component of *mise-en-scène*, color helps Cary's familial and suburban environment seem real.

But color in *All That Heaven Allows* also distracts from the realism of the film. This use of color is complex in that it both remains within the conventions of realist color film practice and diverges from those conventions. This

---

influenced my analysis of color, narrative space, and melodrama in *All That Heaven Allows*. See Christine Gledhill and E. Ann Kaplan, "Dialogue," *Cinema Journal* 25, no. 4 (Summer 1986): 44–53.

2. See Mary Beth Haralovich, "Sitcoms and Suburbs: Positioning the 1950s Homemaker," *Quarterly Review of Film and Video* 11, no. 1 (1989): 61–83.

divergence can be partially explained, I believe, by considering how the needs of melodrama to express ideologies push the conventions of realist narrative space and by examining the ways that *All That Heaven Allows* departs from the conventions of melodrama.

MELODRAMA AND IDEOLOGIES: CHARACTER AND REALIST NARRATIVE SPACE

One goal of textual analysis is to understand how films work ideologies through narrative, character, and style. Melodrama has been of particular interest in this regard because it is a genre whose conventions make ideologies "visible and watchable."[3] Familial and social pressures act on characters to produce narrative conflict—a conflict between the desires of the character and the pressures that impede the satisfaction of those desires. The resolution of the narrative can neither eradicate nor resolve the ideological sources of the conflict. Thus the "happy ending" of melodrama involves a recognition that characters and conflict exist within social forces greater than the characters themselves.

In melodrama, characters are defined as social beings. This attention to the ideologies that underpin social life is an important convention of the melodrama genre (Gledhill 1987, 5–28). Yet melodramas are also well within the conventions of the Hollywood film, which typically represses ideologies rather than analyzing or critiquing them (Mulvey 1987, 75; Nowell-Smith 1987, 74). In many ways melodrama explores the degree to which ideologies can come forward in the Hollywood film. Consider how melodrama makes use of two primary conventions of the Hollywood film: the relationship of character traits and goals to narrative conflict and the verisimilitude of realist narrative space.

Two narrative functions of characters in melodrama correspond to two ways that melodrama critiques ideologies. First, the way the characters engender narrative conflict extends beyond their personal goals and desires to include analysis of the ideological nature of their traits and actions (Elsaesser 1987, 63–65). The narrative asks how these characters can find happiness when their desires lie in opposition to their family, community, class, race, and/or gender identities. In *All That Heaven Allows* Cary's desire for a life

3. How films make ideologies "visible and watchable" is a primary goal of Tony Bennett and Janet Woollacott's methodology for the analysis of popular fiction. See Tony Bennett and Janet Woollacott, *Bond and Beyond: The Political Career of a Popular Hero* (New York: Methuen, 1987), esp. chap. 6, "The Bond Films: 'Determination' and 'Production'."

with Ron is perceived by the other characters as a threat to the foundations of the social formation. Cary's son, daughter, and most of her friends disapprove of her wish to cross the boundaries of class, age, and sexuality.

Yet the film also proceeds toward a "happy ending" in which the ideological pressures of family and community are somewhat dispersed. Kay is en route to forming her own family, and Ned leaves the home and family for a life away. Cary's friends are represented as so bound within social conventions that their influence on her life deserves to be repudiated. Cary eventually finds her place within a "new" social formation with Ron. Melodrama works toward exposing ideologies while also recognizing the pressures of the happy ending that allows characters to find a comfortable place within the patriarchal order (Nowell-Smith, 73).

The second function of characters in melodrama is to live through and to express emotions. Characters are not simply villains or strong hero(in)es. They are not represented as individuals who are able to surmount social pressures through bravery or special physical and emotional strength (Elsaesser, 55–58, 64–67; Gledhill, 31–33). Melodramas are also known as "weepies" because the characters' struggles are tied so strongly to ideologies over which they have no control. The emotions of characters critique ideology because these emotions show how difficult it is to cope with ideological pressures.

Rainer Werner Fassbinder commented about Sirk's *Imitation of Life* (1959) that the audience weeps because it understands why the characters must be in conflict and how social life inevitably engenders the conflict: "The cruelty is that we can understand them both [Annie and Sarah Jane], both are right and no one will be able to help them. Unless we change the world. At this point all of us in the cinema cried. Because changing the world is so difficult" (Fassbinder 1972, 106). Thus one of the ways melodrama brings ideologies to the surface is through explicitly linking character motivation, emotion, and conflict with the ideologies that inform the position of characters in social life: as members of family, community, race, and class and as gendered beings.

The stylistic conventions of realism place these characters and conflicts within a recognizable social world (Gledhill, 37)—that of the home, family, and community. In one way, melodrama uses *mise-en-scène* as other Hollywood films do. Costumes, settings, lighting, and the arrangement of characters in the frame—all help to define the characters and their relationship to each other and to the conflict the film is working through. But the realist narrative space of melodrama also makes evident the social pressures and ideologies that participate in the definition of the characters and the conflict.

In addition to using objects and decor to make ideologies and social pressures concrete, *mise-en-scène* also makes visible the different points of view that participate in the ideological conflict (Elsaesser, 61–62, 67).

In *All That Heaven Allows* there are four significant and contrasting narrative spaces that help underscore Cary's struggle for identity: Cary's and Sara's suburban homes and the oppositional space of Ron's old mill and the Andersons' house. Cary's home serves several functions: a haven for the family secure in the knowledge that everything is as it was; evidence of the restrictive nature of Cary's class and community; the ground on which Cary's alienation from her family takes place; and, finally, a manifestation of the ideological prison from which Cary will escape. The cocktail party at Sara's home confirms the sources of the pressures on Cary while Ron's old mill and the Andersons' party suggest comfortable and pleasurable alternatives to the suburban ideologies.

Mise-en-scène also contributes to the second function of characters in melodrama, the expression of emotions. Many emotions are well within realist expectations: sadness, desire, happiness, frustration, insecurity, and so on. Yet melodrama also deals with more extreme emotions, emotions produced from the deeply fundamental inability of characters to conform to ideological demands, especially in the area of sexual identity. This emotional energy is often expressed through visuals that seem to exceed the possibilities of verisimilitude and realist narrative space (Elsaesser, 59–61; Gledhill, 9; Nowell-Smith, 73–74).

In *All That Heaven Allows* Cary's emotionally charged discussion with her daughter avoids being verbally explicit about Kay's response to her mother's sexuality. What the dialogue cannot say at this point in film history is exhibited in the intense color striations that cross Cary's and her daughter's faces. Because the conventions of melodrama are situated in ideological conflicts and because characters must express the emotions that derive from these fundamental conflicts, the aesthetics of melodrama must sometimes diverge from the verisimilitude of realism in order to vent the emotions important to the genre.

Melodrama, then, works ideologies through narrative and character in multiple ways. Characters are defined and motivated by the contradictory pressures of ideologies. Narrative conflict stems from the desires of characters being at odds with their social and sexual identities. Melodrama uses realist narrative space to both validate the presence of the social world and to identify the ideologies that motivate character and conflict.

The 1950s color melodramas are especially fertile ground for exploring how melodrama can comment upon ideologies within Hollywood film practice. In *All That Heaven Allows* color's participation in realist narrative space helps make evident the ideologies that inform Cary's struggle with her repressive suburban environment and her family. Color also emphasizes the emotional register of the film. Yet analysis of the color system of *All That Heaven Allows* does not merely show that the film is an exemplary instance of color participating in the conventions of melodrama. As we shall see, color has three additional functions in the film: (1) as part of the realist aesthetics of the Hollywood film; (2) as a device for pulling the film away from or decentering it from conventional Hollywood film practice; and (3) as a means of blocking concentration on the story and thereby impeding the emotional trajectory of melodrama.

CONVENTIONS OF COLOR FILM PRACTICE

The complexity of the color system in *All That Heaven Allows* can be understood by considering how it remains within the conventions of realist color film practice and also how it diverges from those conventions. As Steve Neale has shown in his discussion of the history of film industry discourses on color, color had two contradictory impulses: toward realism and toward spectacle. These contradictions were "managed and contained" by the development of filmmaking practices that subordinated color to the primacy of narrative. Color has the ability to reproduce the "natural" look of the world and thereby evoke reality. Yet color can also draw attention to itself and is therefore capable of disrupting realism. While color is "a 'natural' ingredient of visual reality," color can also trouble the integrity of visual reality. Color can exceed its narrative function and thus destroy the illusion of reality important to realist filmmaking (Neale 1985, 145–51).

In some genres the rules of verisimilitude are not tied to conventions of realism. In "genres of stylization and spectacle" (the musical comedy, the historical epic, the adventure story, fantasy), color contributes to an aesthetic of spectacle and fantasy and is therefore not incompatible with concentration on the story (Bordwell, Staiger, and Thompson 1985, 355; Neale, 148–49). In realist drama, on the other hand, color should support the story. Neale has shown how color was considered to be an "intruder" upon realist drama, "usurp[ing] the proper functioning of other more important elements" such as character and story (Neale, 149). This potential of color to exceed realism should be repressed in favor of color that more clearly underscores the narrative.

The color system of *All That Heaven Allows* takes advantage of this double potential of color, breaking the "rules" of color film practice in subtle and complex ways. I discuss below six conventions of classical realist filmmaking that were established to ensure that color would not intrude upon realism or interfere with the primacy of the narrative. These conventions are derived from two principle sources: the "law of emphasis" developed in the 1920s by Natalie Kalmus for use in the Color Advisory Service of the Technicolor Company[4] and the 1957 Society of Motion Picture Technicians and Engineers' (SMPTE) publication on color cinematography. Although Kalmus's "law of emphasis" was developed expressly for use with Technicolor, as Neale has argued, her guidelines for color were not "idiosyncratic" (Neale, 151).

1. *Color should contribute to unobtrusive realism.* The SMPTE manual stresses that in color planning for a film, "color 'normalcy' is generally the goal." Kalmus's "law of emphasis" and the SMPTE agree that color is not an autonomous element in filmmaking and that it should be used in a manner appropriate to the "given story situation." "Don't try to *force* color into a picture," the SMPTE advises. Unless color functions as a specific signifier of narrative meaning, it should contribute to the unobtrusive realism of the film (Neale, 149–50; SMPTE, 43).

2. *Color should be emphasized only when it carries specific meaning.* For Kalmus, "nothing of relative unimportance in a picture shall be emphasized."

4. Natalie Kalmus was head of the Color Advisory Service of the Technicolor Company. She helped enforce the norms of cinematic expression in Technicolor through the avenue of the color consultant. The color consultant advised cinematographers, art directors, costume designers, and directors on how to use Technicolor so that *mise-en-scène* would support the structure and "mood" of the narrative. Technicolor brought with it very strict and particular aesthetic regulations.

Kalmus's "law of emphasis" was designed to ensure that color would not function as an autonomous element in cinematic expression. Scripts were analyzed for the dominant mood or emotion of each scene and then appropriate colors were assigned to the film. Colors were to be harmonious in relation to each other unless the dramatic value of the scene required that color function as a signifier of specific meaning. Thus, it was argued, audiences would not be distracted from the more important elements of the story. See Basten, 66–71; Bordwell, Staiger, and Thompson, 356; and Neale, 150–51.

The credits of *All That Heaven Allows* contain the words "Print by Technicolor." This indicates that Technicolor processes were used only in the final release prints of the film and that the film was not shot in the three-strip Technicolor process. This raises several questions about the conditions of production of the film, including the role of William Fritsche as Technicolor consultant in production planning and the degree to which Technicolor's prescriptions on color would affect the development of the color system of films that were only printed by Technicolor.

For the SMPTE, "color [should] 'act' with the story, never being a separate entity to compete with or to detract from the dramatic content of the picture. . . . if it does not do this, we invariably find it in competition with the story." One should never be "conscious" of color unless it means something (Basten 1980, 70; Neale, 149; SMPTE, 41).

3. *Eliminate distracting focal points*. Color should be used in uncomplicated ways. Distracting focal points should be eliminated within scenes. Kalmus advises that "unnecessary busyness [succeeds] only in disturbing a viewer's concentration and tiring [the] eyes." For the SMPTE, "if a background is a clutter of *color and detail*, it becomes an even stronger visual magnet [than background clutter in a black and white film]. By using fewer and less saturated colors as well as by simplifying background detail, any action of the actors becomes more definite and emphatic, and color plays its proper role as one of the prime factors of story-telling." Thus, color should not intrude upon the balance of the *mise-en-scène* necessary to understanding the narrative (Basten, 70; SMPTE, 41).

4. *Color used in costumes should enhance character traits and separate actors from backgrounds and from each other*. Kalmus advised filmmakers to "clothe [actors] in colors that build up his or her screen personality." The SMPTE was more specific: "The color in costumes cannot be permitted to become 'eye-catchers' unless such an effect is deliberately desired, and so helps rather than hinders the story." Also, "costumes and wardrobe have the added function of punctuating the actors against the background" (Basten, 70; SMPTE, 43).

5. *Color can move through editing*. Color is an important factor in how films are edited. The SMPTE points out that color "moves" not only within the scene with character movement and camera movement but also through editing. A color that was in the background in one shot can be brought to the foreground in the next shot. This color "movement" has the potential to disturb the smooth flow of a film (SMPTE, 41).

6. *The female lead has primacy in color planning*. The role of the female lead is crucial to the development of the color system used in a film. The SMPTE stresses that her "appearance is of paramount concern [and] must be given undisputed priority. . . . If her complexion limits the colors she can wear successfully, this in turn restricts the background colors." Thus the coloring of the lead actress should dominate the color system of a film—her costumes and the sets as well as the casting and costuming of other actors (SMPTE, 40–41).

Melodrama participates in and contradicts these conventions of color film practice. The genre is dependent on the presence of a recognizable social world in order to situate characters and narrative conflict within ideologies. *Mise-en-scène* will therefore underscore what Kalmus and the SMPTE call the "story": the emphasis on understanding characters. However, making ideologies visible is an important part of the story melodrama tells. Within the parameters of unobtrusive narrative space, melodrama must exhibit the material realities that make the ideological pressures on the characters understandable. Thus the function of color in the *mise-en-scène* of melodrama will usually be doubly motivated: by the conventions of melodrama and by the conventions of the color Hollywood film.

Yet color in *All That Heaven Allows* is both natural and intrusive. Because the *mise-en-scène* appears "natural," it contributes to the primacy of narrative and therefore to an understanding of the characters and the story of melodrama. However, in its deviations from the principles of Hollywood film practice, the color system of *All That Heaven Allows* complicates the melodrama and troubles the primacy of narrative.

ALL THAT HEAVEN ALLOWS: COLOR, REALIST NARRATIVE SPACE, AND MELODRAMA

In *All That Heaven Allows* narrative space participates in both the "unobtrusive realism" of conventional film practice and melodrama's analysis of ideologies. An opposition that helps structure the film as melodrama is the contrast between familial and suburban repressiveness and the more open social life of Ron's alternative lifestyle. The values associated with these ways of living are underscored by the realist narrative space in which each character lives. Thus the ideological pressures on Cary's social and sexual identity are made visible. Narrative space helps the film to examine Cary in ideological terms, to explain why she must struggle with herself and why her desires are at odds with those of her family and community.

As Fassbinder has observed about *All That Heaven Allows*, "in Sirk, people are always placed in rooms already heavily marked by their social situation. . . . In Jane's house there is only one way in which one could possibly move" (Fassbinder, 97). Living space, and its attendant possibilities for interaction among characters, is restricted in Cary's living room, where the aesthetics of furniture arrangement creates a single pathway by which one can traverse the room and a designated formal conversation area in front of the fireplace (fig. 4–1). In Ron's old mill and the apartment of his friends, the Andersons, space is open. It is not compartmentalized into separate family or social functions. The Andersons' party shows how this alternative space is adjustable for the serendipity of makeshift dining arrangements and dancing to homemade music. Social interaction is flexible in this adaptable space; it is more intimate, less formal (fig. 4–2).

This opposition is made visible through the design of interior space and the degree to which characters can comfortably move within it. In addition, Cary's home and Ron's old mill have contrasting color tones, which—combined with the arrangement of furniture and objects—underscores the ideologies the film takes up. Cary's home is dominated by cool blue-grey walls, light tones, and tasteful furniture. Ron's space is richer with warm wood hues. It is rougher in texture and the furniture appears more casually placed in the room (fig. 4–3). This use of color in the narrative space has meaning in that it helps to make the contrasts in lifestyle visible. Yet at the same time this narrative space has "normalcy"; it is "unobtrusive" in its realism.

However, the color system and realist narrative space in *All That Heaven Allows* do not simply establish a binary opposition between suburban conformity and an alternative Walden-like existence. Color also functions in excess of narrative primacy in several ways. In many instances where color is "excessive" or has the potential to disturb concentration on the story, the color is doubly motivated: by realist narrative space and by the conventions of melodrama. Color in *All That Heaven Allows* is, then, within the conventions of normalcy at the same time that it "complicates" the narrative space.

The scene in which Cary's daughter, Kay, confronts her mother with the social implications of Cary's relationship with Ron is a well-known and obvious moment of excess (fig. 4–4). Color functions as a signifier of the psychic and sexual energy that cannot be contained or expressed by the narrative in the usual ways. In this scene the potential of color to function as spectacle is not solely motivated by the emotional register of melodrama. A diegetic source for the color striations exists within the realist narrative space of Kay's bedroom (fig. 4–5). The scene begins when Kay enters her room, tossing her jacket down on a chair by a window that is apparently constructed of stained glass. Fabric has been positioned outside the window to give the effect of colored glass. Kay's movement toward this window helps to mark it as the apparent natural source for the intense color that inflects the interchange between Kay and Cary. This "excess" is tempered, to a degree, by realist narrative space. Yet it is also "obtrusive" realism and a signifier of the emotional intensity that underscores the familial and social pressures on Cary.

While this scene is an isolated and conspicuous instance of color that is neither harmonious nor uncomplicated, the film uses red, yellow, and blue in similar ways. These colors are within the conventions of realist color filmmaking, and they also comment on the ideologies the film takes up. Yet they also have the potential to distract from the "more important" elements of character and story.

Red is sometimes obedient to color conventions in that it functions as a specific signifier of character and narrative development. When Cary decides to rejoin the social world on her date with Harvey, her children take notice of her red dress (fig. 4–6). As Laura Mulvey has observed, Cary's red dress is misconstrued by her children as evidence that "the impotent and decrepit Harvey" is the object of Cary's "newly awakened interest in life and love" (Mulvey, 78). In her prior social excursions outside the home Cary wore a black velvet dress more suitable to her status as a widow. The red dress is marked by the characters as evidence of a change in Cary's identity as a sexual being.

The strength of the color red also functions to markedly separate Cary from other characters and from the settings of her home and the country club. She stands out as protagonist as her character progresses through the narrative. In addition, the gathering at the country club is the first time that Cary's sexuality is explicitly shown to be a problem. She is assaulted by Howard who takes Cary's reappearance in social life (and, presumably, her red dress) as evidence of her sexual availability.

Later in the film, at Christmas, when Kay and Ned give Cary a television set as a substitute for living her own life, Kay's red dress functions in ways similar to Cary's—to mark the change in her character and to underscore an emotional moment in the narrative (fig. 4–7). Kay has undergone a transition from an immature and cold intellectual to a woman who is loved. A red dress, already marked by the film as a signifier of woman's sexuality, is incorporated into Kay's new look as object of desire: no longer wearing glasses, her glamour make-up and misty expression enhanced by soft lighting. Kay apologizes to Cary for not understanding Cary's need to be loved by Ron. Cary, having succumbed to the pressure of her children and turned away from a relationship with Ron, listens to Kay in some misery.

The red costumes each woman wears stand out against the more uniform color of the *mise-en-scène*. Yet these costumes also have specific meaning for the narrative and for the development of the characters of Cary and Kay. In addition, the red costumes comment on the ideologies that constrain woman's identity. They are indicative of the role a woman's sexual identity plays in her life and in the life of her family.

However, there are many scenes in the film where red is used as a "visual magnet," creating focal points that distract from the primacy of narrative and character. When Cary walks through the Christmas tree lot after her breakup with Ron, men in red jackets interfere with viewer identification of Ron, who is also in a red jacket, standing on the truck (fig. 4–8). In a scene at the train station Cary's discussion with an unidentified woman in a red-orange scarf provides the information that Cary is waiting for her children to arrive. But Cary's back is to the camera, thus allowing the red-orange scarf to distract attention from the main character. In an early scene in Cary's bedroom Kay picks up an ambiguous red object (a small purse, perhaps) and carries it to the dresser, thus moving the color red (held in an object without narrative significance) within the more uniform color of the bedroom.

The color system of the film does not always use red to separate objects or characters from the setting in order to emphasize the narrative or to comment on ideologies. While these red objects—purse, scarf, jackets—are all "natural" colors, they complicate the realist narrative space, interfere with the emotional trajectory of melodrama, and trouble the attention to the narrative that is important to the conventions of color film practice.

Unlike the color red, the colors blue and yellow appear to participate in more uniform color systems. Throughout the film blue is a signifier for nighttime while yellow indicates warm interior lighting. While both colors are motivated by "natural" sources within the *mise-en-scène* and while neither color is as distractive as red, in combination blue and yellow are neither especially harmonious nor restful to the eye. The evening after Ron and Cary meet, Cary has placed the tree branches Ron has given her in a vase on her dresser. Ned and Kay enter Cary's bedroom, thus intertwining the two forces that will vie for Cary in the rest of the film: Ron and Cary's family. The deep blue from the night and the yellow from the hallway compete for viewer attention, making it unclear where the eye should go in the narrative space (fig. 4–9).

This use of color complicates the otherwise realist narrative space of the bedroom. Its relative lack of visual harmony suggests that Cary's attraction to Ron will be a problem later in the film. But at this point the combination of blue and yellow does not yet function as a specific signifier of narrative meaning. Later in the film, however, the greater problem of Cary's sexual identity is enveloped within blue and yellow. Howard's assault on Cary at the country club takes place outdoors on a terrace (fig. 4–10). The yellow from the interior and the blue from the night are visually contentious. Also, Cary's red dress—already marked as a signifier of her sexual awakening—and Howard's "reading" of Cary's availability supply this narrative space with the troubling meaning that was not made explicit in the earlier scene in Cary's bedroom. Blue and yellow in combination complicate the realist narrative space and help to underscore the fact that Cary's sexual identity—whether

Figure 4-1. Living space is restrictive in Cary's tastefully furnished, blue-grey living room arrangement. (Copyright by Universal Pictures, a division of Universal Studios, Inc. Courtesy of MCA Publishing Rights, a division of MCA, Inc.)

Figure 4-2. The color of Cary's costume shows that she is adaptable within the less formal interior space of the Andersons' home. (Copyright by Universal Pictures, a division of Universal Studios, Inc. Courtesy of MCA Publishing Rights, a division of MCA, Inc.)

Figure 4-3. In Ron's old mill, space is open and the room has rich, warm tones. (Copyright by Universal Pictures, a division of Universal Studios, Inc. Courtesy of MCA Publishing Rights, a division of MCA, Inc.)

Figure 4-4. Obtrusive color functions as a signifier of the ideological pressures that cannot be expressed through dialogue. (Copyright by Universal Pictures, a division of Universal Studios, Inc. Courtesy of MCA Publishing Rights, a division of MCA, Inc.)

Figure 4-5. A diegetic source for the subsequent unrealistic color is suggested as Kay walks toward the colored "glass" of the window. (Copyright by Universal Pictures, a division of Universal Studios, Inc. Courtesy of MCA Publishing Rights, a division of MCA, Inc.)

Figure 4-6. Cary's red dress is clearly marked, setting her apart as protagonist and suggesting a change in her sexual self-identity. (Copyright by Universal Pictures, a division of Universal Studios, Inc. Courtesy of MCA Publishing Rights, a division of MCA, Inc.)

Figure 4-7. In a red dress, Kay, transformed by love, apologizes to Cary for not understanding Cary's need to be loved by Ron. (Copyright by Universal Pictures, a division of Universal Studios, Inc. Courtesy of MCA Publishing Rights, a division of MCA, Inc.)

Figure 4-8. Red jackets create focal points that interfere with the identification of Ron, thus distracting from the primacy of narrative. (Copyright by Universal Pictures, a division of Universal Studios, Inc. Courtesy of MCA Publishing Rights, a division of MCA, Inc.)

Figure 4-9. Blue and yellow compete for attention, complicating the composition of the *mise-en-scène* and looking toward problems with Cary's sexuality. (Copyright by Universal Pictures, a division of Universal Studios, Inc. Courtesy of MCA Publishing Rights, a division of MCA, Inc.)

Figure 4-10. Blue, red, and yellow are visually contentious, confirming that Cary's sexual identity is a problem. (Copyright by Universal Pictures, a division of Universal Studios, Inc. Courtesy of MCA Publishing Rights, a division of MCA, Inc.)

Figure 4-11. Cary pauses in an intense blue light, captured in the confining space of her home. (Copyright by Universal Pictures, a division of Universal Studios, Inc. Courtesy of MCA Publishing Rights, a division of MCA, Inc.)

Figure 4-12. The functions of the female lead in color planning, as central character and as spectacle, are split between Jane Wyman and Agnes Moorehead. (Copyright by Universal Pictures, a division of Universal Studios, Inc. Courtesy of MCA Publishing Rights, a division of MCA, Inc.)

Figure 4-13. Cary's costumes allow her to merge within the narrative space of her home, confirming the ideological pressures that inform her struggle. (Copyright by Universal Pictures, a division of Universal Studios, Inc. Courtesy of MCA Publishing Rights, a division of MCA, Inc.)

Figure 4-14. Cary's dress and Ron's suit are homogeneous with other costumes when Cary tries to integrate Ron into her community. (Copyright by Universal Pictures, a division of Universal Studios, Inc. Courtesy of MCA Publishing Rights, a division of MCA, Inc.)

Figure 4-15. Ron's sad and solitary pose dissolves into housekeeping activities in Cary's bedroom. (Copyright by Universal Pictures, a division of Universal Studios, Inc. Courtesy of MCA Publishing Rights, a division of MCA, Inc.)

Figure 4-16. This distractively busy *mise-en-scène* refuses to sustain a uniform emotion of "sadness" across the cut. (Copyright by Universal Pictures, a division of Universal Studios, Inc. Courtesy of MCA Publishing Rights, a division of MCA, Inc.)

explicitly linked with Ron or not—is an ideological problematic that this melodrama will take up.

In one scene blue comes very close to functioning as an emphasis in itself, intruding on the realist narrative space. After the Christmas scene in which Cary learns that her children have plans to live their own lives outside of the family home, Cary comes to regret her decision not to marry Ron. She wanders around her living room and possessions. It is night and Cary pauses in an intense blue light (fig. 4–11). While this blue is not a specific signifier of narrative meaning, it does serve to capture Cary in this space. Because the intensity of the light exceeds verisimilitude, it is somewhat disruptive to this narrative space. Yet is also underscores Cary's loneliness and her realization that she tied herself to an ideology that will make her unhappy.

In the last area of color I would like to consider—the role of the female lead in relation to the film's color system—*All That Heaven Allows* splits the primacy of the female lead in color planning between Jane Wyman and Agnes Moorehead. In his analysis of the role the female star plays in the development of color aesthetics, Neale observes that "whether conceived and articulated in terms of the discourse of 'natural beauty' or the discourse of 'glamour'," color aesthetics ensured that the female lead would provide spectacle to be looked at at the same time that she carried out her function within the narrative (Neale, 151–55). In *All That Heaven Allows*, however, Moorehead functions more strongly as the source of color spectacle than Wyman does. Moorehead's coloring, make-up, and costumes emphasize the ability of color to capture pastels and flesh tones while Wyman blends into the background (fig. 4–12).

Color accentuates Moorehead, shifting the color emphasis away from the film's female protagonist and thereby deviating from the conventions of color film practice. However, using color to embed Cary within narrative space is also a subtle way of underscoring the primacy of the melodrama narrative. With the exception of the red dress, Wyman's costumes function to place Cary within the monochromatic tones of the narrative space of her suburban home and also to show that she is easily adaptable to Ron's less conformist setting (fig. 4–2).

It is Sara, Cary's best friend, who is costumed more conventionally as the female lead. Sara is separated from the background by color while Cary wears the blue-grey tones of her suburban home. Cary's integration into the home is emphasized through Sara, who appears with Cary in much of the space of the home: outdoors, the kitchen, the living room, Cary's bedroom. Sara's orange coat complements her hair, while Cary's suit allows her to merge with the decor of her living room and dining room (fig. 4–13). Sara wears red "visual magnets" as she visits with Cary in the kitchen, while Cary blends into the setting. In Cary's bedroom Sara's orange dress allows her to stand apart from the setting, while Cary's costume adopts the color of her bedroom.

It can be argued that Sara has a vivacious and scintillating personality that is underscored by her costumes and that Cary's costumes are an indicator of her ability to be comfortable in the oppositional settings of the film. Cary's black velvet dress and Ron's three-piece suit are homogeneous with other costumes at Sara's cocktail party when Cary tries to show that Ron can fit in with her friends (fig. 4–14). In the alternative space of the film Cary is one among the others who look on as Ron opens a wine bottle with his teeth at the Andersons' dinner party. The visually flamboyant Sara would more likely be marked as "different" in this warm-toned environment.

While Cary's adaptability may be one motivation for her costumes, their monochromatic tones also firmly place her within the confining space of her suburban home and thereby into the ideological pressures that inform her struggle. However, even as the color system of *All That Heaven Allows* splits the functions of protagonist and spectacle between Cary and Sara, at a key moment in the film this split subverts the emotional trajectory of the melodrama. After Cary informs Ron that she cannot marry him because of pressure from her family, Ron's sad pose (fig. 4–15) dissolves into a shot of Cary's bedroom (fig. 4–16). A maid is vacuuming the hallway floor in the background while Sara, in an orange dress, talks with Cary about her decision. This shift in color refuses to sustain "sadness" across the cut. In this distractively busy *mise-en-scène* the deep space housekeeping activities and Sara's costume compete for attention. Rather than maintaining a uniform emotional register in this transition, the contrast in color underscores the ideologies that separate Cary from the peace and solitude of Ron's old mill.

One could consider melodrama as another "genre of stylization and spectacle" in that color which appears to deviate from conventional color film practice is motivated by the genre conventions of melodrama. The need to make ideologies visible in melodrama is ultimately not troubling to the primacy of narrative but is well within the stylistic parameters of the genre. However, unlike the musical or fantasy genres, melodrama is much more circumscribed by the need to represent realist narrative space.

The color system in *All That Heaven Allows* is very complex whether considered within the conventions of color film practice or within the conventions of melodrama. In some very orthodox ways the color system of the film helps make ideologies visible by giving material existence to the oppositional social formations that structure the film. Yet even while the realist narrative space provides "normal" sources for all of the colors, *All That Heaven Allows* also uses the ability of color to function as an emphasis in itself: as spectacle, as excess, and as potentially distractive of the primacy of narrative. The film's divergence from conventional Hollywood realism can only be partially explained by the genre conventions and aesthetics of melodrama. Research into the industrial conditions of production of *All That Heaven Allows* and other 1950s color melodramas can further our understanding of the apparent contradictions between melodrama and studio-produced commercial entertainment.

WORKS CITED

Basten, Fred. 1980. *Glorious Technicolor*. Cranbury, N.J.: A. S. Barnes.

Bordwell, David, Janet Staiger, and Kristin Thompson. 1985. *The Classical Hollywood Cinema: Film Style and Mode of Production to 1960*. New York: Columbia University Press.

Elsaesser, Thomas. 1987. "Tales of Sound and Fury: Observations on the Family Melodrama." In *Home Is Where the Heart Is: Studies in Melodrama and the Woman's Film*, edited by Christine Gledhill, 43–69. London: British Film Institute.

Fassbinder, Rainer Werner. 1972. "Six Films by Douglas Sirk." In *Douglas Sirk*, edited by Laura Mulvey and Jon Halliday and translated by Thomas Elsaesser, 95–107. Edinburgh Film Festival.

Gledhill, Christine. 1987. "The Melodramatic Field: An Investigation." In *Home Is Where the Heart Is: Studies in Melodrama and the Woman's Film*, edited by Christine Gledhill, 5–39. London: British Film Institute.

Mulvey, Laura. 1987. "Notes on Sirk and Melodrama." In *Home Is Where the Heart Is: Studies in Melodrama and the Woman's Film*, edited by Christine Gledhill, 75–79. London: British Film Institute.

Neale, Steve. 1985. *Cinema and Technology: Image, Sound, Colour*. Bloomington: Indiana University Press.

Nowell-Smith, Geoffrey. 1987. "Minnelli and Melodrama." In *Home Is Where the Heart Is: Studies in Melodrama and the Woman's Film*, edited by Christine Gledhill, 70–74. London: British Film Institute.

Society of Motion Picture and Television Engineers (SMPTE). 1957. *Elements of Color in Professional Motion Pictures*. SMPTE.

BIBLIOGRAPHY

Color

Branigan, Edward. "Color and Cinema: Problems in the Writing of History." *Film Reader* 4 (1979): 16–34.

ALL THAT HEAVEN ALLOWS

Buscombe, Edward. "Sound and Color." In *Movies and Methods*, vol. 2, edited by Bill Nichols, 83–91. Berkeley: University of California Press, 1985.

Kindem, Gorham. "Hollywood's Conversion to Color: The Technological, Economic, and Aesthetic Factors." In *The American Movie Industry*, edited by Gorham Kindem, 146–58. Carbondale: Southern Illinois University Press, 1982.

Melodrama

Gledhill, Christine, ed. *Home Is Where the Heart Is: Studies in Melodrama and the Woman's Film*. London: British Film Institute. 1987.

5

THE SPACE OF *EQUINOX FLOWER*

Edward Branigan

One critic says of the films of Ozu Yasujiro that "There is generally poetry in exactness" (Gilliatt 1973, 83). Without question the style of Ozu may be termed exact. The precision of Ozu in *Equinox Flower*—made in 1958 and his first color film—is perhaps most obvious in his editing practice. Through editing, the space of a film develops as a flow of spatial fragments which interact to reveal (and imply!) larger physical spaces. In *Equinox Flower* that development of space appears as rigorous as the rectangular latticework that decorates the walls of many of the homes of the film. It encompasses such elements as the choice of camera-to-subject distance, slight variation in angle, the formal pattern of camera set-ups, the introduction of ninety-degree an-

This article emerged from David Bordwell's Spring 1975 seminar in film criticism at the University of Wisconsin–Madison. It is reprinted from *Screen* 17, no. 2 (Summer 1976): 74–105, through the courtesy of the Society for Education in Film and Television Ltd. I have made revisions throughout the article and have expanded my discussions of incremental variation, editing, and graphic space in sections 2, 3, and 5. I wish to thank David Bordwell and Kristin Thompson for their encouragement and assistance and New Yorker Films for their cooperation.

gles and overlapping space, as well as the graphic potential of consecutive spatial fragments. These are the major elements that operate to create the space of *Equinox Flower*. I will examine these elements in an attempt to specify the material correlates of Ozu's style of exactness. Only in this manner will the "poetry" of such a style achieve definition.

First, however, it may be helpful to briefly sketch the plot of *Equinox Flower*. The film, set in Tokyo in postwar Japan, concerns the efforts of Mr. Hirayama—a middle-aged father successful in business—to arrange a marriage for his daughter Setsuko. A younger daughter, Hisako, is not quite ready for marriage. Setsuko, however, is in love with another man and opposes the arranged marriage. Her mother (not named in the film)—whose own marriage was arranged—is more understanding than her father. Hirayama at first refuses to attend the wedding of Setsuko and the man of her choice but then relents and does attend, though he does not finally accept the marriage until later when he decides to visit his daughter in her new home (in Hiroshima!). The plot contains allusions to Japan's samurai tradition, World War II, Westernization, the rise of an upper middle class, and the changing role of women. There are, in addition, two parallel subplots. One involves Mrs. Sasaki and her daughter Yukiko, an unmarried girlfriend of Setsuko; and the second concerns Fumiko, the daughter of Mikami—a close friend of Hirayama—who has left home to live with a man and work at the Luna Bar.

SHOT SCALE

In the classical Hollywood film the scale of the shot varies according to an inverted pyramid structure as illustrated by the following:

1. Establishing Shot (a major variant: we see a detail of the scene, then pull back or cut to the establishing shot)
2. Long Shot (master shot)
3. Medium Two-Shot
4. Reverse Angles (over-the-shoulder shots)
5. Alternating Medium Close-ups (sometimes Point-of-View Shots)
6. Cut-away (or Insert)
7. Alternating Medium Close-ups
8. Reestablishing Shot (usually a reverse angle or two-shot)

Ozu by contrast employs a model based on three different types of shots—the Transition, Full Shot, and Medium Shot—as follows:

1. Transition
2. Full Shot
3. Medium Shot of each individual
4. Full Shot
5. Alternating Medium Shots
6. New Full Shot
7. Alternating Medium Shots
8. Transition (often includes a repetition of the initial full shot)

In his later work Ozu does not use fades and dissolves. The Ozu transition, instead, consists of one or more shots—often still lifes—of outdoor spaces (e.g., an alleyway, bridge, advertising sign, passing train or boat, a distant mountain) usually coupled with indoor spaces (e.g., a vase or table) that as a unit open and close the film as well as operate between the scenes. In the later Ozu films nearly every scene is introduced or mediated by a series of transitional spaces. In *Equinox Flower* only two of the thirty scenes are not enclosed by transitional spaces. The transition device of Ozu has been called a non-narrative "intermediate space," a "pillow-shot," a "curtain shot," and a "coda."[1]

The narrative function of the Ozu transition is rather complex. A few general comments, however, may be useful. First, the Ozu transition establishes the space of the scene and in this respect is like the shot of the exterior of a bank in a classical Hollywood film; we are provided a master grid with which to read subsequent spaces. However, unlike the bank exterior Ozu's transitions often establish the space only obliquely or retrospectively. The two scenes in Yukiko's apartment are identified by shots of a *nearby* hospital (figs. 5–12, 5–13). The reunion scene at a seaside inn opens with two shots

1. Kristin Thompson and David Bordwell, "Space and Narrative in the Films of Ozu," *Screen* 17, no. 2 (Summer 1976): 46–55, and letters to the editor, *Screen* 17, no. 4 (Winter 1976/77): 121–24 ("intermediate space"); Noël Burch, *To the Distant Observer: Form and Meaning in the Japanese Cinema*, revised and edited by Annette Michelson (Berkeley and Los Angeles: University of California Press, 1979), 160–61 ("semi-pillow-shot" and "apparent pillow-shot," 163 n. 14, 168, 169); Tadao Sato, *Currents in Japanese Cinema*, trans. Gregory Barrett (Tokyo: Kodansha International, 1982), 190 ("curtain shot"); Schrader (1972), 27, 29, 33–34, 37. Burch proposes a loose analogy between Ozu's transition and the "pillow-word" and "pivot-word" of classical Japanese poetry. Schrader connects Ozu's "coda" to the Zen Buddhist concept of *mu* (negation, emptiness, silence). The more precise musical analogy is the "modulation," not the "coda." For related views, see Dennis Konshak, "Space and Narrative in *Tokyo Story*," *Film Criticism* 4, no. 3 (Spring 1980):

of stone lanterns, but it is not until many shots later *inside* the inn that we understand where these lanterns are located. Further, the transitions frequently do not establish space in the most economical and efficient way. Between the shot of a Kyoto pagoda and Yukiko walking along a Kyoto street we see a wooded hillside. Thus Ozu's transitions often function to impede the recognition and start of the following scene.

What are the consequences of this strategy? First, space and the objects in space assume a special priority—an existence all their own apart from, independent of, the characters and plot. As Penelope Gilliatt notes, "Ozu's films always convey a sense that the inanimate world existed long before mankind did and will be here long after we are extinct" (83). We see a white vase before it becomes a white vase *in* Hirayama's home. Though we may see people walking down a hallway to Hirayama's office, we also see the hallway at a later time when it is empty—when it is merely a hallway and not a hallway *to* an office. Empty spaces such as the hallways of office and home or the Luna-Bar passageway (which appears nine times) create a tension of uncertainty through repetition and variation for we know that characters have traveled, may travel, actually travel, or sometimes travel through the space. This tension of ambiguity serves to break the identification of character and space.

Quite often we see an unknown person or persons cross through an empty space. Paradoxically it is this nominal movement which may create the perception of emptiness. The function of these persons is made even more formal—and the space more autonomous—when we notice that they often move in step with one another or at regular intervals. At one point in *Equinox Flower* there is a match on motion from a waiter in a white coat crossing the end of a hallway to a woman in a white sweater crossing, in the same direction, the end of an alleyway. In conjunction with the music which is an in-

---

31–40, and Marvin Zeman, "The Serene Poet of Japanese Cinema: The Zen Artistry of Yasujiro Ozu," *The Film Journal* 1, no. 3–4 (Fall-Winter 1972): 62–71.

Thompson and Bordwell have continued their important work on Ozu: *Film Art: An Introduction*, 2d ed. (New York: Alfred A. Knopf, 1986), "A Nonclassical Approach to Narrative, Space, and Time: *Tokyo Story*, 308–14. See also Thompson, " 'Transitions' in *Equinox Flower*" (unpublished paper, University of Wisconsin–Madison, 1975); "Notes on the Spatial System of Ozu's Early Films," *Wide Angle* 1, no. 4 (1977): 8–17; and *Breaking the Glass Armor: Neoformalist Film Analysis* (Princeton, N.J.: Princeton University Press, 1988), chap. 12, "*Late Spring* and Ozu's Unreasonable Style." See also Bordwell, "Our Dream-Cinema: Western Historiography and the Japanese Film," *Film Reader* 4 (Evanston, Ill.: Northwestern University, 1979), 45–62, and *Ozu and the Poetics of Cinema* (Princeton, N.J.: Princeton University Press, 1988).

variable component of the transitions, these regular movements generate a rhythm through the empty spaces and confirm their existence.

The transitional space is not the space of characters. Rarely does a character appear in a transition; even the glance of a character seems to evaporate into these spaces. Both Yukiko and Hirayama will look outdoors and comment on the weather but instead of cutting to what they see—an eyeline match—a transition begins in a distant space. Though characters are often left at the end of a scene staring pensively, the transitional spaces do not mirror the mental or emotional state of the characters; nor do they follow the expectation or natural interest of the viewer. We are surprised when an Ozu character suddenly breaks into tears just as we often fail to recognize the narrative logic which draws us to a space until well into the scene. For example, Hirayama tells Yukiko that he will have his daughter visit her (the classical "transitional hook" through dialogue [Herman 1952, 144]), but the next scene is of Yukiko's mother in the hospital: *then* we move to Yukiko's apartment—which is near the hospital—for the visit (through the device of a quasi-point-of-view shot!). There is even one sub-scene which is never explained by the narrative. During a conversation with Mrs. Sasaki, Hirayama stands up, indicates he will return, and walks down the hall to his office where he sits quietly looking over various papers. There are many possible reasons, including no specific reason (!), why he leaves Mrs. Sasaki; but we never find out.

The transition, then, serves to establish the space of a scene, but more important it establishes the priority of space and generates a rhythm. The transitional shots are followed by the full shot. This shot includes all of the individuals in a new scene from the distance of a long shot (e.g., figs. 5–9, 5–31, 5–42). It is followed, in turn, by medium shots of each individual (e.g., figs. 5–2, 5–18, 5–26, 5–43). Ozu never approaches closer than a medium shot of a character. There are no medium close-ups—shoulders and above—or close-ups. Typically the camera is placed directly *between* two individuals (e.g., figs. 5–40, 5–41) and no matter how close they are sitting in the full shot the alternation between characters will be in medium perspective (e.g., figs. 5–31, 5–32, 5–33; 5–9, 5–38, 5–39). For this reason, the number of different medium shots in a scene is restricted; in a short scene there will be only one type of medium shot of each individual from a single set-up. Hence profile shots stand out in an Ozu film. Generally a character must move to a new sub-space in order to rate a new medium shot. Such movement is uncommon in an Ozu scene and is never used merely to introduce new space for the purpose of relieving the repetition of previous medium shots—a common technique, however, in classical films and television serials where a character talks while he walks to a window, another character ambles over to pour coffee, etc.

Any deviation from the pattern of medium shots would be significant. In the crucial family-dinner scene in which Hirayama announces he will attend the wedding of his daughter, we begin with three persons seated around a table. This arrangement would typically lead to two different types of medium shots for each individual—from set-ups between each pair of individuals—a total of six medium set-ups. Instead we see three set-ups of Hisako, two of Setsuko, and only one of the mother. The mother plays a central role between Setsuko and her father, Hirayama. The mother's narrative importance is here revealed in terms of space.

Ozu does not utilize medium or long two-shots where three or more persons are together. Each person appears alone in his or her own space. If two persons are in a room, they will appear together only in the full shot. The nearest equivalent of a two-shot in an Ozu film will reveal only a small part of the second person's body: a sleeve, a hand, the knees of someone kneeling, or, rarely, part of a shoulder. In these cases the fragment of a body occupies a relatively small portion of the frame and remains absolutely stationary so that it functions less as a synecdoche for a person and more as graphic potential for the composition. There are, in fact, only nine two-shot set-ups in *Equinox Flower* and only four (each appearing only once) in *An Autumn Afternoon* (1962).

As a scene progresses the full shot will be replaced by a new full shot which is a major variant of the first full shot. These full shots are used to punctuate the repetition of medium shots. For example (diagram 5-1), in the family-outing scene the repetition of medium shots (set-ups 7, 8) is divided by a full shot (set-up 6), which sequence is in turn divided by a major variant of that full shot (set-up 3—ninety-degree change in angle), which in addition divides into the transitions on each end of the scene. A similar structure obtains for the Mikami and noodle-restaurant scenes (diagrams

Diagram 5-1. The sequence of set-ups in the family outing scene.

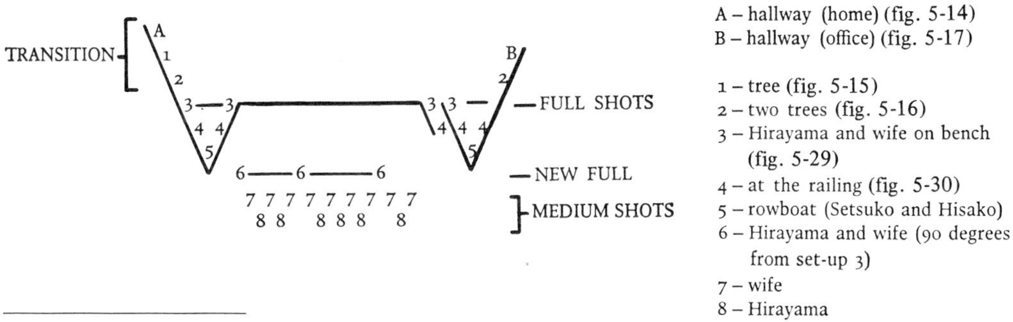

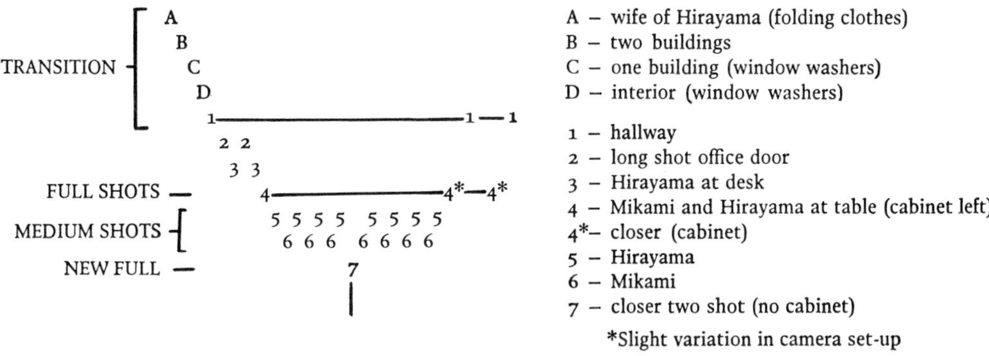

Diagram 5-2. The sequence of set-ups in the first Mikami scene.

5–2 and 5–3) (cf. fig. 5–42—set-up 4 in the noodle restaurant—with fig. 5–44—set-up 9).

In the dinner scene—which is much longer—there are three full shots of the table. The first appears four times (fig. 5–9), then gives way to the second (180-degree shift in angle), which appears five times, then gives way to the third (ninety-degree shift in angle), which appears four times, and finally the first full shot reappears to introduce the final series of medium shots. Again, these full shots function to mark off repeating sets of medium shots with each individual surrounded by a private space. The private space is further emphasized by the fact that Ozu never uses dialogue to bridge two medium shots. Off-camera speech, too, is severely limited.

If the spatial progression of an Ozu scene is highly determined, so also is the narrative progression. Donald Richie finds a five-part pattern beginning with empty space or characters in repose and continuing with preliminary action, followed by dialogue—the main point of the scene—then after-talk which is often humorous, and concluding with a return to repose (1963–64, 15). The narrative codes singled out by Roland Barthes in his study of Bal-

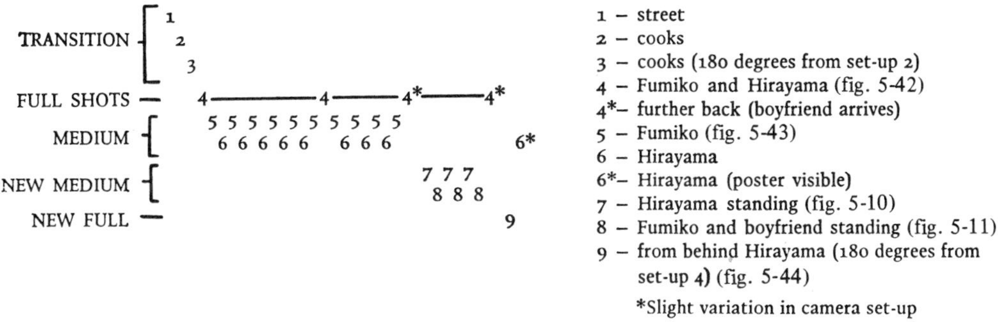

Diagram 5-3. The sequence of set-ups in the noodle restaurant scene.

 zac's *Sarrazine* provide another base for analyzing the Ozu scene. Roughly, the five codes may be defined as follows:

1. The *hermeneutic* code is a series of parallel and interrelated questions threading a narrative. At various times it names a subject, states a condition, proposes a question, delays its answer in multifarious ways, and finally discloses the answer which is the truth of the narrative (1974, sec. 32, 37, 89).
2. The *proairetic* is that code of actions, consequences, gestures, and behavior which become sequences (e.g., stroll, murder, rendezvous) when and because they are given a name in the process of reading. The proairetic is a cause-effect chain whose logic is that of the probable, of practical experience, of psychology, of culture, of history, of what is familiar: the "already-done," "already-written" or "already-seen" (sec. 36, 56, 86).
3. The *semic* is a code which includes the connotations of persons, places, or objects. The semic constructs the characters and ambience of narrative. In this way, a character is nothing but a galaxy of apparently trifling data which has coalesced around a proper name and/or pictorial image (sec. 28, 41, 81).
4. The *cultural* or referential code refers to any generally accepted body of knowledge or wisdom generated by a culture, e.g., psychology, history, science, literature, aphorism (sec. 11, 59, 87).
5. The *symbolic* is a code of meaning and relationships based on the figures of rhetoric, the traits of the body, or economic (exchange) systems (sec. 92, pp. 262–63).

The strategy of the classical text is to intertwine or "braid" these codes. As they intertwine, the codes act to limit each other's polysemic or plural nature in order to direct our attention to particular meanings. Thus the semic is often glued to the hermeneutic; in film narrative, for example, the "stranger" often exists solely to pose an enigma, or an object (e.g., the Maltese Falcon) solely to be the object of inquiry. The device of doubling—the repetition of meaning among codes (Brewster 1973, 33–35; Branigan 1984, 31–34)—is part of the process of limiting the polysemic nature of the codes. Without a process of isolation, the codes in a visual art are infinitely present at any moment, which is to say that an infinity of narratives is possible with no one narrative actualized. For narrative to exist the codes must interact with one another at some minimal level.

If we examine the Ozu scene in these terms, the middle of the scene contains hermeneutic, proairetic, and semic coding; the beginning and especially the end contain semes of character; the transitions contain semes of place and object. This division of narrative codes suggests that the Ozu text is less concerned with intertwining or braiding the codes and more concerned with cutting the codes free of one another to achieve a certain independence, to reaffirm an equality. When a code is alone, Barthes says that it "does no labour, transforms nothing: it *expresses*" (1974, 160; Barthes' emphasis). Put another way, we might say that the character repose at the end of a scene and the transitions because of their singular-code structure operate to empty the text of meaning, to suspend "the obsessional play of symbolic substitutions" (Barthes 1982, 75) and "the compulsive production of meaning."[2] Barthes argues that the "West moistens everything with meaning" using metaphor and syllogism (1982, 70) whereas Japanese society explores a lower limit of language, a pure designation (1982, 83) which, for example, abolishes such Western distinctions as animate/inanimate and inside/outside.[3]

Indeed the strategy of separating the codes, impeding their interaction, may be applied at the level of the scene. It is not until one-third into *Equinox Flower* (scene 11 of 30 scenes) that the central conflict arises. Later there is an entire scene—the reunion—which is irrelevant to the plot of the film. There is also a remarkable shot midway through that reunion scene which takes us to the garden outside the reunion inn (with continuous diegetic sound) as if a transition were beginning; but the next shot returns us to the interior. Thus space not only separates the scenes but may break into the scene itself.

In sum the transition for Ozu is not merely an identification of setting or a connection of narrative spaces from one to the next—a mutual dependence of codes—but the penetration of space as space into the narrative. It is a difference of the order "we see Hirayama" and "we see space and we see Hirayama in space." The transition does not create a narrative hierarchy in which the hidden motives of human personality are allowed to dominate the inanimate world and become the sign of an object's value.

---

2. Quotation from a manuscript version of Noël Burch's *To the Distant Observer* discussed by Jonathan Rosenbaum, "Richie's Ozu: Our Prehistoric Present," *Sight and Sound* 44, no. 3 (Summer 1975): 179. The passage appears in a different form in Burch's book: 161 n. 12, 172. See generally Taihei Imamura's provocative article, "The Japanese Spirit as It Appears in Movies," in *Japanese Popular Culture*, ed. and trans. Hidetoshi Kato (Westport, Conn.: Greenwood, 1973), 137–50 (Ozu's transition "does not contribute to the development of the plot; it stops it," with the result that his "plots are mere changes of composition . . . merely an accumulation of pictures," 144, 146). Imamura explores links between Ozu's techniques and the grammar of the Japanese language, the pattern of everyday conversation, other art forms, Buddhism, and general attitudes toward social change.

3. Barthes (1982), 58–62. By contrast, Kathe Geist, using metaphor freely, purports to discover thematic significance in Ozu's transitions. She says that a happy scene in *Equinox Flower* contains shots of drying laundry because the clothes "flap

The classical Hollywood style will employ the technique of reframing—a small change in camera angle, distance, or lens focal length—in order to hold a character in the center of the frame or to make room for the entrance of a second character. Reframing will also be employed between shots; that is, when a shot is repeated it may have been slightly changed in anticipation that a character will soon stretch out a hand or a door in the background will open. Ozu, like Hollywood, reframes his camera, but—since there are no camera movements in *Equinox Flower*—he uses reframing only between shots. In Ozu films, however, reframing is not a slave to the narrative dominant or character movement.

Consider three set-ups of Setsuko's mother. The first (fig. 5–1) occurs twice prior to the mother leaving the table to meet her daughter who has been accompanied home by the man she wishes to marry. When the mother returns to the table, she sits down exactly where she was before (note the position of the partition and the small bottle), but the first set-up is replaced by a second which occurs five times (fig. 5–2) and features a striped cup in the left foreground. Setsuko refuses the arranged marriage, argues with her parents, and finally leaves the room. A third set-up of the mother then appears four times as she speaks to Hirayama (fig. 5–3). Then he too angrily leaves the room. The scene ends with the fourth repetition of the third set-up as the mother is now as alone as she was at the beginning of the scene. Notice in the third set-up that the striped cup has not moved from the left frame but that a mirror surface, with a cover containing pictures of multicolored birds and previously half visible, is now fully visible. In addition the background lighting has been slightly altered from a flat background to a background which recedes toward a vanishing point not in center frame but off frame left (the linear perspective is created by the angle of the mirror and the two sets of window partitions). The reframed set-ups seem to mark out narrative units here, to mark the shifts in a conversation in which the mother suggests that she will break with Hirayama and support Setsuko. Later in the film there are two further variations utilizing these compositional elements (figs. 5–4, 5–5; cf. fig. 5–26).

Another function of reframing is illustrated by the dinner scene (figs. 5–6

joyously in the wind." "Yasujiro Ozu: Notes on a Retrospective," *Film Quarterly* 37, no. 1 (Fall 1983): 7. See also Geist, "Narrative Style in Ozu's Silent Films," *Film Quarterly* 40, no. 2 (Winter 1986–87): 28–35, and Don Willis, "Yasujiro Ozu: Emotion and Contemplation," *Sight and Sound* 48, no. 1 (Winter 1978–79): 44–49.

Figure 5-1, 5-2, 5-3. (All stills in this chapter courtesy of New Yorker Films.)

through 5–9). The maid (fig. 5–6) looks into a room and sees the mother, Setsuko and Hisako (fig. 5–7). The next shot (fig. 5–8) repeats the set-up of figure 5–6 but now slightly reframed so that a new space opens on the left frame (containing a partition, turquoise towel, and green foliage). The following shot (fig. 5–9) repeats the set-up of figure 5–7 but also slightly reframed so that the foreground table and a vertical partition disappear and a top-frame horizontal is now fully visible, which completes an elaborate matching of vertical lines (both left and right partitions) in these four shots. The reframing functions here to pull us away from one space (figs. 5–6, 5–8) and edge us into another space (figs. 5–7, 5–9) by matching on graphic qualities. The change in distance alone would not accomplish this effect since the change is so slight that if the shots were coupled the result would be a jump cut. Instead the emergence of the left vertical (in figure 5–8) and the disappearance of the table and vase (in figure 5–9)—rather than distance itself—are the physical correlates of movement through space.

A third function of reframing in Ozu is the introduction of new graphic elements into narrative. (The importance of graphic elements will be considered later.) In the noodle-restaurant scene (diagram 5–3) set-up 4 is reframed to 4* (the asterisk indicates reframing) not only to accommodate the arrival of Fumiko's boyfriend but to inaugurate the play of overhead lights with character movement throughout set-ups 4*, 7 (fig. 5–10), and 8 (fig. 5–11). The reframed shot adds three overhead lights which angle into the distance.

A fourth function of reframing in Ozu is more difficult to define but per-

Figure 5-4.

Figure 5-5.

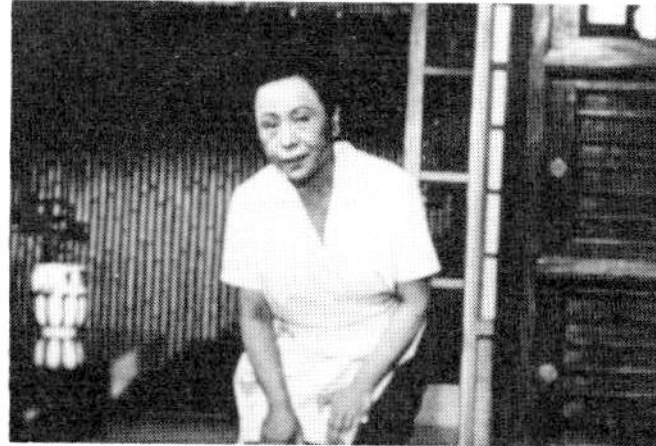
Figure 5-6.

Figure 5-7.

Figure 5-8.

Figure 5-9.

haps has some relation to the spectator's apprehension of time: repetition and variation creating an experience of succession. This notion arises from the fact that a majority of the scenes in his later work contain shots which reveal a slight change of camera position. Often the slight change will appear toward the end of the scene. In the noodle-restaurant scene set-up 6 is slightly reframed to 6* (a poster is revealed on the right frame) even though Hirayama has returned to his chair at the table and there is no further action in the scene. Similarly, at the end of the Mikami scene (diagram 5–2) set-up 4* differs from 4 only in that the shiny silver handles of a cabinet are more prominent in the immediate foreground. (Cf. also figs. 5–18, 5–20, 5–22.)

Schrader claims that Ozu's stylistic tendency to reframe—"a difference, however minute"—springs from the philosophical concern of Zen Buddhism for the uniqueness and differentiation of life. He also speaks of an Ozu film as the expression of the imperceptible movements of the mind in contemplation (1972, 33, 31). Richie would locate these imperceptible movements primarily at the end of scenes where there is a narrative pause, a stasis—a private moment of a character, a "continuous continuation"—before the

Figure 5-10.

Figure 5-11.

transition to the next scene (1963–64, 15). Typically the Ozu scene will end as the conversation turns to incidental matters, then lapses, and a character is left in contemplation (cf. figs. 5–18, 5–22). In any event slight reframing does seem to occur at the end of many scenes and, perhaps, to involve the apprehension of time in a special sense.

Time in an Ozu film would seem to be related to time in a Robbe-Grillet novel. Barthes puts it this way:

> [C]lassical time has no other figure than that of a destroyer of perfection. . . . One might say that the classical object is never anything but the archetype of its own ruin, which means setting against the object's spatial essence a subsequent (hence external) time functioning as a destiny and not as an internal dimension. . . . Robbe-Grillet gives his objects an entirely different type of mutability. It is a mutability whose process is invisible: an object, first described at a moment of novelistic continuity, reappears later on, endowed with a scarcely perceptible difference. This difference is of a spatial, situational order (for instance, what was on the right is now on the left). Time dislocates space and constitutes the object as a series of slices which almost completely overlap each other: in that spatial "almost" lies the object's temporal dimension. . . . Robbe-Grillet's objects never decay, they mystify or disappear: their time is never degradation or cataclysm: it is only change of place or concealment of elements.[4]

A functional equivalent of slight reframing is a slight change in *mise-en-scène* between two identical set-ups. Like reframing, it creates a special apprehension of time and is a common formal device in *Equinox Flower*. In the family outing (diagram 5–1), for instance, the difference between the two occurrences of set-up 5 is that at the end of the scene the boat is further from shore and the waves somewhat larger; otherwise all is the same: the boat is still moving in the same direction, in the center of the frame, with respect to exactly the same landmarks, and the daughters once again wave to their parents.

The slight variation in *mise-en-scène* occurs also between scenes. The two shots of a hospital exterior (figs. 5–12, 5–13) which introduce scenes in Yukiko's apartment differ only in that the later shot does not contain a foreground tree. Similarly the shots of the Luna-Bar alleyway leading into the

---

4. Barthes (1972), 20–21. Susumu Okada argues that the Japanese do not see time as a corruption of the material world. Such a view of time as gradual decay is characteristic of the West and leads to a fundamental opposition between the ephemeral and an essential or transcendental reality. "Japanese Films: Images of a Culture," *Cultures* 2, no. 1 (1974): 210–11.

Figure 5-12.

Figure 5-13.

two Luna-Bar scenes differ in that a car "changes" shape, a red poster becomes yellow and scattered silvery water on the pavement becomes a shiny pool. Two scenes in Hirayama's office are introduced in nearly identical fashion. The first shots of each transitional series are identical and show a vertical space between buildings at the same time of day (shadows cast on the buildings are identical). The second shots are closely related: the earlier scene shows four rows of five windows on the face of one of the buildings; the later scene shows four rows of three windows (fig. 5–36). The third shots of each series show the same row of office workers from the same angle bent over their desks, but in the later scene we see two tanks in the foreground instead of two men washing windows in the room (fig. 5–37).

Still another example of slight variation between scenes: when the street outside Hirayama's home is shown a second time from the same set-up, the same action is repeated (the arrival of Yukiko; later, the arrival of her mother) with two subtle changes: the cab "changes" color from green to white and in the far background a woman in a red sweater and her friend now walk away on the left, rather than right, side of the street. Incidentally, the woman in the red sweater and her friend appear in the far background in two other scenes of *Equinox Flower*: another triumph of delicate variation in an Ozu film. In *An Autumn Afternoon* (1962), a woman in a red sweater appears in fifteen of twenty-eight scenes.

In sum the tactics of slight reframing or slight adjustment of *mise-en-scène* are evidence of a systematic process of spatial nuance—an incremental variation of space. Its purposes are multiple: to mark narrative units through spatial shift, to edge us into or out of space, to introduce graphic elements into space, and, perhaps ultimately, to confront the temporal dimension as it exists within surface by converting an object's duration into a spatial extension. Ozu's representation of time is based not on an object in *motion*—e.g., water flowing—but on an unseen and sporadic interruption of shape and line which can only be inferred *after* the fact by making a series of comparisons. Strangely, the viewer experiences time after its passage with the result that time acquires a static, "distanced" quality more like a matrix than an arrow. A sense of aging gives way to mere place in a nexus of relations.

EDITING

Noël Burch has asserted that the space and time of a film, through editing, is "capable of rigorous development through such devices as rhythmic alternation, recapitulation, retrogression, gradual elimination, cyclical repetition, and serial variation, thus creating structures similar to those of twelve-tone music" (1981, 14). Burch emphasizes the transition from one shot to the next. However it is also possible that a *repetition* of shots and shot sequences may create a large-scale pattern which unites nonadjacent segments of a scene. Indeed I believe that a spectator's understanding of a scene arises from an ability to search for out-of-sequence connections, or "crisscross" matches, between shots; say, between shots 2 and 4, 3 and 7, 4 and 1. Our experience of spatial development will then depend upon global design as well as local juxtapositions. One approach to the description of this global aspect of editing is to concentrate on the arrangement of camera set-ups as diagrammed in diagrams 5–1 through 5–3.

An Ozu scene often displays a rigorous spatial symmetry in terms of its overall arrangement of camera set-ups. Consider the pattern of the family-outing scene (diagram 5–1). The scene ends by reversing the order of the set-ups which opened the scene:

(1, 2, 3, 4, 5, 4, 3) ⟶ (3, 4) (3, 4, 5, 4, –, 2, –)

These two progressions are further set off by the fact that they contain no dialogue—conversation is limited to the middle shots of the scene (set-ups 6, 7, and 8). The scene ends with a preliminary repetition (3, 4): the mother walks to the railing to wave to Setsuko—as she did in the opening set-ups of the scene. Then those opening set-ups appear in reversed order as Hirayama walks to the railing (3, 4, 5, 4) where both wave to Setsuko. In terms of the narrative the mother has acted to mediate[5] between father and daughter at a *spatial* level: she has drawn Hirayama into a new space—the railing—in order to create a certain contact or relation between father and daughter. At a

5. In *Equinox Flower* compare also the mediation of the maid acting between visitors and the family; of Yukiko between Hirayama and Setsuko; of Mrs. Sasaki between Hirayama and his wife; of Hirayama between Mikami and Fumiko; and there are many other examples.

spatial level the contact is of a most tenuous kind, for the space of the daughter (set-up 5) is the only space in the scene which exists solely by virtue of a directed eyeline (a glance, a wave) (diagram 5–4). As previously remarked, the only difference between the two shots of the daughter is that in the second her boat is somewhat further from shore. This is the final outing that the family will take together prior to Setsuko's marriage. In the next scene the father learns that Setsuko plans to defy him, reject the arranged marriage, and marry another man.

Set-up 3 of the bench does not recur in the end sequence because Hirayama and his wife have moved from the bench to the railing and would not be visible even in the background (diagram 5–4). Here the formal pattern actually serves to reinforce their absence from the bench, since it calls to mind that very image (set-up 3—the empty bench) which has *not* reappeared where expected in a larger context or pattern of editing (3, 4, 5, 4, –, 2, –).

Diagram 5-4. Family outing, plan view, 2–8.

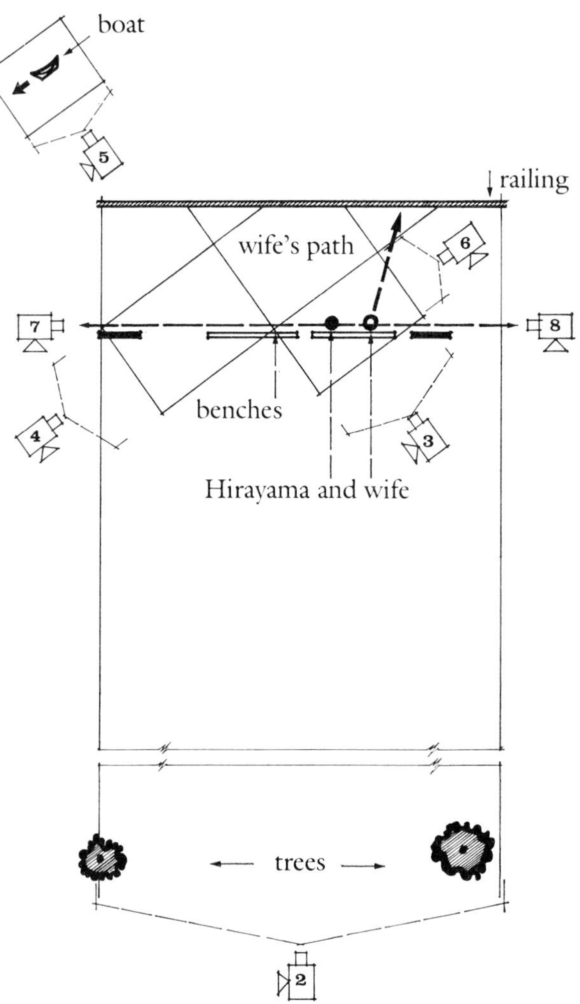

Set-up 1—the final shot—also does not recur in the end sequence. In its place appears the shot of an office hallway which, however, is similar—in graphic terms—to the framed spaces marked out at the beginning of the scene (home hallway, tree, two trees—set-ups A, 1, 2—figs. 5–14, 5–15, 5–16) and repeated at the end (two trees, office hallway—set-ups 2, B—figs. 5–16, 5–17). The repetition of these four framed spaces—particularly the two hallways—serves to formally close the pattern of set-ups which constitutes the family-outing scene.

Another common instance of the formal arrangement of camera set-ups in Ozu films is the appearance of what might be termed a "privileged" set-up. This is a camera placement which occurs only a single time in the scene and divides a long series of alternating medium shots. The first Luna-Bar scene contains the following:

666666

777 777

9

Another privileged set-up (7) occurs in the Mikami scene (diagram 5–2).

A third strategy that permeates Ozu's editing—along with the spatial symmetry of a scene and the privileged set-up configuration—is to force an object in the *mise-en-scène* to undergo formal variation through a succession of shots by manipulation of the camera set-ups. The last thirteen shots in the first Luna-Bar scene feature a white ashtray in the right foreground. Utiliz-

Figure 5-14.

Figure 5-15.

Figure 5-16.

Figure 5-17.

Figure 5-18.

Figure 5-19.

Figure 5-20.

Figure 5-21.

Figure 5-22.

ing a pattern of five camera set-ups (17, 5, 17*, 18, 17**) (figs. 5–18 through 5–22), Ozu makes the ashtray appear and disappear and finally, for the last shot of the scene, appear half on-screen and half off-screen *always* in the right foreground. In the final shot of the scene, Kondo concludes his conversation with the bar hostess and stares sullenly into his drink. The repetition is as follows (1 = appearance; 0 = disappearance):

(1 1 1 1 1 1) (0 1 0 1 0 1) (1/2)

Many critics have noted that objects in an Ozu film exist not, as in classical Hollywood narrative,[6] in relation to a character or plot but rather for themselves, in a phenomenological *there*ness. Barthes notes vis-à-vis the work of Robbe-Grillet that when an artist withdraws from objects a sense of func-

6. The classical Hollywood narrative devours its objects. André Bazin cites the example of a man locked in his cell waiting for the arrival of the executioner. The door handle of the cell exists so that it may be shown in close-up slowly turning. *What Is Cinema?*, vol. 2, trans. Hugh Gray (Berkeley and Los Angeles: University of California Press, 1971), 28. Lewis Herman advises screenwriters that "Props are tools for action movement, story development, character development, acting aids, suspense, comedy, and for countless other purposes" (1952, 248). "Props of all kinds should be introduced early in the story, developed as the story continues and, where possible, paid off at the end of the picture—a sort of pictorial gimmick, as it were" (246). In *She Wore a Yellow Ribbon* (Ford, 1949) we expect a yellow ribbon to be prominent in the narrative. By way of contrast, in *Equinox Flower* there is no reference whatsoever to an equinox, a flower, or an equinox flower.

tion (utility) as well as substance (inner relevance, quality, meaning, relation to man) then what is left is only symmetry and formal arrangement—the object has no further resistance than that of its surfaces.

> [O]ptical apprehension, which prevails everywhere [in Robbe-Grillet's work], cannot establish either correspondences or reductions, only symmetries. (1972, 16; 13–17, 23–24)

Though we may see an object being used in *Equinox Flower*, such as the turquoise towel (Hisako carries the towel into a room briefly near the end of the film) or the chair with the red cushion (at the end of the film, in a climactic moment, Setsuko's mother will sit in the chair), we have invariably also seen that object untouched—from multiple perspectives—through several earlier scenes. A red kettle in various locations appears in seven of the nine scenes in Hirayama's home and only in the first scene is it actually picked up and carried off. (More about the red kettle later.) Even the clothes people wear are at times carefully shown apart from humans: they are ironed, folded, or shown hanging on clothes lines.

One is tempted to observe that a certain formality extends also to the performances in an Ozu film as if the characters were objects with unknowable interiors. Ozu demanded that acting be nonexpressive, opaque, one might even say "atonal."[7] We never know exactly when, or how, Hirayama comes to accept his daughter's marriage. Is it when he arrives home with clothes he will wear to the wedding? Is it during the scene in which Yukiko tricks him into approving the wedding? Is it the family-outing scene, reunion scene, conversations with Kawai and Mikami, or his sudden change of travel plans at the end of the film? Even within the film, characters are unable to penetrate the surface of other characters, to make decisive psychological judgments. Hirayama, asking what kind of man his daughter is in love with, is told that the man used to be a good basketball player. Thus to the viewer, Ozu's story is often constructed less in terms of psychologically driven characters and more in terms of an exhaustion of formal, logical possibility in a framework of parallel anecdotes. *An Autumn Afternoon*, for example, concerns marriage in various states: young married, old married, unmarried, never married, newly married, about to be married, secretly engaged, and widowed.

It should be noted that what makes possible an attention to nuance in the

7. For first-hand accounts of Ozu's handling of actors, see Richie (1974), 143–47. Richie's book should be read with great caution. It contains many factual mistakes in the description of the films. See also Rosenbaum, note 2 above.

 editing of Ozu is the fact that he employs only a limited number of stylistic elements as background. We have already seen, for example, that in general Ozu uses only three different types of shot scales, employs no camera movement, and restricts the number of new set-ups in a scene. (These tendencies are even more pronounced in later films.) In short, spatial nuance is most apparent against the background of an overdetermined, repetitious space. Otherwise the subtlety of variation is lost and perception instead centers on the integration of new adjacent spaces or, if this is not possible, on the existence of fissures or radical discontinuities between spaces.

SPATIAL ARTICULATION

An overdetermined space depends on a system of continuity that serves to anchor and re-anchor space within a scene. The spatial continuity of Ozu has all of the rigor of classical Hollywood cinema but contains fewer elements. There are, in fact, four principles that govern the space within an Ozu scene.

First, Ozu utilizes a 360-degree model of space[8] to generate camera set-ups whereas Hollywood uses a 180-degree model. Ozu's camera is not locked onto one side of a 180-degree line. Second, Ozu usually changes camera position between shots by a multiple of ninety degrees or by zero. He rarely uses intermediate angles.[9] Third, Ozu shots are almost always taken from a slightly low position, two or three feet from the floor—the so-called *tatami* or kneeling position. Fourth, Ozu slightly overlaps adjacent spaces—and only slightly—so as to create a bond or narrow band of commonality between the spaces.

The space of a scene is generally the product of one or both of two types of cutting. Lateral cutting (diagram 5–5) moves in one of two perpendicular directions: in or out, left or right. Theoretically a cut-in would not produce a new field of space as does a cut-back; but in practice, because of Ozu's control of depth of field, *mise-en-scène*, shot scale, etc., a cut-in normally opens new space. For convenience, and because Ozu's camera usually remains at a fixed angle and height, I ignore movement in the third spatial dimension, that of height.

The other major sort of cutting is rotational cutting (diagram 5–6). In

8. I am here using the concepts of 360-degree and ninety-degree space proposed by David Bordwell in several courses at the University of Wisconsin–Madison. The concept of lateral and rotational spaces used below was also developed in conjunction with David Bordwell and Kristin Thompson.

9. But see Thompson and Bordwell, "Space and Narrative," 59.

Diagram 5-5. Lateral cuts.

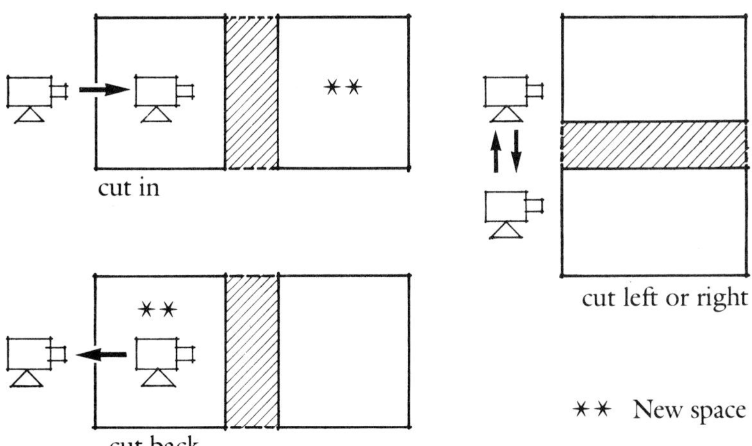

practice such cutting involves, for Ozu, a slight lateral movement as well; in this way space is made to overlap on an edge. Other more complicated spaces are the result of a combination of lateral and rotational spaces (diagrams 5–7, 5–8, 5–11).

We see, then, that Ozu partitions space so as to create a slight overlap or margin between spaces. In the dinner scene, for example (figs. 5–6 through

Diagram 5-6. Rotational cuts.

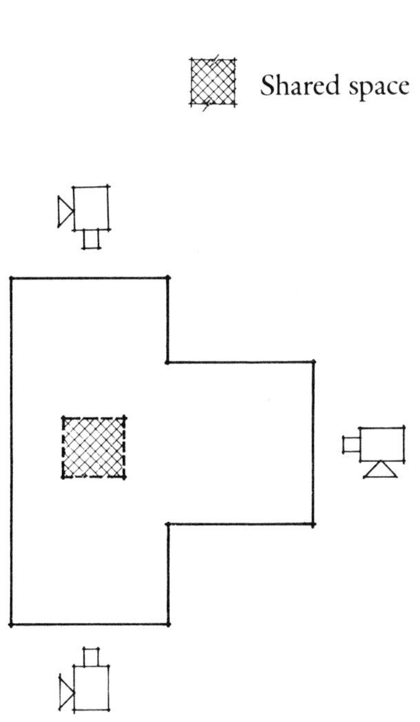

Diagram 5-7. Radial cuts.

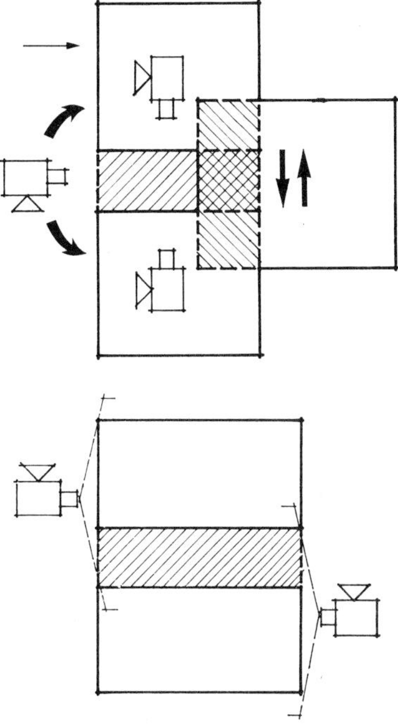

Diagram 5-8. Lateral and rotational cuts.

Diagram 5-9. Noodle restaurant, plan view.

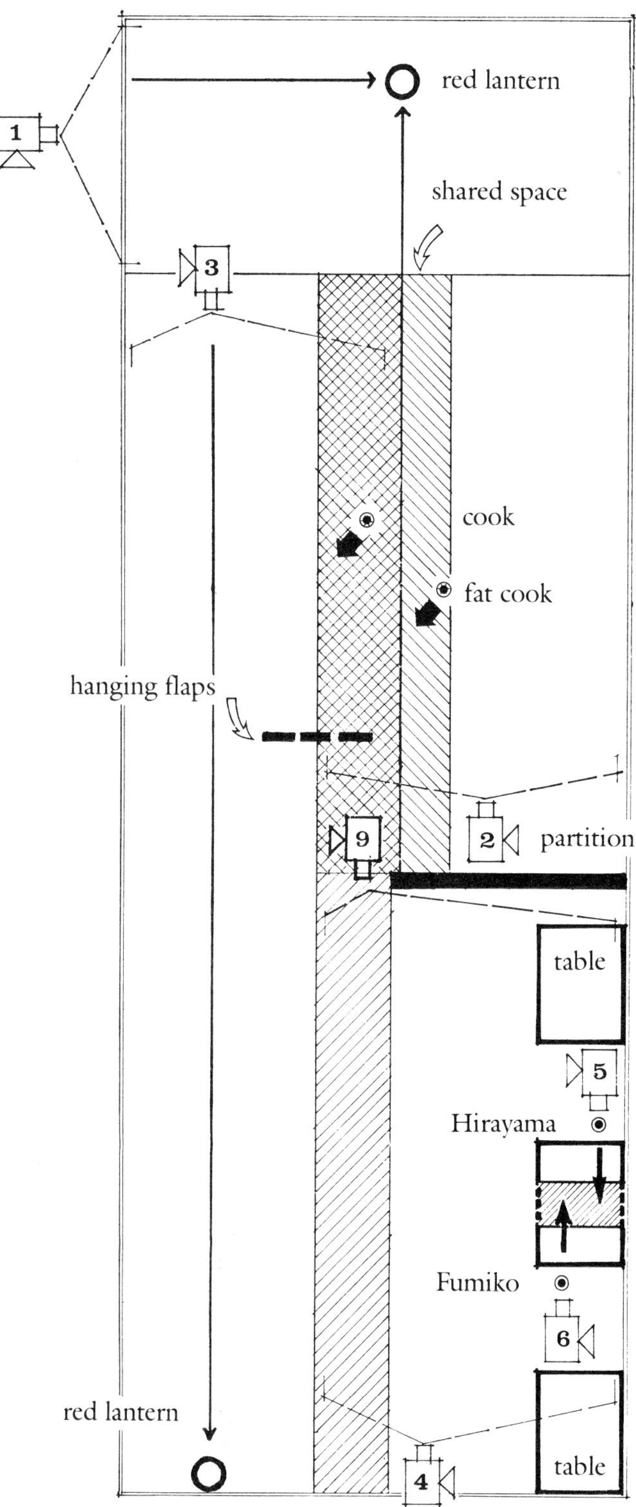

5–9), a table and vase are the common measure between two spaces (figs. 5–6, 5–8 and 5–7, 5–9). In the noodle restaurant (diagram 5–9) the match from set-up 1 to 2 is carried by a (barely visible) hanging red lantern; from 2 to 3 by a broader overlap of space (the cooks); from 3 to 4 by one cook in the distance; from 4 to 5 by Fumiko seated at a table (figs. 5–42, 5–43); from 5 to 6 by objects on the table.

The key, therefore, to Ozu's continuity is for the viewer to recognize the shared space of two shots; stated another way, Ozu's continuity forces the recognition of shared sub-spaces. Frequently these sub-spaces are marked by a single object only. In Hirayama's home (diagram 5–10) four consecutive shots involve a red kettle which pivots between different spaces: in shot 1 the kettle is on the right; in 2, on the left; in 3, on the left; in 4, it has been "replaced" on the right by a red table and red can (figs. 5–23 through 5–26). This sequence in slightly different form is repeated later in the film.

Not only may objects reveal a shared space but also there may be much activity along and across the shared space of two shots. Ozu emphasizes his partitioned space by repeated cuts on motion of ninety degrees or 180 degrees. Even when the margin of commonality is a plane seemingly no wider than a playing card, we will see the spaces joined by movement across the

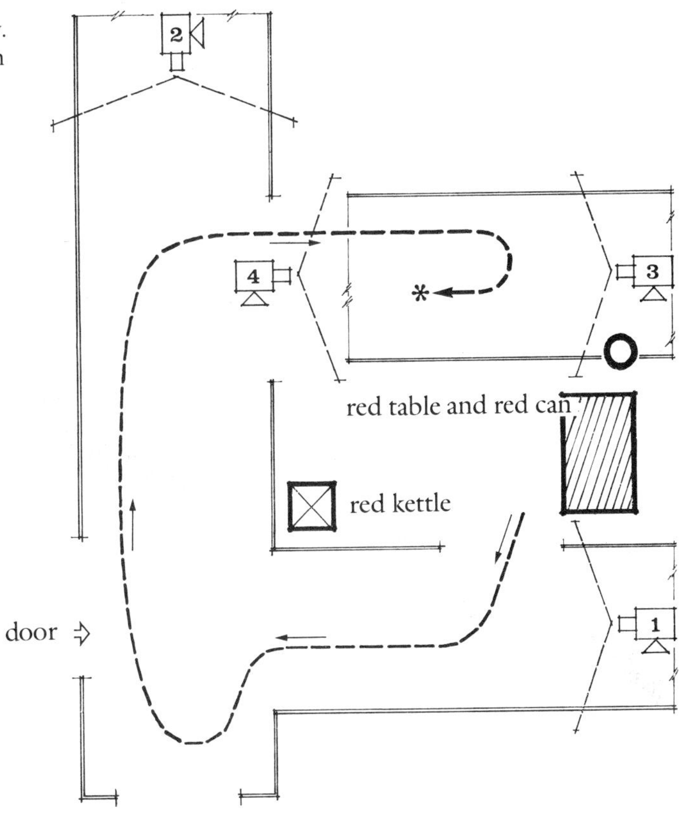

Diagram 5-10. Plan view. Path of Hirayama through four successive shots.

Figure 5-23.

Figure 5-24.

Figure 5-25.

Figure 5-26.

frame lines. Kondo, for example, hands a paper to Hirayama across the shared space of a simple lateral cut left (diagram 5–5; figs. 5–27, 5–28), and Hirayama and his wife walk repeatedly between two spaces in the outing scene (diagrams 5–1, 5–4—set-ups 3, 4; figs. 5–29, 5–30). The latter example illustrates one consequence of abandoning 180-degree space: there is no systematic screen direction—Hirayama's wife exits right and enters right.

More generally, we see that Ozu creates cubistic spaces. By penetrating one spatial cube with another in different places, in different amounts, and with mutually varying angles (multiples of ninety degrees) he creates a staggering number of possible sub-cubes. An object caught in such a sub-cube—

Figure 5-27.

Figure 5-28.

Figure 5-29.

Figure 5-30.

such as the red kettle—is examined from multiple points of view and itself becomes multiplaned.

Broadly speaking, then, Ozu's technique yields sub-cubes or margins of overlapping space. What are the consequences of the technique? There is a stress on objects. Earlier we examined this stress with respect to Ozu's editing practice which creates a sense of phenomenological *there*ness. There is also a sense of depth and completeness not found in classical Hollywood films: Ozu reveals all the walls of a room and not just three. In addition, Ozu's spaces frequently enact the same rhythm that occurs in many of his stories: balance, counterbalance, equality. When Ozu shoots six men working at a table in *Equinox Flower*, each alternating medium shot contains three men. Other compositions are more complex but often still display a careful symmetry of forces.

More fundamentally, the art of Ozu aims to insert the object or the person in an ongoing dialectic of space. For this reason a critic may speak of the "independence" of Ozu objects or exclaim how "alive" the objects seem. What is really meant is that an object does not possess a *single*, absolute relation to its space but rather exists within a certain tension of space. Consider three extraordinary set-ups from *An Autumn Afternoon*, which appear four, sixteen, and thirteen times respectively. There are no other set-ups in the scene. In the first three shots of the scene (figs. 5–31, 5–32, 5–33) we see a soy-sauce bottle "alternate" from frame right to left to right while a beer bottle appears anchored at frame left with its label always turned toward the camera in spite of the 180-degree cuts between the medium shots (figs. 5–32, 5–33). One possible arrangement of the objects is shown in diagram 5–11; another possibility is that the camera occupies a plane marked by *two* soy-sauce bottles, one on either side (both containing the same level of soy sauce!)—one bottle for each man. The fundamental uncertainty (contradiction?) of the space is its most salient characteristic.

Such a spatial articulation in the classical Hollywood cinema would be a scandal. In the classical cinema, the top of the table would be contrived so that the soy-sauce bottle would exhibit a single, unambiguous relation to its

Figure 5-31.

Figure 5-32.

Figure 5-33.

Diagram 5-11. Plan view. A spatial articulation from *An Autumn Afternoon.*

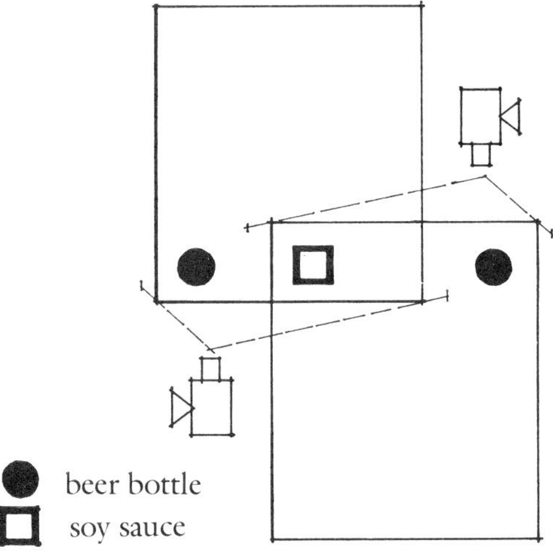

space. Ozu, on the contrary, blocks such a unitary conception of space in favor of a dialectic of space. The soy-sauce bottle cannot exist with respect to a single beer bottle but must exist in relation to two beer bottles, to a second soy-sauce bottle on a far table, and—perhaps even—to a third soy-sauce bottle on the same table. These relations are not evident at the level of the single shot but must be grasped as the complex interaction of three shots. Thus objects (and persons) for Ozu are seen not as subordinate to, or reflecting, a theme or ideological stance, but as a complex organization of space that reveals not meaning in the ordinary sense, but geometry and symmetry in a state of balanced opposition.

GRAPHIC SPACE

In Ozu's *Early Summer* (1951) a woman walks between two parked cars to cross a street. We then see her from the far side of the street as she crosses (figs. 5–34, 5–35). The second shot, however, is framed between two new parked cars in such a manner that the graphic similarity with the first shot almost suggests that there has been *no change* in the scene despite the wom-

Figure 5-34.

Figure 5-35.

an's evident movement. The composition of the shots acts as a counterbalance, working *against* the narrative action. This suggests that Ozu, through his compositions, may be telling a different story—or one more complex—than first appears.

For Ozu, objects in space are not containers of an essence or even function but are bundles of graphic surface qualities which create geometries: line, shape, color, angle, size, mass, volume, texture, plane, and the like. These qualities while being systematically explored not only mark out the dimension of space—cue our perception of narrative space—but are also capable of reacting on the space, and defining a new sort of space. In the first Luna-Bar scene in *Equinox Flower*, for example, we see a pink lamp and a red telephone in the left background. Ozu cuts in, rotates 180 degrees, and contrives the shot so that in the immediate foreground the pink lamp is at the right but, surprisingly, the phone is split away from the lamp and *remains* at frame left. The pink lamp has changed position in the frame—from frame left to right—in accordance with our spatial expectation—a 180-degree reversal of space. The red phone, however, has seemingly defied a three-dimensional conception of space by holding its position. Though the phone is not spatially continuous it is graphically continuous—the redness of the phone remains in the same place within the frame. Thus Ozu pries loose a graphic quality—redness—from its three-dimensional reference. This does not, of course, block our recognition of three-dimensional space so much as offer a certain resistance to that space and open up—or reward—our perception of the film image as a two-dimensional surface: that of frame height and width.

Across this surface, then, the graphic elements of Ozu are free to operate. The dimension of frame width is explored perhaps most of all in Ozu films. This exploration—which is systematic only in the later films—may be described if one simplifies a bit. Consider only two possible movements: first, an object which moves from frame left to right (a reversal) *with* the cut and, second, an object which remains at frame left or right *in spite of* the cut (a stasis). It should be noted that our "natural" inclination is to "follow the angle" and expect an object to change location with a shift in angle (e.g., 180 degrees). In the course of an Ozu film, however, one must also train one's perception to *stay* with space, to discover correspondence by overlap.

With the above two possible movements there may be coupled three possible types of objects: a single object, two identical objects—each seen in only one shot—or two "similar" objects—each seen in only one shot. By "similar" I mean that the objects share only one graphic quality, such as shape or line. Thus with two types of movement and three types of objects there are six basic patterns with which to explore the frame width.[10]

Illustrations of these possibilities in *Equinox Flower* are:

1. One-Object Reversal: the vase in the dinner scene (figs. 5–6, 5–7, 5–8); the red kettle (figs. 5–23, 5–24).
2. One-Object Stasis: the ashtray in the first Luna-Bar scene (figs. 5–18 through 5–22); the centerpiece bowl in the dinner scene (figs. 5–38, 5–39); the red kettle (figs. 5–24, 5–25).
3. Two-Identical-Objects Reversal: two pairs of bottles in the noodle restaurant (figs. 5–42, 5–43).
4. Two-Identical-Objects Stasis: the corners of two chairs in the Mikami scene; two overhead lights in the noodle-restaurant scene (figs. 5–10, 5–11); the peanut cans in the dinner scene (figs. 5–38, 5–39).
5. Two-Similar-Objects Reversal: the red kettle is replaced by a red table and red can (diagram 5–10; figs. 5–25, 5–26); a wallpaper design of green ferns becomes a living fern.
6. Two-Similar-Objects Stasis: three windows on the face of a building become three pictures on a wall (figs. 5–36, 5–37).

A special site for graphic movement in width is an Ozu dinner table—in a restaurant or at home. In the family-dinner scene, a red-striped can of peanuts always appears in the left foreground in spite of right-angled cuts between three people resulting in four different medium shots involving the can. For instance, a set-up of the mother (fig. 5–38) alternates with one of her daughter Setsuko (fig. 5–39). The peanut can and the centerpiece bowl, however, do not change position in spite of a 180-degree shift in angle. (Note the graphic "equinox" of fig. 5–38—the level of half-filled glasses matches the height of the centerpiece bowl.) The peanut can, in fact, serves to anchor a larger circulation of graphics across the table.

A viewer's mind can become quite unwired in an attempt to fix the

10. In order to speak of the graphic match as a structural principle, there must exist the structural possibility of a *non*-match of graphics. And indeed one can find in *Equinox Flower* instances of such non-matches. Ultimately the non-match reduces to empty space, empty of graphics. Ozu's use of empty space within the frame, however, is beyond the scope of this investigation. An example occurs at the start of the reunion scene in *Equinox Flower*. We see five men exit from the room leaving seven men variably spaced around the dinner table. These empty spaces between the men—like the vacant spaces between the branches of a flower arrangement—are used to structure the graphic composition of the scene. The Japanese concept of *ma* (distance, interval, natural pause) is relevant as well as, perhaps, the Zen concept of *mu* (emptiness, stillness).

Figure 5-36.

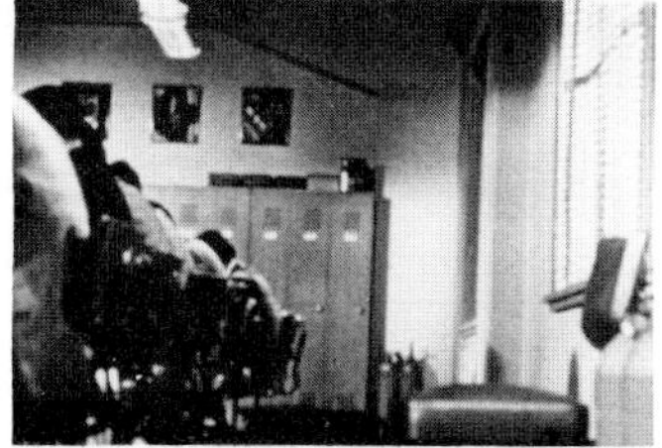

Figure 5-37.

Figure 5-38.

Figure 5-39.

geography of an Ozu dinner table (not to mention the fruit in a centerpiece). Bottles, glasses, cups, dishes, vases, centerpieces shift about in the image because of the editing—marginal, cubistic space (for example, diagram 5–11)—and the acknowledged cheating of object continuity to further graphic continuity (Richie 1974, 125–26; Shinoda 1985, 12–13). In the noodle restaurant, for example (diagram 5–9), there is a graphic match on a red lantern between set-ups 2 and 3 which is *only* a graphic match—it carries *no* spatial continuity. Later in the scene we watch as a beer bottle and glass exchange positions on the frame lines while two small bottles appear and disappear on the left frame. Thus Ozu's tables are the occasion for what might be called a dance of the bottles. One could feast forever at such a mythical table, since food and drink would continue to multiply around the table.

In the family-outing scene Ozu used compositions involving a frame within a frame to graphically link home, outdoors, and office (figs. 5–14 through 5–17). A more complicated use of the two-dimensional surface of the film image is the diagonal construction that operates through four successive scenes in *Equinox Flower* (cf. Richie 1974, 132–34). In the first Luna-Bar scene a set-up of Kondo (fig. 5–40) alternates with one of Hirayama (fig. 5–41). A diagonal is formed by pink lamps, Kondo's head, a pink lamp, and red phone; a diagonal in the opposite direction is formed by Hirayama's hands, a white horse, bottle, and Hirayama's head. In the next scene at the noodle restaurant (diagrams 5–3 and 5–9) a diagonal is formed by two bottles of uneven height which are behind Fumiko (fig. 5–42) and in front of her (fig. 5–43). At the end of the scene three bottles of uneven height are behind Hirayama, who is now alone, and three are in front of him (fig.

Figure 5-40.

Figure 5-41.

Figure 5-42.

Figure 5-43.

Figure 5-44.

5–44). In these two scenes Hirayama confronts the daughter of a close friend who has left home to live with a man and work in a bar. In the next scene Hirayama angrily confronts his own daughter and demands to know if she is sleeping with her boyfriend. The scene concludes with a shot of the RCA building as a giant 'V' lights up from bottom to top (fig. 5–45). A second confrontation with Fumiko follows with diagonals alternating in the manner of the previous Luna-Bar scene (cf. figs. 5–46, 5–47 with 5–40, 5–41).

More generally we see that when the Ozu image is considered as a flat surface, it becomes a mosaic of line, color, and shape. These graphic forms we usually recognize as an arrangement of objects—a red phone, a red-striped peanut can, an ashtray, a red kettle, a soy-sauce bottle—whose logic is not that of a three-dimensional narrative space, but of pure form. It is important to remember that such a two-dimensional mosaic, though without the cues of linear (or other) *perspective*, is nonetheless a space—implying position, direction, movement, relation, and so forth. By allowing graphic elements to define a flat space, Ozu motivates an awareness of the entire frame

Figure 5-45.

Figure 5-46.

Figure 5-47.

and not just the center of the frame (and central perspective), which is all that is usually demanded by classical Hollywood film. Moreover, Ozu's representation of space has an important connection to a uniquely Japanese way of perceiving the world. Space and time are perceived not as a homogeneous and infinite continuum but rather as a juxtaposition of two-dimensional facets, each with a distinct time measurement. Hence the world appears as a collection of spatial and temporal "edges" which limit what can be known. This notion of space and time survives from early epochs and permeates Japanese life today in various forms of architecture, music, theater, painting, religion, gardening, tea ceremony, and more (*Ma*, 12–17, 48, 56–57; Chang 1984–85). In this sense, Ozu's art reanimates certain fundamental Japanese traditions.

THE SPATIAL CODE

Style is a set of laws—a system—that produces formal transformations of the materials of the art medium—in film broadly Metz's five matters of expression: the moving photographic image, music, noise, speech, and the written word (Metz 1973, 90). The result—the trace—of style is structure. The formal transformations most evident in the structure of film occur at the level of graphics—the display of its physical qualities. The play of lines, colors, and objects, however, is actually only the consequence of fundamental shifts in position and direction. In day-to-day life, after all, a red kettle does not leap about and "change into" a red table and red can. The red kettle is a cue for space. The manipulation of this space by the film medium is, in fact, so fundamental that it represents a narrative code on the level of the narrative codes Barthes uses to analyze *Sarrazine* in *S/Z*. In a literary work space can be mapped out only in terms of secondary codes. For example, descriptions in literature incorporating the words "left" and "right" are based on something like Barthes' cultural code; that is, the code summons our experiential knowledge of the direction of our left hand and our right hand. But in film, because it is a visual art, space is perceived—sensed—directly.

Nevertheless, this direct perception of space in film is a coded construction. The code begins with the cues of monocular depth (the cues of classical painting)—overlap, linear and size perspective, familiar size, illumination direction, etc.[11] But these cues do not exhaust the spatial code. The cinema has

11. A summary of thirteen spatial cues appears in Edward Hall, *The Hidden Dimension* (Garden City, N.Y.: Doubleday, 1969), 191–95; see also chap. 7, "Art as a Clue to Perception," 77–90. See generally Virginia Brooks, "Film, Perception and

 added powerful cues of its own, notably camera (distance, angle, height, lens, focus, camera movement) and editing. The early Russians—Eisenstein, Vertov, Kuleshov, and others—were pioneer explorers of the theoretical and practical aspects of the spatial code.

All the above cues, then, are spatial signifiers, spatial indicators. More precisely, the spatial signifier is an event, a cue, which has as its signified a spatial *relation*. If we see, for example, two objects one of which is partially obscured by the other—the cue of overlap—then the spatial relation which is suggested is that the obscured object is further away (and behind) the other object. Through the operation of spatial cues (some in combination, some in opposition) spatial *relations* are forged (implied, contradicted) among objects and persons: thus we perceive a space that has such and such dimensions, that contains objects and persons related in such and such a way, that is related—most importantly—to nearby (other) spaces in such and such a way. The spatial cues uniquely provided by cinema certainly create spatial relations; such as, a man related to a nearby bowl of soup through editing. The operation of certain cinematic signifiers of space is exactly what we have been considering in *Equinox Flower*: shot scale, reframing (incremental variation), the camera set-up, editing (in the sense of spatial articulation), and the graphics of *mise-en-scène*.

Moreover, when the spatial signifiers are given wide play—as opposed to the practice in what are known as "static, theatrical" films—the cinema creates spatial relations that implicate an ever-expanding set of spaces in a process akin to what Barthes calls a "metonymic skid" of space: each space adding to its neighbor some new trait, some new departure (Barthes 1974, sec. 40). It is at this point that a film becomes truly "spatial," that one of its narrative acts *is* the creation of space. The expanding (contracting, pulsating) array of related spaces is as much a part of the film text as the characters, their movement, their words, and it constitutes a narrative in combination with them.[12] An earlier discussion, for example, indicated how the spatial

---

Cognitive Psychology," *Millennium Film Journal*, no. 14/15 (Fall/Winter 1984–85): 105–26.

12. Ozu's space is evidence of a particular *narration* at work in his films. See David Bordwell's concept of "parametric" narration, *Narration in the Fiction Film* (Madison: University of Wisconsin Press, 1985), 274–310, and see his book *Ozu*, esp. chaps. 4–6. Nelson Goodman's concepts of "exemplification" and "expression" are also useful in pinpointing how space may do more than merely represent dramatic action; *Languages of Art: An Approach To A Theory of Symbols*, 2d ed. (Indianapolis: Hackett, 1976), 45–95. See also Catherine Elgin's analysis of Goodman's concepts, *With Reference To Reference* (Indianapolis: Hackett, 1983), 59–95.

aspects of the family-outing scene in *Equinox Flower*—the formal arrangement of set-ups, the unique space created by eyeline—form a narrative of family contact and withdrawal.

In a more fundamental sense, there are no spatial cues in film except filmic cues. The reason is that everyday cues of space—such as linear perspective—are transformed when taken up by the cinema. (Witness the creation of linear perspective from figures 5–2 to 5–3.) The space which appears juxtaposed in two shots of a film is unlike any space on earth. If one could visit the office building in Japan where Ozu made *Equinox Flower* (assuming such a building exists!) and walk its halls, one would still be unable to reconstruct the space of the film, the space implied by the experience of the film. That space exists only at twenty-four frames per second.[13] The impact of Eisenstein's shot scale in *Alexander Nevsky* (1938) when he cuts in along a line is, according to the spatial code, an implosion of space that has no basis in the everyday world. Even the classical film—which aims to create "spatial continuity," i.e., the sense of a three-dimensional surrounding space endowed with independent existence ("natural" space/time) from which a sequence of shots has somehow been excerpted—creates its space carefully and painstakingly, with attention to a great many conventions (spatial codes).[14] In short, film is a constitutive medium where nonfilmic (profilmic) reality is radically transformed—defamiliarized—by the medium. The spatial code of film invites one to perceive space in a new (old) manner.[15]

---

13. See Burch (1981), chap. 3, "Editing as a Plastic Art," 37–40. The camera, too, exists only at twenty-four frames per second. Edward Branigan, "What Is a Camera?" in *Cinema Histories, Cinema Practices*, ed. Patricia Mellencamp and Philip Rosen, American Film Institute Monograph Series, vol. 4 (Frederick, Md.: University Publications of America, 1984), 87–107; Bordwell, *Narration*, 119. Diagrams 5–4 and 5–9 through 5–11 should thus be understood not in relation to real space or to a profilmic camera but as themselves fictional, as a record of the hypotheses and predictions made by a viewer about the underlying connections and structure of a scene. Edward Branigan, "The Spectator and Film Space—Two Theories," *Screen* 22, no. 1 (1981): 74. At a theoretical level Umberto Eco shows that meaning does not depend on real-world objects and referents in *A Theory of Semiotics* (Bloomington: Indiana University Press, 1976), 58–72, 161–71.

14. For the conventions of classical film, see David Bordwell, Janet Staiger, and Kristin Thompson, *The Classical Hollywood Cinema: Film Style and Mode of Production to 1960* (New York: Columbia University Press, 1985).

15. In *Late Spring* (1949)—one of the most noteworthy films in the history of the cinema—Ozu boldly transforms the space of the famous fifteenth-century garden of Ryoanji in Kyoto. In the Japanese culture the garden represents a supreme spatial achievement.

In the films of Ozu the transitions are the site of almost pure movements of the spatial codes. The understanding of a transition depends not on assigning the transition, or one of its spaces, the meaning of another code (such as by consuming the space in a causal chain), but on the realization—gained by "following" the matches—that the transition is a code apart from the others. For the viewer, the Ozu transition is a purely spatial experience. It is this foregrounding of the spatial code in Ozu's films that justifies us in classifying Ozu as a "modernist" filmmaker.

CONCLUSION

Ozu Yasujiro in *Equinox Flower* develops a spatial code which is quite different from that of classical Hollywood's "spatial continuity." This in no way means that the spatial articulations of Ozu are superior to those of classical Hollywood cinema; rather, Ozu's system of spatial coding is merely *another* system, one of many possible systems. We have noticed that as part of his system, Ozu chooses a different set of shot scales (three) and organizes these elements in a structure quite different from the Hollywood pyramid or crisis structure where a progression from establishing shot to close-up concentrates psychological and causal energies. Ozu's organization of shot scales, on the other hand, tends to retard a weaving or braiding of the codes so that at certain points (the transitions) the text is emptied of meaning (the other codes) and expresses only space.

Ozu then utilizes in a systematic fashion minute camera reframing and minute changes in *mise-en-scène*—incremental variations—to reveal fluctuations in space. This sporadically changing space is related to an apprehension of time not as a steady corruption of what we know and desire but as an inner consequence of objects remote and independent of human will. Further, Ozu understands that the pattern of camera set-ups alone may become a large-scale form in the film. Through rigorous camera placement networks of objects are created which are opaque as to essence or function but reveal spatial symmetry and geometry.

Ozu's general articulation of space is based on a 360-degree model of space—rather than Hollywood's 180-degree model—coupled with a system of right-angled (lateral and rotational) cubistic space. The result is that the object or person is not locked into a single, absolute relation with its space but rather exists within a balanced opposition, a dialectic of space. Ozu even explores the possibility of confronting a three-dimensional perception of space with a sequence of two-dimensional facets which yield a fractured mosaic of graphic and temporal qualities. Graphic patterns of objects, in states of reversal and stasis, emphasize the material surface of perception.

Finally it was suggested that all these aspects of spatial development are, in fact, parts of a single code operating throughout film—a spatial code. This code takes, as its expression plane, spatial cues; and as its content plane, spatial relations. The structuring of space and spatial relations is a narrative act which for the viewer is a spatial experience. The exploitation of the spatial code in *Equinox Flower* and more generally in the work of Ozu confirms that he was a modernist filmmaker of the first order.

WORKS CITED

Barthes, Roland. 1972. "Objective Literature." In *Critical Essays*, translated by Richard Howard, 13–24. Evanston, Ill.: Northwestern University Press.

———. 1974. *S/Z*. Translated by Richard Miller. New York: Hill and Wang.

———. 1982. *Empire of Signs*. Translated by Richard Howard. New York: Hill and Wang.

Branigan, Edward. 1984. *Point of View in the Cinema: A Theory of Narration and Subjectivity in Classical Film*. Berlin and New York: Mouton.

Brewster, Ben. 1973. "Notes on the text 'John Ford's *Young Mr. Lincoln*' by the Editors of *Cahiers du Cinéma*." *Screen* 14, no. 3 (Autumn): 29–43.

Burch, Noël. 1981. *Theory of Film Practice*. Translated by Helen Lane. Princeton, N.J.: Princeton University Press.

Chang, Ching-Yu. 1984–85. "Japanese Spatial Conception," eleven parts in *The Japan Architect*, nos. 324–35 (April 1984–March 1985).

Gilliatt, Penelope. 1973. Review of *An Autumn Afternoon*. *New Yorker* 49, no. 13 (19 May): 83–84.

Herman, Lewis. 1952. *A Practical Manual of Screen Playwriting for Theater and Television Films*. New York: New American Library.

Ma: Space-Time in Japan. Exhibition catalogue. Cooper-Hewitt Museum.

Metz, Christian. 1973. "Methodological Propositions for the Analysis of Film." *Screen* 14, no. 1/2 (Spring/Summer): 89–101.

Richie, Donald. 1963–64. "Yasujiro Ozu: The Syntax of his Films." *Film Quarterly* 17, no. 2 (Winter): 11–16.

———. 1974. *Ozu: His Life and Films*. Berkeley and Los Angeles: University of California Press.

Schrader, Paul. 1972. *Transcendental Style in Film: Ozu, Bresson, Dreyer*. Berkeley and Los Angeles: University of California Press.

Shinoda, Masahiro. 1985. Interview. *American Film* 10, no. 7 (May): 10–13.

Bordwell, David. *Ozu and the Poetics of Cinema*. Princeton: Princeton University Press, 1988. (This book contains an extensive bibliography on Ozu.)

Burch, Noël. *To the Distant Observer: Form and Meaning in the Japanese Cinema*. Revised and edited by Annette Michelson. Berkeley and Los Angeles: University of California Press, 1979.

Geist, Kathe. "Narrative Style in Ozu's Silent Films." *Film Quarterly* 40, no. 2 (Winter 1986–87): 28–35.

Imamura, Taihei. "The Japanese Spirit as It Appears in Movies." In *Japanese Popular Culture*, edited and translated by Hidetoshi Kato, 137–150. Westport, Conn.: Greenwood, 1973.

Lehman, Peter. "The Mysterious Orient, The Crystal Clear Orient, The Non-Existent Orient: Dilemmas of Western Scholars of Japanese Film." *The Journal of Film and Video* 39, no. 1 (Winter 1987): 5–15.

———. "To the Dreaming Observer: Response to Kristin Thompson and David Bordwell." *The Journal of Film and Video* 40, no. 1 (Winter 1988): 67–71.

Mellen, Joan. *The Waves at Genji's Door: Japan Through Its Cinema*. New York: Pantheon Books, 1976.

Richie, Donald. *Ozu: His Life and Films*. Berkeley and Los Angeles: University of California Press, 1974.

Rosenbaum, Jonathan. "Richie's Ozu: Our Prehistoric Present." *Sight and Sound* 44, no. 3 (Summer 1975): 175–79.

Sato, Tadao. *Currents in Japanese Cinema*. Translated by Gregory Barrett. Tokyo: Kodansha International, 1982.

Schrader, Paul. *Transcendental Style in Film: Ozu, Bresson, Dreyer*. Berkeley and Los Angeles: University of California Press, 1982.

Thompson, Kristin. *Breaking the Glass Armor: Neoformalist Film Analysis*. Princeton: Princeton University Press, 1988.

Thompson, Kristin, and David Bordwell. "Space and Narrative in the Films of Ozu." *Screen* 17, no. 2 (Summer 1976): 46–55.

Zeman, Marvin. "The Serene Poet of Japanese Cinema: The Zen Artistry of Yasujiro Ozu." *The Film Journal* 1, no. 3–4 (Fall-Winter 1972): 62–71.

6

ORDER AND THE SPACE FOR SPECTACLE IN FELLINI'S 8 1/2

Charles Affron

The explicit subject of Federico Fellini's *8 1/2* is the unsuccessful effort of its protagonist, Guido Anselmi, to begin shooting a movie. Guido is a director in crisis, unable to make the choices necessary for the definition of his project. Scenario, casting, and decor are in a state of flux; they refuse to submit to placement, to order. Guido is powerless to fix them in space, the spectacular space of the film director, a field—however shifting—of comprehensible coordinates on which a film's narrative is meant to unfold. Guido's narrative keeps disappearing over the boundaries of his imagination and his memory, sliding beyond the edge of the frame of his troubled vision. The confusions of this movie director, captured by the unpredictable rhythm of his perception and of the *mise-en-scène* of the film of which he is the hero, oblige the spectator to recognize distinctions between the fields of narrative reenactment in *8 1/2* and those of the classical film narrative.

Guido's unstable relationship to the space required for his film is in fact a crucial narrative principle of *8 1/2*. At first the film must be read through the protagonist's perplexity. As Guido struggles to extricate himself from chaotic spaces that convey the conflict between his fiction and his life, we, the viewers, struggle to make sense out of what is transpiring on the screen. But as the film progresses an ever-widening gap develops between our perception and Guido's. We gain increasing access to the order of the hero's disorder. Long before he does, we learn that what he perceives as disorder is actually the spectacle of his imagination. When Guido finds the key to staging that spectacle he can begin making his film and Fellini can conclude *8 1/2*.

The quest for that key is punctuated by a series of clashes in which Guido's attempts to comprehend the shape and scope of his vision are challenged by orders—religious, economic, bourgeois, intellectual—over which he has little or no control. These various orders are incarnated by characters who, either by implication or directly, are critical of Guido's disordered life and his disordered art. They supply specific definitions to the spaces they occupy. Some of their spatial configurations—those evocative of his childhood (the grandmother's farmhouse and the beach of Saraghina, the woman who signals his sexual initiation)—satisfy the hero at first. They seem apt material for the creation of his fiction. But during the course of the film even these congenial spaces are transformed; the farmhouse-harem and the beach eventually come to inhibit Guido's creativity. Other space/character configurations are threatening from their first appearance: Gudio's hotel room/the curious, ironic doctor and the skeptical critic; the cemetery/Guido's disapproving mother, father, producer, wife; the hotel lobby/the invasive assistants, press agent, journalist, actress; the school and chapel/the censuring, punishing priests; the thermal baths/the admonishing cardinal; the set of the spaceship/the mocking visitors; the movie theater/the exasperated producer.

The opening sequence of *8 1/2* depicts a nightmare in which, locked in his car, the director is stuck in a traffic jam in an underpass. As Guido struggles to free himself from this literal version of problematized space, we the viewers are made aware of a problematized space that is specifically cinematic. The first image we see is that of the back of Guido's head through the rear window of his car. The frame of the window echoes the cinematic frame of the image; here an image that stubbornly withholds the face of the actor. We see an actor in the conventional space of the movie frame but see him unconventionally, from the back. Duration marks this positioning as exceptional. The viewer expects to see a face soon after seeing the back of a head. We will in fact not see Guido's face until several minutes later when, during his physical examination, we learn he is a movie director. At that point the purpose of deferring our view of the hero's face can be related to the reflexivity of *8 1/2*. What is one to make of a film about a movie director, someone who is supposed to be *outside* the space we see on the screen? And how will this director include his subjectivity in the fiction he is creating? Is there a space adequate to both his situation as director, outside the space of the frame, and to his function as protagonist of his own fiction, at the center of the spatial coordinates of that fiction?

The first full disclosure of Guido's face deploys a series of more blatant references to the modalities of cinematic space. Guido snaps on the light in the bathroom, then sees his own face in close-up, framed in a mirror, just as the viewer does (fig. 6–1). This is accompanied by music—Wagner's "Ride of the Valkyries"—that seems to bear no relationship to the image. It neither emanates from a discernible source nor provides appropriate "background" to the situation before our eyes. It signals an apparent disjuncture between image and sound. This disjuncture becomes more pronounced when the bathroom is suddenly flooded with a bright light and an unidentifiable "electric" sound. Later, when we come to associate the light and the sound with the movie soundstage, we grasp the placement of Guido in the space of a movie about to be made (Guido's) and that of a movie that has, of course, already been made (Fellini's). These distinct spaces shape each other throughout the film. They repeatedly pass through a series of relationships, serving sometimes as parallel reflections, sometimes as points of departure from one to the other, sometimes as ironic commentary upon each other. Guido and the figures he encounters inhabit spaces made unstable by the film within the film, by the rhythm of their shifting, blending, echoing, by the uneven pattern of their intersections.

The next sequence, played on the terrace of an elegant spa, demonstrates this pattern. The first eight shots are from Guido's point of view as he observes a crowd of people taking the water cure. The randomness of that point of view is conveyed by restless panning in which the markedly unpredictable

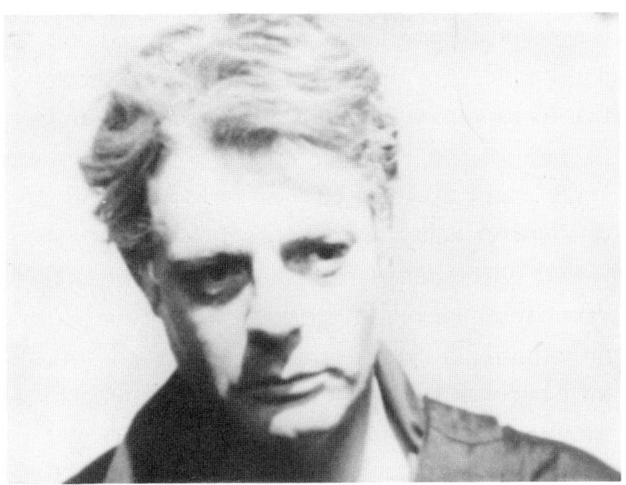

Figure 6-1. (Courtesy of Corinth Films, Inc.)

camera movements sometimes follow, sometimes go counter to the figures. The viewer's sense of near and far, right and left is jeopardized by panning that seems to violate the logic of spatial organization, as if the lens were never content with the situation of the frame lines. The close-up, a conventional means of emphasis of the lens, is incorporated into the expression of randomness. The panning makes it seem that the faces in close-up appear by accident rather than design. During this opening part of the sequence, the director's prerogatives of organization and selection are replaced by the wandering viewpoint of the curious onlooker. Here Guido reads space with the eye of the amateur, someone whose attention is arrested, but only fleetingly, by picturesque details, an onlooker bemused by space but unable or not yet willing to exploit it. The amateur's eye begins to make sense of the narrative space when it locates the source of the music heard in the preceding bathroom sequence: the little orchestra playing on the terrace of the spa. This strategy reminds us that narrative space is logically organized space in which sound and image are causally related. Wagner's music, representative of the wild ride of the mythic Valkyrie maidens, is a comic comment on the leisurely pace of the strollers, whose gazes, oriented in many directions (even right at the lens) add to the instability of the field.

In this same sequence a high-angle long shot of the people moving in orderly lines on the spa terrace is yet another gesture of narrative organization. The conventional master shot of cinematic vocabulary, the shot designed to organize the space as a comprehensive field, gives access to the expanse in which the action is about to take place. Here, however, it is at first withheld; instead of announcing, the master shot is made to summarize. The dislocation of the master shot in the syntax of the sequence reminds us of what has been missing—the control of the omniscient narrator, the confident director. Accompanied by a change of music, that control is finally exerted. The movement in space, as soon as it is located and mapped through the global, detached view of the far-seeing lens, is subjected to the rhythm of the overture to Rossini's *The Barber of Seville*. Music has served an ironic purpose throughout the sequence and now comments on itself. Music drama becomes comic opera. Both, however, turn random strolling into a dance, and we are never quite sure whether the choreographer is Fellini or Guido.

Our uncertainty is banished a moment later when Guido enacts an emphatic instance of directorial intervention. With the help of Claudia, the muse-figure, he transforms the observed space into imagined space. The hurly-burly of the spa terrace is interrupted by a moment of epiphany. As soon as Guido himself is shown in the crowd, moving in line to have his glass filled with the curative water, he stops the action and the music. He slides his dark glasses down the bridge of his noise as if to see more sharply. His vision suddenly sweeps the terrace clear of its crowd. The field becomes a delineated space for another kind of spectacle. Enormous walls frame the entrance of an enchanting female figure, Claudia, who will reappear in many guises throughout *8 1/2*. Here, she traverses the terrace with a dancelike movement, endowing it with her magical presence, demonstrating that it exists of and for Guido's inspiration. But if Claudia's terrace suggests Guido's eventual mastery of space, its sudden disappearance suggests that at this point in the film that mastery is imperfect, fleeting. The radiant Claudia turns into an impatient, perspiring attendant, urging Guido to take his glass of water; the ecstatic silence is replaced by the strongly accented beat of Rossini's music. Guido is once again prey to confusion and apathy.

Claudia's subsequent appearances demonstrate a similar but not identical spatial function. The first of these caps a series of temporally related sequences in the spa hotel. With its corridors, rooms, and lobby, the spa hotel is to some extent predefined by the viewer's knowledge of spaces generic to all hotels. This knowledge is both confirmed and challenged by Fellini's staging strategies and the set design. The lobby, for instance, contains an area where men are working on the unfinished set, thereby acknowledging that what we see is a movie set. Guido's several passages through the corridors are occasions for encounters with characters who fuel his imagination, with others who pester him regarding the film he is unable to make. The director's perambulations are thus a clear metaphor for his halting and stumbling efforts to make a film. The production office is installed in a hotel room that contains, as it should, a bed (replete with three occupants) but also the paraphernalia pertinent to Guido's film: unfinished costumes, models, photographs. Guido's own room is littered with still more photographs. The orderly, functional elements of the hotel are thus invested with the vagaries of Guido's art. The fixed corners of its conventionally rectangular spaces are repeatedly destabilized as once again the camera anxiously pans. The lens is as nervous and fugitive as the gaze of the film's protagonist, a man (a movie director) programmatically identified by the acuity of his vision, a man who seems unable, often unwilling to concentrate that vision.

As before, Claudia provides a moment of focus. On the spa terrace she achieved this on a monumental scale; here she defines a space of intimacy. Guido has passed through lobby, production office, and corridor to the privacy of his bedroom. The room is nearly completely dark, its components hidden in shadow. It is from the shadow that Claudia emerges, first in her white uniform, then in her white slip, finally in bed, in extreme close-up, caressing the white sheet covering her neck (fig. 6–2). She purrs: "I want to

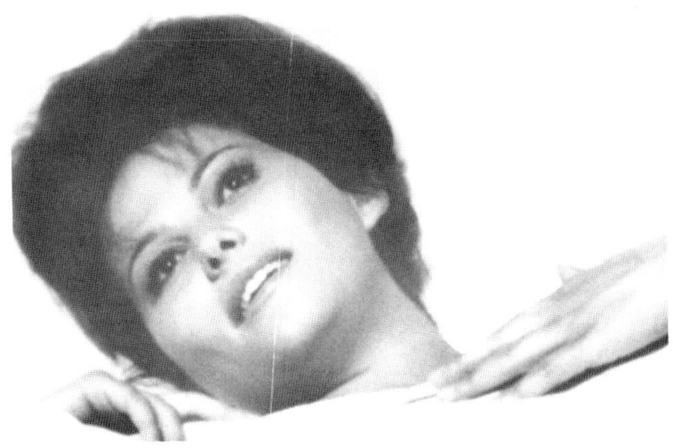

Figure 6-2. (Courtesy of Corinth Films, Inc.)

put things in order. I want to clean up." In these instances, the viewer's ability to capture any sort of spatial configuration is invested in the whiteness of Claudia's face, her costume, and her bare shoulders and arms. In the black, shapeless field there is nearly nothing more. The definition provided by Claudia is therefore without context. Claudia does not organize space. She occupies it fully, thus precluding any dramatic articulation. Claudia is a figure without a dramatic frame, a character without a fiction.

Guido, however, must make a movie, not a portrait in close-up. The spatial dilemma incarnated by Claudia is shifted but not resolved when she materializes as an actual character in the film rather than as a construct of Guido's fantasy. This occurs in a large movie theater, a space whose size recalls the first apparition of the muse figure. The colossal dimensions of the spa terrace contained and were animated by the moving crowd. The auditorium of the movie theater, whose regular rows of seats are meant to be occupied by a full audience (reflecting the space occupied by the viewers of *8 1/2*), dwarfs the randomly placed viewers present for the screen tests of Guido's film. The scale of relationship between human figure and space in the terrace sequence conveys Guido's confusion; the altered scale of that relationship in the auditorium "places" Guido's anxiety, his troubled connection to the fiction and to the characters in his life. Here, in a space constructed for cinematic representation, presided over by the hectoring producer, the director is seated apart from the others, separated from them by empty rows of seats (fig 6–3). And prior to the projection of the screen tests everyone, including Guido, is sharply detached from the large white screen.

As soon as the screenings begin the space is radically disrupted by both the gaps and intersections between screen and auditorium. The viewer's sense of scale is countered by the conflicting spatial coordinates of the film *8 1/2* and those of Guido's screen tests. The viewer must respond to a multiple set

Figure 6-3. (Courtesy of Corinth Films, Inc.)

of off-screen spaces: (1) the virtual off-screen space that hovers beyond the frame of all cinematic images; (2) the off-screen literally inscribed in *8 1/2* by the screening of a screening; (3) the off-screen enacted within the screen tests as the usually silent, invisible director shouts instructions to the actors and finally appears himself in the tests; and (4) the shots of the anxious, depressed Guido sitting in the auditorium as we hear the sound of his doubly "off" voice—off-screen in relation to the image before our eyes and off-screen to the image Guido is watching. The interplay of on/off screen space is intensified as the screen tests, repeatedly intercut and shot from unpredictable camera angles, reach a paroxysm of confusion.

One of the functions of Guido's muselike fantasy figure is precisely to banish confusion, and this is achieved by the entrance of Claudia, the actress who has been engaged to play the muse. Yet Claudia the movie star is no more successful than the previous Claudia in organizing a space other than her own. In silhouette she is the only significant configuration in the frame. Her hair brightly lit by the projection beam, she walks forward, conferring her poise and control on the incoherent space. The exchange between the actress and the inspired director enacted in front of a projection booth is an example of Guido's creative processes, of his ability to arrest space and place the performer in space. Yet the space for Claudia is still excessively circumscribed and therefore insufficient for an imagination as expansive as that of Guido/Fellini. This sense of limits persists through the rest of the encounter as Guido and Claudia walk down a narrow staircase, then converse as they drive in the actress's car (a place of utter calm, in contradistinction to the nightmare car of the opening sequence). The world outside the car's windows, apart from an occasional flashing light, remains invisible in the darkness. For several minutes Fellini abandons the kinetic camera rhythms that characterize much of *8 1/2* and focuses on the faces of the two characters, singly or together. The viewer is allowed to settle into the comfort of conventional action-reaction shots, of a strictly logical editing pattern for both sound and image.

Guido asks Claudia to stop the car in the courtyard of an old building. As the car turns the beams of its headlights play over the edge of the building and the facade; then we see the three sides that form the symmetrical courtyard, an elongated version of a theatrical playing space. Almost immediately Claudia reverts to muse and, dressed once again in her white uniform, appears in an upstairs window of one of the buildings (fig. 6–4). A moment later she descends to the courtyard, where she inspects the place settings on a table incongruously situated in the center (fig. 6–5). Complementing the patent symmetry and frontality of the spatial configuration, she demonstrates the activity she spoke of during the scene in Guido's bedroom: "I want to put things in order."

This order, the order of the pristine surface and the regularity of household economy, echoes two other sequences in *8 1/2*. The first occurs at the end of Guido's love scene with his mistress, Carla. We see the hotel room in a high-angle long shot that occupies a position in the syntax of this sequence similar to that of the high-angle long shot of the spa terrace referred to above. Here, after a series of complex staging strategies (involving two mirrors and shifting planes) intended to disorient the viewer, we are finally permitted to seize the proportions of the room and to locate the disposition of the characters, the walls, the furniture. Guido has fallen asleep; Carla is reading a comic book and munching on a piece of fruit. Without explanation or preparation, a woman dressed in black appears, taking small steps to the left, moving her right arm as if she were wiping something (fig. 6–6). We are about to learn that she is Guido's mother. In his dream she is first placed in the bedroom he shares with his mistress, then in the cemetery in which his father is buried (and reburied). The continuous activity of the Mother—who first dusts an imaginary wall in the bedroom, then dusts the surface of Guido's father's mausoleum—conflates the "real" space and dream space in the fiction, recalling the contiguity of nightmare and awakening in the film's first sequences. This is another of those disquieting intersections between spatially distinct domains where the boundaries of Guido's perception, imagination, memory, desire, and unconscious are jarringly thrust against each other and presided over by a figure representing a specific kind of order. The order of the Mother is that of conventional spatial harmony, the order of the dedicated homemaker.

Figure 6-4. (Courtesy of Corinth Films, Inc.)

Figure 6-5. (Courtesy of Corinth Films, Inc.)

Much later in the film, at the conclusion of the harem sequence, a similar order is expressed but on a different scale. The space of the harem is the enormous farmhouse room shown previously in an evocation of Guido's childhood memory. Now it is inhabited by the dramatis personae of Guido's love life (with the significant exception of Claudia, who always appears in solitude), women who, in this absurdist staging of male wish-fulfillment, flatter, cajole, and seduce the hero, admonish him, revolt against him, and then submit to his will. In a dizzying array of groupings and framings, the women seem to fill and reshape the space with each of the many pans and tracking shots (fig. 6–7). They pose, they walk slowly, they run, they

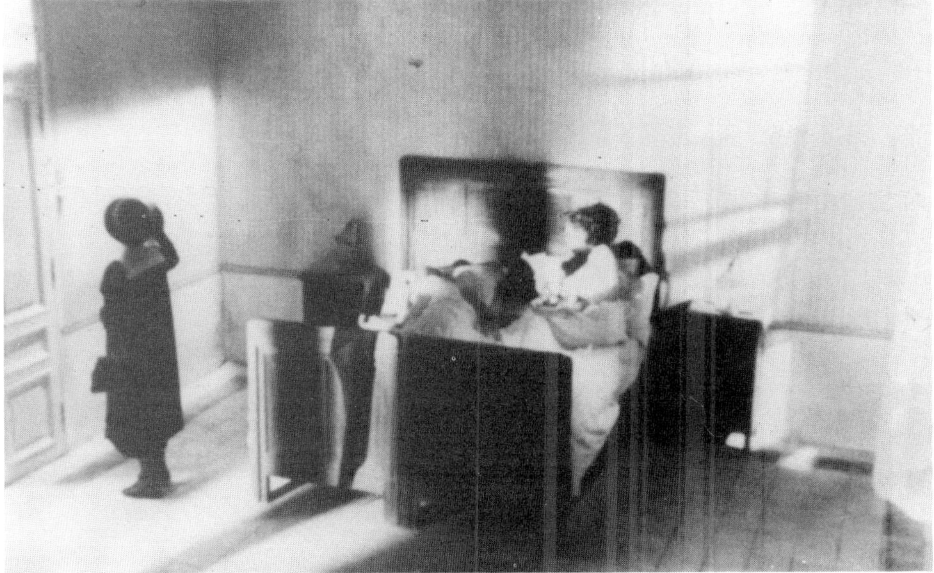

Figure 6-6. (Courtesy of Corinth Films, Inc.)

Figure 6-7. (Courtesy of Corinth Films, Inc.)

dance—one of them even swings through the space on a bedsheet. Guido's imagination and the capacity of his eye and his *mise-en-scène* to contain space without diminishing its flux are given full exercise in this farmhouse/love nest/circus/vaudeville theater. At the end of the sequence, however, that exercise is terminated by the imposition of an order that is, again, not Guido's but instead that of a fantasy wife—the order of domesticity. The modern, intellectual, neurotic Luisa, Guido's "real wife," is costumed in the harem sequence like a simple farm woman who is happy to do all the chores, to keep things clean and tidy. She resolves the riotous movement of the harem as she inscribes her domestic economy on the space, a spotlight following her passage through the space (now emptied of all the other characters), recharting its dimensions as she takes down the hanging laundry, throws it into a large tub, fills her bucket with water, and proceeds to scrub the floor. Echoing the Mother's dusting, she too enacts the muse's desire to "put things in order" and to "clean up."

The order and cleanliness proposed by the Mother, the fantasy Luisa, and Claudia are unsatisfactory solutions to Guido's artistic dilemma. His inspiration withers in spaces that are dust-free, neatly organized, and swept clean. Fellini's attitude toward this sort of order is explicitly conveyed by the ironic and subversive modes in which it is presented: the Mother performs her cleaning up in the room in which Guido and his mistress have just made love; Claudia speaks of order and cleanliness while lying in Guido's bed, seductively caressing the sheet; Luisa scrubs her floor in solitary melancholy and is finally transformed into a figure of theater by the sharp outline of a spotlight, a clear reference to the pathetic vaudeville turn of Jacqueline (the first "artiste" loved by Guido), prominently featured in the harem sequence. The unwelcome Mother, the provocative lover, and the too-perfect wife are discordant to the spaces that they wish to put in order. The Mother reactivates Guido's paralyzing guilt about his dead father and his betrayed wife. Claudia, positioned as the ordering factor in Guido's film, appears in bed when the director is particularly apprehensive about his craft. Luisa's rendition of domestic order is a doomed effort to order his personal life. Guido is unable to stage his film in bed with either Carla or Claudia; nor can he stage his marriage on Luisa's clean kitchen floor.

In *8 1/2* as in so many of his films, Fellini, with characteristic misogyny, tends to put women in what he deems their place, to reduce them to caricatural roles. Dazzlingly beautiful (Claudia), absurdly buxom, vulgar, and devious (Carla, the mistress), frighteningly grotesque (Saraghina), too smart for their own good (Luisa and her friend Rossella), they all serve the caricatural fantasy of male superiority and male domination depicted in the harem sequence. The gender division of the film's dynamics relies upon and perpetuates stereotypical notions of male and female identity. The spaces associated with nearly all the male characters annoy and perturb Guido, but they are spaces in which he is able to navigate, just as he navigates in a male world, exercising male power, the power of money, and the power of hierarchy in the work place. Guido is *the director* to his producer and *the boss* to his assistants, even as they attack him for wastefulness and indecision. Much more threatening are the spaces organized by the women where Guido is vulnerable in his maleness: as son, lover, husband. Guido is infantile, spoiled, egotistical, exploitative, charming, talented; the women are stupid or too intelligent, monstrous, beautiful, nurturing, castrating.

In Fellini's patronizing, self-serving, yet also self-satirizing myth of the male artist, the neat ordering of space represented by and enacted by the "domestic" women is, of course, inimical to the free, creative exercise of Guido's directorial eye. The space of a movie and the space of a monogamous marriage are not compatible. The roving eye of Guido, Luisa's husband, may have seriously jeopardized the couple's relationship; the roving eye of the movie director is personal, eccentric, avid for images, eager to comprehend the complexities of space, to find shifting points of visual and dramatic focus. The director bends space to accommodate present, past, and fantasy, the plural and the singular, many women and one woman. Guido wants to expand spatial configurations to allow for the coexisting, complementary, conflicting locales of his life and his art. He is able to see everything at once, which is part of the dilemma of this man with a roving eye. Space is often filled to overflowing. Guido's vision, in fact, requires overflowing space. From the very start this appears to be the organizing principle of his perception. Excess in space is the order of most of the film's sequences: the cars jammed into the underpass, the crowds of people filling the spa terrace, the hotel lobby, the thermal baths, the public square, and the spaceship set on the beach. The small, private spaces—Guido's room and the production office—are crammed with details, with unexpected objects and planes.

These spaces, large and small alike, show Guido's predilection for instability. In the play of shifting angle and camera position, the viewer is led to share in Guido's anxiety. What will we see next? What relationship will it bear to what we hear, to what we have just seen? But if space conveys the director's instability it also gives us access to an exhilarating amount of material. As we become accustomed to their rhythm, the incessant tracking pan shots that at first destabilize conventional strategies for reading space lead to increased vision. Made to share Guido's anxiety, we are trained to share his acuity and his quickness.

Near the film's end, just as Guido is preparing to abandon his film, the viewer can appreciate the extent of Guido's vision and is able to make sense of it. During the course of a press conference the hero commits a fantasy suicide. The press conference sequence displays all of Fellini's most disorienting staging practices: illogical camera angles, disjointed editing syntax, constant violation of screen direction, rapid shifts in scale, frenetic camera movement. These are precisely the practices that the viewer has been taught to respond to for the preceding two hours of the film's duration. In desperation Guido scurries beneath a table, temporarily blocking out the menace of space before attaining the oblivion of suicide.

In the next scene workmen begin to tear down the colossal set built for the spaceship scene. Daumier, in one of the longest speeches in *8 1/2*, approves Guido's decision to give up his film. His argument reminiscent of the gestures and motto of the figures who advocate domestication, the cynical critic asserts that intellectuals must not add more "disorder" to an already disordered world: "What we really need is some hygiene, some cleanliness, some disinfection." He cites the examples of two French poets—Mallarmé, who celebrates "the white page," and Rimbaud, who abandons poetry altogether. It is precisely during this sermon on the virtue of the silence of the creative artist that Guido finds the inspiration to begin again. Just as we think he has surrendered to the ultimate calls to order through his fantasy suicide and the destruction of the set for his film, there emerges a call stronger than that of the censuring critic—the call to spectacle. Maurice, an old show business friend of Guido's, interrupts Daumier's sour litany with the words, "We're ready to begin." Earlier in the film on the same spa terrace of Claudia's first apparition, Maurice had introduced a mind-reading act in which miraculous links were made between the thoughts of spectators and those of Maya, the telepathist. Maya filled the space with her tricks and her thoughts, invested the space with her powerful imagination. This is exactly what Guido has been trying to do through the course of *8 1/2*. He has been trying to demonstrate his imagination, to render it spatial, to find a form of spectacle that accommodates its shape, its extent, its contents. And this is what now, just as he is stripped of hope, he is suddenly able to achieve. Maurice, with his exaggerated theatricality, releases Guido from his silence and provides a space adequate to Guido's *Big Confusion* (a working title for the film).

While Daumier preaches sententiously off-screen, on-screen, Guido's film truly begins, first with an image of Claudia, again in her white uniform, then with shots of other characters, they too dressed in white, walking along the beach. Guido is filled with happiness. He senses that the disparate elements of his life are joining, ready to inhabit the same field. Claudia's annunciatory appearance followed by the parade of the white-clad characters lead Guido to the congenial space of spectacle. It is there that he comes to accept the confusion whose boundaries are himself, his own identity. He need only assert that identity to find its fitting space, a theatrical, spectacular space—a circus ring. At last he is able to give the signal for the spectacle to begin. The remaining characters of the film, the extras, even the technicians, descend the giant stairway in *random* order. Of course, as they do so that very randomness is ordered by the shape of the stairway, a stairway whose only function is to serve the spectacle.

The unstable, the shifting, the random previously reflected Guido's anxiety, even while they demonstrated Fellini's art. Now, at the conclusion, these conditions persist, but their sense has been altered. They have become positive indications to Guido of his own artistry. The director's art and life reach their final intersection when Guido and Luisa join hands with nearly everyone who appeared in or worked on *8 1/2*. They all dance around the raised perimeter of the circus ring. Guido, the ringmaster, becomes master of the space, master as he was briefly in the harem sequence when, in the manner of a wild animal tamer, he subdued the rebellious women. Now there is no longer need to subdue rebellion. The discrepancies adhere to this sign of inclusion, of comprehension, a sign that makes life into a spectacle. All the differences, all the discontinuities of time and the conflicts between characters submit to this coherent space of spectacle.

8 1/2 does not end, however, in the comfort of coherence. After more than two hours during which we have been made expert in the reading of problematized space, we should not be surprised by the final shot, where spatiality is itself problematized. Fellini expresses this paradox through the use of a device that recurs several times in the film—the spotlight. The spotlight literally focuses attention on theatrical, spectacular space. It creates that space by artificially excluding the surrounding space. Fellini has punctuated *8 1/2* with spotlighted effects, of which the first appearance of Maurice, Jacqueline's vaudeville turn, and Luisa's floor-scrubbing are only several examples. In the final shot the spotlight is a circle within the circle of the circus ring. It illuminates a small band of clown musicians and Guido as a schoolboy who move in time to their own music. The clowns exit, leaving young Guido. The spotlight follows his small figure to the center of the ring, then is extinguished. The boy exits; the remaining lights in the ring are turned off. Just as Guido finds the space in which to begin his film, Fellini concludes *8 1/2* with a series of gestures that signify ending. Guido's desire for the nearly infinite liberty of the imagination submits to the demonstration that the space for spectacle is finite and defined by an ultimate order, the boundaries of the work of art. And here, as the final image is lost, sliding over the border into the nonspace of darkness, the conclusion links Guido's initial anxiety over capturing space to any viewer's sense of exclusion when the experience of the art work is terminated.

BIBLIOGRAPHY

Fellini

Bondanella, Peter, ed. *Federico Fellini, Essays in Criticism*. New York: Oxford University Press, 1978.

Budgen, Suzanne. *Fellini*. London: British Film Institute, 1966.

Metz, Christian. "Mirror Construction in Fellini's *8 1/2*." In *Film Language*. New York: Oxford University Press, 1974.

Perry, Ted. *Filmguide to 8 1/2*. Bloomington and London: Indiana University Press, 1975.

8 1/2

Affron, Charles, ed. *8 1/2*. New Brunswick and London: Rutgers University Press, 1987.

Bazin, André. *What Is Cinema?* Edited and translated by Hugh Gray. Berkeley: University of California Press, 1967.

Bordwell, David. *Narration in the Fiction Film*. Madison: University of Wisconsin Press, 1985.

Braudy, Leo. *The World in a Frame: What We See in Films*. Garden City: Anchor-Doubleday, 1977.

Comolli, Jean-Louis. "Caméra, perspective, profondeur de champ." *Cahiers du cinéma*, nos. 229–32 (May–November 1971); nos. 234–35 (December 1971–February 1972); no. 241 (September–October 1972).

AFFRON

7

BUSTER KEATON, *THE GENERAL*, AND VISIBLE INTELLIGIBILITY

Noël Carroll

While watching a film the spectator undergoes a variety of cognitive experiences—observing, speculating, recognizing, inferring, interpreting, and so on. The film theorist André Bazin drew a distinction between what he considered the two basic types of cinema viewing. The first, which he associated with editing, seems connected primarily to inference since the spectator must fill in so many unseen details as well as spatial and narrative relations. The second, which he associated with the single shot—specifically, those presented via deep-focus photography—is more a matter of observation. That is, with editing, relations are implied that the spectator is supposed to supply by induction; whereas with the single shot done in the deep-focus medium-long shot (a shot in clear focus throughout with two or more planes of action), the spectator is meant to see and to take note of the relevant relations.

It seems to me that there are more categories of cognitive experience than this in cinema viewing and that they are not necessarily linked to editing versus shot composition in a one-to-one correspondence. In this essay I will use an analysis of Buster Keaton's film *The General* to discuss further, more fine-grained distinctions that need not always be mapped onto an opposition between composition versus editing.

My method will be functional, using the language of goals to describe the cinematic organization of an event and analyzing how formal arrangements facilitate those goals. By the end of the essay we should see a functional equivalence between certain editing patterns and compositional formats.

The primary formal strategy in *The General* is the deep-focus long shot. Penelope Houston has speculated that the recent rise of Keaton's critical stock (in the fifties and sixties) can be accounted for partially by Keaton's use of the long shot, a practice that corresponds to the favored strategies of the fifties and sixties—including those of neorealism, the new wave, and cinema-verité. Houston writes that Keaton uses the long shot to authenticate the action.

> [He keeps] as much of the action as possible within a shot. It started presumably with a natural pride in letting the audience see that those leaps and falls and glissades of movement were all his own work. There could be no cutting because to cut into the action would suggest a cheated effect. He was prepared to risk his neck for an effect which might last twenty seconds on the screen. The camera had to get far enough back to take it all in. (1968, 65)

This explanation of use of the long shot is reminiscent of Bazin's thrill when Chaplin enters the lion's cage in *The Circus*. Long shots in such cases vivify the action by establishing that the action performed in the fictional context literally encompasses many of the same risks to life and limb that the represented act entails off-screen.

While the authenticity theory certainly explains Keaton's long shots at least part of the time, it cannot account for Keaton's use of the long shot time and time again in scenes where there are no risks or stunts. A theory that might account for those long shots is that of comic functionality. Much of the humor Keaton employs derives from what Bergson calls the equivocal situation, i.e., one in which two points of view are in evidence—the character's mistaken assessment of the situation and the audience's correct view of how things stand. An example of this sort of gag in *The General* occurs when Johnny Gray enters Union territory. The audience knows Johnny's predicament while at the same time comprehending Johnny's total obliviousness to it as he scrupulously prepares fuel for his engine. The gag, based on Johnny's obsessive inattentiveness, erupts when the audience grasps both the actual situation and another situation, namely the secure one that Johnny wrongly imagines.

One might hypothesize that the long shot is the best way to enact an equivocal situation gag based on obsessive inattention. If this were true, then we would have an adequate comic functionality theory to explain Keaton's use of the long shot, in terms of its being the best cinematic means for articulating his favorite type of gag. And to formulate a comprehensive theory to explain Keaton's use of the long shot we could add comic functionality to authenticity. That is, in this theory, for stunts Keaton uses the long shots to confirm the audience's admiration of his courage and skills, while for equivocal situation gags he uses the long shot to set out simultaneously the character's misperception alongside the correct view of things in the most functionally perspicuous manner available.

The difficulty with the comic functionality approach is that it is simply false that the long shot is the *best* means for representing equivocal situation/inattention gags. Obviously the long shot is one way to do these gags, but it is hardly the only way. Harold Lloyd, for instance, most often favors doing this type of gag by editing, *à la* Griffith. In Lloyd's *The Freshman*, Harold Diddlebock is tricked into giving a public address. As he speaks he holds an épée, whose tip he absentmindedly pushes along the floor. An insert shot of the floor reveals an open light socket threateningly close to the tip of Harold's wayward rapier. One senses that at any moment Harold will unknowingly plunge the sword into the open electrical outlet. Anticipation builds. Clearly the character is unaware of the danger that we, the viewers, know of (thanks to the insert). Suddenly Harold starts dancing frenetically as a shock of electricity courses through the steel sword into his body. Here we have an equivocal situation gag based on inattention. That is, due to his misconstrual, the character believes the situation is safe, while the audience, alerted by the insert, knows it is almost lethal.

The Lloyd example shows that there are ready alternatives to the long shot for representing equivocal situation gags of the obsessive inattention variety. Lloyd uses editing, juxtaposing a detail to a medium shot. Obviously an overhead medium long shot would have turned the trick just as well. Perhaps, were it Keaton's gag, the overhead approach would have been mobilized, with the victim's head in the perpendicular foreground of the shot and the socket, on the floor, in the effective "background" of the composition. However, this means of representing the situation would be no more effective than Lloyd's actual two-shot format, in terms of conveying the information that is crucial to understanding the gag. To respond to the gag, one must know both that the open socket is near the end of the épée and that the victim is unaware of that fact. This knowledge can be communicated by either a two-shot schema or an overhead deep-focus long shot. As regards the formal requirements that make the gag work as a gag, either format is viable. Thus there is no reason to believe that the deep-focus long shot is the best means for representing equivocal situations, though it is one means.

There is a difference, however, between the two approaches. The Lloyd approach conveys the requisite information synthetically, through editing, without ever visualizing all the elements of the gag in one shot. The gag will work if the audience knows that an event, x, has happened. But the long-shot approach gives the audience something above just knowledge. In other words, "knowing that x" is sufficient for an equivocal situation gag to work, and—as we have seen—editing can communicate such knowledge. But the long-shot method goes beyond the requirements of comedy in assuring that the audience sees x happening in its totality, i.e., with all its relevant elements visible. Keaton does not opt for the long-shot format simply because it is comically functional but because he has a concern beyond comedy that the audience experience x in a "seeing that x" mode.

"Seeing that x" in the alternative cited above entails "knowing that x." But the "seeing that" modality contrasts with the cognitive state where the audience merely knows x on the basis of inference from the discrete details of montage. Evoking the experiential modality, "seeing that x" can serve as a basis for understanding all of Keaton's long shots. Thus it is more comprehensive in explicating Keaton's use of the long shot than the authenticity theory, the comic functionality theory, or a combination of the two. By explaining Keaton's use of the long shot in terms of a desire to engender the experience of seeing that an event, x, is happening in its totality, Keaton's project may be differentiated from Lloyd's and, for that matter, from Hitchcock's.

So far, distinguishing between "knowing that x" and "seeing that x" hasn't really gotten us much further than Bazin's distinctions that were introduced in the opening of this essay. Also, our explication of Keaton's long shot is too broad. We may be able to differentiate Keaton from Lloyd with these categories, but what of a comic like Tati, who—especially in his later works—also emphasizes the long shot? Both might be described in terms of attempting to promote the same "seeing that x" cognitive state in the audience.

In order to contrast Keaton with Tati a further category will have to be added. In terms of composition Keaton employs far more determinate structures for guiding audience attention than Tati does. These determinate structures include foreground/background play, where one element of the event is in each region with little detail in intermediary regions. Keaton's high and low angulation and his use of diagonal composition also give a highly predictable and compelling direction to the audience's attention.

Tati's composition, at least in a film like *Playtime*, is much more multifaceted. He often eschews internal structuring devices like the diagonal and angulation, allowing the spectator's eye to wander, to rove, and to savor the kind of ambiguity that Bazin promised as an especially desirable possibility in long shots. This is not to say that Tati shots lack directional devices altogether. Sound and color often direct attention in his films, as they do in all sound color films. But for the sake of a kind of realism Tati has foregone a battery of visual schemas that move the spectator's eye along preordained pathways. Tati aspires to a kind of neorealist comedy. He attempts to enact the belief that comedy originates in everyday life by presenting comic material in a format somewhat analogous to ordinary perception.

Tati's optimal spectator is one who engages in exploration. Tati decenters his comedies, providing simultaneous comic action all over the shot. He renders the perception of comedy more like the perception of everyday social scenes. We observe comedy in a way that is, from the perspective of comic film conventions, relatively analogous to noncinematic perceptual experiences. This has a thematic significance, of course, as it suggests its own converse. That is, an everyday perspective on the comic complements a comic perspective on the quotidian.

Keaton's composition in the long shot is much more architectonic than Tati's. Attention tends to be directed by the highly determinate structure of the shot. It would be too strong to claim that a diagonal causes the viewer to follow a specific pathway of attention. After all, members of the audience who are locomotive enthusiasts may never take their eyes off the General, no matter how strongly the composition and action suggest that they move from one element of an event to the next. Nevertheless, it does seem correct to suppose that a highly determinate composition, such as one employing a diagonal or angulation, does prompt a certain scenario for attention. One tends to scan to and fro along a diagonal; one tends to follow the trajectory of a high-angle shot, much as one follows the sight of a rifle to its target. Such determinate compositions thus can emphasize those objects and actions that are incorporated in the formal structures under discussion. That is, these devices become vehicles for making certain elements of a scene salient. Against Tati's tendency to equalize on-screen elements, Keaton opts for a compositional hierarchy. Given this, it is easy to discover Keaton's program by isolating that which he elevates for attention in his hierarchy.

Here an example seems appropriate. In the first half of the film, when Johnny is chasing the General with the Texas, he stops at a Confederate staging area to pick up reinforcements. Unfortunately, he forgets to attach the platform car loaded with Southern troops to his lumber car. The result is that, unbeknownst to Johnny, he lights out in pursuit alone. The shot I want to consider is the one in which Johnny realizes that he is alone.

It begins as a medium shot. The camera is mounted on the bridge that runs from the cab of the locomotive to the cow-catcher. In the foreground of the shot we see Johnny. He is staring ahead through the window of the engine. We know that the troops are not attached to the train, and we know that Johnny is unaware of this. There is a certain comic reaction to the confidence that Johnny evinces, given its groundlessness. In the screen-left background of the shot we see trees lining the roadway. We can also see a receding line of the tips of the railroad ties that make up the roadbed. But initially we cannot see the track. Because the rails are straight, we also, at first, cannot see behind the train. Given the position of the camera, the locomotive and the lumber car completely block out the track behind. The effect is somewhat like what Keaton achieves in *The Playhouse* when Big Bill Roberts camouflages the entire line of zouaves by standing in front of them with his enormous bulk. Since the trajectory of perception is fixed, since the spectator can't alter her angle of vision, and since the camera can't see around corners, it is easy to interfere with the sheaf of light rays that is being delivered to the audience by interposing objects in that sheaf. Here Keaton exploits the discrepancy between natural vision and cinematic vision—that is, between constantly shifting station points between the subject and the object, and a single fixed station.

In the shot in *The General* the blocking effect is only momentary. Suddenly the train hits a bend in the track. And as the locomotive and the lumber car snake around that bend, the lumber car jostles out of the camera's path of vision and the open, empty track behind the Texas comes into view, pulling off in a diagonal curve toward the upper screen-right corner of the shot. The audience sees evidence of what it already knew, i.e., that there is nothing behind Johnny.

The foreground/background tension is comically exquisite, with Johnny, confident but ignorant, counterpoised against the devastating absence of the Confederates. Eventually Johnny turns around. Initially pausing, he then pokes his head out of the side window of the locomotive. Pausing again, he then thrusts his entire torso out of the aperture—a full-bodied double take! Then, dismayed, he turns his face toward the camera in a look of disbelief that gradually metamorphoses into a mixture of anger and determination.

The use of deep-focus foreground/background play and the slow diagonal recession of the track are hardly necessary for the gag to be effective. A much easier mode of representation would be to break up the scene into four shots. There could be an establishing shot from the side of the train showing the locomotive and the lumber car with nothing behind them. Then there could be a close shot of Johnny turning around followed by a point-of-view shot with the camera moving over an empty track. Then we could return to another close shot of Johnny in order to catch his comic disgruntlement.

Alternatively, the shot might have been done in a single take from alongside the train. Here the camera would pull up from behind the train, at first registering the absence of the troops and then passing by the cab of the train at just the moment when Johnny leans out of the window and realizes that he is alone. This variation of the shot might end with Johnny turning forlornly to the camera.

In the montage alternative, the audience would know that Johnny was alone. It is well-known about point-of-view shots that though they tell you what a character sees, they often do not supply evidence of how she manages to see what she sees. There is a striking example in Ford's *Fort Apache*. The main character, played by Henry Fonda, is killed in a box canyon. Aided by binoculars, another character, portrayed by John Wayne, sees the death. Or at least this is what the point-of-view shot establishes. One would have thought that, given the distance, the narrowness of the canyon, and all the smoke and fury of the battle, this vision on Wayne's part would be quite spectacular. Given the point-of-view format, we understand that the Wayne character sees the Fonda character die. But we have no idea how this incredible feat is accomplished.

In the alternative single-shot method for shooting the scene in *The General*, the audience does *see* that Johnny learns that he is alone; it does not just *know* that he learns this. However, in the alternative single-shot variation, the audience does not see how it is suddenly physically possible for Johnny to learn what he knows. Keaton's actual approach makes the swerve in the track absolutely salient. Shooting from the side would in all probability flatten out such a subtle curve. But even if the lateral shooting angle did not obliterate the bend, it would still require an extremely thoughtful viewer to make the inferential connection between the curve and Johnny's rude awakening. The viewer would have to reconceptualize the lateral scene frontally. Keaton's approach, of course, begins frontally. To account for why he does this we have to go beyond what is required to make the gag work, for—as previously outlined—there are at least two other formal structures that could make the gag successful: one that relies on a "knowing that *x*" mode of cognition and another that is a case of "seeing that *x*." Keaton's choice has more behind it than evoking either of these states.

That "more" is the desire to engender what we may isolate as a third category of audience attention. This new category is predicated on eliciting a cognitive experience in which the audience sees *how* an event happens. For Keaton in *The General*, physical processes provide the basic subject of the film. Engines are stoked, uncoupled, derailed; artillery is loaded, fired, and transported. Keaton approaches this material from a distinct compositional perspective. He employs a battery of highly determinate compositional structures to enable the audience *to see how* the depicted physical processes happened; he uses these compositional structures in order to give visual salience to the key elements in the causal interactions he presents.

From the above we see that there are at least three distinct cognitive experiences that a director may elicit through stylization. To summarize: as regards depicting an event *x*, an audience may simply know that *x* occurs. Here knowledge is based on inference from conventions and on inferences that make the details of the decoupage conform with the information and expectations that the story supplies. Perhaps we should add another distinction here: that of "believing that *x*"—where the difference between "believing that *x*" and "knowing that *x*" might be drawn by claiming that in the former the event truly occurs in the fictional world of the film, while in the latter the event is implied by the editing and the narrative, but it does not occur in the fictional world. An example of this might be one of Hitchcock's red herrings.

"Seeing that *x*" differs from "knowing that *x*" in that in the former case one sees the event in its totality, i.e., all the key human and physical elements that make up the event are visible on screen. This in turn differs from the category of "seeing *how x* happens," in that with "seeing how" all the key elements and their interaction are not only presented but also made *salient* by the composition.

To make the contrast between "seeing that" and "seeing how" clearer, consider an extreme case of "seeing that." In Edwin S. Porter's compositions one sometimes finds shots where the shot is so broad, the actors so chaotically arrayed, and the shot so decentered that one can easily miss the basic action. In *The Great Train Robbery* and *The Kleptomaniac* Porter presents strong examples of multifaceted composition, cases where the arrangement of details is so disorganized that one "sees that *x*" sometimes only in the special sense that the event is imprinted on the viewer's retina. With Porter one can literally fail to recognize an event despite the fact that all the elements are visible. Keaton's composition contrasts strongly with this. Porter approaches an exaggerated case of the "seeing that *x*" modality. With Porter the viewer may sometimes merely technically see all the elements of the action, but she sees them in such a way that the action is not recognized.

A less extreme case of "seeing that *x*" is the example cited as the single-shot alternative to Keaton's frontal long shot of the discovery that the Confederates are not behind him. Here all the elements of the event are visible, and the event is recognized. Nevertheless, a contrast may still be drawn between Keaton's method and "seeing that *x*," insofar as a case of "seeing how *x*" involves a more directive composition, which not only displays the whole event but also makes the key elements and their significant interrelations salient.

Obviously the range of phenomena that can fall under the category of "seeing that *x*" is broad and varied. In the Porter cases the entire event is not made salient, while in our proposed single-shot alternative to Keaton's frontal long shot, only the relation between the track and Johnny Gray's perceptual field is obscured. Between these two examples there is a wealth of further variations that might be balkanized elaborately as a continuous set of gradations. Many refinements are possible here, but I will emphasize only one—a distinction between "seeing that *x*" without recognition of the event and "seeing that *x*" with recognition. The former, more extreme, case approached by Porter may be labeled "seeing that *x*"(1), while the other may be given the suffix (2).

Given the above distinctions, we can note the logical relations among some of the categories. A case of "seeing that *x*" (2) entails that the spectator "knows that *x*." A case of "seeing how *x* happens" entails that the spectator "sees that *x*"(2) and that she "knows that *x*."

Since "seeing how" is such an awkward locution, it may be better to refer to this phenomenon as "visible intelligibility." This might be understood informally as a case where one comprehends an event at a glance in terms of the interaction of the relevant causal processes.

One value in introducing these categories is their pragmatic value to criticism. The styles of different directors may be characterized in terms of tendencies favoring one or another of these categories. In my research I have found that in *The General* Keaton manifests a commitment to visible intelligibility. This seemed to me especially significant because it suggests a parallel between Keaton's cinematic style and the comic content of the film. That is, many of Keaton's gags involve successes or failures in the mastery of physical tasks. Key here is the question of intelligence, significantly concrete intelligence. An important thematic aspect of the film is Keaton's development of intelligent behaviors vis-à-vis physical processes. On the level of the audience's experience of the film, physical understanding and intelligence are also important for Keaton. He strives for shots that maximize the visible intelligibility of scenes to the audience. For the character, then, concrete intelligence is the theme, while for the audience the visible intelligibility of physical processes is the key cinematic commitment. Both in style and content Keaton shows a basic interest in the understanding of the physical world. Perhaps no film is quite as pervasively concerned with the comprehension of physical processes as *The General*.

In employing visible intelligibility as a critical tool certain methodological restraints seem appropriate. In order to corroborate that a given shot is a significant case of visible intelligibility it is advisable to formulate, as I have done above, alternative means of shooting the scene, where the formal arrangement of details would promote either "knowing that *x* happens" or "seeing that *x* happens"(2), rather than "seeing how *x* happens" (i.e., visible intelligibility). The purpose of these thought experiments is to propose that since there are live alternatives to the method actually employed, artistic choice of some sort can be inferred to be operative. In supporting a claim of an artistic concern with visible intelligibility in any film, it is important that one's foils—i.e., one's imagined alternative treatments—be historically plausible in terms of conventions of the context of the film and in terms of the probable aims of the film (given its cultural role). Also, a claim that a shot is a significant instance of visible intelligibility cannot be well supported by using outlandish foils. For instance, shooting a scene from a mile away may supply you with a "seeing that" alternative to your claim of a significant case of visible intelligibility. However, this alternative is so implausible that it is hard to imagine it entering most choice procedures. The degree to which the alternatives to a given procedure are improbable, in general, determines the degree to which a claim of a significant instance of visible intelligibility is implausible.

Discovering cases of visible intelligibility is a matter of intuition. Explicating them is a matter of tracing the compositional variations that make key items in the event salient, once one has a clear description of what event one is dealing with. Confirming a discovery as a significant artistic instance of visible intelligibility involves demonstrating through thought experiments that the given scene could have been one of several plausible alternatives in an artistic choice procedure.

To supply a fuller sense of what is involved in explicating instances of visible intelligibility, let us consider some examples. In the section of *The General* devoted to Johnny's pursuit of the spies, the Union hijackers disconnect one of the boxcars of the General, hoping it will roll back and impede the progress of the Texas. When he sees the obstacle, Johnny has the idea of pushing the boxcar onto a siding, thereby clearing his path. Johnny stops his locomotive, leaps from the cab, and rushes to pull a device that switches tracks, in order to send the heavy boxcar onto a siding. Next, in an overhead shot, we see Johnny in the foreground of the cab of the Texas; and in the background we see the boxcar in the top screen-left corner of the image. The boxcar is rolling freely on a spur parallel to Johnny's. In the background, unbeknownst to Johnny, the spur the boxcar is on reunites with his spur. While Johnny rushes around the cab, the boxcar slips in ahead of him.

Obviously, if Johnny had been attentive, he would have seen that the tracks converged, and he would have raced his engine so that he would have been far past the point of connection by the time the boxcar slid back onto his track. But he was preoccupied. In a close shot following that shot where we see the boxcar in the lead, we see Johnny framed by the window of the cab. His mouth drops open; he sees the boxcar in front of him. Then he closes his eyes, as if to envision the environment as he had pictured it. Then he turns around—that is where his mental map places the boxcar. Finally, he looks forlorn, as if the entire transaction were incomprehensible, perhaps magical.

The overhead long shot in this sequence seems to me to be a case of visible intelligibility. To explicate it one must attend to the particular strategies or formal articulations in the *mise-en-scène* that render the key elements of the event salient. The camera is mounted high on the tender. We see Johnny busy in the cab. He is in the center of the foreground of the shot. Off in the background in the upper screen-left corner, we see the wayward boxcar on the parallel track. There is no action in the intermediary regions of the image to avert our natural tendency to scan from near to far. The rectangular boxcar echoes the edge of the frame while the rectangular edge of the window of the locomotive sets up a third resounding formal echo. We move naturally through this formal pattern. Johnny is bending down under the window fiddling with this or that. The high-angle long shot not only shows us the key elements of the situation but also shows us how the boxcar winds up in front of the Texas and why Johnny is insensible to the situation. Here the elaboration of sharply demarcated foreground/background regions, the use of angulation, and the use of rhyming rectangular edges are individual formal articulations that, when coordinated, emphasize how Johnny becomes befuddled by the mechanics of the situation.

The above boxcar gag is followed by another where, unbeknownst to Johnny, the boxcar is derailed when it strikes a piece of debris—a railroad tie—that the Union spies have thrown there to impede the Texas. The shot that represents this is a low-angle long shot. Here angulation substitutes for editing in terms of selecting the relevant aspects of the situation. The low angulation directs the audience to the track and to the wheels of the boxcar. We anticipate and then understand how the crash has occurred. Rather than starting with a close shot of the tie on the track and then shifting to a standard lateral medium shot of the crash, Keaton employs a single long shot with low angulation. The eye follows the subtly rising trajectory of the low angle to the center of the screen where on the track we find the tie—made larger by the angulation—that overturned the car. At a glance the whole event is pellucid, comprehensible because the low angle immediately gives salience to the tie and thus sensitizes us to the key physical variables of the situation.

The process of explicating a case of visible intelligibility involves an enumeration of the formal articulations of the image whose coordination emphasizes the key causal relations of the depicted event. In our examples, foreground/background play, the diagonal, angulation, and repetitive shapes have been singled out as constitutive elements of the visible intelligibility of the shots discussed. Of course, these are not the only available strategies. Indeed, even in Keaton there are techniques other than these that promote visible intelligibility. In explicating instances of visible intelligibility the task is not to reduce every case to the operation of a handful of recurrent strategies. One would suspect that the list of strategies would grow as filmmakers experiment with new ways of prompting attention.

Though the examples of visible intelligibility so far have been derived from single-shot compositions, since the concept is a functionalist one it may also be applied to editing. That is, visible intelligibility is a goal that can be pursued through or instantiated in a system of editing as well as a compositional system. Here Keaton's variation of the field/reverse field structure is important. In *The General* Keaton reverses the field of a long shot on several occasions. What seems distinctive about this technique is precisely that it is a long shot being reversed. Everyone employs a shot-countershot convention for interpolating close shots in the representation of dialogue. But in *The General* Keaton also uses field reversals with long shots. The reason for Keaton's use of long-shot field reversals seems to be that this particular structure is closely connected with Keaton's use of the foreground/background regions in his single-shot compositions. That is, editing of this sort functions as a means to accentuate foreground/background juxtapositions of elements by systematically rotating those elements in relation to their screen position and prominence. Used in this way editing is an added means of yielding salience, while the use of long shots maintains the constant visibility of all the relevant elements of the scene.

Examples of this use of long-shot field reversal occur in the eleven-shot sequence in *The General* where Johnny narrowly misses blowing himself to smithereens. Keaton begins this sequence with a handful of lateral shots, which include Johnny's priming the gun and getting his foot entangled in a chain between two railroad cars. The mortar is jostled by the roadbed, and the lowered barrel of the gun points right at him.

The fifth shot in this scene is from behind the mortar, with Johnny in the background of the shot. His foot is caught in the chain. He is stuck on top of the ladder on the back of the tender. Our sightline runs along the trajectory the mortar shell will take. Here the foreground/background position aligns all the crucial elements of the scene as well as underscoring the key physical relation, the trajectory of the projectile. In the foreground we see the mortar, its fuse, and its inexorable target. The shot also emphasizes the interrelations of the elements, since the line of vision of the camera is virtually the same as the line of fire of the mortar.

Shot six is a slightly closer version of shot five, in which we see Johnny shake off the chain. Shot seven is a long-shot reversal of shot five. It is a frontal long shot with the camera mounted on the tender. In the foreground there is lumber; in the mid-ground Johnny climbs onto the top of the car; and in the background we see the implacable gun, its fuse steaming and its muzzle lowered directly at the Texas. Johnny throws several chunks of wood at the mortar, hoping to alter its elevation, but to no avail.

This shot is especially important. First of all, it reverses the field of shot five. In this way it frontally underscores the two crucial features of the scene—the cannon and the Texas. The foreground/background juxtaposition of shot five already achieved this. Shot seven further accentuates this formal emphasis by systematically rotating the visual field so that the gun and the Texas exchange the most prominent screen positions. This is a powerful means of giving utmost salience to key elements. This field reversal also gives the audience more perceptual data about the relative positions of the two objects, provoking a refined sense of depth via the systematic permutation of screen configurations. That is, by reversing the screen position more depth cues about the distance between the two objects are supplied, providing a richer comprehension of the space involved.

Last, shot seven alerts the audience to the fact that there is a curve in the track. The curve, of course, is exactly what saves the Texas from obliteration. By emphasizing the track in shot five as a straightaway and then reversing the field in shot seven, where the track curves, the audience is sensitized to the physical fact about the track that accounts for how the Texas is saved.

The most famous shot in this interpolation is the tenth. It is an overhead long shot with extreme depth of field. In the foreground, in the lower screen-left corner of the image, the mortar rolls into the frame. In the mid-ground there is the Texas, and in the background we can see the General.

From behind the mortar we can no longer see its fuse smoking. It is about to discharge. Between the Texas and the mortar, however, we see that the track is curved. The Texas is pulled from the trajectory of the volley by the swerve in the roadbed. The gun fires, the shell whizzes past the Texas, and the shell detonates a mile or so away, just missing the last boxcar of the General, deep in the background of the shot. In the foreground, a cloud of white smoke hovers over that part of the track where the mortar fired; it is just before the curve.

Shot ten is certainly composed in a way that maximizes the visible intelligibility of the scene in and of itself. Nevertheless, the earlier field/reverse field alternation of shots five and seven enhances the clarity of the physical situation, not only by emphasizing the basic physical elements but also by emphasizing their alignment—first along a straightaway and then along a curve. The field/reverse field here primes the audience for the basic physical insight concerning the curve in shot ten, thereby facilitating the audience's capacity to see at a glance how the event happens.

Although thus far visible intelligibility has been elucidated in terms of causal relations within events, the preceding discussion of the alternation of shots five and seven suggests a spatial application as well. The systematic alternation of striking long-shot compositions may enhance one's sense of the depth of a shot, specifically in terms of the distance relations between objects. That is, the addition of perceptual cues about the space of the event yields a heightened sense of the distance relations. The data base for the audience's judgment is augmented, supplying a stronger understanding of how pertinent objects stand in relation to each other.

Closely related to the goal of visible intelligibility as regards its application to spatial relations is what might be described as geographical intelligibility. An example of this occurs, for instance, in the sequence in which Annabelle removes the linking pin from the General so that she and Johnny can hijack the General from the Yankees. There is a frontal shot of men heaving provisions into a freight car. In the foreground a bearded Union officer directs the activities. With Annabelle hidden in a bag on his shoulders Johnny walks past the point where he should have loaded the sack into the freight car. Instead he walks to the lower screen-left corner of the frame, where there is a junction between two freight cars. The Union officer gesticulates. Then Keaton cuts to a lateral shot. This shot is mounted from behind Johnny. The camera looks down the alley between the two freight cars. A hand—Annabelle's—reaches out from the sack and lifts the pin from between the two cars, disengaging them. In the background of the shot, over the top of the sack, we see the Union officer from the previous shot still gesticulating.

He orders Johnny to put his sack in the freight car Johnny has just passed. Keaton then cuts back to the frontal long-shot set-up and Johnny throws the sack, with Annabelle and the pin, among the provisions.

The second shot in this chain is crucial. By repeating the officer from the foreground of the first shot in the background of the second shot the spectator can concretely locate the action of the second shot in regard to the action of the first shot. A tighter shot of Annabelle's removal of the pin that did not include the officer would have rendered the geography of the scene more abstract. By *systematically cross-referencing* elements—specifically, the officer—from one shot to the next, Keaton conveys *a concrete sense of orientation* about the relation of the spaces depicted in the disparate shots. The evocation of a sense of geographical intelligibility is not merely a function of the fact that Keaton tends to edit-in-the-round (by which I mean shooting a scene from frontal, lateral, rear, and overhead angles, rather than from a merely frontal perspective). Eisensteinian montage also edits-in-the-round, but it does not evoke a sense of geographical intelligibility, because pains are not taken to perspicuously cross-reference the elements in successive shots.

In the preceding example, geographical intelligibility differs from visible intelligibility in that in the former the audience's strong sense of the directional relations in adjacent spaces is more a matter of construction than of observation. However, even though it is a matter of construction, the spectator has a very concrete and articulate map of the spatial relations between objects, because the audience is provided with more visual cues about the relation between the two shots than is usual. And also those cues are saliently composed. As in the baseball sequence in Keaton's own *College* or in the return of Dave Waggoman's remains in Anthony Mann's *The Man from Laramie*, the audience is given an evidential basis for a powerful mental map of the geography; one feels particularly well-oriented to the space. And even though the space is constructed, it is internally articulated well enough with cross-referenced elements that one has the sense that one would know how to move in it.

Though there are differences between our examples of visible intelligibility and geographical intelligibility—especially in terms of degrees of observation versus construction—nevertheless both have the effect of giving the viewer a heightened sense of understanding. In the case of visible intelligibility that heightened understanding pertains to causal processes and interactions, while in the case of geographical intelligibility it is a matter of spatial orientation. At the level of style, in *The General* Keaton is concerned to portray the physical world and its relations with a clarity perhaps unmatched in the history of film. This interest is of course also reflected in the composition and editing of other Keaton films. And it obviously also corresponds at the level of style to some of the most recurrent themes in Keaton's narratives and gags: the question of understanding and mastering causal relations in a world of things, on the one hand, and the question of precisely locating and correctly orienting oneself within one's environment, on the other hand. The issues Keaton explores in his physical clowning, that is, become central issues of his cinematic style.

WORKS CITED

Houston, Penelope. 1968. "The Great Blank Page." *Sight and Sound* 37 (April).

BIBLIOGRAPHY

On Buster Keaton's *The General*

Carroll, Noël. *An In-Depth Analysis of Buster Keaton's The General*. Ph.D. dissertation, New York University, 1976.

Rubinstein, E. *Filmguide to The General*. Bloomington: Indiana University Press, 1973.

On Film Composition

Bazin, André. "The Evolution of the Language of Cinema." In vol. 1 of *What Is Cinema?*, by André Bazin, translated by Hugh Gray. Berkeley: University of California Press, 1967.

Carroll, Noël. "The Power of Movies." *Daedalus* 4 (Fall 1985): 114.

8

THE SOUNDS OF *MASH*

Robert T. Self

Film conveys information through five means: images, written language, spoken language, music, and sound effects. Although three of these tracks are aural, scholarship and reviewing have tended to address film primarily as a visual medium. This emphasis results in part from the secondary development of sound and the "talkie" in the history of film and in part from a belief that sight is a more dominant sense than hearing (Altman 1980a, 14–15). In recent years a growing body of film theory and criticism has sought to correct this imbalance and to focus attention not only on the complexities of film sound but on the diversities of the functions of sound within the various systems and styles of film. Rick Altman urges the necessity of recognizing that "neither track [sound or visual] accompanies the other, neither track is redundant; the two are locked in a dialectic where each is alternately master and slave to the other" (1980b, 79). Any number of well-known narrative films can illustrate the intricate power of sound to support, extend, contradict visual imagery—from such early sound films as *M* (1930) to the recent historical epic *The Last Emperor* (1987). As in cinematography, improved technology in recording and reproduction has continuously provided sound technicians with ever-larger ranges of choice in their manipulation and construction of the sound track. The knowledgeable film viewer must learn to listen to a film's sound as discriminatingly as he/she looks at its images.

Among contemporary American filmmakers few directors have been as innovative and challenging to the audience's ability to hear, see, and understand feature films as Robert Altman. Beginning with the highly successful *MASH* (1970) and continuing through *Beyond Therapy* (1986), Altman has made over two dozen movies that work aggressively to broaden, revise, and interrogate the ways Hollywood has traditionally constructed its stories and the stylistic features employed to tell those stories. *Nashville* (1975) and *A Wedding* (1978), for example, develop stories around twenty-four and forty-eight major characters, and *California Split* (1974) and *Nashville* were among the first films in the film industry to use the multitrack recording systems already widely used in the recording industry to produce a sound track that mixes as many as sixteen different original tracks. A close analysis of the sound in *MASH*, Altman's most popular film, illustrates both the complex potential of sound in traditional or classical Hollywood cinema and the innovative possibilities of sound for the development of a more modernist narrative discourse.

To attend closely to sound involves a twofold critical procedure: the recognition of the formal properties of sound within the range of technical possibilities and the analysis of the particular functions of those sounds within the systems of an individual film. Sound, along with editing, cinematography, and *mise-en-scène*, is one of the four technical bases of cinematic style and always helps to establish the three systems—spatial, temporal, and logical—of filmic discourse. The sophisticated film viewer is able to distinguish among the different voices, music, and effects of any film and also to comprehend their significance for the overall construction of meanings in the film.

In story cinema, the dominant form of the movies, sound has traditionally functioned to establish dramatic time and scenographic space as a context subordinate to the causally connected action of fictional characters. Sound contributes to (delineates, describes, denotes, determines) the viewer's sense (literally, ironically, ambiguously, metaphorically, reliably, or unreliably) of story situation, place, time, point of view, action, or character. Of the three kinds of sound—dialogue, sound effects, and music—the first has played the greatest role because stories circulate around characters. Christian Metz has observed that "the only cinematographic aspects that interest everyone, and not just some specialists, are the image and speech" (1980, 28), and that because classical narrative film is concerned with the "*mise-en-scène* of bodies"

(Doane 1980, 37). Just as the spatial and temporal systems of film are subordinate to the dominance of narrative logic, the other two kinds of sound are subservient to the needs of characterization. Mary Ann Doane states, "Sound and image, 'married' together, propose a drama of the individual, of psychological realism" (1985, 61).

Although Altman films—like those of such other American directors of the 1970s as Francis Ford Coppola, John Cassavetes, Stanley Kubrick, Martin Scorsese, and Arthur Penn—work to disrupt and criticize the traditional style of the classical Hollywood cinema, the various categories of sound may nevertheless be recognized in *MASH* within the functional boundaries of narrative. As the sound engineer for *Health* (1980) observes, "Altman demands a full rich multi-layered track which will color, highlight and augment his story . . . , one which will give nuance to each character" (Lear Levin 1980, 368–69). It is first necessary, however, to identify formally the kinds of sound that generate such effects.[1]

The location or source of dialogue, sound effects, and music is a major consideration in the categorization of sound, and the most important categories here are *on-screen* and *synchronous*. Such sound emanates from some source within the space enclosed by the frame and is synchronized to that source. A simple illustration is the two-note whistle so characteristic of Hawkeye in *MASH*; we see his lips pucker on the screen, and we hear the whistle on the sound track. During the last supper sequence, we see a singer and guitarist performing on-screen, and we hear their song on the sound track synchronized with the movement of their lips and fingers. The dominant use of this category occurs during the dramatic scenes located throughout the film when two or more of the story's characters are gathered within the frame to converse with each other. Dago's conversation with Hawkeye about Painless's "problem," for instance, or Duke's and Hawkeye's effort to persuade the colonel to get Major Burns out of their tent and to secure the services of a chest surgeon take place in scenes where we watch their lips move and we hear their voices at the same time.

A variation of these categories is sound that is *off-screen* and *simultaneous*. Such sound regularly accompanies a paramount feature of the classical narrative style—shot/reverse shot editing wherein we watch the face of a listener while we hear a voice, sound, or music whose source is off-screen, that is, not visible within the frame but occurring simultaneously with the dramatic

1. The categories of sound defined in this essay derive from work by Claudia Gorbman (1976), David Bordwell and Kristin Thompson (1979), and Daniel Percheron (1980).

time of the listener. *MASH* illustrates this familiar narrative device on several occasions: when Duke and Hawkeye meet Frank Burns; when Trapper John shows up initially in "The Swamp"; and when the colonel expresses his pique over Trapper's fight with Burns. In such instances the shot/reverse shot editing intimately situates the audience within the dramatic space. We read an expression of incredulity on Duke's face as we and he listen to Burns reciting the Lord's Prayer. We watch signs of pleased delight on Trapper's face as we and he hear the vehement expression of the colonel's anger at him. Viewers thus share the act of audition with a character in the fiction; the off-screen voice elicits interest in the character psychology that motivates classical causality, and the fictional space is extended beyond the borders of the frame. Other sounds emanating from off-screen serve to ground the reality of dramatic space, such as the barking dogs, trickling stream, and roaring jet heard on the sound track as the resting surgeons begin their plot to expose Hot Lips or the ubiquitous announcements from the loudspeaker addressed not only to the limited space visible within the frame but to the whole "camp compound."

Just as on-screen sound works in dialectic with off-screen sound, so synchronous and simultaneous sounds indicate another aspect of temporal order that is *nonsynchronous* or *nonsimultaneous*. Sounds not associated with the apparent time of the action visibly occurring at any given moment in a film involve a complex set of additional categories and require us to distinguish between those sounds deriving from some other story time than that visually present and those sounds deriving not from the story time at all. This distinction is between *diegetic* and *nondiegetic* sounds. Speech, sound effects, or music that would be audible to characters within the fiction, within the action of the story, is diegetic; sounds audible only to the audience derive from the narration of the film and are nondiegetic. David Bordwell and Kristin Thompson further distinguish between off-screen sounds that occur simultaneously with the time of the story's image and have their source in the story space—*simple diegetic* sound—and sound that emanates from a time prior to or following the time of the visible image of the story—*displaced diegetic* sound (1979, 204).

MASH effectively demonstrates this divergency in sound categories. The examples of *off-screen, simultaneous* sound mentioned above are also *simple diegetic* sounds, a category Altman uses at times with much complexity. During the scene celebrating Trapper's being named chief-of-staff, we watch one aspect of the party while overhearing a variety of conversations, including Radar's half-singing, half-speaking new lyrics to the song "Hail to the Chief," without ever seeing the off-screen sources of those conversations.

Simple diegetic sound here vastly multiplies the density of the space only partially visible within the frame. The simple diegetic sound of Hawkeye and Duke singing "Onward Christian Soldiers" becomes off-screen as the camera pans to observe outside their tent a procession of others in the camp who add their voices to those inside the tent; the sound is thus both on- and off-screen at the same time. The sound of the hymn continues across the cut to a shot of Burns praying and becomes an example of off-screen, simultaneous, simple diegetic music that ironically contrasts with the shifting, glaring eyes of the pious major seen in extreme close-up.

Two striking examples of displaced diegetic sound occur in the film as well. Story sound that is *earlier* than the time of the image is audible in the scene between the colonel, Duke, and Hawkeye when they discuss Burns and the new chest surgeon. The flow of sound categories here is remarkable: the on-screen, synchronous dialogue among these three actors becomes off-screen and simultaneous as the camera cuts to a shot of the colonel's ante-office to show Radar entering the colonel's office. The camera holds on this space as we overhear Radar's message to the colonel, then cuts to a scene later in the pre-op ward where Hawkeye and Duke check patients while their voices and the colonel's continue on the sound track. The scene works like this:

Shot	**Dialogue**
1. *Medium three-shot: Duke, colonel, Hawkeye around colonel's desk.*	DUKE: We got to get a A-1 chest cutter in here quick or we're gonna be
2. *Medium shot of colonel's outer office; Volmer at switchboard to left; Radar enters right, crosses, exits left.*	in a helluva lot of trouble. COL: Forget it. No MASH unit has a chest surgeon, and we're not about to get one. RADAR: Excuse me, Sir; they're behind in OR and the
3. *Medium shot of pre-op ward with Duke and Hawkeye bending and checking wounded as they weave their way among the nurses and the large number of men who lie on stretchers all over the floor. Camera pans left to follow their progress.*	pre-op ward is all jammed up. The helicopters and ambulances are coming in full. COL: You guys are going to have to go to work early today. DUKE: What! Add overtime to a twelve-hour day! What the hell is

that. The union will raise all kinds of cane with you, Henry.

HAWK: Boy, Henry, you work those kind of hours you sure need your rest. You can't get it with a sky pilot jabbering away to Heaven all night.

COL: Major Burns will be out of your tent in twenty-four hours. Tell'em that Captain Pierce and Captain Forest are on their way.

HAWK: Henry, you're forgetting something . . . , a chest cutter!

COL: I'll try, dammit . . . !

The sound in shot 1 is simple diegetic, on-screen, and synchronous; in shot 2 it is still simple diegetic but has become off-screen and simultaneous; and in shot 3 it is off-screen, nonsimultaneous, and displaced diegetic. The effect of this sound shift is to show that while in dialogue the surgeons argue about ways to improve their and the unit's operating efficiency, in action they have already moved to meet pressing medical needs. Altman thus adds a deeper, more positive resonance to their characterization as we simultaneously hear them badger the colonel for improved medical conditions and watch them work sympathetically and professionally with the wounded soldiers.

Another example of displaced diegetic sound where the sound is later (as opposed to earlier) than the image occurs in the scene when Major Houlihan questions Hawkeye about the performance of the nurses on his shift. As the sound track carries Hawkeye's voice saying, "You would like to know what I think of the nurses on my team. Well, I'll tell you. I think they're fine; I think they're just great," the scene has shifted away from the two of them in the mess tent to a shot of the operating room; the brief scene during which the lights momentarily go out appears to be a flashback motivated by Hawkeye's (briefly voice-over) evaluation of his nurses; his off-screen, nonsimultaneous, displaced diegetic voice yields on the sound track to the sounds of surgical equipment, the conversation of nurses and doctors, and when the lights return, a spontaneous song by the staff—a mixture now of on-screen and off-screen simple diegetic sound. The scene concludes with a return to the on-screen diegetic voice of Major Houlihan synchronized with her face as she contrarily observes that "Major Burns is far from satisfied." The effect of this scene, as will be more fully analyzed later, is to expand and endorse Hawkeye's critical and subjective point of view.

Nondiegetic sounds, that is, sounds that are not part of the story space and are audible on the sound track only to the audience, are usually off-screen since their source is not within the fictional, dramatic space designated by the frame. They are also usually nonsimultaneous since the time of the story and the time of its telling—the filmic discourse—are discrete and dissimilar. Bordwell and Thompson remark, "When 'mood' music comes up over a tense scene, it would be irrelevant for us to ask if it is happening at the same time as the images since the music has no relation to the space of the story" (1979, 206). Thus the "Washington Post March" is not heard by the football players in the game toward the end of *MASH* and is nondiegetic; the violin rendition of "Reveille"—which takes place during Painless's last supper, is performed by one of the characters in the story, and is audible to both the celebrants of that supper and to us the audience—is diegetic.

The film provides few examples of nondiegetic sound effects—such as, for instance, the whistling noisemaker heard during the raucous music toward the end of the football sequence. Nondiegetic sound, like nondiegetic music, usually works to color, condition, and direct audience reaction to events, situations, characters, and themes in the story proper, and occasionally diegetic sounds will serve this rhetorical purpose of narrative discourse. A comic example of this usage occurs in the scene in which Hot Lips and Burns first feverishly embrace; in mid-embrace, Hot Lips suddenly breaks away, straightens her uniform, and walks off the screen. Burns is left looking quite dazed, and on the sound track we hear the spitting, sputtering sound of static as the camp loudspeaker comes on for another of its ubiquitous announcements. While emanating diegetically from the story space, it comments comically and nondiegetically on the physical condition in which the suddenly aborted passion has left the major.

The film uses no nondiegetic speech—that is, spoken language addressed only to the audience, unheard by story characters—the traditional form of dialogue called *voice-over* narration. One of the film's most notable and well-known sound devices, however, the camp loudspeaker, reflects the complex use of sound that has been a trademark of nearly all of Altman's films. The voice can be synchronized with its apparent source, the loudspeaker, only by the editorial juxtaposition of the mechanically reproduced voice and a close-up shot of a loudspeaker,[2] but it has a variety of diegetic functions: to convey

2. Juxtaposition of the loudspeaker with the voice that emanates from it is of

the larger presence of the camp compound beyond the visually truncated spaces delineated by the camera; to establish an effect of militarylike realism; and to provide a dramatic continuity across contiguous shots of discontiguous spaces. The twenty-one different pronouncements from the loudspeaker also serve structural, comic, and thematic functions (as will be analyzed later) and work overall to give the film the kind of unity frequently achieved by the nondiegetic musical score that accompanies the story in classical narrative films. A simple illustration of its function as diegetic continuity is the three-shot sequence that shows (1) the sexually aroused Burns, (2) Burns and Hot Lips mailing their joint letter to headquarters, and (3) Burns saying good night to Hot Lips outside her tent. Across these shots is heard the unbroken announcement from the loudspeaker that three cases of amphetamines had been stolen for the third time in a month. Here are three shots—three separate times and spaces—whose integrity derives from the coherence of the announcement.

This juxtaposition makes a number of thematic points, too: the pious Major Burns contemplating adultery is linked to the medical component of the military that runs on drugs—an ironic mix of positive and negative values associated with both "heroes" and "villains" that gives preference to neither. This complex effect is reinforced by the next announcement about a planned lecture on "blood and fluid replacement" that is heard during the shot of a refrigerated blood container being opened to show a supply of beer during the party for Trapper. The sounds coming from the loudspeaker are occasionally on-screen, synchronic, and diegetic; more often they are off-screen, simultaneous, and diegetic. But the messages from the loudspeaker move progressively from a purely diegetic effect of realism ("The following men will report to the departure area . . .") to an increasingly nondiegetic effect of thematic commentary ("Tonight's movie has been *MASH* . . ."), although it is speech constantly grounded in the story.[3]

Music is the most familiar example in classical Hollywood cinema of

---

course only an approximate synchronization since the "true" source of the words within the diegesis is a depersonalized army clerk who makes the announcements.

3. Gorbman uses the terms "extradiegetic" and "metadiegetic" sound to distinguish between sound not deriving from the diegesis at all and sound such as dialogue that may emanate from a character within the diegesis but that is being heard as though it were nondiegetic commentary; she further notes that this is an arbitrary but sometimes useful distinction. The loudspeaker, then, as part of the diegesis that regularly seems not simply to be in the story but to be a gloss on the story, would thus be an example of metadiegetic sound (1976, 450).

nondiegetic sound and is copiously illustrated in *MASH*. Claudia Gorbman notes the necessity for attending to three different levels of coding in analyzing film music: the purely musical codes, the cultural codes, and the narrative codes (1980, 185). Her categories ask us to recognize the particular kind of music employed (jazz, classical, folk, etc.), its cultural connotations, and its special pertinence in the narrative context. Thus we recognize the diegetic singing of "Onward Christian Soldiers" as religious hymnology; as a "battle hymn" with patriotic, militaristic, and religious associations; and as an ironic comment on the pious values of Major Burns, whose prayer provokes it. The nondiegetic music playing on the sound track as we first glimpse Hawkeye is musically a marching tune and culturally a sound of military pomp and circumstance, but narratively it is a contrast in its stateliness with the image of the informally attired Captain Pierce leaving the officers' latrine. The orchestral music accompanying Hawkeye's and Trapper's apprehension by the MPs in the Tokyo hospital scene is "suspense" music that connotes both the generic context of spy films and the "mickey mousing" sounds employed in countless cat-and-mouse chases in Hollywood cartoons; its particular significance at this point in the story is humorous and supports the diegetic playfulness of the two surgeons who in their dialogue mimic the Hollywood spy and detective film. The dignity of the march music played over the football game at the end of the film connotes the fall collegiate football scene, but its use with the game here is comedic; the game is neither stately nor collegiate but cynical and farcical.

MASH clearly demonstrates the wide range of sounds at the filmmaker's disposal for the purposes of constructing both a literal and an expressive realism in film narratives. To this point we have looked closely at some of the minute functions each category may play in the spatial and temporal delineations of the narrative. Sound, like the other stylistic aspects of film—editing, *mise-en-scène*, and cinematography—also works across a film to establish larger patterns of significance that determine the viewer's overall responses and understandings. In *MASH* these patterns invoke interest in at least three major areas: They critique and unsettle the means of telling realistic stories in the manner of the classical Hollywood cinema. They participate in a tradition of literary and cinematic comedy and social commentary. They raise philosophical and psychological questions about the relationship of sound to signification in the cinema.

Sound, especially speech, in the classical cinema has been employed since its inception to promote the popular and critical myth that the essence of film as a form of discourse derives from its ability to capture "literal reality." The film industry has historically devoted a great deal of energy to coordinate the acoustic with the visual apparatus in order to enhance the illusion of realism. John Belton points out in this regard that the evolution of sound technology represents "the quest for a sound track that captures an idealized reality, a world carefully filtered to eliminate sounds that fall outside of understanding or significance" (1985, 66). As sound technology has vastly improved the ability to reduce mechanical noise from its tracks, leaving a clean sound of dialogue, effects, and music, the effort of the movies to portray "true-to-life" fiction has also greatly improved. Merely to scrutinize the lengthy credits that have been placed at the end of Hollywood films since the 1960s is to become aware of the large number of technical personnel—sound recorder, sound editor, sound rerecorder, sound effects editor, music recorder, music editor, etc.—required to construct this quality of realism. A popular critical generalization about Robert Altman's films credits them with advancing the state of this "art." Speaking of Altman's *McCabe and Mrs. Miller* (1971), for instance, one textbook states: "Sound is often stacked on sound, voice on voice, but stacked in new ways so that we get an incredible sense of *being there*—in a different place and a different time. The texture is so real that we feel the rain and the cold wind and even smell the smoke" (Boggs 1985, 181–82). We have already heard how the loudspeaker enhances the reality effect in *MASH*. And the constant overlapping of ambient sound and dialogue is another striking characteristic of sound in the film that may be heard as contributing to this effect: When Hawkeye and Duke arrive at the mess tent at the beginning of the film, for instance, the sound track is filled with the hum of many voices in dinner conversation and the sounds of clattering silverware and plates. During the twelve scenes in operating rooms—which punctuate and structure the film in much the same manner as the loudspeaker announcements—we hear the constantly overlapping dialogue of doctors and nurses and the sounds of surgical tools from the several operations usually occurring at the same time.

Robert Altman as a major innovator of sound technology during the 1970s would seem to be a candidate for praise in the industry, but the opposite is the case. Altman was fired by Jack Warner from the production of *Countdown* (1968) because of this "new way" of constructing sound; while it may increase some sense of "being there," it vastly complicates the viewer's ability to follow the story, and classical cinema gives precedence to dramatic realism and credibility before the capturing of literal experience. Overlapping sound and dialogue was not new in 1970. Such filmmakers as Howard Hawks and Orson Welles employed it with dramatic effect in the 1930s and 1940s. What is striking is Altman's violation of a boundary with regard to the traditional foregrounding of story. James G. Stewart, one of the principal sound engineers during the "Golden Age" of Hollywood, writes of this boundary:

> I do not go along with the present trend to see how difficult you can make it for an audience to understand the dialogue. There is a definite limit past which you must not go, or you lose the attention of your audience. Once you have lost that you have ceased to communicate. There is a basic principle: before you can communicate you must have the attention of the listener or the viewer. In poor intelligibility there is an element of irritation which causes the audience to reject what you are telling them. (1980, 62)

Altman's films demonstrate an interest in a dense texture of sound that from one perspective may be more realistic—that is, more like the act of listening in actual experience—as it requires the viewer to select from among the conflicting number of sounds that will be heard. But an important divergence from the classical yoking of sound to the demands of the story in *MASH* is Altman's attitude toward storytelling itself:

> Sound is supposed to be heard, but words are not necessarily to be heard. I am trying to divorce the audience somewhat from literature and from theater, which is based on literature. In those areas it's the words that the character uses that [are] important. I think in film it's what the character does not say, what you don't hear. (Leyda 1977, 6)

Stephen Heath writes, "To disturb the achieved relations of sound and image in the apparatus is to disturb the performance, to break the whole coherence of vision" (1981, 121). Altman's use of sound in *MASH* reveals not a concern with presence, a concern to authenticate and valorize some reality, but a realization of fragmentation. Coherence of story is broken into the film's four major sequences, none of which is linked by any narrative causality; and coherence of personality is fractured into disconnected action. This depiction of fragmentation and brokenness reflects the film's antiwar thematics; it marks the renegade director whose work disrupts classical canons of style, and it reveals not only a hostility toward military authority but a profoundly contradictory attitude toward the authority of discourse as well.

Altman's work, like that of other American directors during the 1970s, is influenced by the international art cinema of directors like Fellini, Bergman, Godard, and others who value narrative realism less than authorial expressivity. In this cinema, the viewer is puzzled not by enigmas developed in the story but by questions raised in the act of storytelling, in the process of narration, in the dissonance perceived within the cinematic apparatus itself. One of the most striking examples of this destabilization of diegetic reality occurs at the very beginning of the film as the *MASH* theme plays over the opening scenes of helicopters bearing wounded soldiers on stretchers: What is the relationship between these initial shots of the diegesis that denotes war and the nondiegetic lyrics of the lilting ballad: "Suicide is painless; it brings on many changes, and I can take or leave it if I please"? The questions generated by this music's commentary on the story are multiplied in the first dialogue of the film:

> *Medium shot, zoom lens, of Colonel Blake and Radar staring off-screen right, apparently at the arriving wounded seen in opening shots, with rotating helicopter blades out of focus in extreme left foreground.*
>
> COL: Radar, get a hold of Major Burns and tell him that we're going to have to hold a couple of surgeons over from the day shift to the night shift. Get General Hammond down there in Seoul; tell him we gotta have two new surgeons right away!
>
> RADAR: I guess I'd better call Major Burns and tell him to put another day shift in our night shift. I'll put in a call to General Hammond in Seoul. I hope he sends us those two new surgeons; we're sure going to need 'em!

This dialogue summarizes the effects that large numbers of newly arriving wounded have on the MASH unit; in turn it becomes the cause motivating the arrival in the next scene of Duke and Hawkeye—except that these words so crucial to the viewer's understanding of the initial situation in the story—that set in motion the whole cause-effect chain of the narrative logic—are spoken by both characters simultaneously and are incomprehensible. It is possible only after several listenings to fully decipher the content of their speech. Laughter at what becomes part of the comic business in the film, the overlapping of the colonel's commands with Radar's simultaneous statement of them, occurs at the expense of clarity in the development of the story. At the crucial stage of the story's beginning, this shot disrupts causality, what David Bordwell calls "the armature of the classical story" (1979, 13). In describing such disruptions in films of the international art cinema, the authors of *The Classical Hollywood Cinema* argue: "The author comes forward chiefly as patterned violations of the classical norm. Deviations from the classical canon . . . any failure to motivate cinematic space and time by cause-effect logic—can be read as 'authorial commentary' " (374). One technical analysis of Altman's use of multiple dialogue tracks described his work not in terms of story but of painting: "His wish was to create a condition figuratively similar to that of a painter who might coat his canvas with layer upon layer of color, allowing each brush stroke to give character and texture to the final rendering" (Lear Levin, 336).

Part of the authorial—or directorial—expressivity in *MASH* lies in the reflexivity of the film, in those moments when the film as discourse addressed to an audience, rather than simply a series of story events unrolling innocently before our eyes, becomes apparent. When the black singer performs "Suicide Is Painless" during the last supper scene, the sound of the song is diegetic, heard from within the story, rather than nondiegetic as it is during the opening credit sequence; however, the singer looks directly into the lens of the camera as he sings and performs not for the other characters in the scene but for us in the audience. This direct address of us with his eyes deflects our attention from the "reality" of story events to the artifice of the filmic discourse. The film again self-consciously places the audience in the position of the camera and thus of the addressee of the scene where Hawkeye, ostensibly speaking into a newsreel camera, looks directly at us and says, "Hi, Dad!" At another point the film actually foregrounds the whole process of narrational sound—the unseen, off-screen placement of a microphone to eavesdrop on characters speaking to each other in ignorance of the audience listening and watching on the other side of that invisible wall that separates us and them—in the scene in which Radar places the microphone under Hot Lips' bed.

We have already observed that the announcements on the loudspeaker shift from the function of establishing diegetic space to one of diegetic commentary on the action. A realistic effect is achieved when announcements about camp movies are heard, but the nondiegetic function is simultaneously served by the fact that all of the movies screened in this MASH unit are war films, recalling reflexively that *MASH* too participates in this genre. The humorous anachronism of the announcements is only apparent to the viewer who knows that while *When Willie Comes Marching Home* (1950) is a film about World War II, the film *The Glory Brigade*, like *MASH*, is about the Korean War and was released in 1953, a year later than the time of the story in *MASH*. The concluding announcement of the film marks the end of the story as the diegetic sound becomes the nondiegetic summary (and anachronistic anticipation!) of the film we have just seen: "Tonight's movie has been *MASH*. Follow the zany antics of our combat surgeons as they cut and stitch their way along the front lines operating as bombs—[laughter] as bombs and bullets burst around them, snatching laughs and love between amputations and penicillin. Follow Hawkeye, Trapper John, Duke. . . . Starring Donald Sutherland, Elliott Gould, Tom Skerritt. . . . That is all."

Self-reflexive narration has long been a staple of classical film comedy, as evidenced by films like Buster Keaton's *Sherlock Jr.* (1924), which "is, above all, a movie about a movie—a film within a film within a film" (Mast 1973,

133), and Woody Allen's more recent *Purple Rose of Cairo* (1984), in which much of the humor emerges as the diegetic and nondiegetic voices of the film actually converse with one another. *MASH* is a comedy, and a good many of the uses of sound discussed here contribute to its humor. The dialogue contains much of it: A voice during surgery commands, "Make the stitches bigger; he's an enlisted man." The general talks about betting on football games, then says, "Special Services says it's the best gimmick we've got to keep the American way of life going here in Asia." The colonel humorously confuses the antecedent of "it" and asks, "Betting?" The loudspeaker at one point parentally admonishes the camp to remove pictures from walls "so that our rooms will look clean and orderly." In both the episode devoted to Burns and Hot Lips and the episode devoted to the visit to Japan, the film establishes villains whose discrediting motivates much of the film's comedy. Thus Burns's solemn voice reciting the Lord's Prayer is replaced by the childish plea "Don't tell on me" reverberating across the camp from the microphone hidden under the bed.

Such moments are also marked by sound effects—as when the sound of a gong signals the humiliation of the hospital director and the dispatching of Burns—and by music—as when the loudspeaker broadcasts the singing of "It's Time for Us To Say Sayonara" upon the departure of Burns. Music functions comically in several other places: the boisterous music on the sound track complements the farcical pratfalls and slapstick of the football game in the film's last major sequence. It also helps to create a density of humor in the episode devoted to Painless: As Lieutenant Dish raises the sheet to look at the "best equipped dentist in the army," we hear on the sound track the rising chorus of humming voices and violins performing the *MASH* theme, followed by a high-angle shot from outside the tent in which the erect tent pole matches the shape of the sheet uplifted over the "Painless Pole" in the previous shot, in which the song's lyrics juxtaposing "painless" and "suicide" evoke the metaphorical association of death and sexual intercourse and in which the crescendo of voices and violins appropriately brings the whole sequence to a climax.

Upon its release, many critics compared *MASH* to the tradition in comedy represented by novels like *Catch-22* and *Slaughterhouse Five* and by films like *The General* (1926) and *Dr. Strangelove, Or, How I Stopped Worrying and Learned to Love the Bomb* (1963). "Black humor" is comedy characterized by laughter evoked in face of violence, death, and destruction; its laughter may be therapeutic against the traumas of life, and its message always takes the form of social commentary against the negative aspects of established values. All of these works are antiwar comedies, and a good many of their thematic values are represented on the sound track in *MASH*. At one point the sound track brings in a direct verdict of collusion among manufacturers of war materials; during the air-borne shot of the MASH landing area at the beginning of the Japanese episode we hear what sounds like a radio broadcast announcing that "A federal court ruled that E. I. Dupont de-Lamours, Remington Arms Company Incorporated, and the Imperial Chemical Industries Limited had conspired to divide the chemical market." Again, during Hawkeye's and Trapper's brief interview with the hospital director in Japan, the same kind of radio voice is overheard, here more ironic than direct: "UPI today voted the Korean War the top news story of 1951." There are other ironies in loudspeaker voices, like the Armed Forces Radio that plays songs in Japanese and Radio Tokyo that plays songs in English by Japanese singers—a humorous mix of voices and a confusion of national identities. Hawkeye and Trapper operate together twice, on the wounded enemy soldier following the end of the Painless sequence and on the baby in the Japanese sequence; the shared suffering and shared circumstances of war emerge explicitly here in both action and words. A nurse complains in the former operation, "That man is a prisoner of war, Doctor." Trapper replies, "So are you, sweetheart, only you don't know it." In the latter scene, when the nurses officiously complain about the sick baby (of American and Japanese parents) as an illegal patient, Hawkeye reacts, "We stumbled on him; we don't want him but feel we can't back away from him." This dialogue explicitly contrasts the authoritarian negativism and the humanitarian professionalism that grounds social commentary in the film.

Such dialogue represents a central role played by sound in dominant cinema's creation and realization of a diegetic world. Stephen Heath observes that "the sound cinema is the development of a powerful standard of the body and of the voice as hold of the body in image, the voice literarily ordered and delimited as speech for an intelligibility of the body, of people—agents and characters—fixed in the order of the narrative and its meanings, its unities and resolutions" (1981, 191). At one level the storied world of *MASH* contests and unfixes human desire with violence and death. But just as its characters struggle against the constraints of military authority, so the film struggles against the rigor of traditional narrative order. Nowhere is this combat more apparent than in the acoustic refusals of fidelity, of clarity, and of synchronization with the visual scene. Sound calls attention to itself as a separate register disconnected from the coherence of narrative voice. Asking to be heard in distinction from rather than in collusion with the image, the sounds of *MASH* convey a complex and cacophonous range of aural discourse. They work traditionally to create a story of human characters. They work nontraditionally to distance the presence of those characters. They echo the fragmentations of war, and they fragment the authority of narrative heroes. They subvert the pomposities of power and laugh at the subversion.

". . . That is all. . . ."

WORKS CITED

Altman, Rick. 1980a. "Introduction." *Yale French Studies* 60, no. 1: 3–15.

———. 1980b. "Moving Lips: Cinema as Ventriloquism." *Yale French Studies* 60, no. 1: 67–79.

Belton, John. 1985. "Technology and Aesthetics of Film Sound." In *Film Sound: Theory and Practice*, edited by Elisabeth Weis and John Belton, 63–72. New York: Columbia University Press.

Boggs, Joseph M. 1985. *The Art of Watching Films*. 2d ed. Palo Alto, Calif.: Mayfield.

Bordwell, David, and Kristin Thompson. 1979. *Film Art: An Introduction*. Reading, Mass.: Addison-Wesley.

Bordwell, David, Kristin Thompson, and Janet Staiger. 1985. *The Classical Hollywood Cinema: Film Style and Mode of Production to 1960*. New York: Columbia University Press.

Doane, Mary Ann. 1980. "The Voice in the Cinema: The Articulation of Body and Space." *Yale French Studies* 60, no. 1: 33–50.

———. 1985. "Ideology and the Practice of Sound Editing and Mixing." In *Film Sound: Theory and Practice*, edited by Elisabeth Weis and John Belton, 54–62. New York: Columbia University Press.

Gorbman, Claudia. 1976. "Teaching the Soundtrack." *Quarterly Review of Film Studies* 1: 446–52.

———. 1980. "Narrative Film Music." *Yale French Studies* 60, no. 1: 183–203.

———. 1985. "Annotated Bibliography on Sound in Film (Excluding Music)." In *Film Sound: Theory and Practice*, edited by Elisabeth Weis and John Belton, 427–45. New York: Columbia University Press.

Heath, Stephen. 1981. *Questions of Cinema*. Bloomington: Indiana University Press.

Levin, Lear. 1980. "Robert Altman's Innovative Sound Techniques." *American Cinematographer* 61: 336–84.

Leyda, Jay, ed. 1977. *Film Makers Speak: Voices of Experience*. New York: Da Capo.

Mast, Gerald. 1973. *The Comic Mind: Comedy and the Movies*. Indianapolis: Bobbs-Merrill.

Metz, Christian. 1980. "Aural Objects." *Yale French Studies* 60, no. 1: 24–32.

Percheron, Daniel. 1980. "Sound in Cinema and Its Relationship to Image and Diegesis." *Yale French Studies* 60, no. 1: 16–23.

Stewart, James G. 1980. "The Evolution of Cinematic Sound: A Personal Report."

In *Sound and the Cinema: The Coming of Sound to the American Film*, edited by Evan William Cameron, 38–68. Pleasantville, N.Y.: Redgrave.

BIBLIOGRAPHY

Barthes, Roland. 1977. "The Grain of the Voice." In *Image-Music-Text*, edited and translated by Stephen Heath. New York: Hill and Wang.

Black, David Alan. 1987. "Cinematic Realism and the Phonographic Analogy." *Cinema Journal* 26: 39–50.

Frith, Simon. 1984. "Mood Music: An Inquiry into Narrative Film Music." *Screen* 25: 78–87.

Gorbman, Claudia. 1986. *Unheard Melodies: Narrative Film Music*. Bloomington: Indiana University Press.

Johnson, William. 1985. "The Liberation of Echo: A New Hearing for Film Sound." *Film Quarterly* 38: 2–12.

Kozloff, Sarah. 1987. *Invisible Storytellers: Voice-Over Narration in American Fiction Film*. Berkeley: University of California Press.

Levin, Tom. 1984. "The Acoustic Dimension: Notes on Cinema Sound." *Screen* 25: 55–68.

Neale, Steve. 1985. *Cinema and Technology: Image, Sound, Colour*. Bloomington: Indiana University Press.

Pudovkin, V. I. 1985. "Asynchronism as a Principle of Sound Film." In *Film Sound: Theory and Practice*, edited by Elisabeth Weis and John Belton, 86–91. New York: Columbia University Press.

Silverman, Kaja. 1988. *The Acoustic Mirror: The Female Voice in Psychoanalysis and Cinema*. Bloomington: Indiana University Press.

Williams, Alan. 1980. "Is Sound Recording Like a Language?" *Yale French Studies* 60, no. 1: 51–66.

9

SOUND IN *LES VACANCES DE MONSIEUR HULOT*

Donald Kirihara

Few films delight the ear more than Jacques Tati's *Les Vacances de Monsieur Hulot* (*Mr. Hulot's Holiday*). From its 1953 release critics have remarked on its sonic richness and the complex interaction between sounds and images, striving to put into words the film's unusual approach to the construction of the audio track. One critic, for instance, compared its repudiation of conventional film sound practices to modern painting, calling it a kind of "auditory cubism" (Amengual 1954, 40). The nature of the sound track of *Les Vacances* poses problems for a viewer used to a diet of films with more informative dialogue and more plausible noises. It is Tati's particular genius that the sound track of *Les Vacances* comes forward to a degree unheard of in conventional narrative filmmaking. In its complexity the sound style of *Les Vacances* helps to expose the processes of perceptual organization at work in all film viewing.

The film's story is a sparse one.[1] A group of tourists gathers at a seaside

1. The version of *Les Vacances* studied here is an American print of the film. An analysis of another print may well differ in detail from mine, but my focus is on the functions of sound in the film, not on an exhaustive listing of gags.

resort for a summer vacation. Their holiday activities always seem disrupted by Mr. Hulot, whose travels in a sputtering auto and participation in events distract vacationers and residents of the town. His actions are scorned by most of them, but a few appreciate Hulot's efforts to break up the regimentation of resort life. Like Tati's other films (*Jour de fête, Mon Oncle, Playtime, Traffic*), the story premise of *Les Vacances* blends with a celebration of nonconformity in the face of the impersonality of modern everyday life. Also like his other films, *Les Vacances* is marked by the extraordinary care taken with images and sounds. Although Tati's work is often compared with the comedies of Chaplin and Keaton, his films are hardly silent. Tati's legendary devotion to the sound tracks of his films included months spent in sound studios carefully postsynchronizing voice, music, and noise with the timing and scale of his gags. Coupled with this is Tati's often-stated warning that audiences should enter his films attuned to a different set of expectations. Indeed, few films make more demands upon their listeners than *Les Vacances*.

FIDELITY AND AUDITOR EXPECTATIONS

We can begin by saying that sound in *Les Vacances* gains our attention in unusual ways. Sound is neither a "natural" rendering of everyday noise nor simply a support for the slim narrative action. Tati's careful selection and control of sound takes advantage of our sonic expectations formed by everyday activities. Fidelity—a sound's linkage to a represented source—serves as the basis for many of the film's gags.[2] Sounds often seem wholly inappropriate for their function. For example, Hulot's unique automobile horn seems funny initially for its inability to intimidate a lazy dog. Our interest in its dysfunctional quality compounds later when a hunter mistakes the horn for a flight of birds. Noises (or the lack of them) pierce the modulated background: a slap explodes with the volume of a shot while at the other extreme footsteps fall without making a sound. Actions produce unexpectedly strange noises: a swinging door produces the distinct tone of a plucked cello string; shoes scrape against sandpaperlike doormats; tennis balls bounce with the hollowness of coconuts.

Just as sound in *Les Vacances* is not always "natural" in the sense of its fidelity to everyday experience, sound technique is not simply incidental to and supportive of the events of the narrative. In a classical film, sounds typically possess a particular significance to the story action, helping us to focus our

2. David Bordwell and Kristin Thompson discuss the importance of fidelity as a dimension of film sound and the richness of Tati's films in this regard (1986, 240–41).

attention on the depth and development of the narrative. That is, speech offers the opportunity for characterization (through accents, voice timbre, pacing, etc.) and an avenue of information (e.g., reviewing what has happened or predicting what will happen); noise can provide the sudden change associated with a plot twist (e.g., a rap at the door, a shot in the dark) or the sonic wallpaper for background ambience; music may comment on a story situation or signal the presence of a character.

In comparison with the functions of sound in a classical narrative, we find in *Les Vacances* a lack of prominence of the voice. The dialogue comes forth not only in several languages but also sporadically and in disjointed phrases. More peculiar is that we do not usually *see* characters speak. The synchronization between heard words and faces addressing the camera that we take for granted in other films finds only intermittent expression in the film; most speech originates off-screen. In addition, noise distracts from the action in the image as often as it complements it. Even music refuses surreptitious placement in the background of scenes, surging forward to obliterate all other sound or insistently repeating in the form of a familiar melody.

This play with fidelity thus marks the spectator's role in the consumption of a film by actively comparing sound techniques in *Les Vacances* with film sound conventions and "real life." But assumptions about a sound's fidelity to a source may be established and reinforced through events *within* the film as well, playing with viewer/listener expectations through the associations set up early in the film and varied later. For instance, we do not see Hulot until well into the film; we associate him initially with his backfiring auto in the long trek to the resort. The sound is so unique and the association so strong that the sputtering gradually alerts the viewer as well as characters in the film to expect his presence. At one point Martine, a young woman who encounters Hulot in several scenes, is trapped in a car next to a boring intellectual. At the sound of Hulot's backfiring auto off-screen she starts and smiles in recognition of the familiar sound. In a similar way we see early in the film that the distinct ring of the dinner bell has the effect of drawing the vacationers into the hotel, and in time it prompts our own expectation of dinner as well; after a tennis match when the players search for some lost balls the bell prompts our anticipation of a shift in locale back to the hotel.

The difference in sound technique in *Les Vacances* is not due simply to the fact that odd sounds lie at the heart of many of the film's gags. Sound also works to present the processes of sonic inferences and expectations at work in narrative film and in doing so makes the film auditor more aware of the activity of listening. There may be no better example of this than the loudspeaker scene at the railroad station near the opening of the film. A graphic example of Tati's mockery of self-important speech, the gag turns words into a gnarled jumble of pops and sizzles. The resulting passenger confusion is also a commentary on the sonic demands to be made in our upcoming journey through *Les Vacances*: the sound track still channels the listener's attention, but instead of directing it toward a literal interpretation of the story information we are made to focus on the film's systems of space and time.

SOUND SOURCE AND SPATIAL RELATIONS

Sound plays a key role in defining the spatial relations of a narrative film. The sensitivity to space that the listener exercises during a film is fundamentally one of locating the source of a sound in the space of the scene using cues of direction and distance. This construction of an auditory space borrows from our contact with the world at large. It is of some importance to be able to locate sounds indicating, for instance, danger (Is that a siren?) or to use sounds to help us decide where to direct our visual attention (What direction is it coming from?). The concept of auditory space applied to film is handy for another reason: just as the auditory space that surrounds us standing on a street corner must be largely inferred—it is the totality of all sound events perceived from all distances and directions, seen and unseen—the auditory space that we must construct from the vibrations of a theater loudspeaker is also the product of the listener's inferences (Blauert 1983, 2–5; Moore 1982, 150).

In classical film practice, location of a sound source is seldom an issue because the viewer's construction of space remains consistent with the film's causal chain of events. The notion of "sound perspective" describes the manipulation of film sound, mainly through volume and reverberation, to correspond to shot scale. A close-up of a character speaking, for instance, will be accompanied by that character's voice similarly centered for our attention. Noise coming from sources in the background, say, from figures conversing in the depth of the shot, will be comparatively muted and indistinct. The narrational function of such selection is obvious: the voice of the character relates information pertinent to the story without distraction from other sounds.[3]

Typically in classical films, then, the voice is the center of attention, but in

3. For the historical background of this practice see Bordwell, Staiger, and Thompson (1985, esp. 53–54 and 301–3).

Les Vacances Tati neatly reverses this. Sound techniques in the film help to defeat our expectations of a space at the service of the narrative, thanks primarily to what may be its most obvious sonic property, the lack of a dominant voice track.

This reversal has much to do with the film's overall use of techniques to imply space. Tati's preferred visual style favors the use of decentered compositions in long shot, with gags often staged in the depth of the shot. Sound often accentuates this decentralization, primarily by manipulating volume to be an unreliable indicator of the direction and distance of a sound source. High-angle long shots of the guests in the hotel lobby, for example, are accompanied by noises or snippets of conversation that are momentarily difficult to locate in the space of the frame; an exchange of dialogue may come from figures positioned at the edge of the image. Exteriors exhibit the same tendency, with tiny figures or vehicles in the background producing shouts or revving disproportionate to their size.

We can also note that the dialogue in the film that we do pick up often presents information of little pertinence to the action in the image: banal observations about recipes or past war experiences mix in equal portions with commands ("Come along, Henry"), questions ("Why is that boat in the water?"), or explanations (of a picnic about to begin or the meaning of a boat's name). Characters—the conventional vehicle for the transmission of story information—tend to be mute; although it often has been observed that Hulot's utterances are rare and monosyllabic, other characters share his silent tendencies. Martine, for instance, has practically nothing to say at all. The function of voice quality as a distinguishing characteristic is undercut as well, placing more emphasis upon gestures and figure movements to identify characters. A few characters do stand out against this preference for demonstration versus speech, but those more garrulous individuals such as the leftist intellectual or the retired military man are singled out as humorous for their verbal pomposity.

Instead of standing front and center as the focus of our aural attention, voices tend to fill the backgrounds of scenes. They form part of the ubiquitous off-screen ambience, of no more consequence than the sounds of the surf or the birds. All told, this is a reversal of the importance of the voice in classical narratives; the utterances remain clear but the primacy of dialogue and its close relationship with the narrative action has been removed. As André Bazin observed of *Les Vacances*, dialogue is not so much incomprehensible as insignificant (Bazin 1983, 152).

With the removal of the voice as the center of our aural attention, elements that more conventionally would remain in the "background" gain new force. In particular, sounds that seem to originate off-screen play a more prominent role in guiding our spatial expectations.

One characteristic of sound in the film is the dense and almost ever-present mix of noise and speech that implies a teeming world beyond the frame: e.g., chirping birds, children's voices, and rolling surf. This mix is promoted in the film immediately by the long introductory section leading up to Martine's arrival at the resort. After the credits music does not reappear until Martine takes her bags from the bus driver. The first lines of dialogue we see delivered do not occur until Hulot's arrival at the hotel. The journey establishes noise—and the concomitant downplaying of enacted speech and music—as a major player in the film's sound track.

The prominence of off-screen sound heightens our awareness of off-screen space and our own anticipation in locating a source for the sound. This may occur by delaying the revelation of the sound source. For example, two women sit on the beach when a loud grinding noise incongruously appears on the sound track; a quick pan reveals its source to be a runaway boat winch. But more complex are incidents when off-screen sounds affect action in the image in unexpected or absurd ways. In one scene the off-screen noise of the kitchen staff shouting appears to cue the diners to begin their meal. When some exercisers dutifully squat to their leader's off-screen whistle, a long pause forces them to hold their awkward positions, and the *absence* of noise in this case creates the anticipation of an edit. The cut provides the retroactive explanation for the pause: Hulot is talking to the instructor.

Such anticipatory and retroactive play with the source of off-screen sounds also exploits the diegetic status of music in the film. Diegetic sound here refers to sound elements whose source is implied to originate from the space of the story, for example the voice of a character, or noise or music from some enacted event. An example of nondiegetic music would be "mood" music added to comment upon story events. That the use of music creates tension between diegetic and nondiegetic space may be seen in the use of radios and phonographs in the film. The first morning at the resort begins when Martine places a record on her phonograph and the film's theme music starts up on the sound track. The theme continues uninterrupted, however, as the setting shifts to a series of vignettes on the beach, and the music's diegetic status becomes ambiguous. Later in the film another day begins with the theme apparently emanating from some nondiegetic source. Hulot appears at Martine's boarding house in preparation for a horse ride, and only then a cut to Martine getting ready reveals the source of the music: a phonograph next to her dressing table.

Music's ambiguous diegetic status is also reflected in one of the few instances that involves music other than the theme song. At the end of Hulot's adventure at the cemetery a fast-paced and seemingly nondiegetic tune comes up on the sound track and continues across the fade to the next scene that evening back at the resort. As Martine looks downstairs from her room, her point of view reveals a man in a chair listening to a radio and contentedly keeping time to the music. We have been misled again, and this time the delayed revelation of the music's source crosses not only several locales but a temporal ellipsis between scenes as well.

But more daring for its baring of the process of locating sound sources is Tati's use of silences as a structuring element of the sound track. In *Les Vacances* silence can fill a scene as readily as any noise. Expected sources of sound generate no sound at all. Part of the disorienting comedy of Hulot running up behind the unknowing hotel owner are his noiseless footfalls. When Hulot plays ping-pong in the background of one scene, the game first dominates the sound track but later disappears altogether when our attention shifts to the card game in the foreground. The spatial presence of silence is also signaled by the disappearance of sound: the arrival of Hulot's backfiring auto at the tennis courts is marked by a final explosion that freezes the action and silences even the birds.

A summary example of how our activity of locating sound in space is forwarded in the film may be Hulot's disruptive arrival at the hotel. The backfiring of Hulot's auto bleeds under the first shot of the lobby and continues off-screen to a waiter's double takes. As the sputtering dies away, the waiter moves from table to table establishing individual pockets of sound with every new reframing; then a squeal of someone trying to lock onto a radio signal comes up. We expect to see the source of this new sound, but instead of cutting to a radio operator Tati cuts to a high-angle long shot establishing the space of the lobby, with the radio operator at the bottom of the frame. Sound's peculiar alliance with action appears as well. During Hulot's entrance the timbre, cadence, and pauses of a lilting Irish song ("The Kerry Dance") synchronize with cutting and visual gags (e.g., the fluttering mustache of one hapless tourist, the wind-blown tea pouring) as well as other sound elements (the wind, the exclamations of the residents) to the climax of the sequence, the abrupt suspension of the song's conclusion and the hotel owner's coincidental off-balance lunge to close the door. The interplay of on- and off-screen sound and space, the careful mixing and timing of familiar and unfamiliar noises, and the manipulation of anticipated actions and space indicate that locating a sound's source can be an unusually abstract activity in *Les Vacances*.

If the lack of a narrative center causes us to refamiliarize ourselves in relation to the space of *Les Vacances*, it is also the case that our temporal orientation does not proceed from the classical film's usual cause-effect chain of events. Tati's theme of the fragility of regimented relaxation develops through a leisurely pacing of successive events, with no central conflict inexorably driving the narrative and few deadlines set by which characters seek to solve long-term enigmas or gain specific goals. The result is what Bazin described as an involved sense of time almost palpable in its deliberateness, with the sound track's contribution tangling the spectator in a sound "skein" (Bazin, 152).

This entanglement and the difference it implies for the use of sound in *Les Vacances* may be seen in terms of how we perceive temporal patterns of sounds. We may consider the temporal dimension of sounds—their patterning in time—along two lines: through rhythm and sound streaming. Rhythm is the ordering of elements in temporal succession; music may be the most obvious category of film sound for such ordering, but speech and noise also offer rhythmic possibilities. Sound streaming is somewhat more complicated. A stream is our organization of a group of acoustical elements into a coherent whole, one that appears to originate from a single source. Psychologists have noted how we fix on separate streams of a sound mix; streaming describes how we separate and organize the swarm of auditory impulses that surround us into coherent sounds (e.g., singling out a voice overheard in a crowded room). In the cinema, rhythm and sound streaming are important means by which a filmmaker can manipulate a listener's temporal expectations of order and duration, for both depend upon the filmgoer's perceptual activity and his or her psychological process of forming sonic patterns in time (Fraisse 1978, 235; Moore 1982, 194–98; Bregman and Pinker 1978, 19).

We seldom take note of temporal patterns for their own sake in conventional films, yet in *Les Vacances* they are foregrounded for our attention. The importance of dialogue in a classical film helps break up duration into discrete units, as evidenced by our tendency to mark time in terms of complete sentences spoken by the characters. In *Les Vacances* the unambiguous stream of speech is replaced by an emphasis on music and noise; instead of relying upon speech to provide a measure of the duration of a shot or the tempo of the cutting in a scene, music and noise furnish a different sense of continuous time. For example, we can note the broad alternations established at the beginning of the film, from the opening credits where the theme music and sound of the surf alternate in a rhythm of the incoming waves. The first two shots of the narrative proper play out this alternation more fully, with a jarring cut from a deserted beach and oceanside sounds to the bustle and noise of a crowded train station. Separated as major elements in the film's sound mix, this opening alternation gives way to an increasingly complex intermix of sound streams.

Music can coincide with the duration of a scene or the timing of gags, as the Irish ditty does during Hulot's arrival at the hotel, but usually music insists on its own durational boundaries. The film's theme melody is the best illustration of this, for it nearly always runs to completion, no matter when introduced. This insistence on a unified pattern can be seen at the end of the hiking episode. After his stumbling exit Hulot reenters the hikers' shack, and we hear their shouting off-screen and a harmonica playing the theme. Fade out on image and sound, although the theme has not run its course. Fade up on the hotel as its lights come on: the hikers' voices and harmonica return, along with the conclusion of the melody.

In addition to fixing the theme song in the spectator's memory, the repetition of the entire melody sets up a durational framework in which a set of actions can occur. This is rather different from the classical film's insistence that duration be secondary to the narrative demands of the scene. Put another way, where in a classical film the duration of music will typically take its cue from the action, in *Les Vacances* the actions arrange themselves within the song's running time. The result is a certain "timeless" quality in the music—a set pattern that goes through a series of rhythmic metamorphoses. Our expectations set up by the theme show this pliability: once established at the beginning of the film it reappears from many diegetic sources (e.g., via phonograph recordings, whistling, harmonica, the singing hikers) and in many different versions. When a little boy balancing a pair of frozen treats carefully walks up a flight of stairs and twists a door handle open, the music—another variation of the theme—conveys the hesitating delicacy of the situation. The arrangement and tempo shift without stopping when the boy reaches his friend and shift again when we move to a new locale (the businessman's son is given a hat for the evening ball), finally concluding after the transition to the next scene (the evening ball). The theme song has an unpredictability that is not simply attached to character or situation; over the course of the film the suppleness of the constantly changing melody is interesting in itself. Part of the pleasure we derive from it comes from its familiarity tempered by its many transformations.

Noise also participates in the film's durational play by insisting on the sanctity of its own rhythm. We usually associate continuous diegetic sound with uninterrupted duration in the story film, and background noise or music furnish powerful cues that imply temporal continuity across the cuts of a scene. But in *Les Vacances* diegetic sound may double as connectors that link abstract ideas or visual similarities rather than temporal continuity. For instance, during the vacationers' journey to the resort, Hulot's auto struggles up a hill before sputtering to a stop. As its motor dies away the sound of birds comes up on the sound track. Cut to two bicyclists as the chirping flows under the edit. Another vehicle passes the cyclists and its hum flows under the following cut as the narration's journey to the resort resumes. Diegetic sound (the birds, the motorcar) extends under the edits to link the shots, but the spatial and temporal connection is vague since the cyclists have not been seen before and Hulot's auto is nowhere to be found in the second shot. Instead, the association is an abstract one, a "relay" in which separate sound streams allow the journey to be completed. This is a different, and momentarily disorienting, way of signaling duration.

Another example of this system of abstract sonic connectors, one that *compresses* time, may be seen in the events of the first full day at the resort. From Martine's playing of the phonograph, to the incident with the boat painters, to the first lunch scene (where Hulot wipes his companion's mouth with his sleeve), to Hulot's assistance with the suitcases, to Henry and his wife sitting down to dinner, diegetic sound (primarily undifferentiated offscreen voices but also whistling, a radio announcer, and sounds from the hotel kitchen) bleeds over the edits so that elapsed time seems greatly condensed: half a day is collapsed into 12½ minutes of screen time with no detectable durational gaps.[4] The rhythm of successive events in this enacted time span seems based less on clear causal connections and more on abstract connections of motion and duration, space and time.

The skein of auditory patterns shows itself best at the end of the film in the final fireworks scene.[5] The scene is set up in one sense by the earlier masked ball, where the rise and fall of the lobby radio and Hulot's phonograph produce a conflict that is as much a sonic struggle for dominance through volume as it is a battle for our attention between the rationality of a news broadcast and our by now intimate acquaintance with the theme song.

---

4. Compression and an even more complex example from Tati's *Play Time*—the Royal Garden scene—is discussed in Bordwell (1985, 82).

5. In terms of the overall form of the film, Kristin Thompson has shown that the fireworks scene marks a culminating reversal of the initial order of the resort society, as Hulot's final disruption manages to drag the tourists into unwilling revelry (1977, 26–30).

The fireworks scene itself is a final intermix of familiar sonic elements in a carefully woven design. A dog barking is introduced well before the explosions begin and only finds gradual integration into the action—first in the background as the waiter and the businessman's son wait in the deserted dining room, then bleeding under successive cuts to Hulot being driven into a fireworks shed, and finally closing the sequence after the din has died away. The jazz recording runs through the sequence in a somewhat different way; suspended once earlier in the film and again early in this scene by the irate guests, it finally concludes thanks to the hotel owner's unintended reincarnation of the phonograph, its completion magically coinciding with the last fizzle of the fireworks. Where at the masked ball the sonic streams square off against each other in a tug-of-war, in the fireworks scene they rise, ebb, and intertwine into a series of playful associations.

Les Vacances does not allow its listeners passive acceptance of its work. The dense weave of its sonic components, the temporal and spatial interrelations of sound and image, and the clever manipulation of our expectations all call upon the spectator to better appreciate his or her perceptual systems for understanding and describing the auditory world. Tati would go on to the even greater challenges offered by 70mm, multichannel sound in *Playtime* (Thompson 1979), but *Les Vacances* remains a remarkable achievement, rich both in sonic technique and in the demands—and respect—it accords the film auditor.

WORKS CITED

Amengual, Barthélémy. 1954. "L'Etrange Comique de Monsieur Tati, Part II." *Cahiers du cinéma* 34 (April): 39–45.

Bazin, André. 1983. "Mr. Hulot and Time." Translated by Walter Albert. In *Jacques Tati: A Guide to References and Resources*, edited by Lucy Fischer, 149–53. Boston: G.K. Hall.

Blauert, Jens. 1983. *Spatial Hearing: The Psychophysics of Human Sound Localization*. Translated by John S. Allen. Cambridge, Mass.: MIT Press.

Bordwell, David. 1985. *Narration in the Fiction Film*. Madison: University of Wisconsin Press.

Bordwell, David, Janet Staiger, and Kristin Thompson. 1985. *The Classical Hollywood Cinema: Film Style and Mode of Production to 1960*. New York: Columbia University Press.

Bordwell, David, and Kristin Thompson. 1986. *Film Art: An Introduction*. 2d ed. New York: Knopf.

Bregman, Albert S., and Steven Pinker. 1978. "Auditory Streaming and the Building of Timbre." *Canadian Journal of Psychology* 32: 19–31.

Fraisse, Paul. 1978. "Time and Rhythm Perception." In *Handbook of Perception VIII: Perceptual Coding*, edited by Edward C. Carterette and Morton P. Friedman, 203–54. New York: Academic Press.

Moore, Brian C.J. 1982. *An Introduction to the Psychology of Hearing*. 2d ed. London: Academic Press.

Thompson, Kristin. 1977. "Parameters of the Open Film: *Les Vacances de Monsieur Hulot*." *Wide Angle* 2, no. 1: 22–30.

———. 1979. "*Playtime*: Comedy on the Edge of Perception." *Wide Angle* 3, no. 2: 18–25.

BIBLIOGRAPHY

Jacques Tati and *Les Vacances de Monsieur Hulot*

Bazin, André. "Mr. Hulot and Time." Translated by Walter Albert. In *Jacques Tati: A Guide to References and Resources*, edited by Lucy Fischer, 149–53. Boston: G.K. Hall, 1983.

Fieschi, Jean-André. "Jacques Tati." In *Cinema: A Critical Dictionary*, edited by Richard Roud, vol. 2, 1000–1005. New York: Viking, 1980.

Fischer, Lucy. *Jacques Tati: A Guide to References and Resources*. Boston: G.K. Hall, 1983.

Gilliatt, Penelope. *Jacques Tati*. London: Woburn Press, 1976.

Kehr, Dave. "Les Vacances de Monsieur Hulot." In *The International Dictionary of Films and Filmmakers*, vol. 1, *Films*, edited by Christopher Lyon, 497–98. Chicago: St. James, 1984.

Maddock, Brent. *The Films of Jacques Tati*. Metuchen, N.J.: Scarecrow Press, 1977.

Rosenbaum, Jonathan. "Paris Journal." *Film Comment* 7, no. 4 (Winter 1971): 2–6.

———. "Tati's Democracy: An Interview and Introduction." *Film Comment* 9, no. 3 (May–June 1973): 36–41.

Studlar, Gaylyn. "Mr. Hulot's Holiday (Les Vacances de Monsieur Hulot)." In *Magill's Survey of Cinema: Foreign Language Films*, edited by Frank N. Magill, 2075–79. Englewood Cliffs, N.J.: Salem Press, 1985.

Thompson, Kristin. "The Parameters of the Open Film: *Les Vacances de Monsieur Hulot*." *Wide Angle* 2, no. 1 (1977): 22–30.

———. 1979. "*Playtime*: Comedy on the Edge of Perception." *Wide Angle* 3, no. 2 (1979): 18–25.

Film Sound

Balázs, Béla. *Theory of the Film: Character and Growth of a New Art*. Translated by Edith Bone. New York: Dover, 1970, 194–241.

Belton, John, and Elisabeth Weis, eds. *Film Sound: Theory and Practice*. New York: Columbia University Press, 1985.

Bordwell, David, and Kristin Thompson. *Film Art: An Introduction*. 2d ed. New York: Knopf, 1986, 232–60. Excerpted in Belton and Weis.

Burch, Noël. *Theory of Film Practice*. Translated by Helen R. Lane. Princeton: Princeton University Press, 1981, 90–101. Included in Belton and Weis.

Gorbman, Claudia. *Unheard Melodies: Narrative Film Music*. Bloomington: Indiana University Press, 1987.

Kracauer, Siegfried. *Theory of Film: The Redemption of Physical Reality*. New York: Oxford University Press, 1965, 102–56.

Nisbett, Alec. *The Technique of the Sound Studio: For Radio, Recording Studio, Television, and Film*. 4th ed. London: Focal Press, 1979.

Reisz, Karel, and Gavin Millar. *The Technique of Film Editing*. London: Focal Press, 1968, 256–72.

Screen 25, no. 3 (May–June 1984). Special issue, "On the Soundtrack."

Yale French Studies, no. 60 (1980). Special issue, "Cinema/Sound."

Part 2

CULTURAL ANALYSIS

INTRODUCTION

Peter Lehman

Narrative structure, space, composition, color, sound—none of these things is simply a matter of aesthetics. Why we find certain stories interesting and exciting and others boring and why some compositions are pleasing and others unattractive or unsettling are matters of cultural complexity. The essays in this section address some of those cultural issues using methods of analysis informed by history, psychoanalysis, Marxism, economics, and feminism.

Patricia Mellencamp analyzes the representation of women in *Gold Diggers of 1933* and argues that women's and men's roles in that film are more complex and contradictory than those described in Laura Mulvey's influential account of the classical Hollywood cinema. Lucy Fischer investigates Susan Seidelman's contemporary film *Desperately Seeking Susan*, in which stereotypical distinctions between the good woman and the bad woman are rejected and reworked. Russell Merritt studies the disturbing representation of blacks in the notorious *Birth of a Nation* and finds contradiction and unexpected ambiguity at the center of the controversial rape scene. Thomas Cripps also examines racial representation in the more recent film *Sweet Sweetback's*

 Baadasssss Song, written and directed by Melvin Van Peebles, who used his public persona of the cool, streetwise black man to shape the film's reception. Van Peebles's image as well as that of his film hero contrast significantly with Sidney Poitier's once popular portrayal of virtuous nobility. The contrast between *The Birth of a Nation* and *Sweet Sweetback's Baadasssss Song* is not surprising, since one was made by whites at a critical period in the development of the feature narrative and the other was made by blacks during a recent period of political activism and change.

Another pair of essays also yields informative contrasts between films. Robert Eberwein applies psychoanalysis to *Blow-Up*, a film in the European art cinema tradition, and Janet Walker and Diane Waldman examine psychoanalysis in *Freud*, a Hollywood film. After reviewing traditional psychoanalytical criticism of *Blow-Up* that attempts to understand character behavior and motivation with reference to psychoanalytic models such as the Oedipus complex, Eberwein attempts a more complex application of such concepts to the way in which the film is constructed and we as spectators respond to it. Somewhat similarly, Janet Walker and Diane Waldman review feminist perspectives on the value of psychoanalysis as a critical tool before analyzing a film about the figure most identified with the development of psychoanalysis. They concentrate on the way in which *Freud* represses crucial issues of the representation of childhood molestation and infantile sexuality and how that repression returns in the form of textual disturbance of both sound and image.

Charles Wolfe analyzes *Mr. Smith Goes to Washington* (1939) historically by relating the way in which that film depicts Washington to the way in which other image-making institutions such as newsreels depict it during World War II. The social relations in which the film was embedded at the time of its release are then related to the specific ways in which narrative, image, and sound work to transform the social material the film engages. Mike Budd also considers the historical production and reception context of an important film, *The Cabinet of Doctor Caligari* (1920), a context that includes German expressionism and the classical realist cinema and, in America, some historically specific elements such as anti-German sentiment at the time of the film's release. The form of the film emphasizes the rereading aspect inherent in all film viewing since the ending throws all that has gone before into an unexpected light that encourages the viewer to go back and rethink what he or she has seen.

Judith Mayne's analysis of *Ali: Fear Eats the Soul* examines cinema's potential to create radical social critique, in this instance by employing melodrama without the usual emphasis on intense emotion and by rejecting the usual distinction between the personal and the political—social behavior is seen as a function of class and economics, and capitalism is linked to the alienation the characters experience due to the division between their work and their personal lives. Douglas Gomery examines economics not as they are represented in the film but as they shape the very film itself, his example being *The Singing Fool* (1928), which was released during the coming of sound by Warner Bros. This historical juncture combined with the film's star, Al Jolson, and Warner's previous silent vaudeville shorts help to explain both the form of the film and its immense box office success. Gomery focuses on the industry and production context of the film, which is central to the detailed analyses of films presented in this section since it foregrounds the importance of the economic context in which all films are made, distributed, and exhibited.

10

THE SEXUAL ECONOMICS OF *GOLD DIGGERS OF 1933*

Patricia Mellencamp

On 24 October 1929, the U.S. stockmarket crashed, an economic catastrophe that was remembered by television during the October 1987 Black Monday coverage. Television was on crisis alert, continually breaking and entering entertainment, anticipating a financial catastrophe that did not occur. The 1929 crash resulted in an estimated 1932 unemployment figure of 13 million out of a population of 123 million, with wages 33 percent less than in 1929. In spite of this decline in income, movie attendance was estimated at between 60 to 75 million/week, attracting a regular audience indicated by the development of codified genres (as well as sequels, series, and remakes) and distinct studio styles (U.S. Bureau of the Census 1976, 135, 164). According to one critic: "At Warner Brothers . . . films were made for and about the working class. Their musicals, born of the depression, combined stories of hard-working chorus girls and ambitious young tenors with opulent production numbers. . . . Lighting was low key. . . . Cutting corners became an art. Stars were contracted at low salaries. . . . Directors worked at an incredible rate, producing as many as five features per year. The basic film at Warners . . . was a melodrama . . . which ran for 70 minutes. Pace was more than Warner's trademark—it was a necessity" (Baxter 1968, 50–51). If one momentarily accepts the undocumented assertion that Warner Brothers films were made "for and about the working class," which raises issues of address and enunciation, then the 1930s struggle by labor to organize would be a critical social/political context for this historical audience's reception.

Thus a few cursory details are in order. Unions were just beginning to gain power and demand benefits in an era before Social Security, unemployment and health insurance, minimum wage, and other labor laws such as proscribed working hours and conditions. Demonstrations by the unemployed occurred around the country, often involving violent encounters with the police. For example, thirty-five thousand demonstrators for unemployment insurance in New York were attacked by police, as were ten thousand protestors in Cleveland. On 7 March 1932, three thousand protestors marched on the Ford factory demanding jobs. Police, armed with pistols and machine guns, fired; four protestors died and were declared to be communists by gossipers, the conservative press, and politicians. In Toledo a large crowd of the unemployed marched on grocery stores and took food (Wallechinsky and Wallace 1975, 226–27). The fear of the overthrow of capitalism, like the "red scares" of the twenties, was real—the Soviet revolution, it must be remembered, had occurred less than two decades prior. The New Deal, with its versions of socialist practice such as federally funded corporations (TVA), helped elect Roosevelt president. He enacted Social Security in 1934–35; unions gained benefits, with collective bargaining granted in 1935.

Signs of economic chaos and poverty (such as street people today) visibly demonstrated a gap between rich and poor—an estimated seventy thousand children were homeless, living in shanty towns, as in William Wellman's *Wild Boys of the Road*. Rather than interpreting these events as economically and socially determined, thereby questioning capitalism, some members of Congress viewed them as personal—inspired and instigated by communists—and created a committee to investigate radical activities. Thus began the House Un-American Activities Committee, which would investigate Hollywood, particularly the screenwriters' guild, in the forties under its infamous acronym, HUAC. (It should be pointed out that Hollywood unionized early and thoroughly, with the exception of studio executives and producers; by the mid-thirties there were guilds for writers, actors, directors, and cinematographers.) Along the way, Prohibition was repealed in 1933; the Catholic Legion of Decency was founded in 1934 to "select" (censor) movies for Catholic audiences.

In 1933 the Warner Brothers film *Gold Diggers of 1933* was listed by *Motion Picture Herald* as the second top money-maker of 1933 (another Ruby Keeler/Dick Powell/Busby Berkeley extravaganza, *42nd Street*, was third). *Gold Diggers* is symptomatic of these issues of unemployment and homelessness: from the irony of the first spectacle, "We're in the Money," and the initial apartment sequence of unemployed chorus girls with the montage of unpaid bills and the theft of milk, to the concluding "Remember My Forgotten Man" spectacle. The latter takes us on a theatrical Hale's tour of recent U.S. history as Hollywood sociology—with demarcating wipes like stage curtains separating the acts, or scenes, first of marching soldiers, then the wounded, bandaged veterans of World War I, and finally the bread lines and soup kitchens of the post–World War I years, "explaining" the depression by World War I. Carol (Joan Blondell) sings, "Remember my forgotten man. You put a rifle in his hand. You sent him far away. You shouted hip-hooray. Just look at him today." The film symmetrically and resolutely moves from the erotic spectacle of women interchangeable with money in "We're in the Money" (the cheery irony of "Gone are my blues and gone are my tears. I've got good news to shout in your ears. The long lost dollar has come back to the folds. With silver you can turn your dreams to gold") to the dark blues of "Remember My Forgotten Man" with its backlighted, tiered set of marching soldiers rhyming the women's silhouetted dressing rooms in "Pettin' in the Park."

Other signs of social unrest strangely permeate the opulently surreal world of the film, functioning like dream mechanisms of condensation and displacement. The presence of police, whose image circulates throughout the film, is perhaps the most displaced image: the sheriff interrupts (censors) and stops "We're in the Money" (initiating the narrative pattern of interruption and delay of both story and show), literally stripping the women of their costumes; police are the roller-skating male chorus of "Pettin' in the Park," with Trixie, the comedienne (Aline MacMahon), cross-dressed as a policewoman (although wearing a flower in her lapel); a policeman on the stage of "Forgotten Man" confronts a "bum" who is revealed as a veteran by Carol; the sheriff is uncovered near the end by Barney, the producer, as an out-of-work actor. Thus police are rendered harmless, their image contained but still suggestive.

Prohibition is alluded to by Gigolo Eddy's guitar case (like the violins in "Shadow Waltz," a female emblem), which contains booze (that he dumps behind a backstage flat when the sheriff interrupts "We're in the Money"), equating two prohibitions—women's bodies and sex—with the illegality of alcohol; and by the speakeasies where Trixie and Carol seduce J. Lawrence

 Bradford and Fanuel Peabody. After the Legion of Decency began to condemn films for Catholic audiences in 1934, the scanty costumes and virtual nakedness of the "Pettin' in the Park" sequence were censored in the *Gold Diggers* sequel.

Like classical Hollywood film and musical comedy in general, the film also operates via the containment of sexuality, moving from single women (and men, separated by class) to a triad of perfectly paired, married (classless) couples, taking women out of the erotic spectacle, with a moral for women in the last sequence: without men (or capitalism), women (the working class), including a black woman singing the blues, will be old, haggard, alone, poor, and bleakly figured by German expressionist lighting—indeed a barren fate worse than death. For women, alone means living without men. Together and united as they are in this film, women are not enough; critically, they do not have access, except through sexual wiles, to the "conditions of production," particularly financing. As the lyrics of "Remember My Forgotten Man" inform us: "And once he used to love me. I was happy then. He used to take care of me. Won't you bring him back again? Cuz ever since the world began, a woman's got to have a man. Forgetting him you see, means you're forgetting me, like my forgotten man." Warner Brothers' explanation for social and economic ills resembles Congress's conspiracy theory, with rampant female sexuality (elided with the effects of World War I on the family) rather than communism as the guilty party.

Thus the film's solution to the depression, unemployment, and unbridled, anxiety-provoking female sexuality is the family under capitalism, narratively figured as marriage to Back Bay Boston investment bankers (who save the show from bankruptcy with Brad's critical check of $15,000 and his reluctant willingness to perform in the spectacle—rhymed by J. Lawrence's $10,000 payment to Carol for nonsex, a check later transformed into a wedding gift), collapsing the inequities of both class and gender into marital salvation. The film equates marriage and the couple—the happy ending—with capitalism. By uniting the working-class chorus girls (as Polly [Ruby Keeler] tells us in the upper-class nightclub scene on the balcony, her father was a postman) with upper-class, inherited wealth in a backstage triple whammy of Polly/Brad, Trixie/Fanuel (Trixie is wearing her policeman's garb—a comment on older/comic women's lack of eroticism), and Carol/J. Lawrence, presumably the nation will be restored. Within the film's economy the only significant "difference" is sexual difference; other cultural, social differences—the inequities of class, race, politics, economics, and age—are secondary. While the female lead characters are represented as working class, one must question the enunciation of this film, the specificity of its address "to the working class"; at the same time the film is in many ways addressed to women. (That the two investment bankers are parodied must also be taken into account. J. Lawrence and Fanuel are naive and inept—hardly savvy corporate scions—and are shown at their club, not at work; they are the representatives of inherited rather than earned wealth. What is valued is working for a living.)

With the crucial qualification that Berkeley's spectacles are addressed to the male spectator, literally coded as voyeur or fetishist, Leroy's narrative demonstrates the pleasures of female friendship—the solidarity between Trixie, Carol, and Polly—and is propelled by fast-talking, inventive women (who are transformed into identical, anonymous, Freudian symbols in the spectacles that stop the advance of the story) who are infinitely more interesting, idiosyncratic, and clever than the wimpy men (particularly Warren William, who as J. Lawrence has top billing albeit less screen time, and the ever-present, eager-puppy tenor Dick Powell, in this instance as Brad Roberts or Robert Bradford). In one reading the end functions as a resolute, albeit "logical" containment of women, which includes separating them. In another interpretation one can historically imagine marital rescue preceded by a spending spree on luxury items as an acculturated fantasy of the historical women in the audience—with few other options available to them in the thirties. The women use men's false notions about women's character to get what they want; masquerade becomes story, with the audience keyed in on the deception that is told from the women's point of view. Thus even the marital trajectory/inevitability, manipulated by the women for economic pleasure and gain as much as or more than romance, suggests an address and appeal to women—who are let in on the joke, which is on J. Lawrence and Fanuel. These "chorus girls" are not stupid, inexperienced characters, particularly Trixie: "It's the depression, dearie." However, knowledge, which the women have about men, is not power; money is.

To elucidate the sexual economics of *Gold Diggers*—including the use of women's bodies as emblems of plenitude, as interchangeable parts in an era of assembly line mass production; and the use of women as infinite, available, luxurious commodities (suggesting that there is no scarcity, no deprivation, in a word, no depression) that are celebrated/flaunted then denied/contained by a filmic system in which the female body is both desirable and terrifying, at least to Freud, Fanuel, and J. Lawrence—I will use arguments derived from the writings of Michel Foucault, particularly *The History of Sexuality*, and Sigmund Freud on sexual aberrations. I will also use Laura Mulvey's influential formulation derived from a close reading of Hitchcock's films as well as Lacanian rereadings of Freud. I will then return to "the female body under capitalism," using what Foucault assesses as "the docile body" in *Discipline and Punish: the Birth of the Prison*, eliding his analysis of "repetition and difference" with the business principles of "standardization and specialization," and applying these assembly line, disciplinary practices to the techniques of (1) precision dancing, (2) the conventions of the classical text and musicals, with consideration of (3) the film's conditions of production.

I

Within the historical parameters of the classical text, cinema *is* an everyday machine of the ideology of the family. It is an institution that relays and constructs objects of desire, finally conscripted within the family through film's endless creation of new, youthful couples. The representation of the erotic, promenaded female body—the figure of exploitation and the source of pleasure—then the denial and containment of that dangerous and unacceptable eroticism by death, marriage, or German expressionist lighting (of women living alone, i.e., without a man) in The End is both the paradox and obsession of classic film. These film discourses of sexuality parallel Foucault's analysis of the historical, rhetorical terrain, an analysis *against* Freud's repression hypothesis: "What is peculiar to modern societies, in fact, is not that they consigned sex to a shadow existence, but they dedicated themselves to speaking of it *ad infinitum* while exploiting it as *the* secret" (1978, 35).

In film the shouted secret is embedded in the fade to black, protected by the safety and closure of "The End." In Berkeley's fantasies the secret is a proclamation. Foucault defines sexuality as "the name that can be given to a historical construct . . . one relay of which is the body that produces and consumes" (195). The on-screen female body is produced as a representation for male consumption by the narrative and through the eyes of the male protagonist, for the male spectator. (However, one must complicate this by now accepted division of pleasure—women have always comprised a large audience for cinema, presumably not going to the movies only for displeasure.) Foucault further describes this historical body, which dates from the middle of the eighteenth century to the present and future, as a class body: One of the bourgeoisie's primary concerns was to provide itself with a body and a sexuality, resulting in "the endogamy of sex and the body." This class body was defined by "health, hygiene, descent, and race. While blood determined and defined the aristocratic body, sex determined the bourgeoisie body. The bourgeoisie's 'blood' was its sex" (124). Thus sexuality, conducted on the plane of the body, is a particular production—a historical construct rather than a natural, biological given—erected since the eighteenth century by the institution of the family. This version of the family is the locus of a critical conjuncture between what Foucault labels the "deployment of sexuality" and "the deployment of alliance": the family, later supported and analyzed by psychoanalysis, anchors sexuality *and* the circulation of wealth and reproduction whereas before these functions and discourses had been distinct. For example, the gloriously sexed and air-brushed body of Rita Hayworth, fashioned in gold lamé for eroticism (the deployment of sexuality) in *Cover Girl* is in the end coupled with Gene Kelly's middle-class, Brooklyn body (the deployment of alliance).

This collapse of two formerly separate systems within the family, enacted in the conclusion of the *Gold Diggers*, in the backstage ring of happy couples and the successful show, occurs because, among other reasons, mechanisms of power and knowledge are now centered on sex. Foucault's analysis of power is of particular interest in relation to classic texts. He defines power as "a multiplicity of force relations, a process . . . a chain . . . with domination and subordination as its terminal form" (86). In his construct power is tolerable only on the condition that it mask a substantial part of its operations. "Its success is proportional to its ability to hide its mechanism" (86). This depiction of an apparatus of sexuality matches analyses of the technical and narrative conventions of classical films, as well as the relations between on-screen male and female protagonists as poles of the domination/subordination split. To place eroticism within the family and consequently to put women in their place of subordination within that family is often The End of the classical film. (Whether the women of *Gold Diggers* would be subordinate is open to question.) It is not insignificant that in order to accomplish this task of power the apparatus must be masked.

Yet paradoxically enough a parallel tactic is accentuation or excess, particularly apparent in musicals that foreground the body and the cinematic apparatus. Foucault locates one of power's four major strategies as the "hysterization" of women's bodies, an apt concept for Berkeley's visions. This strategy constructs the female body as "thoroughly saturated with sexuality."

> In the process of hysterization of women, "sex" was defined in three ways: as that which belongs in common to men and women; as that which belongs, *par excellence*, to men, and is hence lacking in women; but at the same time, as that which by itself constitutes woman's body, ordering it wholly in terms of the functions of reproduction and keeping it in constant agitation. (153)

The history of cinema could be written as an agitation of women's bodies.[1]

In cinema, sexuality becomes image—framed, fragmented, then unified for consumption. Lucy Fischer's 1976 essay on *Dames*, which emphasizes the wit of Berkeley's literalisms ("Thus, in the Berkeley numbers the notion of women as sexual *objects* takes on a deviously witty relevance"), concludes that the film concerns "the image of woman as image" (awareness, hence, via reflexivity, excess) celebrating not her presence "as much as her synthetic, cinematic *image*" (5, 10). The addition of spoken language in its historical subservience to the image, like the couple, marrying the image, increases the fragmentation, unified into a singular coherence in the end. J. Lawrence's assessment of "cheap and vulgar gold diggers," repeated by Carol, silenced by a kiss, and applied to Carol and Polly (a case of mistaken identity) is materialized in "We're in the Money," which equates women's bodies with coins, strategically and fetishistically placed, turning into waves, circles, with pans over identical, infinite smiling faces—there, available. The camera dollies in (with a brief loss of focus) on Fay Fortune's face (Ginger Rogers), then closes in on an extreme close-up of her lips singing in pig Latin, literally nonsense, outside language as Lacan would analyze it. After the perverted and parodic voyeurism of "Pettin' in the Park" with the midget/baby turned raincoated master of voyeuristic ceremonies—his leers directly addressed to the camera—intercut shots of legs, ankles, and transparent costumes, and "female" symbolized by huge snowballs and beach balls, comes the next spectacle, "Shadow Waltz." This number transforms the gold-digging strippers of "Pettin' " encased in chastity steel costumes, their virginity undone by can openers, into petals of a flower, playing appropriately Freudian violins, softened symbols of more legitimate, upper-class femininity. Before marriage can occur, the film cleans up the image (and presumably class) of women, making them more respectably sexual. Berkeley took Freud (a recent import to the United States) very literally, agitating women's bodies into fetishistic excess or surplus voyeurism. In the end, with the exception of Carol, the Parisian-garbed prostitute of countless well-made plays who compassionately wails a blues song about the depression, the exhibitionist women are gone.

The main currency of exchange is the erotically coded image of the sexed female—high-lighted, halo-haired, feathered, furred, air-brushed by Technicolor, costumed by Adrian, and made up by Max Factor. This gorgeous, tan-

1. For recent revivals of hysteria (both male and female, which it always was [think of Gregory Peck swooning into Ingrid Bergman's arms in *Spellbound*, granted its Oedipal overtones] and which Foucault fails to emphasize), see, for example, *Fatal Attraction, Slam Dancing* and *Baby Boom*.

talizing concoction (attractive to women as well as men) uncontrollably, often powerfully, circulates through eighty-nine minutes of the film, only to be contained/possessed in the privileged seconds of the end by a usually middle-class male/husband. The moment of metamorphosis from sexuality to alliance is an immaculate conception, keeping cinema's virginal code intact in the unseen and the unheard of, the fade to black—the secret that is sex. Sex "by itself constitutes woman's body" and yet is "lacking in women." This is film's paradox and women's historical double-bind. Film's solution—fade/family—keeps the secret of sex in the dark of censorship or romance while imaging its manifestations in the "agitated" female body. The couple's passage through the film into the fade then into The End literalized Foucault's analysis:

> It is through sex—in fact an imaginary point determined by the deployment of sexuality—that each individual has to pass in order to have access to his own intelligibility . . . to his body . . . to his identity. (155)

II

This Foucauldian analysis elicits results similar to Laura Mulvey's oft-cited psychoanalytic construct in "Visual Pleasure and Narrative Cinema." Drawing on Freud's "Three Essays on Sexuality," particularly "The Sexual Aberrations," his very short elucidation of fetishism, and on Jacques Lacan's writing on the mirror phase and narcissism, Mulvey reiterates Freud's assessment of scopophilia: "in these perversions the sexual aim occurs in two forms, an *active* and a *passive* one" (Freud [S.E. 7, 157]). Like Freud, Mulvey (whom I will paraphrase/quote) sexually differentiates these roles: "Women in their traditional exhibitionist role are simultaneously looked at and displayed, with their appearance coded for strong visual and erotic impact." In both story and spectacle what counts is what the heroine provokes; she functions as an erotic object for the characters within the film and for the spectator within the auditorium, as the by now very famous "bearer rather than maker of meaning." In this bipolar system the man forwards the story and is the bearer of the look of the spectator—the possessor of power (1975, 1–16, 11). (Although they must manipulate men in order to do so, the women of *Gold Diggers* make things happen.) In almost every page of Freud, woman as the sign of sexual difference embodies the threat of castration, which, as Freud never tires of telling us, evokes original anxiety—J. Lawrence says to Peabody: "I'm afraid . . . that woman is fascinating. We don't have to give in, do we?"

Mulvey argues that turning the woman into a fetishized object is one way to control male anxiety—the Berkeley spectacles are the quintessential examples of this technology of gender. The other avenue lies in ascertaining guilt, asserting control, and subjecting the guilty women through either punishment or forgiveness. This means of control, sadism, is suited to a story, dependent on making something happen, forcing a change. The story of Carol and J. Lawrence, which interrupts and postpones the spectacles, is an example of this tactic.

However attractive and perfectly applicable Mulvey's dichotomous system is to this film, as it is as system to most classical texts, recently including the history of painting, the "either/or" analysis has limitations. A model of contradiction, a "both/and" logic, might be more pertinent, particularly for women. Other readings, including female bonding, female pleasure, and even the gendered techniques of duplicity, simulation, and masquerade, are possible. In fact, an opposite case could be made regarding this film, at least on first glance: that the women get what they want, including the security and respectability that rich, upper-class men provide and close friendship with each other; that the women move the narrative forward, finding a backer for Barney's show and husbands for themselves, albeit through manipulation, trickery, deceit, and seduction (including the pretense of sex after getting J. Lawrence drunk). However, a cautionary note is added to this celebratory interpretation if, as does Freud in the next paragraph, masochism is added to the techniques of sadism (and fetishism).

Masochism might more aptly describe J. Lawrence and the extreme anxiety of Fanuel Peabody, his cohort. As Sonja Rein has so lucidly argued in an unpublished seminar paper (via Gilles Deleuze yet significantly against the recent rewriting arguing masochism *for* feminism as a female, spectatorial mechanism[2]): "what is important in masochism is the desire to return to the mother . . . thus, the masochist demands that he be beaten in order that the image of his father in him . . . is diminished." The scene in which Carol gets J. Lawrence drunk, strips him of his clothes, and puts him in her bed under the pretense of having had sex, like their entire story and that echoed by Trixie and Fanuel, could be read as a masochist scenario. Furthermore, as Rein points out, "What is important for Deleuze is the nature of the agreement made between the masochist and his torturer. . . . the contract functions . . . to invest the mother image with the symbolic power of the law."

2. One principle text on the theory of masochism is that of Gilles Deleuze, *Sacher-Masoch: An Interpretation*, trans. Jean McNeil (London: Faber and Faber, 1971). Film critics employing models of masochism include Gaylyn Studlar and Kaja Silverman (whose assessments Rein strongly challenges).

(Think of Trixie garbed as a policewoman.) In the concluding "Forgotten Man" sequence Carol is mother, invested "with the symbolic power of the law" in her connection to the policeman.

Critically, the masochist manipulates the mother image *with the victim's consent*; and thus, according to Deleuze, the masochist or victim "generates" the contract. (That a contract has been made is suggested by the character of Fay, who constantly threatens to upset the agreement. More generally the question of who is the victim and who is the torturer is a crucial one for feminist analysis, for within this model of masochism even the torturer, if female, is under male control, acting for his pleasure.) Rein argues that even within masochism "woman is man-made": "In Deleuze's scenario, women are by no means powerful. What power they do possess is only conferred by the man and is specified by him; women act solely in his interests and most definitely not in their own." In whose interest Carol and Trixie act is again open to question or interpretation. However, this model goes a long way toward explaining the war spectacle of the film's conclusion. "As Deleuze suggests, in both masochism and sadism there is the formation of the mother-image, but in the former she is appropriated as the ideal image while in the latter she is tortured and cast out." Masochism makes sense of the last scene with its various images of mother and war as a spectacle of masculinity, with the suffering of the soldiers/victims as masochistic, male pleasure.

III

Other discourses permeate the film. One is an older version of Freudian symbol analysis, ahistorical approaches still popular in literary criticism, derived from *The Interpretation of Dreams*; Freudian psychoanalysis was in 1933 a recent import to the United States—along with German and Austrian expatriates moving to Los Angeles—and one enthusiastically adopted and endorsed by Hollywood whose role in popularizing and simplifying psychoanalysis is surely incalculable. Freud was alive and writing, although he would eventually die of writer's cramp.

The unrelated second is Taylorism (and a plethora of similar studies as theories)—functional, scientific, efficiency studies of management that included descriptions of the body as/working in tandem with a machine. Assembly lines (echoed in the symmetrical rows of matching chorus girls and the parading soldiers on conveyer belts) were fairly recent inventions in this era of mass production technology (not the least of which was cinema itself)—with Henry Ford as the international emblem of U.S. mass production expertise. Like the Hollywood studio structure (with the vertically integrated monopolies of the Big Five well ensconced), corporate, factory principles of standardization (and for the studios, specialization) were operative in Berkeley's female formations of assembly line symmetry, harmony, anonymity, perfection—combinations of Freud's sexual fetish and Marx's commodity fetish linking up with mechanical studies of human labor.

Specialization is detailed by the division of women (and men) into types, for the show within the film, and as characters: Polly, the sweet, young ingenue; Trixie, the older comedienne; Carol, the tough, ageless, sexy woman with, yes, the heart of gold; and Fay, the true gold digger. That these types are standardized is documented by the changing physical fashions in women's bodies in the twenties, thirties, and forties. The three couples represent three versions, or three stages, of romance, a marital typology that accords with character traits; Polly and Brad represent young, innocent, virginal love; Carol and J. Lawrence, middle-age sexual desire; and Trixie and Fanuel, asexual, childish, older companionship. Significantly, because all the women are young, the age of the man defines each relationship, suggesting that our interpretation of the women is, to a degree, determined by the men. The film, like the history of Hollywood cinema, upholds the double standard of chronological difference, wherein women must forever be young while men can vary in age and even grow old. The older man and the younger woman is the norm for cinema, rarely the reverse. Specialization also describes the film's (and Hollywood's) conditions of production—detailed in the credits via department heads (design by Anton Grot and Carl Jules Weyl; costumes by John "Orry" Kelly; camera, Gaetano Gardio, Barney McGill, Sol Polito; music by Harry Warren and Al Dubin, mentioned in the film by Barney) and divided between Mervyn Le Roy, a contract studio director (like the rest of studio employees, on a monthly salary) who made over fifty films in eight years, and Berkeley. Standardization via the evolution of conventions of classic Hollywood style and genres, in this case the conventions of the musical comedy (with motifs and figures circulating throughout both spectacle and narrative segments, gluing them together despite their vastly different "styles") is also operative. More of this later.

That these are capitalist, corporate practices is not without implication. In fact the Berkeley sequences are spectacles of the glories of capitalist technique and hence are visual demonstrations of the narrative—salvation via investment bankers (a reference to and parody of the role investment bankers [perhaps Waddill Catchings] played in Warner Brothers' massive and expensive conversion to sound in 1927–28). This connection is argued by Siegfried Kracauer in a 1931 essay (whose thesis is later picked up in Bazin's essay on pin-ups), "Girls and Crisis": "In that postwar era, in which prosperity appeared limitless and which could scarcely conceive of unemployment, the girls were artificially manufactured in the USA and exported to Europe by the dozens. Not only were they American products; at the same time they demonstrated the greatness of American production. . . . When they formed an undulating snake, they radiantly illustrated the virtues of the conveyor belt; when they tapped their feet in fast tempo, it sounded like *business*, business; when they kicked their legs with mathematic precision, they joyously affirmed the progress of rationalization; and when they kept repeating the same movements without ever interrupting their routine, one envisioned an uninterrupted chain of autos gliding from the factories into the world, and believed that the blessings of prosperity had no end" (63–64). Regarding the Rockettes and their sanitized routines, perhaps he is right. Equally, in the midst of the real and the film's depression, Berkeley's scenes suggest that "prosperity had no end." Rather than operating technology, women are cogs of and for technology, like the machine, submissive, dominated usually by a male leader who can mold many into a singular uniformity.

Although often treated as idiosyncratic and unique, Berkeley's girls were not new or unique. However, their B-movie versions (for example, in *Stand Up and Cheer* the chorus of lead-footed chorines in costumes that just hang rather than reveal, who awkwardly try to move let alone dance, with frontal, static, mid-height camera placement, virtually no moving camera shots, and editing void of any metric or rhythmic patterns) demonstrate just how very good and complex Berkeley's kaleidoscopic realizations are. His scenes celebrate technologies other than just the body (or, the female body as technology, a technology of gender, in perfect historical harmony with cinema technology), including, in "Shadow Waltz," electricity in the neon-lighted violins and huge violin formation. Along with turning women into objects fraught with Freudian symbolism so crassly obvious as to historically turn to parody—evidenced by contemporary audiences' gasps of bemused amazement during the viewing—and reassembling fragmented, fetishized body parts as symbolic puzzles, his scenes depict the wonders of film technology and its ability to transform space and time—a very modern concern of painters, novelists, and philosophers in the early twentieth century. As Fischer writes: "If the geography of the numbers is unchartable, their temporality is unmeasurable" (4). Berkeley combines the oldest technology, sex, with the modernist technology par excellence, cinema.

As Carolyn Marvin argues in "Dazzling the Multitude," around the turn of the century engineers and entrepreneurs believed that electricity—particularly in manufacturing and transportation—would "heal the breach between classes . . . democratize luxury and eliminate conflict based on competition for scarce resources" (258). (The breach, it was argued, was fostered by the inequities of steam power. The modernist belief that technology will bring social progress is an old argument that ignores social and political configurations.) Along with its imagined role in industry, electricity, along with other newly developed technologies like the automobile and the cinema, was also a novelty, a spectacle, a passing fancy or fad, and a medium of entertainment. Electrical light shows were popular, outdoor events, with elaborate performances against the sky at World's Fairs and expositions.

However, even more directly pertinent as a forerunner to the electrical virtuosity of cinema (here specifically the "Shadow Waltz" extravaganza but including all the tour-de-force spectacles) is Marvin's description of the 1884 Electric Girl Lighting Company, which "offered to supply illuminated girls" for various occasions and parties. These girls of "fifty-candle power" were "fed and clothed by the company" (260), and could be examined in the warehouse by the prospective customers hiring them as waitresses or hostesses—exotic, high-tech, high-voltage servers. Electric girls, their bodies adorned with light, also appeared at public entertainments as "ornamental objects," and performed electrical feats in revues. The term *ornamental* echoes Kracauer's use of the concept of mass ornament in relation to mass culture (a model that argued the mirroring relationship between the spectator and the spectacle), and is perhaps a term taken from architecture, Kracauer's field. The electric girls combine the arguments of Kracauer regarding chorus lines with the visions of the early entrepreneurs of electricity.

What is intriguing to me is the persistent contradiction between yoking the female body either to nature or technology, presumably opposite interpretations. As I argued a long time ago in an essay on *Metropolis*, this historical equation of the female body with technology represents the female body as a special effect, one that suggests both the danger and the fascination of spectacle, an aberration which must be held in check (Mellencamp, 1981). However, whether as old-fashioned nature or modern technique, the technology of gender functions to keep women in line: the electric girls, like Berkeley's and Carroll's girls and the robot in Rotwang's laboratory of electricity, were there, in the end, to serve their masters.

As in most musicals, Berkeley combined these techniques of the stage with cinematic technique; his girls are the modern, abstracted, often faceless descendants of revues, vaudeville (for example, Earl Carroll's *Vanities*) and, in England, music halls. Their exhausted reincarnations parade today as aging women with sagging breasts at the Folies Bergère in Paris; strut as imitations in glitzy Las Vegas "shows"; perform holiday shows for families at Radio City Music Hall; are TV commercials for pantyhose; and appear on reruns as the June Taylor dancers, in strange alliance with Jackie Gleason.

As the story goes, recently reported by John Lahr, the Rockettes were the U.S. version of England's Tiller Girls and first materialized in St. Louis in 1925 as the Missouri Rockets: "sixteen dancers were strung out across the stage like beads on a necklace: thirty-two hands, thirty-two legs moving as one" (1977, 83). This sounds remarkably like Berkeley, quoted by Fischer: "My sixteen regular girls were sitting on the side waiting; so after I picked the three girls I put them next to my special sixteen and they matched, just like pearls" (4). Russell Markert was the inventive U.S. entrepreneur who "put the shortest dancers at the outside of the line and the tallest in the center to create the illusion of uniform size" (Lahr, 83). Installed in 1927 at the Roxy, the girls expanded in number to 32 Roxiettes. When they moved to Radio City Music Hall they were renamed the Rockettes. Conformity was the key; their "style was efficient, dehumanized, perfect, the last vestige of Twenties Bauhaus design in human form." The key was group discipline and submission. The worst thing a Rockette could do was "kick out," literally "step out of line." "If any girl got wide in the hips or thighs, I'd have the costume department measure her size. . . . I'd tell her to reduce back to her original Rockette measurements." Rockettes were not allowed to tan—the Rockettes all were the same color, white. Markert was the coach until he retired in 1971; the dance, with the trademark kick that still elicits applause, is the same, as is their rigid, upright posture and style of movement. They don't bump or wriggle (Lahr, 83). Berkeley's "girls" did not need to dance: "I never cared whether a girl knew her right foot from her left so long as she was beautiful" (Fischer, 6).

Interestingly enough, the analyses of various dance-line daddies are almost identical fantasies of power over women. A 1940 interview with Earl Carroll remembering his "Vanities" could have been spoken by Markert or Berkeley (quoted in Fischer's opening epigram: "I love beautiful girls and I love to gather and show many beautiful girls with regular features and well-made bodies"). The commentaries of the various leaders are as uniform as the precision female lines they order:

> I soon realized that the most exciting thing one could put on a stage was a breathtakingly beautiful girl. She did not need to know how to dance or even sing . . . there were no talent requirements. . . . They are assembled on the stage and then segregated according to height. Then in lines of twenty, they step forward, count off, make quarter turns and face forward. . . . The fol-

> lowing points of beauty are given careful consideration: color and texture of hair, brilliancy and size of eyes, regularity of teeth, general coloring, texture of skin, formation of hands and feet, posture and personality. . . . There are times (and this was particularly true during the war) when it was necessary to engage girls who do not have all the necessary qualifications. We replace them when it is possible.[3]

Carroll, sitting at the center of Foucault's panopticon, details an inch-by-inch ideal: a 6-inch wrist, a 12-inch neck, a 19 1/2-inch thigh, and a 9-inch ankle. Carroll was also a cultural historian, perhaps an early film theorist: "Turnover is much greater than it used to be; those with talent go on to the films and those less gifted soon settle down into a quiet matrimony." As in film, women have two choices: showgirl or wife/mother.

There is something truly perverse about creating beauty through precision control that abstracts women's bodies; I am reminded of Freud's remarks on beauty derived from vision that were stated just prior to his discussion of scopophilia (and the relation between scopophilia with its active/passive components and Foucault's model of the panopticon with the see/seen dyad). Freud writes: "The progressive concealment of the body . . . keeps sexual curiosity awake. This curiosity seeks to complete the sexual object by revealing its hidden parts. [Think of the midget raising the curtain on the strip tease in "Pettin' in the Park," the peeking intercuts of women dressing, changing costumes, backstage or in their apartments.] It can, however, be diverted (sublimated) in the direction of art, if its interest can be shifted away from the genitals on to the shape of the body as a whole" (S.E. 7, 156). Male desire thus transforms female sex into Art as an excuse, a cover-up for male desire. The film shifts from an emphasis on the women's genitals, the strategic coin placement of "We're in the Money," to the abstract shape of the female body as a neon violin, collectively bowed! in "Shadow Waltz," thereby legitimizing as art a sublimation, making respectable what was illegal, uncivilized (at least for Freud and Berkeley)—women, female sexuality. Berkeley verges on real perversion, which in history has turned to parody in its excess.

Foucault's concepts of the surveyed, docile, disciplined body in *Discipline and Punish: The Birth of the Prison* are perfectly apt, as would manuals for horse or dog breeders also apply to the training and analysis of these chorus

3. I cannot find the anthology of 1940s fan magazine commentary quoted here, particularly interviews with forties stars. Earl Carroll by then had a dinner theater that included performances by his "girls."

lines. Foucault outlines tactics for subjecting bodies, drawing on arguments from the end of the seventeenth century and drawing his model from the military and pedagogy. "The individual body becomes an element that may be placed, moved . . . a fragment of mobile space. . . . in order to obtain an efficient machine . . . the body is constituted as a part of a multi-segmentary machine [which] requires a precise system of command" (1979, 164, 165). The contemporary, post-modern or classically Spartan version of precision dancing is of course aerobics, with its emphasis on taut, exercised buttocks rather than breasts.[4]

The conventions of the classical text also function via the disciplinary techniques of seriated repetition and calculated difference. Moving inexorably to resolution through an intricate balancing of symmetry/asymmetry by constant repetitions and rhymings on the sound and image tracks, classical narrative meticulously follows the disciplined rules of its well-made game. Pleasure is provided by the spectatorial play of these shared conventions: relays of anticipations and delays that alternately create expectations and provide gratification for the audience. Rhyming and repetition within the *Gold Diggers*, as in many classical texts, is complex, amazing in its minuteness. In

---

4. Members of aerobic classes move in tandem with the instructor, imitating confined, inward-turning movements rather than modern dance movements of extension, isolating muscles rather than working them together, as Margaret Morse argued in March 1988 at the NEMLA conference in Providence. Aerobics involves series, repetitions, and other tactics of discipline: "Divide duration into successive or parallel segments, each of which must end at a specific time" (Foucault 1979, 157). We count and repeat during aerobics and are told that we only have four left. To paraphrase Foucault: exercise involves techniques which impose on the body repetitive and different tasks, which are graduated. Think of high, low, and intermediate impact aerobics, graduated weights on the machines, color coded as to normality, divided into male and female color coded scales of strength—definitely a coercion of the body. The exhibitionist body, each fold detailed in the skin-tight outfits, is, however, bisexual, equally visible.

Upon entering programs, instructors measure the body, a standard against which the tightened future of loss is assessed. Nautilus, Kaiser, and Eagle machines isolate and exercise our individual muscles, one at a time, in clubs of rigid dress codes and costly memberships (a combination of the school and the country club, the return of the public baths); our bodies are interchangeable with machines, our sweaty labor resembling leisure, individual versions of assembly line production. Also, the new clubs are panoptic spaces patrolled by surveillance cameras, surrounded by mirrors, distorting and deflecting the gaze, places, strangely enough, of active exhibitionism and passive voyeurism.

one trivial example Barney closes his office door "before the acrobats and midgets" arrive, which rhymes with the real midget of the "Pettin' in the Park" sequence; I have already mentioned the character of Gigolo Eddy, who next appears in Barney's office while they await Brad's $15,000 check; he is seen backstage rubbing alcohol on the "aging juvenile's" back; his guitar case of booze is replicated by the Kentucky Hillbillys and is transformed into the neon image of women as violins; the violin symbol is taken from vaudeville to the legit stage, from a lowly image to a lofty image. In "Shadow Waltz" Polly wears a blonde wig, resembling Carol; backstage we briefly glimpse her holding her blonde wig. Via condensation and displacement, or repetition with a difference, the work is done for and with us. Like aerobics, repetition and careful instruction are as essential as is the move toward closure and conclusion. From the very beginning we await the pleasure of the end.

The narrative of musical comedy coincides with classical narrative. In fact musicals depict a literal version of "family romance," a thematic often embedded within another story in other genres. Musicals virtually reenact the ritual of re-creation/procreation of privileged heterosexual couples, the nucleus of patriarchy.[5] As in classical narratives, the work of musicals is the last-second containment of potentially disruptive sexuality, a threat to the sanctity of marriage and the family. However, musicals, and particularly Berkeley sequences, are set apart from other genres by the coded presence of spectacles, enclosed units within the larger narrative that are set off by a system of visual and aural brackets. These spectacles mirror the narrative, have beginnings and endings, and presumably might rupture the filmic illusion of reality and halt the forward movement of the story.

First and foremost, spectacles are bracketed by complete musical scores. Thus it is significant that "We're in the Money" is not completed; it remains an interrupted spectacle. Music is a foregrounded code that symmetrically reoccurs as functional scoring in the narrative segments and under titles, thereby either anticipating or re-calling the spectacle. "We're in the Money" occurs under the opening titles; then in the Fay Fortune spectacle where it is played slowly during the "no jobs" montage just prior to the decision to take the boys for an expensive ride; and is last heard being played by the orchestra in the fancy night club. "Shadow Waltz" is first played on the piano by Brad for Polly (the fun couple) through the cute, cloying window. Next it is heard

---

5. These are fragments from my essay "Spectacle and Spectator: Looking Through the American Musical Comedy," *Cine-tracts* 1, 2 (Summer 1977), being reprinted in an anthology currently being edited by Ron Burnett.

as a motif when they speak through the backstage door during the interruption of "Pettin' in the Park," then at the speakeasy, later at the night club in a medley following "We're in the Money," and finally in the spectacle of the same name.

"I've Got to Sing a Torch Song" is heard under titles, then sung by Brad in the apartment for Barney and the girls, heard in the apartment before the first entrance of J. Lawrence and Fanuel Peabody, sung by Trixie in the bathtub. The melody is next heard on the balcony while J. Lawrence and Polly discuss her past, and then in the apartment during the kissing sequences between Carol and J. Lawrence. Reportedly this was another production number for Ginger Rogers as Fay Fortune—just beginning her climb to stardom and top billing, here seventh in the credits—that was subsequently cut from the released version. It is the only song that does not have its own spectacle.

"Remember My Forgotten Man" is first played by Brad, repeated through the window, heard backstage when he is reluctantly assuming his place in the show, and at the end. It is obviously a key thematic song, but more important, it is a stammer, a stutter; the film cannot end until Brad writes the lyrics. The conclusion, like all good classical films, works via delay, with the end reiterating the beginning, circling back and tying up all the loose ends. Remember the apartment scene with Barney and the girls. Brad Roberts says: "I've got something about a forgotten man, but I don't have the words to it yet. . . . I got the idea for it last night. I was down at Times Square, watching those men in the bread lines, standing there in the rain waiting for coffee and doughnuts, men out of a job, around the soup kitchen." In one of my favorite moments of cinema, Barney says: "That's it! That's it! That's what the show is about, the depression, men marching, marching in the rain, doughnuts, men marching, jobs, jobs! In the background, Carol, the spirit of the depression, a blues song, no, not a blues song, but a wailing, a wailing! and this gorgeous woman singing a song that will tear their hearts out. The big parade, the big parade of tears! That's it! That's it! Work on it! Work on it!" When Brad writes the lyrics, the film can end. The end shows us what is denied in the lyrics of "We're in the Money": "We've never seen a bread line, a bread line today. . . ."

Singing and dancing are the usual performance modes but not necessary components of the genre. After all, Berkeley's "girls" neither danced nor sang—they smiled, walked, existed. Because music is the dominant code, the performer can sing, dance, skate, swim, or tumble to its rhythms. Editing, camerawork, and stupendous *mise-en-scènes* did the rest. Hence the term "musical comedy." When the music concludes, so do the spectacle and the movie. The opening and closing musical notes are re-marked by another system of mirrored bracketing shots. Identical shots of theater stages, curtains rising, orchestras and conductors, and/or on-screen audiences open and close the spectacles. This theatrical iconography refers both to the origins of the genre and to the spectator in the movie theater, often a proscenium stage with an inserted screen. The erotic messages of the spectacles, however subdued by Hollywood convention and regulation, are celebrations of body, voice, and cinema, intensified by the interaction/duplication of visual and aural codes. *Mise-en-scène*, camera movement, editing, and sound rhythmically and vertically re-mark each other with a high degree of redundancy. These bracketed and rhythmically marked spectacles, set in and apart from the overall movement of the narrative, make explicit and even exhibit certain operations that other genres work to suppress. The spectator is clearly alerted to filmic illusion, as well as to immobility in the dark movie theater. Spectacles can be considered as excessively pleasurable moments in musicals; ironically, the moments of greatest fantasy coincide with maximum spectator alertness. These breaks displace the temporal advance of the narrative, providing immediate, regular doses of narcissistic gratification, satiating the spectator with several "ends."

However, spectacles are ultimately contained, like the interruption of the sheriff, by the process of narrativisation; spectacles mirror rather than rupture, at once anticipating and delaying the resolution of the narrative, thus functioning as a strip tease—a metaphor that is an apt one for the *Gold Diggers*. Interruptus is another. "Pettin' in the Park," like the sheriff stopping "We're in the Money," is a strip tease, as are the many shots of women (un)-dressing. Fay Fortune is stripped of her dress to be used as a lure for Barney: "Remember to stand in the light, Carol." Even J. Lawrence is stripped and put to bed. In a sense the film is foreplay for the end, the Broadway Show, with interruption narratively enacted. First, the interruption of "We're in the Money"; then the delay of "Pettin' " while Brad, threatened with the responsibility for creating prostitutes, decides to enter the spectacle; the "intermission," with a shot of the playbill at the end of "Pettin' "; then the postponement of "Remember My Forgotten Man" while the marital crisis is resolved backstage. Fay continually breaks into the narrative and is kicked out by Trixie—in the apartment with the girls, in the apartment scene with Barney, in the speakeasy, and finally from the night club. Like her missing production number, she is a loose end, a real gold digger who threatens to unbalance the film's symmetry (and a source of female envy and competition).

Cinema's courtship ritual, the endless creation of families, of couples, maps a landscape of the film body: (1) film's material body of light, grain, sounds, and techniques that have accumulated narrative "meanings"; (2) figurations of the human body, uniting as "couple"; and (3) the spectator/auditor's body in the movie theater. A triple seduction—of on-screen couples in classical films, of the audience in the theater, of the critic/theorist by the film text—outlines the film body, tracing "around bodies and sexes not boundaries not to be crossed, but perpetual spirals of pleasure" (Foucault, 1978, 45). The on-screen objects of desire are figurations of the human body, seduced and captured by narrative's inexorable movement to closure—usually the implied consummation of the couple in the brief seconds before "The End," the legal seal of film's narrative/marital contract. This foreplay of exchange, within history and marked by sexual economics, flickers over the spectator/auditor's body.

The dating ritual of "going to the movies," cinema's second seduction, tactilely and tacitly conducted in the anonymous, discreet dark of the movie theater, replays the film's foreplay. Darkness is not only the essential condition of the film's visibility but for Roland Barthes "also the color of a very diffuse eroticism" and the movie theater "a place of disponsibility, with the idleness of bodies that best characterizes modern eroticism" (1979, 3). Barthes further describes the movie theater as "urban darkness, a cinematographic cocoon" in which "the body's freedom luxuriates." He then extends the sexual (or sleep/dream) metaphor of moviegoing: "How many spectators slip into their seat as they slip into bed, coat and feet on the seat in front of them?" (3).

The actual conditions of film exhibition—its past of live performances, prologues, orchestras, and bank nights and other give-aways (movies' various versions of radio and TV game shows that were instituted during the depression, along with double and triple features); film genre mixtures of cartoons, news, travelogues, shorts and features; the introduction of food and drink, particularly popcorn, as well as the pleasures of air conditioning and plush decor; conducted in an intense darkness (before recent fire codes) that required ushers garbed in pseudomilitary uniforms carrying flashlights in sumptuous movie palaces with fetishized, lavish "ladies' rooms" and lounges—elucidate, as I tried to do in my initial remarks, a historical rather than timeless audience, one that includes women (who went to the movies not just for punishment) and their historical pleasure.

Barthes, Roland. 1979. "Upon Leaving the Movie Theater." *University Publishing* (Winter). Reprinted from *Communications*, no. 23 (1975).
Baxter, John. 1968. *Hollywood in the Thirties*. New York: A.S. Barnes & Co.
Fischer, Lucy. 1976. "The Image of Woman as Image: The Optical Politics of *Dames*." *Film Quarterly* 30, no. 1 (Fall).
Foucault, Michel. 1978. *The History of Sexuality*. Volume 1, *An Introduction*, translated by Robert Hurley. New York: Random House.
———. 1979. *Discipline and Punish: The Birth of the Prison*. New York: Vintage Books.
Freud, Sigmund. "Three Essays on Sexuality." 1959. In *The Standard Edition of the Complete Psychological Works of Sigmund Freud*. London: Hogarth Press.
Kracauer, Siegfried. 1931; reprint, 1975. "The Mass Ornament." *New German Critique* 5 (Spring); this source was suggested to me by Patrice Petro.
Lahr, John. 1977. "Fearful Symmetry." *Harper's* (July). Janet Staiger supplied this piece.
Marvin, Carolyn. 1987. "Dazzling the Multitude: Imagining the Electric Light as a Communication Medium." In *Mass Communication Review Yearbook*, edited by Michael Gurevitch and Mark R. Ley. Newbury Park, Calif.: Sage.
Mellencamp, Patricia, 1981. "Oedipus and the Robot in *Metropolis*." *Enclitic* 5, 1 (Spring).
Mulvey, Laura. 1975. "Visual Pleasure and Narrative Cinema." *Screen* 16 (Autumn).
Rein, Sonja. 1978. "Whose Whip Is It Anyway?" Department of English, University of Wisconsin-Milwaukee. Photocopy.
United States Bureau of the Census. 1976. *The Statistical History of the United States from Colonial Times to the Present*. New York: Basic Books.
Wallechinsky, David, and Irving Wallace. 1975. *The People's Almanac*. New York: Doubleday & Company, Inc.

BIBLIOGRAPHY

Methodology

De Lauretis, Teresa. *Alice Doesn't*. Bloomington: Indiana University Press, 1984.
Doane, Mary Ann, Patricia Mellencamp, and Linda Williams. *Re-Vision: Essays in Feminist Film Criticism*. Frederick: University Publishing, 1984.
Heath, Stephen. *Questions of Cinema*. Bloomington: Indiana University Press, 1984.
Modleski, Tania, ed. *Studies in Entertainment*. Bloomington: Indiana University Press, 1986.
Morris, Meaghan. *The Pirate's Fiancee*. London: Verso, 1989.

MELLENCAMP

Petro, Patrice. *Joyless Streets: Women and Melodramatic Representation in Weimar Germany*. Princeton: Princeton Press, 1989.

Film

Bergman, Andrew. *We're In the Money*. New York: Harper & Row, 1971.
Thomas, Tony, and Jim Terry with Busby Berkeley. *The Busby Berkeley Book*. New York: New York Graphic Society, 1973.

11

THE DESIRE TO DESIRE: *DESPERATELY SEEKING SUSAN*

Lucy Fischer

THE DIALOGIC TEXT

> *Every age re-accentuates in its own way the works of its most immediate past. The historical life of classic works is in fact the uninterrupted process of their social and ideological re-accentuation.*
>
> —Mikhail Bakhtin (1981, 420–21)

For many people, the task of performing a close reading of a text connotes placing a hermetic seal around it—studying in great detail the bounded words on a page or images on a screen. While close reading surely involves such a process of self-scrutiny, it can also entail a wider project: going beyond the frame of a particular work to include others that it suggests, invokes, or calls into question. This is an *intertextual* approach—that sees the individual artifact as part of a web of connected discourses. As literary critic Michael Riffaterre states, the proper "intertext" for any work "is the corpus of texts the reader may legitimately connect with the one before his eyes, that is, the texts brought to mind by what he is reading" (1980, 626–27). In a similar vein, Soviet theorist Mikhail Bakhtin has referred to literary works as "dialogic"—in their conversational interaction with myriad cultural and artistic systems. He has also noted how new texts "re-accentuate" the old, recasting them in another form.

It is such an intertextual perspective that I will bring to Susan Seidelman's *Desperately Seeking Susan* (1985)—a work in which I find the traces, echoes, and ghosts of many others. In addition to executing a close formal and thematic analysis of the movie I will situate it within a network of films drawn from the American classical and European art cinemas—texts it reaccentuates and rewrites. Through this dialogue, or argument of texts, a reading of the Seidelman film will emerge.

THE GOOD, THE BAD, AND THE UGLY

There is no figurative image of woman which does not call up at once its opposite: she is Life and Death, Nature and Artifice, Daylight and Night. Under whatever aspect we consider her, we always find the same shifting back and forth.
—Simone de Beauvoir (1974, 210)

In *The Second Sex*, Simone de Beauvoir expounds on the contradictory manner in which woman has been portrayed in western culture: if she is angel, she is whore; if she is victim, she is oppressor; if she is benign, she is perverse.

If stereotypes of woman have circulated in the broad culture, they have also obtained in the arts. De Beauvoir uncovers them in the work of renowned authors: Breton, Lawrence, Montherlant, Claudel, Stendhal. And film scholars have located them in the discourse of popular cinema. In *Movies: A Psychological Study*, Martha Wolfenstein and Nathan Leites devote a section to the dichotomies of "good" girls and "bad" and conclude that their popularity as screen archetypes reveals that the "difficulty of choosing between [them] is one of the major problems of love-life in western culture" (1950, 25).

In the history of cinema there are certain works that foreground the "oppositions" of femininity of which De Beauvoir, Wolfenstein, and Leites speak. In the silent era one thinks of F.W. Murnau's *Sunrise* (1927), in which the seductive "City Woman" lures a country man away from his saintly wife, leaving the family on the brink of ruin. In the sound era one thinks of a group of Hollywood films in which the alleged "poles" of female nature are more starkly drawn. Rather than being dramatized in two unrelated women they are depicted in identical twins (played by the same actress), one of whom is beatific and the other, malign. There is: *A Stolen Life* (1946) with Bette Davis; *The Dark Mirror* (1946) with Olivia De Havilland; and *Cobra Woman* (1944) with Maria Montez (Fischer 1983, 24–43). That the "polarities" of female nature are represented in identical twins only indicates that male culture has never seen them as separate but rather as "doubles" of the composite female soul.

In the classical film narrative the conflict between opposing females is resolved in a morally "agreeable" manner: the good woman triumphs and the bad one is defeated or destroyed. In *Sunrise*, just as the farmer is about to commit murder (in order to elope with his mistress) his wife's incandescent holiness thwarts him from the heinous act. The couple is reunited and the evil woman slinks off in the night like a vampire scurrying away at daybreak. In *The Dark Mirror* (where the twins are suspects in a murder) the psychotic, Terry, is arrested for the crime while Ruth is exonerated and freed from her sister's sadistic torture. In *A Stolen Life* the vampish Pat marries her sister's lover and then is drowned in a boating accident (in which her twin survives). Katy assumes Pat's identity in order to win back her *beau*—playing the part of his wife. When she learns of the couple's estrangement she reveals the truth and is joined with her man. In all of these films the good woman's traits are those aligned with conventional "femininity" (passivity, sweetness, emotionality, asexuality), and the bad one's are associated with "masculinity" (assertiveness, acerbity, intelligence, and eroticism).

THE DIVIDED SELF

> *A feminist practice can only be negative, at odds with what already exists.*
>
> —Julia Kristeva (1981, 169)

Contemporary criticism has revealed that films directed by women frequently oppose the mainstream tradition of works made by men. Claire Johnston speaks of a "counter-cinema" and states that "new meanings have to be created by disrupting the fabric of the male bourgeois cinema within the text of the film" (1976, 214). More recently, Mary Ann Doane, Linda Williams, and Patricia Mellencamp have asserted that a "feminist discourse on film can only be written as a . . . re-vision of a more orthodox canon" (1984, 2). While many feminist theorists believe that a cinema of resistance can only exist in "a politically and aesthetically avant-garde" camp, others are more sanguine about the popular arena (Mulvey 1985, 804). In characterizing the "new woman's film" Annette Kuhn states:

> The pleasure for the female spectator of films of this kind lies in several possible identifications: with a central character who is not only also a woman, but who may be similar in some respects to the spectator herself; or with fiction events which evoke a degree of recognition; or with a resolution that constitutes a "victory" for the central character. . . . it may consequently offer the female spectator a degree of affirmation. (1982, 136)

Desperately Seeking Susan is a "new woman's film"—in a farcical rather than serious vein. Director Susan Seidelman began work in the independent sector with a low-budget feature, *Smithereens* (1984). *Desperately*, however, was more economically ambitious and was given a broad commercial release by Orion Pictures. While on one level it seems a rather traditional romantic comedy, on another it confronts and reformulates the stereotypical dualities with which women have been portrayed (Shumway).

The film concerns an upper-middle-class, New Jersey housewife, Roberta Glass (Rosanna Arquette), who follows the "personals" columns of New York City newspapers. Bored by her marriage to a hot tub salesman, Gary (Mark Blum), she is attracted to the passion expressed in the tabloids. In particular she keeps track of messages for a woman named Susan (Madonna), whose boyfriend, Jim (Robert Joy), sets up trysts with her through newspaper communiques.

One day after noticing a "Desperately Seeking Susan" ad Roberta shows up at the appointed spot: Battery Park. After identifying Susan she tails her around the city all day but loses her in a second-hand clothing store, where Susan has traded a jacket for a pair of sequined boots. Disappointed, Roberta consoles herself by purchasing Susan's jacket, then returns to her suburban home. As she removes her clothing that evening, she finds a key to a locker at the Port Authority. Attempting to return it, she places a "Desperately Seeking Susan" message in the press, which is read by its intended subject.

Roberta returns to lower Manhattan to meet Susan, dressed in her idol's jacket. But just as Susan is about to claim her key, she is arrested for failing to pay her cab fare. Meanwhile Roberta is pursued by a gangster who mistakes her for Susan. (The latter has become unwittingly enmeshed in a murder and in the theft of ancient Egyptian earrings.) As Roberta flees her assailant she collides with a pole and falls unconscious; her pocketbook rolls into the sea. When she awakens she is assisted by Des (Aidan Quinn), a friend that Jim has asked to keep an eye on Susan. Because Roberta is wearing Susan's jacket Des assumes that she is Jim's girl, although he has never met her. Since Roberta experiences amnesia (and has lost all identifying papers), she accepts Des's interpretation of events.

The film charts the ramifications of this initial mix-up: Roberta's comic misadventures as "Susan" and her growing attraction to Des; Susan's attempts to reclaim her possessions; and Gary's essays to locate his wife. When Roberta falls again (in a later scuffle with the gangster) she regains her memory. But rather than return to Gary and her bourgeois life she stays with Des, a penniless projectionist at the Bleecker Street Cinema.

In many ways *Desperately* invokes the dialectics of womanhood so prevalent in the mainstream cinema. Roberta Glass is the quintessential good girl: she is white, married, obedient, well-off, and she displays little autonomy or sexual sophistication. Susan, on the other hand, is the classic *bête noire*. She is single and promiscuous and dresses like a "slut"—in black lingerie, garters, and junk jewelry. She carries a valise decorated with skulls. She operates on the boundary of the law—engaging in one-night stands with mobsters, becoming embroiled in theft and murder plots. She is also an inveterate con woman: breaking into public lockers, imposing on her friends, failing to pay her bills, lying incessantly. The two opposing women in *Desperately* are also seen as Doppelgängers. They literally exchange identities—like the twins in *A Stolen Life*. As Katy became Pat, so Roberta becomes Susan. Susan, then, is herself "transformed" into Roberta: inhabiting the Glass house (to help Gary find his wife), swimming in their pool, wearing Roberta's sequined jacket.

Throughout the film the contrast between women is accentuated by parallel editing structures: as Roberta drives to New York in her expensive car, Susan walks down a grubby city street eating Fritos; as Susan goes to a second-hand clothing store, Roberta writes her personals ad; as Roberta chokes on a cigarette (during her first moments as "Susan"), a prison matron gives the real Susan a light in jail.

While invoking certain paradigms of the classical cinema, *Desperately* ultimately dismantles them, and it does so on diverse registers. Crucial to an understanding of the film is its whimsical tone. While Roberta is represented as a good girl, she is *mocked* (rather than revered) for that status. The film's satire begins in the credit sequence that depicts Roberta and her sister-in-law, Leslie (Laurie Metcalf), at the beauty parlor. As we watch women's legs being waxed, their hair shorn, and their nails manicured, a woman tells an operator, "If my husband calls, tell him I'm not here." Other sequences caustically characterize Roberta's life. As she races back from her day in New York her oven turns on automatically and her coffee pot begins to brew. As she frantically rushes into the kitchen to prepare dinner, she turns on the *Julia Child Show* and does just as she is told. Her husband waltzes in and announces that he cannot stay for supper.

What becomes apparent is that Roberta's life is humorous because it—like her Perrier—is so flat, so devoid of desire. Clearly "Gary's Oasis" cannot quench her thirst. Although his television ads promise that his spas can make "fantasies come true," he fails to liberate *her* unconscious. It is for this reason that she reads ludicrous self-help books (*I'm Okay, You're Okay, Dr. Ruth's Guide To Good Sex*) and writes a diary that Susan finds so boring that "it must be a cover" and that she follows the personals, hoping to steal a personal life of her own. In the beauty parlor she sighs at the excessive emotions expressed in Jim's ad: "*Desperate*, I love that word," she intones. If hers is a life of "quiet desperation," she yearns for existence on a more raucous note. When Leslie sees Roberta reading the personals, she shouts, "I thought you were looking at the *want* ads," misunderstanding the true nature of Roberta's needs. Writing of the 1940s melodrama, Mary Ann Doane characterizes its heroines and viewers as having the "desire to desire" (rather than as having passion itself). She states:

> The woman's film, in its insistent address to the female spectator-consumer, confronts all the difficulties and blockages . . . in the attempt to conceptualize female subjectivity . . . and [woman's] purportedly deficient and highly mediated access to desire. (1987, 13)

This apt phrase applies to Roberta Glass as well—an eighties victim of this forties syndrome.

Significantly, Roberta's fantasies attach to Susan—a hip femme fatale. In the classic cinema the good girl's affect is aimed at a male: the farmer's wife wants her husband back; Katy desires her ex-lover. Neither woman has much interest in her female counterpart. In *Desperately*, however, Roberta's emotions are (at least initially) directed at a woman—one whom she both desires and desires to be. Hence the double-entendre involved in the film's title: while it is Jim who first desperately seeks Susan, Roberta later fills his shoes.

In fact, Roberta is positioned as a typical voyeur, assuming the male stance. As she follows Susan around town shot/countershot editing figures her in the act of looking and Susan as the object of her gaze. At one point during their ill-fated meeting at Battery Park, Roberta peers at Susan through a pay telescope. The image shuts down when her money and time expire—as though to indicate the "illicit" nature of her vision. Perhaps this dynamic accounts for the uneasy jokes about homosexuality in the film. When Gary finds Roberta in jail (mistakenly arrested for soliciting), Leslie informs him that most whores are lesbians. Ultimately, if homoerotic impulses subtend the film, they are "safely" recouped in the reestablishment of symmetrical heterosexual liaisons for the two women.

But if Susan is a questionable love object for Roberta, she is certainly a heroine—and Roberta's fascination with her is a kind of "romance of identification" (Shumway). In fact, Roberta's spying on Susan mimics the position of the female film viewer. Recent feminist criticism has shown that in the classical cinema woman is frustrated from sympathizing with the actions and actors on-screen. As Laura Mulvey notes, the female spectator must either align herself with the passive woman (as demeaned object of the masculine look) or she must identify (in a gender-crossed manner) with the triumphant male bearer of the gaze: a clear double-bind. She writes that "for women (from childhood onwards) trans-sex identification is a *habit* that very easily becomes second *Nature*. However, this Nature does not sit easily and shifts restlessly in its borrowed transvestite clothes" (1985; 1981, 13).

As though to illustrate that phenomenon Seidelman includes a sequence of Roberta watching a movie. After her party guests have left one evening, Roberta sits in her kitchen (obsessively eating leftover cake) as *Rebecca* (1940) plays on television. Significantly, the Hitchcock film is about good girls and bad: the two Mrs. de Winters. In the clip selected Maxim de Winter (Laurence Olivier) tells his new wife (Joan Fontaine) that she has lost her innocence upon her learning the sordid details of his first marriage. As a female spectator Roberta faces the usual dilemma: does she accept her assigned role and identify with the passive, masochistic heroine? Or does she appropriate the male position and choose Maxim, the hero? She is prevented from empathizing with the bad woman, Rebecca, who has been conveniently excised from the text.

In seeking Susan, however, Roberta finally finds a dramatic protagonist to whom she can relate and, like Uncle Josh at the moving picture show, when she locates her, she tries to enter the fictional world.[1] Significantly, she identifies with the "wrong" woman: rather than emulating a good girl—figured on screen for her moral edification—she chooses a bad. Rebecca lives.

This metaphorical search for a heroine in *Desperately* also makes clear how the film's narrative structure differs from the classical paradigm. In *Alice Doesn't: Feminism, Semiotics, Cinema*, Teresa de Lauretis outlines the traditional story as represented in ancient myth. It is one in which the male hero is central and traverses an obstacle-ridden space associated with woman. As she writes: "The mythical subject is constructed as . . . male; he is the active principle of culture. . . . Female is what is not susceptible to transfor-

1. I am referring to the Edison film *Uncle Josh at the Moving Picture Show* (ca. 1902), in which a male film spectator jumps out of his seat and attempts to enter the world depicted on the film screen.

mation, to life or death; she (it) is an element of plot-space, a topos, a resistance" (1984, 119). As an example of such a female narrative force she mentions the Sphinx—clearly a "resistance" in the path of Oedipus. *Desperately* revises this traditional pattern in various ways. Roberta, a woman, is the central character, and it is she (not a male hero) who experiences a significant "transformation." Furthermore, whereas a figure like Susan might have typified the "obstacle" in a classical text (like a *film noir*), here she is no such thing. Rather, she is the means toward Roberta's liberation from the real obstacle, Gary, and his bourgeois life. As though to ridicule her potential Sphinx role, Susan's infamous jacket is emblazoned with a pyramid.

If Roberta is not the typical good girl, Susan is not her conventional foil: she is a parody of that figuration. Obviously Susan's depiction draws on Madonna's preexistent persona of a rock singer. Dressed in trashy underwear and Frederick's of Hollywood garb, Madonna is a caricature of the lower-class "tramp," a posture ironized by her inappropriate name. (She is not "Like a Virgin," after all.) In interviews she cultivates this image: in one article, she confesses: "When I was a Campfire Girl, I'd camp out with the boys and get into trouble" (Cohen 1985, 45). In this respect Madonna functions much like Mae West—a star who also made a travesty of male conceptions of femininity. As female viewers, many of us find these "material girls" preferable to their ethereal counterparts. Part of what attracts us is their consummate narcissism—a quality taken to comic extremes. Mae West flaunted her sexual allure with lines like: "Do you have a gun in your pocket, or are you just glad to see me?" Madonna rivals West in her interview statements. She tells Scott Cohen: "My favorite button is my belly button," and "If I were a girl and knew me, I'd want to dress like me" (Cohen 1985, 44).

And Roberta does. Significantly, she first expresses interest in Susan during her beauty parlor session. While the stylist is fabricating an acceptable image for her (beehive hair-do, red polished nails), Roberta is imagining another role: that of the declassé Susan—her quintessential Other. In this respect Roberta can also be seen to seek "popular culture" in her quest rather than the more high-toned milieu assigned to her (of mineral water, hors d'oeuvres, and Carly Simon music). For Roberta following the personals is a variation on following the soaps—translated from the television screen into the real world.

While in the classical Hollywood film the narrative eliminates the bad girl and delivers the good girl to the appropriate male (*The Dark Mirror, A Stolen Life, Cobra Woman, Rebecca*), in *Desperately* this pattern is somewhat displaced. Susan not only survives but she triumphs, ultimately leading police to the gangsters and winning back her boyfriend (despite her infidelities). While Roberta is restored to a man (defusing any radical sexual politics), she rejects the *assigned* male: her husband, Gary. Instead she prefers Des, who is associated with Susan and the underworld she inhabits. While Roberta eventually regains her memory (and with it her true identity) she is significantly changed, and it has been her "double" who has facilitated the transformation through a gift of a persona. Thus Roberta has desperately sought not only Susan but she has desperately sought (and found) her *self*. Significantly, she achieves this not through conformity but through acts of transgression: she begins as an upstanding housewife and ends up a "prostitute"—a role that merely literalizes her prior status as well-paid marital companion. She begins in the upper economic echelons and winds up on the skids. This is clearly not the fate of the good girls in the canonical cinema. In fact, Roberta's amnesia allows her to forget not only her own identity but those of the saintly women she has been raised to heed.

Roberta's search for self is figuratively represented in a sequence of the film. When we are first introduced to Susan she inhabits an Atlantic City hotel room in which her mobster/lover sleeps. She sits on the floor taking Polaroid snapshots of herself. It is one of these that Roberta later finds in Susan's jacket pocket and carries around with her. Susan's narcissistic photography stands as an emblem not only of her sense of self but of her refusal of male configurations of her (be they photographic or otherwise). Rather, she appropriates the literal and metaphorical masculine gaze. As Susan's photos provide a mirror for herself, so Susan constitutes a mirror for Roberta—one in which the latter's nature is finally reflected.

There are aspects of *Desperately* that also directly critique the male bifurcation of woman into discrete poles. One of Susan's friends works in a sleazy midtown night club as a magician's assistant. She is fired when she insists on wearing her glasses during the act, a gesture that negates her showgirl status. When Roberta "becomes" Susan she finds a card for the club in her pocket and goes there to jog her memory. When she walks in the proprietor mistakes her for a job applicant and drafts her into the magic act. In one of the final scenes of the film (when all the main characters descend upon the club) Roberta appears in the illusion of being sawed in half. Upon seeing her both Des and Gary run up to the stage and try to free her from the two-part box. Here the magic act stands as a metaphor for the artificial division of woman's nature and for the manner in which she is imprisoned and dismembered by that process. At the end of the film, when Susan and Roberta become famous for catching the criminal, the newspaper headline reads: "What a Pair!" This statement transcends the level of plot to focus on the women's synthesis of the false dichotomies of the female that have conventionally circulated. It is also significant that throughout the film each woman wears a single earring (of the stolen set), as though to encapsulate her representation as a single "lobe" of male-conceived feminine consciousness. Though the women in *Desperately* make a joke of patriarchal magic (being sawed in half, making bluebirds disappear), they manage to perform "tricks" of their own—transforming identities, mending woman's divided self.

DESPERATELY SEEKING SUSY

Sexist ideology is no less present in the European art cinema because stereotyping appears less obvious.
—Claire Johnston (1976, 210)

Though I have focused on the American classical cinema, the false dichotomies of womanhood have surfaced in the art film as well. Federico Fellini's *Juliet of the Spirits* (1965) is a case in point that makes another provocative intertext for interpreting the Seidelman film.

Juliet concerns a middle-aged, Italian, suburban housewife (Giulietta Masina) whose husband, Giorgio, is wrapped up in business and having an affair with a younger woman. Juliet is unhappy but only faintly aware of the psychic conflicts that torment her. Over the course of the film she has a series of bizarre experiences that catapult her into a journey toward self-discovery. One night when some friends come over they bring a clairvoyant and he conducts a seance. Juliet makes contact with a spirit named Iris, who tells her that she is "nothing." Another day she accompanies a friend to visit a hermaphrodite occult leader who has come to town. Bishma tells Juliet to get in touch with her eroticism (to be more "sexy") and implies that she is not pleasing her husband in bed. As these spirits and psychics descend upon Juliet's world she is haunted by memories of a repressive Catholic upbringing in which she was taught martyrdom as the female goal. Juliet also befriends her neighbor, an outrageously seductive woman named Susy (Sandra Milo). As Juliet becomes aware of her husband's philandering she gravitates toward Susy and is told by her spirit that Susy will be her "teacher." At one of her neighbor's orgies Juliet arrives boldly dressed in red and almost makes love with a young boy that Susy has chosen for her. Frightened and repelled, Juliet returns home. Although by the end of the film Juliet banishes her destructive spirits and recollections—and seems to be freer—she has made no significant changes in her life. Giorgio has left for a trip with his mistress, and Juliet has not protested. She walks outside the white picket fence surrounding her house but does not entirely leave it.[2]

There are clear parallels between the Fellini film and *Desperately*. Both concern traditional housewives; we might think of Juliet as Roberta seen some ten years later. Both women have unfaithful husbands, and both are sexually repressed. When Gary learns that Roberta has been arrested for prostitution, his sister inquires about the couple's sex life, about whether or not Roberta had orgasms. Gary finds it impossible to believe his wife is a whore because she "didn't like [sex] enough." The case for Juliet's restraint is more clear. Played by the waifish Giulietta Masina, she is a small, childlike woman, a fact accentuated by the Amazonian females who surround her in the film (Susy, Juliet's mother and sisters). She is almost always dressed in white and frequently wears a nunlike hood. Her most disturbing childhood memory is that of playing a saint in a convent play—of being tied to a "burning" grill and raised to heaven amidst crepe paper flames. Her status as good girl is not in question—here is a true madonna (or "angel," as Giorgio calls her).

Like Roberta, Juliet is also associated with magic—in the form of her spirits and demons. Like Seidelman's heroine, she is also vaguely dissatisfied with her life and undergoes an emotional mid-life crisis in which she searches for alternate role models. In the beginning of the film we see Juliet getting ready for dinner, trying on various wigs and dresses like so many disguises. As Roberta finds the bad girl, Susan, so Juliet finds the gaudy Susy—an ersatz burlesque queen. On the rebound from Giorgio, Juliet emulates her neighbor but cannot play the part. Susy and the spirits of eroticism are banished (as well as the voices of martyrdom). Though Juliet learns to be less punitive and guilty, good girl and bad girl have no real rapprochement.

Juliet has had the "desire to desire," but when given the chance to satisfy it she remains in her fantasy realm. In a vision she frees her child-self from the convent play "grill," but she cannot use that liberty in the real world. Rather, Juliet will exchange one set of reveries for another—perhaps more benign, but hardly more radical. Rather than have wants of her own she re-

2. Toward the end of the film Juliet speaks with a female psychiatrist who is visiting her house. This woman's statements come closest to suggesting a progressive denouement for Juliet. The psychiatrist tells her not to fight her passions and desires. She tells her that she secretly wants Giorgio to go away and that without him she would find herself. The psychiatrist's words are not, however, given any more weight in the film than those of others, who advise Juliet quite differently.

mains trapped by her husband's desire: she has him tailed by detectives to find out if *he* loves *her*. In fact, female desire is routinely mocked in *Juliet* through the bevy of lascivious women who populate its terrain. In particular one thinks of Juliet's sculptress friend who cavorts with young boys and makes statues of God figured as her male paramours.

While Juliet remains trapped in her imagination, Roberta passes through the "looking glass" and lives out her obsessions—a fact metaphorically figured in her move from Perrier to vodka. Once she does, there is no turning back: the desire to desire has become desire itself. In the beginning of the film, as Roberta sits in a beauty parlor getting dolled up for her husband, an old rock-and-roll song plays on the sound track—rendered by a girl group. The lyric is addressed to women and tells them that "if [they] want to know if he loves [them] so, it's in his kiss." The song articulates the classic female position: that of Sleeping Beauty awaiting Prince Charming, whose embrace confers the power of love. By the end of the film Roberta is not so much interested in what's in his kiss as what's in hers—not so much concerned with his desires as with her own.

In entering her punk Wonderland Roberta can also be seen to have moved through stages that parallel the film experience. She begins as a classic female spectator who follows (through personals ads) the exciting lives of others and watches Gothics on TV. However, her identification with a real-life heroine (Susan) catapults her from voyeur to participant in the exciting fictional world. Significantly, the female protagonist is a bad girl—one with whom she is not supposed to identify. When Roberta becomes a narrative actant, she finds romance in the form of her attraction to Des (whose name hints both at *des*peration and *des*ire). Significantly, he works as a projectionist at the Bleecker Street Cinema and his liaisons with Roberta continually interfere with his film job. When Des is first introduced he is in the projection booth. Jim telephones Des (on his way out of town) and asks him to keep an eye on Susan—the event that will lead him to Roberta. While on the phone a reel of the horror film that he is projecting falls down, and the audience boos. In the final scene of the narrative Des is projecting a science fiction drama. Roberta (who has left her husband) enters the booth and the couple embraces, leaning on the reel. We then see a shot of the theater screen with the film image burning—a flip metaphor for the sexual desire figured in the closing kiss.

Roberta has managed to use the dynamics of classic female film spectatorship to "get into the picture," but she has subverted the process by enacting the "wrong" part and drama. She has chosen not the good girl but the bad—

not the assigned love interest but another. Once within the diegetic space she destroys its illusions (as she sabotages its magic tricks), "burning" and deforming its representational frame. Once he meets Roberta, Des can no longer project his films, as we can no longer project on her the false dichotomies of womanhood. If in classical cinema, for Teresa de Lauretis, Alice Doesn't—in *Desperately Seeking Susan*, Alice Does.

WORKS CITED

Bakhtin, Mikhail. 1981. *The Dialogic Imagination*. Edited by Michael Holquist. Translated by Caryl Emerson and Michael Holquist. Austin and London: University of Texas Press.

Beauvoir, Simone de. 1974. *The Second Sex*. Translated by H.M. Parshley. New York: Vintage.

Cohen, Scott. 1985. "Confessions of a Madonna." *Spin* 1, no. 1 (May).

Doane, Mary Ann. 1987. *The Desire to Desire: The Woman's Film of the 1940s*. Bloomington and Indianapolis: Indiana University Press.

Doane, Mary Ann, Patricia Mellencamp, and Linda Williams. 1984. *Re-Vision: Essays in Feminist Film Criticism*. Frederick, Md.: University Publications Of America and The American Film Institute.

Fischer, Lucy. 1983. "Two-Faced Women: The 'Double' in Women's Melodrama of the 1940s." *Cinema Journal* 23, no. 1 (Fall).

Johnston, Claire. 1976. "Woman's Cinema as Counter Cinema." In *Movies and Methods: An Anthology*, edited by Bill Nichols. Berkeley, Los Angeles, and London: University of California Press.

Kristeva, Julia. 1981. *About Chinese Women*. Quoted in Gayatri Spivak, "French Feminism in an International Frame," *Yale French Studies*, no. 62.

Kuhn, Annette. 1982. *Women's Pictures: Feminism and Cinema*. London: Routledge and Kegan Paul.

Lauretis, Teresa de. 1984. *Alice Doesn't: Feminism, Semiotics, Cinema*. Bloomington: Indiana University Press.

Mulvey, Laura. 1981. "Afterthoughts on 'Visual Pleasure and Narrative Cinema' Inspired by *Duel in the Sun*." *Framework*, nos. 15–17.

———. 1985. "Visual Pleasure and Narrative Cinema." In *Film Theory and Criticism*, 3d ed., edited by Gerald Mast and Marshall Cohen. New York: Oxford University Press.

Riffaterre, Michael. 1980. "Syllepsis." *Critical Inquiry* 6.

Shumway, David. "Screwball Comedies: Constructing Romance. Mystifying Marriage." Department of English, Carnegie Mellon University. Photocopy.

Wolfenstein, Martha, and Nathan Leites. 1950. *Movies: A Psychological Study*. Glencoe, Ill.: The Free Press.

Feminist Film Criticism

Doane, Mary Ann. *The Desire to Desire: The Woman's Film of the 1940s*. Bloomington and Indianapolis: Indiana University Press, 1987.

Doane, Mary Ann, Patricia Mellencamp, and Linda Williams. *Re-Vision: Essays in Feminist Film Criticism*. Frederick, Md.: University Publications Of America and The American Film Institute, 1984.

Erens, Patricia, ed. *Sexual Stratagems: The World of Women In Film*. New York: Horizon, 1979.

Fischer, Lucy. *Shot/Countershot: Film Tradition and Women's Cinema*. Princeton: Princeton University Press, 1989.

Gentile, Mary. *Film Feminisms: Theory and Practice*. Westport, Conn.: Greenwood Press, 1985.

Haskell, Molly. *From Reverence to Rape: The Treatment of Women in the Movies*. Baltimore, Md.: Penguin, 1971.

Higashi, Sumiko. *Virgins, Vamps and Flappers: The American Silent Movie Heroine*. St. Albans, Vt.: Eden Press Women's Publications, 1978.

Kaplan, E. Ann. *Women and Film: Both Sides of the Camera*. New York: Methuen, 1983.

Kaplan, E. Ann, ed. *Women in Film Noir*. London: British Film Institute, 1980.

Kay, Karyn, and Gerald Peary. *Women and the Cinema: A Critical Anthology*. New York: Dutton, 1977.

Kuhn, Annette. *Women's Pictures: Feminism and Cinema*. London: Routledge and Kegan Paul, 1982.

Lauretis, Teresa de. *Alice Doesn't: Feminism, Semiotics, Cinema*. Bloomington: Indiana University Press, 1984.

Rosen, Marjorie. *Popcorn Venus: Women, Movies and the American Dream*. New York: Avon, 1973.

Desperately Seeking Susan

Andrews, N. "*Desperately Seeking Susan*." *Film Directions* 8, no. 30 (1986): 24–25.

Ansen, David. "Movies: Manhattan Identity Transfer." *Newsweek* 185 (8 April 1985): 85.

Canby, Vincent. "Screen: *Desperately Seeking Susan*." *New York Times* 134 (29 March 1985): C5.

———. "Susan Seidelman Strikes a Blow for Independent." *New York Times*, 134 (31 May 1985).

Cook, P. "*Desperately Seeking Susan*." *Monthly Film Bulletin* 52 (September 1985): 276–77.

Denby, David. "Movies: Coasting." *New York* 18 (1 April 1985).

———. "Movies: Trading Places." *New York* 18 (22 April 1985): 86–87.

Edelstein, D. "Cheerfully Grilling Susan." *Village Voice* 30 (2 April 1985): 47.

———. "Films: Seek and Ye Shall Founder." *Village Voice* 30 (2 April 1985): 56.

Frost, P. "The Current Cinema: Passion." *New Yorker* 61 (22 April 1985): 132–38.

Golden, P. "Susan Seidelman: An Interview." *Films in Review* 36 (June/July 1985): 349–51.

Gray, M. "*Desperately Seeking Susan*." *Photoplay* 36 (September 1985): 19.

Greenwood, H. "*Desperately Seeking Susan*." *Cinema Papers*, no. 53 (September 1985): 69.

Kauffmann, S. "Stanley Kauffmann on Films: Familiar Stories." *New Republic* 192 (22 April 1985): 24–25.

Kopkind, A. "Films: *Mask*; *Desperately Seeking Susan*." *Nation* 240 (11 May 1985): 568.

Maslin, J. "At the Movies." *New York Times* 134 (22 March 1985): C4.

———. "At the Movies: Finding 56 Actors for *Susan*." *New York Times* 135 (3 May 1985): C8.

Morrison, S. "Girls on Film: Fantasy, Desire and Desperation." *Cinéaction*, no. 2 (Fall 1985): 2–6.

Padroff, J. "Lachman Films *Desperately Seeking Susan*." *American Cinematographer* 66 (July 1985): 28–34.

———. "A Splash of Seidelman." *Millimeter* 13 (March 1985): 271.

Schickel, R. "Cinema: Beautiful Dreamer in a Minefield." *Time* 125 (1 April 1985): 76.

Van Gelder, L. "Media: On the Set of *Desperately Seeking Susan*." *Ms*. 13 (April 1985).

Weinstein, W. "*Desperately Seeking Susan*." *Film Journal* 88 (February 1985): 27.

Welsh, J. "*Desperately Seeking Susan.*" *Films in Review* 36 (August/September 1985): 418–19.

Yakir, D. "Celine and Julie Go Lightly: Edward Lachman: The Look." *Film Comment* 21 (May/June 1985): 17–19.

———. "Celine and Julie Go Lightly: Leora Barish: Scraps and Pieces." *Film Comment* 21 (May/June 1985).

———. "Celine and Julie Go Lightly: The Mover: Susan Seidelman." *Film Comment* 21 (May/June 1985).

12

D. W. GRIFFITH'S *THE BIRTH OF A NATION*: GOING AFTER LITTLE SISTER

Russell Merritt

Except as a specimen of American negrophobia, Griffith's *The Birth of a Nation* has suffered almost total eclipse. Symptomatically, when in autumn 1982 *Sight and Sound* conducted its international poll for the ten best films, the movie once called "the greatest film ever made" drew a pitiful two votes. It used to be that in praise of *Birth*'s spectacle and Griffith's contribution to film narrative technique there was hardly anything new to say. Within the past twenty years we have heard significantly less of such matters. Instead we have had a steady outpouring of sociopolitical studies analyzing *Birth*'s racist propaganda and its distortion of Reconstruction history. These are the aspects of the film that are becoming best known—the only aspects many people know. *Birth* is seldom screened outside the classroom and even as a class assignment it occasionally stirs protests.[1]

Those earlier historians who lionized the film as a landmark in film narra-

1. "Top Ten 1982," *Sight and Sound* 51 (Autumn 1982): 242–46. The following are examples of recent approaches toward *The Birth of a Nation*: John Hope Franklin (1979); Ed Simmons and Pat Keeton, "Teaching Racism as 'Great Film Art' Is Questioned," *The Independent* (July/August 1983): 12–13; Mark Pinsky, "Racism,

tive technique have themselves been attacked for a particularly naive kind of form-content split that separates Griffith's skills as a craftsman from Thomas Dixon's race-baiting story. As one revisionist has written: "Against the evidence before their eyes they split Griffith's 'gift for making powerful emotional connections' from 'Thomas Dixon's racial message.' They imitate Griffith's split between good and evil, white and black, by blaming Dixon for the perversions in Griffith's movie" (Rogin 1985, 150).[2]

Moreover, amidst resurgent interest in the evolving style of Hollywood film even *Birth*'s role as the pivotal Hollywood epic, "the film that started it all," has also come under attack. Griffith's influence over Hollywood narrative, we are learning, was neither as substantial nor as pervasive as we were once told, and *The Birth of a Nation*, far from providing a narrative model for future Hollywood epics or American movies in general, was in many ways an extremely odd case. Eisenstein's simplistic notion that Griffith and silent American film were synonymous has been eclipsed by the discovery that Hollywood narrative films developed a variety of competing systems of expression. Other filmmakers were establishing important narrative conventions—especially in the areas of continuity editing, three-point lighting, organically integrated set design, subjective camera movements, and manipulation of narrative chronology and point of view—that owed little to Griffith.

History and Mass Media," *Jump Cut* 28 (April 1983): 66–67; Mimi White, "*The Birth of a Nation*: History as Pretext," *Enclitic* 1, no. 2 (1981–82): 17–24.

2. The standard studies of *The Birth of a Nation* include Milton Mackaye, "The Birth of a Nation," *Scribner's Magazine*, November 1937, 40–46, 69; Iris Barry, *D.W. Griffith: American Film Master*, series 1 (New York: Museum of Modern Art, 1940), 20–22, 34–37; Lewis Jacobs, *The Rise of the American Film* (1939; New York: Teachers College Press, 1968), 171–88; Terry Ramsaye, *A Million and One Nights* (1926; New York: Simon, 1964), 635–44; A. Nicholas Vardac, *Stage to Screen* (Cambridge: Harvard University Press, 1949), 223–26; and, more recently, Richard Schickel, *D.W. Griffith: An American Life* (New York: Simon, 1984), 212–302.

James Agee cut through the usual critical cant in his Griffith obituary notice, *Nation*, 4 Sept. 1948, reprinted in *Agee on Film*, vol. 1 (McDowell: New York, 1958), 313–18. See Edward Wagenknecht, *The Movies in the Age of Innocence* (Norman: Oklahoma University Press, 1962), 99–109, for a scholarly approach to the film with an analysis of previous critics' work. Jay Leyda (1949, 350–56) contains the best critical analysis of *The Birth of a Nation* from the old school. For valuable, hitherto inaccessible, primary material buried underneath unreadable prose and unreliable scholarship, see Seymour Stern, "Griffith: 1–'The Birth of a Nation,' " *Film Culture* 36 (1965).

In the long run the demise of this part of the Griffith legend is a healthy step toward seriously assessing him as a film director. It says something about the shallowness of conventional Griffith studies that his quality as an artist has so often been linked to his influence over other directors or his popularity with early film audiences, as though artistry should be measured by influence and prestige. Rationalizing the study of Griffith and *The Birth of a Nation* exclusively on grounds of original mass appeal only postponed an inevitable critical reckoning about the intrinsic quality of Griffith's film that came due in the late 1960s.

The current harsh focus on the racism in *The Birth of a Nation* is welcome as a corrective to too many analyses that dismissed the bigotry as understandable ("everyone thought that way") or unconscious. But the danger in dwelling exclusively on the film's racial themes is that in belaboring the obvious such analyses miss too much and through omission distort and oversimplify the complexity of the film's narrative. They tacitly assume that *Birth* could only appeal to racists because both formally and thematically it is designed mainly as a racist tract. From the perspective of these studies it becomes difficult to imagine an audience member—particularly an original 1915 audience member—who could have been absorbed by the film while being repelled, embarrassed, or simply indifferent to the film's racial stereotypes. The sociological reading assumes that all pleasures of *Birth*'s text are necessarily guilty pleasures, so offensive is the film's racial theme.

And the film does pose formidable ethical problems. Escape routes available for other controversial works cannot be so easily made to work here. This is not a case of a virulent bigot (like Wagner or D.H. Lawrence) producing a masterwork in which direct expression of the racism is either marginal or nonexistent. Nor is it an instance of a work producing stereotypes like Shylock, Fagin, Uncle Remus, or Sportin' Life, who, though created through bigoted perspectives, remain grand, resilient characters. Instead we confront a work that proudly proclaims its racism. The controversy Griffith and Dixon engender is not whether their portraits of black characters are offensive. The authors make no apology for depicting the behavior of an entire race in uncomplicated, grossly insulting terms. They risk stepping on toes, as Dixon openly admits in articles and interviews, to show the need for black disenfranchisement and strict enforcement of racial segregation policies.[3]

3. Thomas Dixon, Jr. (1906, 22). Dixon, letter to Woodrow Wilson, 5 September 1915, cited in Arthur Link, *Wilson: The New Freedom* (Princeton: Princeton University Press), 253–54. Dixon, interview with Rolfe Cobleigh, cited in N.A.A.C.P., *Fighting a Vicious Film* (Boston, 1915), 26.

Against its racial slanders and the harm they may have caused, claims for the film's formal achievements inevitably sound thin. As Jay Leyda wrote almost forty years ago: "This film is a constant anxiety to honest critics: 'How can I admit artistic or even technical greatness in a film that has written such a history of injury and misuse?' " (Leyda 1949, 352).

Unsurprisingly, the film is most comfortably treated as an example of racial propaganda or as a World War I period piece. Yet were the film no more complicated than the Dixon play on which it is based, it would have been forgotten long ago—as are the other race-baiting films of its day like *Pagan Passions, Yellow Fingers*, or DeMille's silent version of *The Ten Commandments*. The enigma we confront and which historical analyses persistently skirt is how a work can remain so effective when so much of its content is repugnant. Jay Leyda rightly saw that denying the film's richness was an important evasion. But even dividing the film into two parts, as Leyda and others do, proclaiming the first half a self-contained masterpiece and the second half pathological racist melodrama, oversimplifies the problem. The disturbing fact is that Griffith invests even his most offensive sequences with skillfulness that repays minute examination.

To repeat: How can a work remain so effective when so much of its content is repugnant?

In an earlier essay I tried to answer that by a detailed examination of the content itself, suggesting that the racial stereotypes were part of broader social and familial themes perceived by many at the time (and by many still today) as harmless and attractive (Merritt 1972). My argument was that Griffith refashioned familiar Southern legends around what had become for him a signature motif, the woman-centered home, and that the Civil War and its aftermath provided him with an opportunity to expand his idea of the family to epic proportions. However, Griffith did more than simply resurrect old myths. Working from his Dixon sources, he turned familiar legends about the Old South, the Civil War, and Reconstruction into a grandiose populist parable for a nation on the brink of war, creating a cautionary tale for a country in the throes of assimilating blacks and immigrants. By now this argument is a familiar one, and I am no longer entirely comfortable with it. It provides a rather splendid example of the naive form/content split I complained about a moment ago, and rather too neatly historicizes the film's racial venom.

We can get further, I think, by concentrating on the formal aspects of Griffith's work. My argument is that when we do isolate Griffith's formal designs, we discover that his form shapes his content in no consistent or ordinary way. Customarily Griffith is regarded as a master craftsman in full control of his medium, his shots and editing patterns consciously or intuitively designed with considerable precision. Although isolated sequences in *Birth* illustrate that truism, I will argue that at its most interesting points the film becomes formally ungovernable, even incoherent, and that "by letting into his film more than he can handle"—Peter Lehman's evocative phrase—Griffith gets back into stylistic corners that reveal important tears and fissures (1981, 69). Michael Rogin, I believe, was the first to study *The Birth of a Nation* from this perspective and has usefully drawn out the psychoanalytic implications of Griffith's formal obsessions. My own argument is that these spasmodic bursts of uncontrollability are at the center of what keeps *Birth* such a resilient text that defies the banalities and offenses of its source material.

Consider, for example, the scenes in which Gus, a black freedman, frightens Ben Cameron's sister into jumping from a cliff to her death. From the start this was a sequence that the film's opponents found particularly obnoxious and made an immediate target for censorship. In communities where blacks could not get *Birth* banned outright they made the elimination or bowdlerization of Little Sister's death a top priority. Indeed, parts of the sequence in its present form may have been coauthored by the National Board of Censors. A news report on the confrontation between Griffith and the N.B.C. includes the following:

> Various changes [in the film] were suggested [by the Board] which were made. These are said to have been chiefly a substantial reduction in the details of the chase of the white girl by the renegade Negro, which in the original is said to have been the most dreadful portrayal of rape ever offered for public view; the insertion of various soothing captions such as, "I won't hurt you, little Missy"; [and] the excision of [the renegade's] actual lynching were among the changes made.[4]

As best we can tell, this modified version is the text we currently confront.

Chopped up and incomplete, vitiated by the tawdriest racial cliches, it is nonetheless an altogether remarkable sequence.[5] In design it is yet another

4. *The Survey* (3 April 1915): 4.

5. The analysis that follows is taken from two prints of *The Birth of a Nation*, Epoch Producing Corp., 1915. First, a black and white circulation print from the Museum of Modern Art Film Library, New York City. This is identical to the 16mm print distributed by Killiam Shows and the super 8mm print sold by Blackhawk Films.

Second, a 35mm tinted nitrate print with minor variations from the black and

patented chase/last-minute rescue segment, the kind that Griffith had turned out endlessly at Biograph. It has few claims to intellectual subtlety; on the contrary, one of the chief functions of the chase is to cut off intellectual analysis with a nerve-wracking assault on the spectator's emotional faculties. Further, this particular chase triggers off later sequences that become even more overwrought.

Functionally, Flora's death unleashes the wrath of the Klan; Klan activities in fact pivot around her death. Her assault is the primal outrage, the grim culmination of a broad variety of black impertinences that until now were portrayed as insulting but not murderous. Up to this point the Klan likewise had been limited to nocturnal pranks that played off black superstitions. Now, prompted by revenge, the Klan is galvanized to launch an all-out anti-black crusade with no quarter asked and none given.

Structurally, too, the chase prepares for the film's ultimate outpouring, those grandiose races to save Elsie and the Cameron household. Those final chases which culminate in successful rescues that are denied in this sequence are meant to counterbalance and overwhelm this failed rescue, closing the film at a hysterical pitch. Flora's flight, in short, starts us on a roller coaster ride in which our vicarious adventurousness is meant to get the better of our critical understanding.

But even if it had nothing more to offer, Flora's flight is a textbook diagram of Griffith's cunning in setting up chase scenes. Its most apparent virtues are clarity, striking pictorial composition, and irresistible forward momentum. The sequence is also marked by terrific economy, compressing the action into four concise and distinct phases. Part 1: the "renegade" Gus sights Flora on her way to the woods and secretly follows her; part 2: Gus openly approaches Flora, she runs away, Gus runs after her; part 3: brother Ben, apprehensive that his sister is alone in the woods, goes into the forest to look for her; part 4: Flora, terrified at Gus's approach, jumps off a cliff and Ben finds her dying on the ground below.

What keeps these four parts integrated is Griffith's meticulous sense of design. Following the system he had worked out at Biograph, Griffith breaks

---

white print, preserved by the American Film Institute in 1974. A 16mm reduction color print is now also circulated by the Museum of Modern Art; this is the source of the videotape version distributed by Video Classics.

The shot numbers in my text are taken from John Cuniberti (1979). This supersedes Theodore Huff's 1940 shot analysis. In his introduction, Cuniberti describes in detail variations between prints of *The Birth of a Nation* and the archival history of those prints.

his forest down into separate but contiguous compartments, each segment of the forest a tightly defined, autonomous physical locale. There is no overlapping space between one composition and the next, and there are no spatial gaps to permit openings between locales. It is as though we were watching a cross-section of a freight train, each segment of the forest a boxcar, the characters chasing each other from one boxcar to the next. Just as we never see more than three sides of any Griffith room, so here we see only one face of each part of the forest, the vantage point of the shot never changing. In a style reminiscent of the proscenium stage, Griffith's compositions are invariably straight on (no dramatic high or low angles even when we reach the cliffs), and the margins of the frame are treated like stage entranceways. Griffith invariably motivates cuts by having characters pass from one area to another or by having characters peer out from one space into another.

One consequence of this style is that Griffith can yoke together wildly disparate, even incompatible patches of woodland scenery and from them create a seamless, wholly synthetic geographic backdrop. Flora's pine forest is a botanical absurdity, bound on one side by a cotton field (shot 812) and shrubs (816), on the other by the San Bernadino mountains and Big Bear Lake (877)—farmland, barren cliffs, and cathedral pines cheek by jowl.

Yet this ever-changing backdrop never seems confused or jumbled, mainly because Griffith counterbalances the extreme variety of locale—by my count, eighteen sharply differentiated boxcars—with strict uniformity of screen angle (no locale shot from more than one angle, no matter how many times Griffith returns to it) and the constant repetition of these locales as he cuts back and forth between his players. Because they are so sharply differentiated and so frequently repeated, these recurring compositions featuring a brook, pine trees, meadow, forest floor, culvert, and cliff become signposts that remorselessly tally the distance that separates characters. The Cameron picket fence (809), for instance, is always three spaces away from the woodland stream (818)—characters must pass through a shot of a wooden farm fence, then another shot of a meadow, before they can reach it. The cliff (877) is inflexibly separated from the forest floor (866) by four shots of pines and firs. These compositions become cumbersome blocks of space the players must penetrate to either catch up with each other or escape capture. But this rigorous arrangement also tells us how well Flora is doing in keeping ahead of her pursuer. Ben, too, is kept at a precise interval as he races to find her. Even though he is far behind, we can without difficulty keep track of his progress because he enters not merely identical terrain but also the identical compositions that Gus and Flora passed through moments before.

Having put this contraption in motion, Griffith can then tease his au-

Figure 12-1. The Cameron picket fence (shot 809). (Library of Congress.)

Figure 12-2. The farm fence. (Library of Congress.)

Figure 12-3. The meadow. (Library of Congress.)

Figure 12-4. The woodland stream (shot 818). (Library of Congress.)

dience by inserting or erasing blocks of space at will. When, for example, late in the sequence Ben appears to be gaining on Flora, raising the possibility that he might catch up with her after all, Griffith tosses in his path an additional spatial block (shot 892, a piece of forest floor with a fallen log in the back) that he omitted for Flora and Gus. Contrarily, Griffith generates surprise—even shock—when he suddenly erases two blocks of space that have kept Flora two jumps ahead of Gus, so that Gus unexpectedly shows up in a long shot (866) that by rights she should be occupying alone.

This deceptively simple arrangement works particularly well here because of the way it crystallizes Flora's dilemma. In Griffith's hands, the pine forest she wanders into becomes a succession of boxes that permits her little effective maneuvering or freedom of action. This orderly forest isolates Flora without providing her cover or protection. Its spatial opposite is the labyrinth whose tangled skein can provide sanctuary from pursuers and a wide variety of surprises. Characteristically, the labyrinth provides sudden confrontations with mysterious forest denizens à la *Snow White* or *Babes in the*

Woods that may protect the escapee or cast her into new adventures. If the labyrinth implies an open-ended space that disorients the pursued but rewards improvisation, Flora's forest is a meticulously designed, grindingly fatalistic closed system that mocks Flora's flurried gestures and futile efforts at improvised escape routes.

Griffith is no less concise or fatalistic in his manipulation of props. Elsewhere I have referred to Griffith's prop-oriented style (Merritt 1979), and one of the pleasures this sequence provides is the ingenuity with which Griffith has characters interact with an assortment of inanimate objects. Throughout the scene the players are continually brought into contact with objects that make concrete an idea or reaction. On the simplest level, when Gus espies Flora at the brook (815), he holds his military jacket in his hand and exposes a long sleeve shirt that manages to unbutton itself one button at a time as the sequence progresses. One result: when he starts conversing with Flora ("You see, I'm a Captain now—and I want to marry") he can more naturally illustrate by pointing to the jacket's brevet he holds in front of him. Second result: when he runs after Flora (853), he impulsively drops the jacket in the same way that Flora loses track of her water bucket, leaving the jacket for Ben to find and read as a clue. Later a fir branch brushes his hat off (881)—another clue for Ben (904). Still later both hat and jacket will reappear during Gus's Klan trial—these props, not Dr. Cameron's hypnotic talents, providing "evidence" of Gus's guilt.

Even Flora's bucket acquires a curious miniature history that extends back to the scene in the sewing parlor. What prompts Flora to go to the woods in the first place? The scene is set up to suggest childish carelessness. She acts, a title says, "against the brother's warning," and once she reaches the brook she idles her time tossing pine cones at a squirrel. Further, she has a record of thoughtlessness and lack of self-discipline that are meant to seem part of her childish charm. In the first section of the film she breaks into a fit of giggles that jeopardizes her family hiding from Yankee guerrillas; in the second she forgets to shut the parlor door, putting mother and sister at risk while they sew Klan costumes.

But the bucket points to other aspects of Flora's character. Flora, the budding adolescent, is trying to be helpful to her mother, who tends to patronize her. Her mother won't let Flora join in sewing Klan costumes but finally compromises by giving her the exciting if menial task of hiding completed Klan outfits inside sofa pillows. When mother winces at the taste of the stale drinking water, Flora jumps off a sofa arm volunteering to fetch a fresh supply from the spring in the woods. The resistance comes not from brother Ben, who is nowhere in sight, but from her mother who mimes that

Figure 12-5. Gus uses his jacket to illustrate his improved status (shot 815). (Library of Congress.)

Figure 12-6. Gus drops his jacket while he pursues Flora (shot 853). (Library of Congress.)

Figure 12-7. Ben finds the jacket (shot 904); he later uses it to provide "evidence" of Gus's guilt. (Library of Congress.)

Figure 12-8. Flora jumps off the sofa, volunteering to fetch water. (Library of Congress.)

Figure 12-9. Mother tries to dissuade Flora. (Library of Congress.)

the trip is not worth Flora's effort. But Flora grabs the water bucket with determination, proving she is a grown-up and can be useful.

Other details, such as the pillow Ben uses to rest the dead Flora's head upon, reward careful attention. But of all the props used in this scene the most intricate is the handkerchief Ben uses to wipe the blood from Flora's mouth as she lies dying, naming Gus as her pursuer (911). This is the handkerchief that will later be used to sacramentalize Flora's death at a nocturnal Klan meeting. Dipping it in the water her bucket was meant to draw, Ben speaks some Klan mumbo jumbo and holds it aloft like a sacred relic (978). But where has this handkerchief come from? Flora has been using it as a belt, a cinch that loosened when she hurled herself off the cliff. And what is it doing around her waist? It is, in fact, a miniature Confederate flag, the one Flora draped over her shoulder and swore upon when Ben pledged her to si-

Figure 12-10. The Signifying Sash: as the handkerchief that wipes Flora's blood . . . (Library of Congress.)

Figure 12-11. . . . as the sacred relic used in the Klan meeting . . . (Library of Congress.)

Figure 12-12. . . . as the Confederate flag used by Flora as a belt. (Library of Congress.)

lence about Klan activities (795). Like the bucket it is a token of Flora's determination to become a responsible Southern grown-up; having taken her oath of silence, she ties the flag around her waist and shows it off to her brother, just as earlier she had draped long strands of cotton—"Southern ermine," according to a title—over her dress in an effort to impress him with her new grown-up look. Ben now takes the flag from her waist, just as he had earlier sadly picked the cotton from her dress. But if those wisps of cotton personalized the permanent economic loss and ruin brought by the Civil War, this miniature flag becomes the device by which Flora and the South are resurrected. Soaked up by a flag that is both her flag and the flag of The Cause, her blood becomes communion blood. Her death is transformed into the new-found cause for a new Southern Crusade.

Even had the sequence no more to offer than this, we might admire it as the kind of intricately designed scene that we associate with Hitchcock and early Disney. But when we press the sequence somewhat harder, issues of "mastery" and clarity become more complicated.

Having considered what brings Flora into the forest, we turn to what brings her to the cliff. The entire sequence—not to mention the subsequent Klan trial—depends upon the idea that Gus is trying to attack her and that she jumps to save herself from rape. That the pursuer has rape in mind is the vital point that all three Dixon sources have in common.[6]

Yet in *The Birth of a Nation* Flora's pursuer is curiously restrained; Gus keeps insisting he merely wants to talk with her. Even his talk of marriage is oddly indirect. Several commentators have noticed that Flora, trained by her brother to be wary of blacks, may be overreacting hysterically. There is no ev-

---

6. A parenthetical note about those sources: Dixon invented the episode in 1902 for his first Reconstruction novel, *The Leopard's Spots*. There Flora is a minor character, the daughter of an embittered one-armed Civil War vet. She is raped and her skull crushed by a black when she goes to a spring for water. She doesn't run, and she doesn't jump from a cliff. Back home doctors vainly try to save her, and the black man who raped her—a childhood friend of the hero—is burned alive.

In Dixon's novel *The Clansman*, there is no Flora. Her part is taken by a woman named Marion Lenoir to whom Ben Cameron was once engaged. Gus invades her house with a scalawag patrol and rapes her; the victim and her mother, feeling themselves defiled, jump off a cliff after the rapists leave.

It is in the Dixon play, also called *The Clansman* and adapted from the novel in 1905, that Flora is turned into Ben Cameron's sister, goes to the woodland spring to feed a squirrel, and jumps from the cliff to escape Gus. All this is recounted by Gus at a Klan trial, where he is made to confess under the hypnotic stare of Ben's father. Gus is then taken off-stage and hanged from a balcony of the state capitol.

 idence from what Gus says or does that he wants in any way to harm Flora. This is what James Baldwin and Paul Goodman had in mind when they wisecracked that *The Birth of a Nation* was actually a civil rights movie, subtly exposing how the Ku Klux Klan kills innocent blackfaces.[7]

As actor Walter Long plays him, Gus starts with hesitant half steps; he is fearful of being seen and tentative in his furtive stares at Flora. In contrast to the broad, grandiose gestures customarily attached to Griffith villains, Long's Gus is built on intimate microgestures that until now Griffith had reserved for sympathetic figures. Gus begins in a crouched position, slowly trailing Flora from behind a picket fence, alternately looking at her and pretending to inspect a twig he holds in his hand (811). At another fence he looks off-screen to watch where Flora is going, starts to move after her, hesitates, and then moves in the opposite direction (815, 817). Nothing could be further from George Siegmann's Silas Lynch, who when left alone is forever grimacing, clenching his fists, or attacking some mute object—shaking a dog by its ears or smashing a vase on the floor. Gus is not even sure he wants to start after Flora.

When Gus finally does approach her, it is as a trembling suitor who nervously tips his cap, tries to keep his hand from shivering, and, with a gulp, tentatively puts his hand on Flora's arm. Flora slaps him, makes a run for it, and the foot race is on. But even as a villain in pursuit, Gus oscillates between gestures of pleading (one arm outstretched as though hailing a taxi) and cautious stalking. In this segment Flora gets all the close-ups; with a single exception Gus is kept entirely in long shot or in the background of the shots Flora dominates. The exception comes at the climax of the scene, when Gus moves into the camera and Flora makes good her threat to jump. But if Flora's terror is vividly communicated with flailing gestures and screams, Gus's behavior is so underplayed as to verge on inscrutability.

In short, the scene is structured to include the possibility of a tragic misunderstanding. Even Gus's dramatic reaction to Flora's jump—legs astride, arms stretched over his head, his head flung back—is an image fraught with horrible ambiguity, especially since it is taken in extreme long shot (902). Is Gus expressing animallike rage at having missed his prey or is this a gesture of fear turned to despair? To permit such alternative readings makes nonsense of the rest of the film, and Griffith never sustains such tantalizing resonances for long (within minutes Gus the brute is cowering in a gin mill and then shoots an unarmed white man). But it suggests how Griffith is constantly tearing the fabric of his narrative with provocative nuances that sug-

7. Paul Goodman, letter, *New York Times*, 28 Feb. 1965, sec. 6: 40.

gest possibilities the director only dimly perceives and is unwilling or unable to pursue.

Even the way Griffith introduces us to Gus calls into question what Griffith has in mind. When do we first meet Gus? His naming and formal introduction come in an intertitle just before he prowls behind Elsie and Flora out for a stroll. The language teeters between naming Gus aggressor and victim: "Gus, the renegade, a product of the vicious doctrines spread by the carpetbaggers" (Title, 716).

But in fact he is already a vaguely familiar face, one of Silas Lynch's anonymous, brutal minions who figures prominently in assorted anti-Reconstruction vignettes. He is almost always in the background, easy to miss but actively participating in most of the expositional scenes that illustrate the cruelty of the carpetbagger's regime. Linked together, his pretitle appearances even form a crude mini-narrative of sorts, the story of a nameless bully apprentice first seen helping Lynch with his luggage at his new offices (552ff.) who then wins his spurs pushing whites around and finally winds up supervising the Union League's corrupt giveaway food program (562, 604). In one shot he shoves a father and his children into the street after they have lost their home (670). In the next he chivvies a crippled old man who has trouble keeping up with his own dispossessed children (671). When an elderly black man tries to protect the Camerons' "faithful soul" from a flogging, Gus is the soldier who guns him down (679). Later he helps out in bushwhacking a party of Klansmen (769ff.).

Again, this is a provocative way to introduce a would-be rapist: the director teases us with details unnecessary to the encounter between Gus and Flora—details doled out as rewards to the attentive spectator, but details that

Figure 12-13. Gus as underplayed by Walter Long (shot 811). (Library of Congress.)

Figure 12-14. Gus pleads with Flora in long shot. (Library of Congress.)

also subvert our first official picture of Gus as a friendless idler with too much time on his hands.

The details we have just listed are comprehended by the on-screen characters as well as alert viewers, as seen in the Klan's disposition of Gus's corpse. In dumping his body on Lynch's front porch the Klan fuses Gus's role as a brutal Reconstruction enforcer with that of Flora's attacker. The Klan's

Figure 12-15. Flora gesticulates wildly. (Library of Congress.)

Figure 12-16. Gus at his most inscrutable. (Library of Congress.)

flamboyant disposal of a well-known thug who even before chasing Flora had brazenly killed and assaulted citizens in public is plainly meant as a warning to other henchmen in Lynch's organization. The tantalizing details we discover in those vignettes are no news to Piedmont's citizenry. In discovering them we are only learning what seems to be public knowledge among the characters in the fiction.

Figure 12-17. Gus as Reconstruction enforcer (shot 671). (Library of Congress.)

But what makes Griffith's control over these details problematic is what he reveals about Gus in the first half of his film. Griffith includes Gus in two earlier vignettes that give the audience a privileged perspective on Gus that is evocative, unshared by the fictional characters, and as radical a break with Griffith's formulations of villainy as the director ever created. Gus first appears as the happy slave in the background who leads the clapping while two men dance for Ben Cameron and his guests (78ff.). But more suggestive is his second appearance: he is the slave who watches helplessly as black guerrillas burn down a house—presumably owned by Gus's master (214). A mother and two children run out to Gus; the father materializes and is shot down by a black guerrilla on the front porch. The incident passes in seconds. We cannot even be certain that Griffith intended Walter Long in blackface to represent Gus this time; Griffith cast actors in multiple minor roles throughout

Figure 12-18. Gus as the happy slave, leading the clapping (between two black dancers whose backs are to the camera). (Library of Congress.)

Figure 12-19. Gus as the faithful slave, with the mother and daughters of his master, during the guerrilla raid (shot 214). (Library of Congress.)

the picture. At most the scene functions as a kind of Freudian slip, giving us a sympathetic glimpse of a character who becomes a hardened thug. Nowhere else has Griffith given his villains such histories or made them so mysterious. It would be absurd to claim that these nuances add up to a fully rounded character; for the melodrama to work we must believe in the harsh justice that the Klan metes out. But it is important to see that when we are made uncomfortable by the Klan's lynch law we are not simply reacting against the crudity of Griffith's text. The text itself bristles with discordant elements, overtones out of control, that fight the dominant themes. Peter Lehman has examined the problem of textual coherence in his analysis of John Ford's *The Searchers*, and what he finds true of Ford can be applied usefully here. Far from always indicating aesthetic failure, incongruity may also point to a kind of daring (1981, 69).

The sequence we have been analyzing had a reputation long before Griffith filmed it. The rape or attempted rape by a black freedman of an innocent white teen-age girl was something of a set piece in Dixon's Reconstruction stories. Its dramatization on the stage became the focus of protests that met *The Clansman* when it toured in 1905, and nothing better illustrates Griffith's disingenuousness in claiming that he did not mean to offend "any race or people" with *The Birth of a Nation* than his decision to include it. Dixon had been offending blacks on and off for ten years with a variation of this scene, provoking occasional demonstrations and riots.[8] The scene was Dixon's equivalent to the chariot race in *Ben-Hur* or the slavers' pursuit of Eliza on the ice in *Uncle Tom's Cabin*.

Yet Griffith's decision to choose a rape story for his first epic remains haunting. Oddly, it has generally been overlooked in representational histories of rape; it is a curious oversight. In a provocative essay on rape and the rise of the psychological novel, Frances Ferguson argues that the centrality of rape in the birth of the novel was hardly fortuitous (1987). Rape, she argues, is the crime par excellence that requires investigation of the mental states of both the accused and the victim. The crime, she argues, becomes differentiated from the noncriminal act of seduction only on the level of frame of mind.

What interests Ferguson in the rape of Richardson's heroine in *Clarissa* is the importance Richardson attaches to psychology in delineating the struggles both Clarissa and Lovelace go through in interpreting the ambiguities of a traumatic event. In a particularly suggestive passage Ferguson juxtaposes

8. For reactions to Dixon's play see: Durant Da Ponte (1957, 17–22); Dixon (1984, 287–89); *New York Times*, 9 Jan. 1906, 9; 4 Feb. 1906, 1; 24 Oct. 1906, 9.

 three famous tales of rape to mark a progressive history of symbolic representation. Ferguson is struck by how each of the three rape stories—the Bible story of the Levite of Ephraim, Ovid's tale of Philomela, and Richardson's novel—generates new modes of representation, each one more abstract than the previous, each creating greater ambiguity of signs.

At first glance Griffith's version appears a direct throwback to Old Testament efficiency. Violation precedes execution, which in turn leads to mass extermination. In the Bible story the Levite tells the tribes of Israel the story of his wife's rape by sending out her hacked-up body. Ferguson quotes Rousseau's summary:

> When the Levite of Ephraim wanted to avenge the death of his wife, he wrote nothing to the tribes of Israel, but divided her body into twelve sections which he sent to them. At this horrible sight they rushed to arms, crying with one voice: *never has such a thing happened in Israel* . . . ! And the tribe of Benjamin was exterminated. (108)

Griffith's tale retains a similar revenge formula, outrage begetting outrage, the Klan's retaliation gauged as imprecisely and as broadly as the Israelites'. What psychological nuances intrude from the later psychological model provided by Richardson and the eighteenth-century novel only interfere with the logic of Griffith's narrative. It is as though the ambiguities trailing Gus were pesky mosquitoes flying in the face of the narrative, easily brushed away or squashed. The events in the woods are melded with Gus's earlier crimes to make the need for his elimination a foregone conclusion and to generate an all-encompassing attack on Gus's tribal conspirators. Even the methods of communicating and recalling Flora's death have a primitive, ritualistic ring, depending less on words than on the display of Flora's body, bloodstained flags, fiery crosses, and discarded garments. If Ferguson's straight-lined progressive history culminates in a rape story foregrounding ambiguity and depictions of wavering mental states, Griffith's twentieth-century tale introduces an arc in which psychological ambiguity is invoked only to be frantically repressed.

What is heightened by the new medium, however, is the sense of taboo. If the arrivals of the photograph and the motion picture camera represent advances in standards of *vraisemblance* and pictorial realism, a rape story provides a particular challenge: how to depict the taboo graphically. In later silent films, notably Maurice Tourneur's *The Last of the Mohicans* and Victor Seastrom's *The Wind*, the problem is settled with straightforward symbolic devices: a wild, bucking horse; shadows on a wall. Here, however, optical illusions pile upon optical illusions. It is all play, of course, but the play here displaces one taboo after another; the entire scene is so heavily encoded that the sequence can stipulate its own opposite. A white actor pretends to be a black man pretending to want only to talk with an actress who pretends to be a frightened girl who is so young and innocent she may or may not know what he really wants or doesn't want. Flora is tracked down by a brother who has seen nothing but will recount the entire event. Before he is captured, the black/white man kills a white man, just as earlier he has killed a black/white man; these crimes are ignored, but he is justly tried and executed, we are told, for a crime—a rape—we have seen he did not commit. From first to last the scene works to put a veil over the events it purports to bring out in the open.

By the time he shot it, Griffith had become a master of directing and deflecting would-be assaults on women. Usually the displacement took the form of a Prize of Great Worth—a pearl necklace worn on the neck, a baby clutched to the chest, or a letter held in the hand—that enabled the villain to touch and struggle with the woman without actually stipulating a rape attempt. In *A Girl and Her Trust* Griffith gives Dorothy Bernard a Wells-Fargo chest to protect, which as the drama is worked out becomes inseparable from the woman herself as an object of attack. In *The Birth of a Nation* Silas Lynch's pursuit of Elsie Stoneman resembles the classic configuration: a chase around a room is fraught with sexual overtones (he is attempting a forced marriage), but the pursuit, presented as a rape attempt, is in fact an effort to restrain Elsie until the minister comes.

Gus's pursuit of Flora, however, is a far more complex representation. We have moved from a world—represented in Richardson's *Clarissa*—in which principal characters constantly fluctuate in their mental states trying to come to terms with a rape, to a world in which the artist himself is in a state of frenetic fluctuation.

WORKS CITED

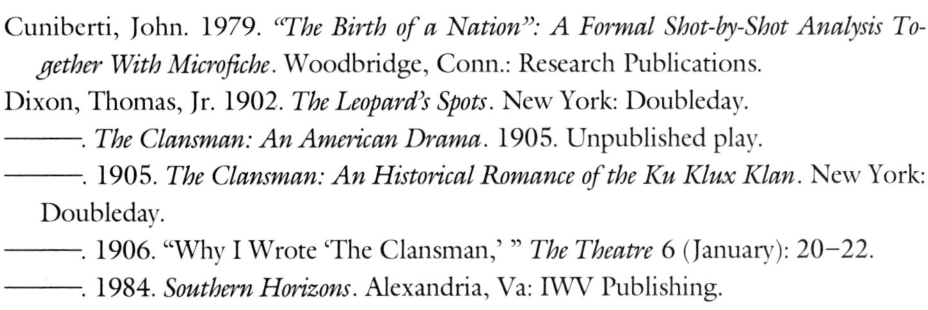

Cuniberti, John. 1979. *"The Birth of a Nation": A Formal Shot-by-Shot Analysis Together With Microfiche*. Woodbridge, Conn.: Research Publications.

Dixon, Thomas, Jr. 1902. *The Leopard's Spots*. New York: Doubleday.

———. *The Clansman: An American Drama*. 1905. Unpublished play.

———. 1905. *The Clansman: An Historical Romance of the Ku Klux Klan*. New York: Doubleday.

———. 1906. "Why I Wrote 'The Clansman,' " *The Theatre* 6 (January): 20–22.

———. 1984. *Southern Horizons*. Alexandria, Va: IWV Publishing.

THE BIRTH OF A NATION

Da Ponte, Durant. 1957. " 'The Greatest Play of the South.' " *Tennessee Studies in Literature* 2: 15–24.

Ferguson, Frances. 1987. "Rape and the Rise of the Novel." *Representations* 20 (Fall): 88–112.

Franklin, John Hope. 1979. " 'Birth of a Nation'—Propaganda as History." *The Massachusetts Review* 20 (Autumn): 417–34.

Lehman, Peter. 1981. "Looking at Look's Missing Reverse Shot: Psychoanalysis and Style in John Ford's *The Searchers*." *Wide Angle* 4: 65–70.

Leyda, Jay. 1949. "The Art and Death of D.W. Griffith." *The Sewanee Review* 57: 350–56.

Merritt, Russell. 1972. "Dixon, Griffith, and the Southern Legend," *Cinema Journal* 12 (Fall): 26–45; reprinted in *Cinema Examined*, edited by Richard Dyer MacCann, 165–61. New York: Dover, 1982.

———. 1979. "Mr. Griffith, *The Painted Lady*, and the Distractive Frame." In *"Image" on the Art and Evolution of the Film*, edited by Marshall Deutelbaum, 147–52. New York: Dover.

Rogin, Michael. 1985. " 'The Sword Became a Flashing Vision': D.W. Griffith's *The Birth of a Nation*." *Representations* 9 (Winter): 150–95.

BIBLIOGRAPHY

The Birth of a Nation

Barry, Iris. *D.W. Griffith: American Film Master*. Revised by Eileen Bowser. New York: Simon, 1965.

Brown, Karl. *Adventures with D.W. Griffith*. 2d ed. New York: Da Capo, 1976.

Cripps, Thomas. "The Reaction of the Negro to the Motion Picture *Birth of a Nation*." *The Historian* 25 (May 1963): 344–62.

Dixon, Thomas, Jr. "The Story of the Ku Klux Klan." *The Metropolitan Magazine* 22 (September 1905): 657–69.

Fleener, Nickie. "Answering Film with Film: The Hampton Epilogue, a Positive Alternative to the Negative Black Stereotypes Presented in *The Birth of a Nation*." *Journal of Popular Film* 7 (1980) 400–425.

Fleener-Marzec, Nickiann. "D.W. Griffith's *The Birth of a Nation*: Controversy, Suppression, and the First Amendment as It Applies to Filmic Expression, 1915–1973." Ph.D. diss., University of Wisconsin, Madison, 1977.

Neale, Steve. "The Same Old Story: Stereotypes and Difference." *Screen Education* 32–33 (1979–80): 33–37.

Oms, Marcel. "*Naissance d'une nation*, oeuvre maconnique." *Les Cahiers de la Cinémathèque* 17 (Christmas 1975): 99–106.

Schickel, Richard. *D.W. Griffith: An American Life*. New York: Simon and Schuster, 1984.

Simcovitch, Maxim. "The Impact of Griffith's *Birth of a Nation* on the Modern Ku Klux Klan." *Journal of Popular Film*: 45–54.

Sorlin, Pierre. "*La naissance d'une nation* ou la reconstruction de la famille." *L'Avant-Scene* (October 1977): 4–13.

White, Mimi. "*The Birth of a Nation*: History as Pretext." *Enclitic* 1/2 (1981–82): 17–24.

Racial Criticism

Baldwin, James. *The Devil Finds Work*. New York: Dial, 1976.

Bogle, Donald. " 'B' . . . for Black." *Film Comment* 21 (September/October 1985): 28–38.

———. *Coons, Mulattos, Mammies, and Bucks*. New York: Viking, 1973.

Cripps, Thomas. *Black Film As Genre*. Bloomington: Indiana University Press, 1978.

———. *Slow Fade to Black*. New York: Oxford University Press, 1977.

Gabriel, Teshoma H. *Images of Black People in the Cinema*. Los Angeles: African Activist Assn., 1976.

Hyatt, Marshall. *The Afro-American Cinematic Experience: An Annotated Bibliography and Filmography*. Wilmington: Scholarly Resources Inc., 1983.

Klotman, Phyllis Rauch. *Frame By Frame: A Black Filmography*. Bloomington: Indiana University Press, 1979.

Leab, Daniel. *From Sambo to Superspade*. Boston: Houghton-Mifflin, 1975.

Leff, Leonard J. "David Selznick's *Gone With the Wind*: 'The Negro Problem.' " *Georgia Review* 38 (1984): 146–64.

Murray, James P. *To Find an Image: Black Films From Uncle Tom to Superfly*. Indianapolis: Bobbs-Merrill, 1973.

Powers, Anne. *Blacks in American Movies: A Selected Bibliography*. Metuchen: Scarecrow, 1974.

Revue du Cinema 363 (July/August 1981). Special issue on blacks in American film.

Sampson, Henry T. *Blacks in Black and White*. Metuchen: Scarecrow, 1977.

Seward, Adrienne Lanier. *Early Black Film and Folk Tradition*. San Diego, 1985.

Stam, Robert, and Louise Spence. "Colonialism, Racism, and Representation." *Screen* 24 (March/April 1983): 2–20.

White, Armond. "Telling It on the Mountain." *Film Comment* 21 (September/October 1985): 39–46.

William Reese Co. *Blacks and Film, 1894–Present: Popular Culture as Socio/Ideological Barometer*. New Haven: William Reese Co., 1985. Catalog of publicity materials relating to black film.

Yearwood, Gladstone. *Black Cinema Aesthetics: Issues in Independent Black Filmmaking*. Athens, Ohio: Center for Afro-American Studies, 1982.

———. "The Hero in Black Film." *Wide Angle* 5, no. 2 (1983): 42–50.

13

SWEET SWEETBACK'S BAADASSSSS SONG AND THE CHANGING POLITICS OF GENRE FILM

Thomas Cripps

Sweet Sweetback's Baadasssss Song (1971) helped introduce black (and to a lesser extent, white) youth to a fresh genre of film that transformed urban moviegoing from a passive toleration of Sidney Poitier's bland movies into a rousing, black, politico-religious experience. In contrast to the upstanding, prim, overtrained characters played by Poitier, Sweetback set forth new outlines of heroic behavior. He killed remorselessly; swaggered; lived off black allies in a squalid, neon-lit streetscape; wore the cool mask behind which black youngsters carried their private selves; performed feats of sexual athleticism; walked with the loose gait affected by armies of black youths as though they walked to a backbeat audible only to themselves; and wore clothes in a stylish mode that seemed insultingly casual. Indeed so insouciant was Sweetback's style that its ensemble of behaviors might be called an *aesthétique du cool*—a style meant to convey a black politics (Cripps 1978a, 10; Robert Thompson, 12–16).

*The author is grateful for a residency at the Rockefeller Foundation Study Center in the Villa Serbelloni, Lake Como, Italy, during which a draft of this essay was written.

In order to heft the political weight of *Sweetback* and gauge its effect on blacks of the 1970s we must first pause to sketch a working definition of *genre* and to set apart from the general case a specifically black genre. Otherwise *Sweetback* at a glance may seem no more than one more bloody exploitation film. The idea of genres, or categories, of films such as westerns and musicals grew out of the historical evolution of the American system of highly commercial studios whose search for profits led them to minimize risk by producing only movies grounded in familiar forms, characters, and stories. This yearning for a proven, dependable product led to the creation of a number of forms and conventions that were reinvented in each new movie of the genre. In this way studios and their audiences negotiated in a cumulative process in which viewers' expectations were bargained against the moviemakers' tastes and the constraints imposed by budgets and sales departments.

In the case of the western genre, for example, over many years and many films a distinct cluster of qualities grew into the conventions that defined the genre and set it apart from other movies. Those conventions included a *community* of social types—sidekicks, marshals, deputies, gandydancers, schoolmarms—acting in a familiar network; an *iconography* of material goods such as white hats for heroes, black for heavies; *casting* decisions that included regularly appearing heroes such as John Wayne and stock players such as Dub Taylor or Olive Cooper; *an arena of conflict* defined by the West itself and its vastness and the paradoxically tight social circles of its towns with the resulting tensions between the clashing codes of civilization and wilderness. All of these conventions were set in imaginative dramatic conflicts that were resolved in the last reel (Pye 1986, 145–46; Lenihan 1980, 12–13).

But there is more at stake than whether or not the audience is pleased. Not only do viewers have an emotional and financial investment in the outcome of the movie—did they like it enough to warrant the ten dollars spent for tickets—but they also derive a politics from their movies. The completed picture, said Herbert Gans, is a negotiated synthesis that becomes, as Peggy Harper has written of tribal art, "not mere entertainment" but "a significant part of the cohesion of its peoples" (Harper 1967, 10; Gans 1974, 69–75). This view of the social function of movies is, of course, a conservative one that reaches beyond forming a mere taste-culture to the forming of an ideology in which the politics of movies, as T. W. Adorno has put it, "are always those of the status quo" (quoted in Hess 1974, 16).

Clearly for black Americans movie politics were inadequate to the political task at hand, particularly after the rising tide of the civil rights movement in the 1960s. Before World War II, black efforts on behalf of the group were limited to "race movies," which by their segregated nature in creating a world of black cops, crooks, and judges, with no sign of the whites who held them in thrall, were implicated in the racial status quo. The war itself, however, brought with it a propaganda of, in the words of various slogans, "unity, tolerance, and brotherhood," which led to an anticipation of the postwar civil rights movement. In keeping with the wartime spirit the government appeared to promise a postwar improvement in black status while Hollywood took up a cycle of "message movies" whose box office success suggested that Americans were ready to accept such a liberalization of their racial arrangements. This is where Poitier's career came in: his first movies such as *No Way Out* (1950) were in the van of this political cinema, but over almost a quarter of a century his work itself became a sort of status quo that presented no new thickets of racial politics to be sorted out. As late as the breakup of the national phase of the civil rights movement following the death of Martin Luther King in 1968, Poitier's image dominated the screen, leaving scant room for a more aggressive black cinema politics.

At this crucial moment in the late 1960s the political agenda of American race relations fell into the hands of "the brother on the block," the enraged, vandalistic, violent young people who appeared on the nation's television screens night after night, sweeping through the streets of Watts, Detroit, and even in the shadow of the Capitol in Washington, looting, challenging the police, and effectively repudiating the pacifist tactics of Martin Luther King. TV documentaries like *A Time for Burning* and *Still a Brother* confirmed and elaborated the news stories of truculence and a new black nationalism rooted in the headiness of standing up to the cops (Cripps 1975; Jersey 1988).

Embedded in this visible, televised actuality was a new black formula waiting to be teased out by a black filmmaker with the vision to discern a new black politics of the screen to replace the accommodationism of Poitier's era. Melvin Van Peebles filled the role with a flair that gave a political dimension to the sometimes politically drifting genre of black films. Moreover, he did so with a penchant for self-advertisement that contributed to the accelerated formulation of the genre by grafting onto it fragments of his own outlaw legend that once gained him access to the studio. In other words, as Hitchcock and Ford over a period of years had entwined their movies and their personal legends into an inseparable image that sharpened the genre and whetted audiences' appetites for each new twist on it, so Van Peebles used his legend to introduce the black genre to the screen full-blown.

Van Peebles penetrated a Hollywood establishment that had been grudgingly opening, motivated partly by a liberal temper and partly by pressure from federal agencies such as the Equal Employment Opportunity Commission. He brought with him an autobiographical legend that paralleled the many "bad nigger" stories of black urban lore. His movies, particularly *Sweetback*, were then portrayed as merely predictable extensions of an actual life. Up to that point, other than the virtuous celibates portrayed by Poitier (who won an Oscar for his role in *Lilies of the Field* [1963]), there had been no black movie hero—except perhaps Stepin Fetchit, an old clown who had been a sort of ironic hero, less heroic than both the white men around him and their world but nonetheless surviving in it as his own version of Joel Chandler Harris's Br'er Rabbit, who was descended from various folkloric African tricksters. Van Peebles's hero, on the other hand, would inspire a decade's worth of black Byronic heroes—injured by (white) life but not fatally, capable of using his *aesthétique du cool* to glide through any crisis, facile in the jive idiom of black urban expression, rooted in a black brotherhood of fellow victims whose community the movie celebrates and provides an anatomy of, and colored by a rhetoric of advocacy of an abrasive black nationalism. But for the unexpected take-off of a Hollywood epigone called *Superfly*, Van Peebles and his *Sweetback* might have given *their* names to the entire era of black exploitation movies that soon constituted the only fresh movie genre to come along in the last quarter of a century (Cripps, 1978, 128–40).

Van Peebles's audience stood poised to embrace some particularly angry black hero whose crudeness promised that he would *not* be "the credit to his race" that every black hero since World War II had been expected to be. Somehow for this generation of black youngsters the old images no longer worked. Those images were developed in 1942, when Walter White of the National Association for the Advancement of Colored People (NAACP) held his group's first wartime convention in Los Angeles with the specific intention of affecting black movie images at their source and William Nunn of the *Pittsburgh Courier* began advocating to his black readers a "Double V" for a dual victory over foreign fascism *and* domestic racism. During the war both Hollywood and the Office of War Information joined in retailing a new black image that reflected this propaganda of national unity across racial lines: the studios with *Sahara, Crash Dive, Bataan, Lifeboat*, and others; the government with its own *The Negro Soldier, Wings for This Man, Henry Browne, Farmer*, and others. Following the war the paragons who had peopled these movies turned up in a cycle of "message movies"—*Pinky, No Way Out, Lost Boundaries*, and others—as chaste, upright, and ultimately "square" Negroes (Cripps 1978b; Cripps and Culbert 1979). Poitier's era embellished them, gave them new spins; but mainly it codified them into a genre of his own which, as the civil rights movement intensified, provided ever less sustenance to young, street-tested activists.

Moreover, American social geography had changed in ways that helped shape a new, young black audience that testily awaited meatier fare. Young moviegoers had always been noticeable by their conduct, and with respect to black movies they seemed more so. Ranging from the message movie era when theatermen reported their touchiness, quickness to take offense, and proneness to fight for a sort of tribal ethnicity ("Negro Teenagers Rampage" ran a *Variety* headline, [1 January 1969, 1]), through the 1950s cycle of teen-angled sagas of beach and dragstrip, to 1960 when bookers noticed an "underground" black market for Elvis Presley's *Flaming Star* (1960) with its Indian/white struggle for the loyalty of Pacer (Presley)—a *mischling* who belonged to neither tribe (Richard Thompson 1975, 207)—to the end of the decade, not only had their tastes sharpened, but black youths in Lyndon Johnson's "Great Society" also had money in their pockets and had moved into urban neighborhoods that had once been home to white people who had been served by all but disused downtown movie palaces. Their parents stood poised to dominate urban politics, counted themselves as of a "sizeable middle class" (*Monthly Labor Bulletin* [May-June 1965]: 502), and decided not to follow whites into the do-it-yourself and crab-grass frontiers. This meant that blacks had proportionally more income to spend on the immediate gratifications of entertainments such as movies. Thus an era that had begun, as *Variety* (15 December 1954, 26) reported, as a "classy suburbs vs. 'Rundown' Rialto" segmented market, ended with the studios holding "special previews" in the Harlems of America and fishing for material to serve the "Negro clientele [that] is now an important factor in box office performances" (*Variety*, 16 May 1962, 70). Reinforcing this drift were Herbert Hill, the aggressive labor secretary of the NAACP, and federal agencies that sought to alter Hollywood hiring practices and open the studio guilds at every level to black personnel.

Not that moviemen leapt to feed this rising market. Mostly they wanted no part of "problem pictures" except for the odd, self-consciously "bold" picture such as Harry Belafonte's *The World, the Flesh and the Devil* (1959), and even then they pulled back, leading reviewers to complain of a movie that "bites off more than it wants to chew" (*Time*, 3 June 1959, 60). Even when they bit into a meaty project, such as Howard Sackler's biopic of the black boxer Jack Johnson, the still active Production Code Administration—the "Breen Office"—balked at certain aspects of black life, obliging, for example, Twentieth-Century Fox to settle for "mothergrabber" as a substitute for the timeworn black portmanteau word, "motherfucker" (Lawrence Turman correspondence, *Great White Hope* file, Twentieth-Century Fox Archive, UCLA).

Into this empty arena stepped Van Peebles, complete with a backstory of a life spent on the rimlands of society, a *demimonde* "bio" that he used as a substitute for the years of filmmaking that he might have used to evolve a genre of black outlaw film. In press releases, negotiations, working lunches, and public appearances, the story, give or take an adornment or so, unfolded and grew like a weed into the legend of a bad dude who scored in Hollywood, and in the process it anticipated *Sweetback* and teased its audience with hints of the black outlaw on his way to their neighborhood. Variously his legend included stints as an "honors" graduate in literature from Ohio Wesleyan, an Air Force navigator, a cablecar gripman in San Francisco (from which experience he milked a book), a sixteen millimeter *cinéaste* who financed his short films by selling his car, a Hollywood reject who had been offered a post as elevatorman, a novelist unpublished because he did not write "enough like a Negro," a graduate student in astronomy in Amsterdam, an actor in a Dutch production of *The Hostage*, a busker on the streets of Paris (where he cultivated the Cinémathèque Française, which had taken an interest in his shorts), a translator of his own novel, *A Bear for the FBI*, into French, an author of two more novels written in French (which earned him a union card and thus a shot at filmmaking), and finally director of *The Story of a Three Day Pass*, a little movie shot in six days on a $200,000 "nut," which earned him a place in the San Francisco Film Festival as the "French" delegate. Larding the basic legend were stories that certified Van Peebles's impulsiveness, coolness in the face of risk, glibness in jiving his way through gatekeepers, and ambivalently dangerous rascality. Variously, he affected "the casual dress and inarticulate speech of the man in the ghetto street"; turned out an opera, a ballet, and a humor magazine; and lived off "being mean" and the favors of "obliging ladies" and by playing the "street blood 'gone bad' " (Gussow 1972).

Few people saw his movies; it was the legend that would shape the genre that *Sweetback* eventually defined. The first two were pale, over-exposed one-reelers, vignettes, actually, of black life—one about a desperate man who goes to jail for a petty crime motivated by his daughter's expensive wedding; the other a tense moment as black men stand as in a slave auction while a white contractor selects a likely worker. Together with *The Story of a Three Day Pass* they were merely the surviving evidence of the credibility of the legend. As he told a TV interviewer (WMPB-TV [Baltimore], 12 December 1971), *Three Day Pass* was important as a form of "blackology"—accomplishing his goals by flattering the French and thereby cadging an invitation

Figure 13-1. Many *Sweetback* advertisements reinforced the legend of Van Peebles as a frame of reference for the film. Images of black victims are dominated by Van Peebles's own impassively cool visage, which promises that "you won't bleed me"—all of it rendered blackly authentic by the arch imprimatur at the bottom of the ad. (Courtesy of Melvin Van Peebles, YEAH, Inc.)

to San Francisco. Not that the films contributed nothing to the genre. *Sweetback*'s outlawry is foreshadowed in the first of the shorts, *Sunlight*, when in the last moments the convict reappears as an outsider looking in on his daughter's wedding; and in *Three Pickup Men for Herrick* the unchosen walk off, baffled by their inability to crack the world of work. In *Three Day Pass* Van Peebles hazes and parodies the "good Negro" by contrasting his tight little presentation-self with his fantasies of sexual conquest dreamt of as though he were a torero donning his suit-of-lights before entering the arena (Peavy 1973). And in his one American film, *Watermelon Man*, he converted his hero (Godfrey Cambridge) from a loudmouthed white bigot into an armed, black, militant rebel.

Here the attentive observer could almost catch the outlines of the emerging angry black genre. As early as the summer of 1969, *Variety* (24 September) reported that *Watermelon Man* had been rebudgeted to include an uncommonly large number of minority apprentices, an accomplishment Van Peebles would credit to his skill at gulling moguls. Thereafter he fought both Columbia and his writer, Herman Raucher, into tolerating political changes and then took exaggerated credit as "the first one to attack the citadel itself." By then he had narrowed his rhetoric to "man," "groovy," and "dig," and affected a permanent costume of jeans, boots, and unlighted cigarillo. "I mean, I'm good," he told an interviewer. "Fuck, what I got to be grateful for?" (Welch 1970). By the summer of 1970, *Variety* (3 June) pieced together the stories and began to see "a dubious commercial trend" marked by R-ratings and black scatology that pointed toward "narrowing the potential audience" at a time when the studios had begun to suffer a terrible slump. The legend and the movies had become one, and the black outlaw genre was conceived and began to slouch toward Hollywood to be born. If only Van Peebles could get it right the first time, trading on his outlaw legend for the richness of a detailed anatomy of a black underworld capable of simultaneously entertaining and politicizing a young black audience primed by years of viewing urban violence on TV.[1]

1. On various aspects of the gradual embroidery of the Van Peebles personal legend, see Peavy (1973), for his early movies; Judy Stone, "An American Who Went to Paris," *New York Times*, 12 Nov. 1967, on Van Peebles's adventures ranging from his obliging women to writing operas; Brock Garland, "Interview: Melvin Van Peebles," *Players* (October 1982): 14ff., on his composing for a ballet and working on a "Ph.D." in astronomy in the Netherlands; Rick Setlowe, undated clipping titled "Saga of Negro Director," comparing San Francisco cablecar gripmen (one of Van Peebles's jobs) to "the gondoliers of Venice" and recounting a story of seeking Hol-

Already the studios had released a string of bloody streetscape melodramas, most of them exploiting rather than addressing the yearning of their audiences, limiting themselves to a politics of lone wolf revanchism rather than of a community-based black social cohesiveness and portraying racism as no more than the greed of a few witless, corrupt, almost slobbering white criminals whose empires and fortunes are so quickly smashed and their women so handily bedded by the black hero that the audiences must have marveled at the ease with which white people could be toppled.

It remained for Van Peebles to codify the discrete elements of his legend into a genre, stiffen it with a spine of political advocacy, set it in a reportorially credible black community, and center its theme in a black hero capable of dramatizing the racial issues at stake. At the center of the frame would be Sweetback himself, an amalgam of all the supercool "bad niggers" whose stories had been endlessly recounted on streetcorners and around the fires of hobo jungles or had crept into the tales of Staggerlee, the sexual outlaw of black urban folklore, or even of Br'er Rabbit, the African trickster to whom Van Peebles likened himself. Unlike the heroes of other nations—El Cid or King Arthur or King Chaka of the Zulus—Sweetback was not to be a man on horseback but a picaresque hero, a rogue, perhaps a little like the *bravos* in Alessandro Manzoni's novel of seventeenth-century Milan, *I Promessi Sposi* (1827), who are indeed rogues but more than mere highwaymen in that they are armed and their rascality is in the service of their liege, church, or other polity; that is, it is more like Jesse James's or Belle Starr's legendary outlawry

lywood employment only to be offered an elevatorman's job; *Variety*, 5 June 1968, 3, 17, on the possibility of his making *two* French films as a result of his output of French language novels rising to four; *Variety*, 11 Dec. 1968, 22, recording his interest in a humor magazine, a possible movie called *Harlem Party* to be made from a play he had produced in Belgium, and his ballet; Mel Gussow, "The Baadasssss Success of Melvin Van Peebles," *New York Times*, 20 Aug. 1972, reported a French version of a story of his neck tattoo, "Couper sur la ligne," and another moment in which he dropped his pants to show yet another tattoo—in Bambara—as well as other stories of "selling second-hand clothes to winos" and of drifting to Mexico to "paint" after a particularly "bratty" adolescence; William A. Raidy, *Sunday Star-Ledger* (Newark), 7 Nov. 1971, who updates the story by including his living out of a suitcase with no fixed address, along with his heightening sense of linkages to "grass roots," "black survival," and "black pride"; *Time*, 99 (16 Aug. 1971): 47, adds variations on his Hollywood experiences such as parking cars, along with an account of an invitation by Henri Langlois of the Cinémathèque Française to visit France, where his flair for street entertainment broadened to include playing the kazoo and panhandling, his French novels rose in number to five—resulting in his earning a di-

directed against greedy railroads or political enemies. Sweetback, then, was to be more than merely a touchy bad dude. He began in Van Peebles's scripts as an apolitical sexual athlete but gradually evolved into a picaroon on the run whose adventures lead him toward a political future.

Moreover, even as he worked on the movie Van Peebles kept his legend and that of Sweetback linked in the public eye, as though to prepare the audience for its eventual familiarity with the black film genre—that is, to accomplish with one film the rich detailing of recognizable casting, typing, mood, setting, and action that white genre makers had taken years to cultivate into their characteristic style. Ford and Hitchcock took decades to mold a specifically Ford or Hitchcock genre; Van Peebles's was to be defined in a single stroke derived from his own public persona. Alluding to his debate with Jack Valenti over *Sweetback*'s initial X-rating, for example, his advertising proclaimed that *Sweetback* had been "rated X by an all-white jury" (Van Peebles 1971, 1–7; *Variety*, 31 March 1971). From script to screen every day seemed to issue forth another outlaw story: a balky assistant director suffered a head-banging on the studio floor; when untrained black technicians fell short, the boss himself stepped in; they "shot on the run in Watts" as though one step ahead of the cops; when "threatened" they drew "real" guns; they worked nonunion by gulling the guilds into thinking the film was a porno quickie; they softened a Detroit booker by dangling him from a thirteenth-story window; they finished in only twenty days, keeping their product in black hands by borrowing completion money from Bill Cosby;

---

rector's card and "a stipend from a wealthy Frenchwoman"—his tattoo reverted to English, and an edge of ghetto cornerboy violence entered in the form of a story of his banging the head of an assistant director on the floor at Columbia; *The David Frost Show* (10 June 1971), which added a term in jail (for panhandling); the *Sun* (Baltimore), 13 Feb. 1971, expanded his creativity to include five record albums, "more film shorts," sleeping on park benches, living in the "slums" of Chicago (rather than in his actual middle-class neighborhood), and his affinity for a "constituency" that embraced "the nitty gritty people"; and Louis Botto, "Work in Progress: Melvin Van Peebles," *Intellectual Digest* 2 (August 1972): 6–10, in which a reporter did not ask to see the tattoos but merely described them as "reportedly" in place. Taken together, this journalistic canon, or at least a sample of it, contributed to a legend that grew in variety and proportion until on the eve of the release of the movie the audiences' expectations were sharpened into an appetite for a genre that they had never seen but already, a priori, knew the traits of. In this way, Van Peebles's retailing of his autobiography as the history of an outlaw saint substituted for a canon of films such as the ones that helped define more formal genres such as Ford westerns or Hitchcock suspense films.

Figure 13-2. Van Peebles surrounded by Columbia Pictures executives in a Hollywood production still, designed to affirm Hollywood's self-advertised accessibility to black filmmakers. For black moviegoers this was a subversive image of the outlaw who had somehow gotten inside the fort. (Copyright 1970 by Columbia Pictures Industries, Inc. All rights reserved. Courtesy of Columbia Pictures.)

they proclaimed their forthcoming work "guerrilla cinema" and "revolutionary film"; and in the end when making the usual deals for marketing tee shirts and ancillary products, Van Peebles imagined they were using "a viable commercial product" to reveal the "power base" which "in the long term [would] liberate the third world people," the entire project being so arcane to white people that it constituted "a new kind of foreign film" (Van Peebles 1971, 8–10; Peavy, 193–96). The legend and the emerging genre had become one. The result was a startling anatomy of black Los Angeles and its errant picaroon in saturated color, punctuated by a ritual mayhem that seemed to stir orgasmic—rather than cathartic—release. "I damn near got a nut," said one critic about watching a beating given two white cops (Coleman 1971, 373).

Like a television pilot that is obliged to introduce all its elements in quick succession before the attention span of its more skeptical than loyal audience lapsed, *Sweetback* took on the form and structure of the genre most readily adapted to successive episodic introduction of generic traits—the quest

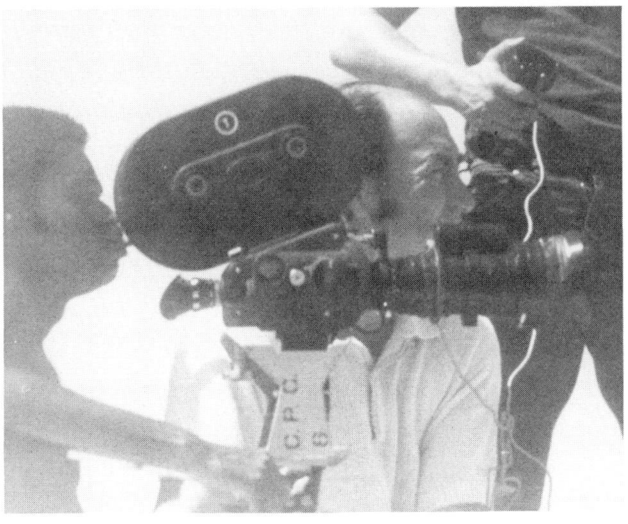

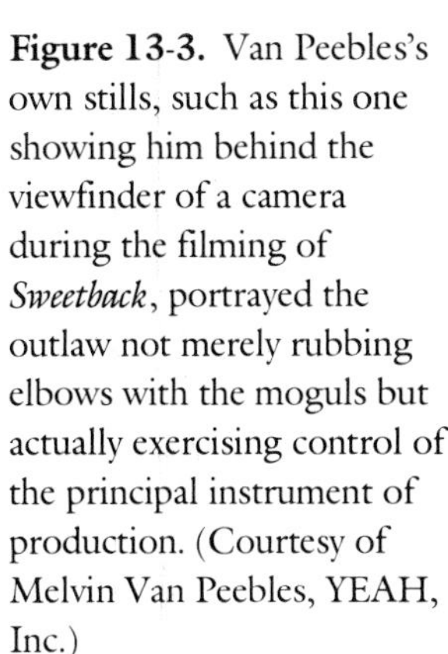
Figure 13-3. Van Peebles's own stills, such as this one showing him behind the viewfinder of a camera during the filming of *Sweetback*, portrayed the outlaw not merely rubbing elbows with the moguls but actually exercising control of the principal instrument of production. (Courtesy of Melvin Van Peebles, YEAH, Inc.)

movie (enameled over with a coating of seamy urbanity borrowed from a particular variant of the lone wolf detective genre known as *film noir*). In other words, *Sweetback* needed no substantive plot, only a ninety-minute strand on which to hang episodes that alternately revealed Sweetback's maturity from apolitical sexual athlete to a sort of black Emiliano Zapata—a revolutionary outlaw—and the responses of both blacks and whites to his evolution. Along the way, as each episode revealed Sweetback and his friends and enemies, the film also in parallel provided a reportorial anatomy of black life and began to speak in an increasingly strident tone of political advocacy, with all of the elements working in a supercool nutrient black idiom.

From the main titles through the credits the message was clear. The audience was to witness "a hymn from the mouth of reality" starring "The Black Community" and "Br'er Soul," and the setting was to be a combat zone peopled by "all the black brothers and sisters who have had enough of The Man"—the latter a refrain reinforced throughout by a music track featuring Earth, Wind, and Fire.

Once these political fundamentals are set forth, the visual aspect tightens to Sweetback himself. At first he is no more than a towelboy and a plaything of the prostitutes who take him as a waif into their brothel. But the spectator knows that destiny is at work here and that the child is the father of the man, for intercut with the shots of young Sweetback (Mario Peebles) shoveling in a square meal, ministering to the whores, and finally servicing one quietly horny one, are shots of the mature Sweetback (Melvin Van Peebles) already on the run through the alleys of L.A. From these beginnings Sweetback soon becomes the star of the house's crowded sex shows, mounting both the women and a transvestite "fairy godmother" as the camera catches close-ups of leering, glistening faces in the tightly packed audience.

In the brothel, of course, politics has no place, at least until a couple of white homicide-division cops enter in search of a patsy to spend the night in jail as evidence of their desultory work on a murder case. Moomoo, the boss, readily gives them Sweetback, who goes quietly, presuming that everyone understands this ghetto game and that he will routinely be released after a night in the cooler. But moments later the angry politics of the street intrude on the well-ordered rules of the game. Their dispatcher orders the cops to pick up a black prisoner, apparently a rioter from the inflamed streets. Here too the film's rules change in that in contrast to the brothel, everything is political. The cops' bust is done with all the flash and jangle that a hand-held camera can provide, and the ride to jail is seen in a long traveling shot of the passing streetscape over which is laid a montage of still more urban graphics capped by a red-bathed "Jesus Saves" sign. Clearly, Sweetback is in for a

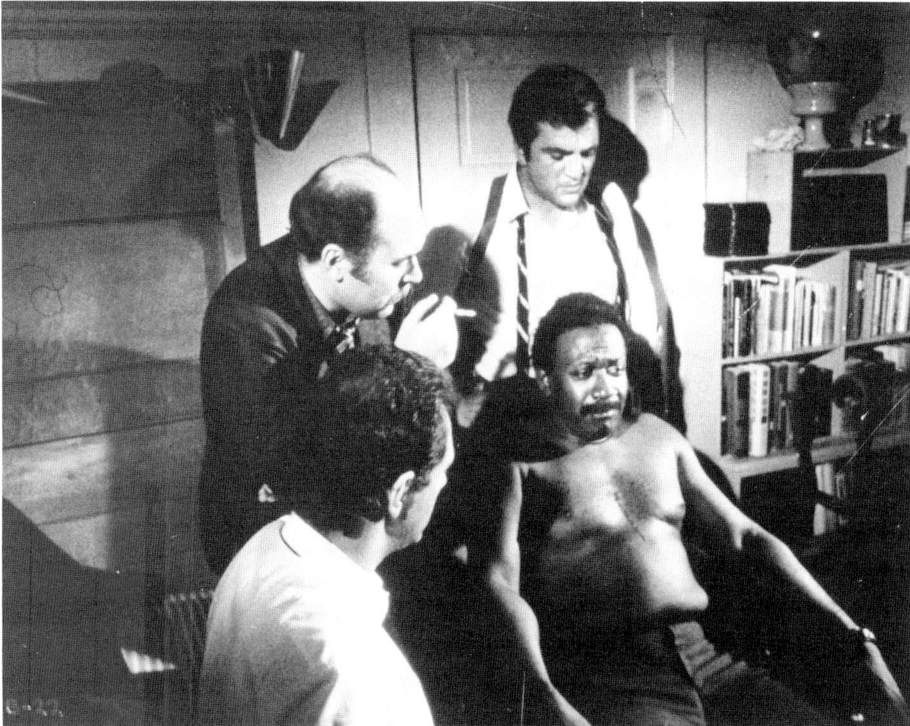

Figure 13-4. Production stills distributed to herald a forthcoming film do not always reflect the actual substance of the film but may be concocted to signal the filmmaker's intentions. In this one for *Sweetback* the plight of blacks is asserted ironically; though centered in the frame, the black prisoner is shown in a tilted-down shot, a rhetorical film device for suggesting powerlessness and vulnerability at the hands of brutal white policemen. (Courtesy of Melvin Van Peebles, YEAH, Inc.)

descent into the same mean streets that the audience has become inured to in a decade of television news of the movement. The difference is that Sweetback is alone rather than in a community of purposeful, singing black activists—alone, that is, save for the suspect the police have picked up and to whom they decide to give a gratuitous licking. "I'm sorry man," one says to the yet apolitical Sweetback, sorry that he has had to handcuff Sweetback to the sullen suspect whom they are about to work over.

As in all quest tales—whether for the holy grail or for revenge against the bushwhackers of one's parents—the real story is in the growth of self-knowledge and in the transformation of character. Sweetback's story is no different. At this moment, as though anticipating critics like Lerone Bennett (1971, 106) who would sneer that "fucking will not set you free," Sweetback changes from a mere sexual mechanic into the totally *engaged* brother on the block. His cuffs loosened by the accommodating cops as they set upon their other prisoner, Sweetback silently switches sides and begins amid flashes of color on the darkened screen to pummel and kick the police. Not yet comfortable with his conversion, however, when the man whom he has saved from a beating asks what "we" are to do next, Sweetback can only snap back, "Where you get that 'we' shit?"

Indeed, for a time he is all flight and no politics. He lights out for the safety of the black neighborhoods and the industrial slums. Amid flashes of saturated cadmium yellows and ochres and carmines and blues he jogs through a slice of black Los Angeles and into the dull brown fields of oil rigs pumping away like birds feeding. Flash frames of color and cuts to police raids show a white Los Angeles heating up in its pursuit of the new outlaw Sweetback. "Caution," says a traffic sign as Sweetback finds an old house in which the brothel owner is visually set apart from Sweetback—showering in an absurd plastic cap, refracted through a mirror, squatting on a toilet, he is as apolitical as Sweetback has been. "Lay out a while," he says, implying that it will all blow over. At first the black community in which he hopes to lose himself remains in a similar political torpor, all mere reactive defiance and truculence rather than political sensibility, like Sicilian *banditi* rather than Garibaldi's nationalist Red Shirts. An old woman-friend agrees to help him but only after first things first—a routine sexual romp accompanied by her ecstatic moans. A preacher dressed in appropriately political vestments—a zebra buba and leopard alb—seems an opportunity to link up with black circles, but Sweetback merely seems an interruption at a wake and he soon resumes his run through the alleys as the mourners call "take him to glory, Lord." The preacher only says "he died of black misery." Meanwhile, the cops give the blacks every provocation to politicize—indeed, they are overdrawn cartoon brutes, and too much so to be taken as the *real* white enemy. The police commissioner, for example, keeps telephone contact with his forces in the field as they nab Sweetback and allows the press to monitor the incoming reports while cynically, cruelly, in a private verbal code, ordering his cops to thrash their prisoner.

It is this last set piece that Van Peebles used to link the movie with the actuality in American streets and to exhort blacks to collective action. As the two policemen beat Sweetback in the open daylight, black kids set fire to their cruiser, and one of them opens a door for Sweetback, hoping to pin the cops inside. It is the only actual coordinated engagement between forces in the movie.

But the movie lacked the political will to define or anticipate the audience's response to white cupidity; after all, while every filmmaker might wish to inspire viewers to direct social action, none would wish to bear responsibility for sending a newly made zealot to his death against the guns of real-life policemen. Thus the blacks in the movie embraced their time-tested *aesthétique du cool*, stiffening against Sweetback's plight but giving the police only silence. The preacher in the zebra skin buba offers only "a black ave maria for you"; the cardplayers around a table reply cynically to his plea for money, "what does a dead man need bread for"; and so on through the movie.

At last, instead of a frontal assault on white America, Van Peebles chose a broadly played sexual metaphor that teased around the one racial stereotype that few blacks ever bothered to deny—sexual prowess. In an interlude in his flight Sweetback encounters a white motorcycle gang. The scene is all blue smoke, popping engines, and chiaroscuro lights and flashes as the gang ruminates on seeking action. "Something sporting," one of them says, "like a duel," as they turn to Sweetback, ever the outsider, who of course gets to choose the weapon. "Fucking," he says under the same lidded eyes that had marked his sexual coolness in the brothel. The gang's champion emerges in silhouette, looming, stocky, Viking-like. As though donning his suit of lights prior to a bullfight, Sweetback undresses save for the derby and white collar he wore in his live shows and mounts his partner/adversary (all of these couplings have been in a missionary posture). As they throb rhythmically to the revving bike engines she screams in ecstasy and the gang rides off, sparing Sweetback as though in tribute to his rutting skills. But the scene also set the political agenda for the entire movie in that it provided the sole moment when Sweetback elected to confront white America rather than cut and run. In this sense it constituted in dramaturgical terms a genuine climax of the film.

Figure 13-5. In a sequence centering on Sweetback's encounter with a white motorcycle gang, Van Peebles advances the plot of the movie while reinforcing his own outlaw legend. The savagery of the bikers is established by echoing scores of Hollywood movies showing Africans and Indians dancing around their fires, thereby subverting Hollywood racial ideology. Meanwhile, inside the circle Sweetback accepts their challenge to a duel, choosing as his weapon his sexual prowess. Thus Van Peebles has it both ways: he manages to portray the white outlaws as savages, while still having Sweetback best them on their own violently sexual terms. (Courtesy of Melvin Van Peebles, YEAH, Inc.)

In fact this will be the last moment in the film in which Sweetback is to be found in a social circle of any sort. Having to choose between a movie about a quest for a political leader under whom blacks will rise as one—a Zapata or Parnell or Juarez—and a movie about a quest for individual political evolution, Van Peebles in midmovie chose the latter. In the last reels the drift toward a black community politics startlingly shifts toward a politics of individual sacrifice and endurance as though Sweetback wishes to become not Zapata but Simon of the Desert or St. Augustine. Sweetback's last social gesture is in a disused poolroom where he is hiding. As the cops kick in the door he makes a one-handed, two-ball combination, as though paying homage to one last stereotype—the black poolroom lounger. Thereafter, every adventure is personal rather than communal, in the desert rather than the city, and so empty of incidents that might engage blacks that the sound track begins to dominate. In the absence of visual metaphor that might engage the black community that Sweetback has abandoned back in Los Angeles, Earth, Wind, and Fire takes up the burden of the message.

Clearly at this point Van Peebles had erected a scaffolding for a black genre film even though the product awaited political refinement. So far the genre embraced the traits of its author's own outlaw legend, but like the Sicilian *banditi* described in Eric Hobsbawm's *Primitive Rebels* he stopped short of cloaking outlawry in political terms. Nonetheless, he had brought into sharp focus a genre-world modeled on his legend. That genre-world was drawn from the black demimonde of Los Angeles; set in an urban, folk, jive idiom through which to address its audience; and resonant with a tone of advocacy for a black polity. It was also complete with a hero capable of operatically expansive, value-laden actions, all performed in the mode of the classic black *aesthétique du cool*, the black mask of insouciance that every black homeboy put on when he faced cops, teachers, parents, and other adversaries.

As to the political message, as we shall see, it was to be embedded in subsequent mutations of the genre after only a rhetorical introduction into the last reels of *Sweetback* in the form of an evocative voiceover by Earth, Wind, and Fire. Indeed, the end of the quest, visually at least, is only incrementally more communal in rhetoric than the apolitical lone wolf with which it began. Sweetback escapes from arrest at the poolroom by strangling one cop with his own handcuffs and impaling another on a pool cue. What shall become of him now? Will he be a guerrilla leader on horseback? Or only another cop killer? The answer quickly follows. A black biker (John Amos) seeks him out. "They told me," he says in a moody day-for-night scene, "he's our future, Br'er, take him." But Sweetback's answer is on the sound track. "Come on feet, do your thing," sings Earth, Wind, and Fire as Sweetback trots through the dry concrete bed of the Los Angeles River, past the electrical and industrial towers of southcentral L.A. Instead of a song of community, the sound track only wails, "Who put the bad mouth on me?"

Sweetback's retreat from the political prospects accruing from his past actions is so off the mark anticipated by a black audience's sympathetic reading of the movie that even the cops are baffled. "Could be an uprising," says the commissioner, "no patrol will be safe in their area." He tries to close ranks by apologizing to two black cops for his casual use of "nigger." Raids wrack the ghetto as the police scour the neighborhoods in search of the outlaw whom they imagine to be the leader of a movement. But Sweetback is already all but gone. And the black community is far from the stalwart "little people" in a Frank Capra movie who wait for their champion. They are toothless winos, obsequious bootblacks, drug-addicted saloon singers, shattered women who cannot even remember their kids' names because "they [urban social agencies] take them away when they get older and bad." Even Earth, Wind, and Fire grows circumspect, singing that "they bled your mama, they bled your [family] . . . but they won't bleed me." Among the occasional flash frames of metaphors is a fish ominously having its head chopped off by a fishmonger.

Jumpy helicopter shots carry the action to the desert where Sweetback's alienation from blacks is complete. The setting is yellow sagebrush rather than Central Avenue. A ruse that allows him a few moments' lead is contrived with a *white* drifter; the appropriate intercut is to a skittish rabbit; and when he is wounded and must make a poultice of mud from his own urine—the ultimate in alienation metaphors—the episode confirms his aloneness. By then, Earth, Wind, and Fire wavers between a familiar chorus of "wade in the water" and the despairing cry of a slogan of the times, "a nigger ain't shit." Living off the desert (he beheads and eats a salamander and drinks from a mudhole) and the kindness of Mexican migrant workers, he makes for the

Figure 13-6. *Sweetback* is intended to celebrate black folklife. But Sweetback's last-reel flight into the desert, coupled with the failure of black communal figures such as this charismatic preacher (West Gale) to aid him, tend to subvert the theme of the movie while affirming the theme of the filmmaker's personal legend.

 border, desperately killing a brace of trailing dogs on his way (pausing, it must be said, for one last coupling with yet another overly appreciative female). Here the quest runs into the ground, exhausted by its own lack of prospects. All that a sympathetic spectator can hope for is Sweetback's return in the van of an army of the poor in some future movie. In fact, Van Peebles tells them so. As in a television spot for a car dealer a graphic text appears across the frame. "Watch out," it says, "WATCH OUT." "A baad asssss nigger is coming back to collect some dues." Even this promise may have rung hollow in that any black media-wise audience might easily have read it for its commercial resonance rather than for its politics and therefore taken the assertion as a pitchman's spiel rather than a zealot's oath.

Nonetheless, black youngsters gave *Sweetback* a reading that credited it for its departure from Hollywood convention and gave it good word-of-mouth, thereby, according to Van Peebles, setting house records at its spring 1971 opening in Detroit and Atlanta, not to mention sales from recording tie-ins. Critics, when it occurred to them, joined the audiences in a sort of homage to the new genre by reviewing the audiences along with the movie and sometimes by measuring the movie against its backstory embedded in the legend of its maker. Indeed for the trades such as *Variety* this tactic quickly became an obligatory reviewing strategy because the emerging black exploitation genre, which often followed so few of the conventions of dramaturgy, required close observation of the audience's response as an index of the prospects of each new movie. In effect, the reader-response criticism that a new generation of critics had begun to introduce into academic circles became an essential tool of tradepaper critics.

Clearly the new genre had *arrived* when critics not only tried on for size the socioartistic standards of the audience but even took up its argot. "Any hip black in the audience would recognize in that look the sure sign of a badass cat," wrote one critic who had sat in an audience whose response fell in two camps—white "stony silence" and black "delighted exclamations." Probing deeper, he reckoned that Sweetback "answers a psychic need of black audiences" (Peavy 1973, 195–96; Gussow 1972; Coleman 1971). Even a mass-circulation "white" magazine, *Time* (16 Aug. 1971, 47), addressed the movie by means of a quotation from Huey Newton, a founder of the Black Panther party, who thought it "the first truly revolutionary black film." Van Peebles, of course, concurred in this notion of *Sweetback* as an insurrectionary tract. "Fortunately the bloods on the street are not fooled [by Hollywood]," he told the editor of *Chamba Notes* (Fall 1979, 5–7). "They relate to what I'm saying."

Every serious black critic, favorable to *Sweetback* or not, took up this matter of the traits of a genre as they contributed to its reception by its intended audience. Lerone Bennett and Don Lee in *Ebony* (1971, 106) not only waved aside its putative revolutionary angle as largely an "illusion" but even found it "reactionary" in its obsession with the lone rather than collective actions of its last half. Others predictably saw what Van Peebles had claimed as a goal or at least put the best face on what they had seen. St. Claire Bourne of the Black Filmmakers Foundation, an advocacy and distribution group, marveled that Sweetback the outlaw had found equal favor among both the " 'street' " folk and the " 'boojies' "—the hip patois for "black bourgeoisie." Clayton Riley, writing in the *New York Times* (9 May 1971), thought its ambivalent ending south of the border was not so much an evasion of the black political dilemma of integrationism versus separatism as it was a reasonable wish to avoid a too pat "victorious" ending. On second viewing Riley liked it even more as a "terrifying vision . . . unadorned by faith." In any case, they seemed agreed that Van Peebles had effectively set Sweetback apart from Hollywood genres that seemed bent on compromising every black protagonist by embedding him in a formula in which, as Nelson George argued, he was "driven by some majority mainstream motivation" (George 1979, 19–20). In this way they implicitly granted that *Sweetback* represented such a deviance from Hollywood convention as to constitute a fresh genre capable of setting its own agenda embedded in its own formulas.

This is not to argue that Van Peebles's work singlehandedly defined a genre that persisted and evolved in the same sort of straight line along which westerns or police procedurals or any other genre matured. Black movies went too quickly from Van Peebles's primitivism to maturity, baroque, rococo, and declining stages. But *Sweetback* did help define its age, contribute to the genre on its own terms, reveal the presence of a heretofore unrequited audience, shape its expectations and thus forecast its receptivity, and, finally, force Hollywood movies (and television) to adjust its vision to the present day.

Moreover, *Sweetback* forced a reconsideration of a notion widely held, particularly among Marxist critics, that popular culture works only to preserve the status quo. Clearly *Sweetback* had demonstrated not only that in the short term it was *possible* to create a genre from the fragments of wishes of a barely perceived audience but also that a popular medium might serve to advocate a cause antithetical to the sensibilities of the mainstream. Indeed, Van Peebles even drew the black center into his orbit, or at least into the theaters, alongside the yelping cornerboys; after all, the film took in more than ten million dollars in rentals—double that figure by Van Peebles's count—and earned an "Image" award from the Hollywood branch of the NAACP. So

Van Peebles challenged the patronizing notion that poor people were no more than putty in the hands of shrewd lords of popular culture. Moreover, he accomplished this in an age-old Hollywood style by inventing a legend with himself at the center, much as Tom Mix or John Ford had done, and then locating his legend at the center of his movie. In this way he combined a distinctly black point of view; a familiar style of conduct and costume that I have called an *aesthétique du cool*; a voice of advocacy, even urgency; a lovingly detailed anatomy of the society from which the moviegoers themselves came; and an outlaw hero who served the dramatic and social function of other outlaws in other cultures—Robin Hood in England, Jesse James in Missouri, Ned Kelly in Australia, and Br'er Rabbit in Africa and Georgia. His prototype lacked only the will to follow the implications of its own logic through to the end. If only Sweetback had stayed in the city among friends rooted in the lower depths he might have remained susceptible to the politicizing that any number of real-life black outlaws had undergone, much as Eldridge Cleaver had moved from convicted rapist to author of *Soul on Ice* and founder of the Black Panther party. As it was, Sweetback's prepolitical rage against whites so sadistic as to seem more gargoyles than recognizable people ended with so little resolution that his author felt obliged to promise a vengeful return. Nonetheless, the fact that a generation of black moviegoers have spent millions in search of a sequel or equal to *Sweetback* and the fact that hundreds of feckless imitations and hundreds more of revanchist Chinese martial arts movies have earned still more millions by imitating Sweetback's style, testify to the place that *Sweetback* holds in the lore of Hollywood genre films.

WORKS CITED

Bennett, Lerone, and Don L. Lee. 1971. "The Emancipation Orgasm: Sweetback in Wonderland." *Ebony* (September): 106–8.

Coleman, Horace W. 1971. "Melvin Van Peebles." *Journal of Popular Culture* 5 (Fall): 368–84.

Cripps, Thomas. 1975. "The Noble Black Savage: A Problem in the Politics of Television Art." *Journal of Popular Culture* 8 (Spring): 687–95.

———. 1978a. *Black Film as Genre*. Bloomington: Indiana University Press.

———. 1978b. "*Casablanca, Tennessee Johnson*, and *The Negro Soldier*—Hollywood Liberals and World War II." In *Feature Films as History*, edited by K. R. M. Short, 138–56. London: Croom.

Cripps, Thomas, and David Culbert. 1979. "*The Negro Soldier* (1944): Film Propaganda in Black and White." *American Quarterly* 31 (Winter): 616–40.

Gans, Herbert J. 1974. *Popular Culture and High Culture: An Analysis and Evaluation of Taste*. New York: Basic.

George, Nelson. 1979. "Life After Sweetback." *Routes* 2 (June): 19–20.

Great White Hope file. Twentieth-Century Fox Archive. UCLA.

Gussow, Mel. 1972. "The Baadasssss Success of Melvin Van Peebles." *New York Times* (20 August).

Harper, Peggy. 1967. "Dance in a Changing Society." *African Arts/Arts Afrique* 1 (Autumn): 10ff.

Hess, Judith W. 1974. "Genre Films and the Status Quo." *Jump Cut* 1 (May-June): 16–18.

Jersey, William. 1988. Telephone interview with author, Spring.

Lenihan, John H. 1980. *Showdown: Confronting Modern America in the Western Film*. Urbana: University of Illinois Press.

Peavy, Charles D. 1973. "Black Consciousness and the Contemporary Cinema." In *Popular Culture and Expanding Consciousness*. Edited by Ray B. Browne, 189–200. New York: Wiley.

Pye, Douglas. 1986. "The Western (Genre and Movies)." In *Film Genre Reader*, edited by Barry Keith Grant, 143–48. Austin: University of Texas Press.

Riley, Clayton. 1971. "What Makes Sweetback Run?" *New York Times* (9 May).

Thompson, Richard. 1975. "Thunder Road: Maudit—'The Devil Got Him First.' " In *Kings of the Bs: Working within the Hollywood System: An Anthology of Film History and Criticism*, edited by Todd McCarthy and Charles Flynn. New York: Dutton.

Thompson, Robert Farris. 1984. *Flash of the Spirit: African and Afro-American Art and Philosophy*. New York: Vintage.

Van Peebles, Melvin. 1971. *Sweet Sweetback's Baadasssss Song*. New York: Lancer.

Welch, Myron. 1970. "I Got the Blood." *Coast FM & Fine Arts* (11 January): 26–30.

BIBLIOGRAPHY

Sweetback

Canby, Vincent. " 'Sweetback': Does It Exploit Injustice?" *New York Times* (9 May 1971).

Euvrard, Michel. " 'Sweet Sweetback's Baadasssss Song.' Melvin Van Peebles: 'Revaliser avec Hollywood sur son propre terrain.' " *CinémAction: Le cinéma noir américain*, no. 46 (1988): 144–50.

Kuumba Workshop. *From a Black Perspective: A Searching and Critical Analysis of the Hit Film—Sweet Sweetback's Baadasssss Song*. Chicago: Kuumba Workshop, 1978.

Lee, Don L. "The Bittersweet of *Sweetback*: Or, Shake Yo' Money Maker." *Black World* 21 (November 1971): 70–79.

Murray, James P. "Melvin Van Peebles." In *To Find an Image: Black Films from Uncle Tom to Super Fly*. Indianapolis: Bobbs, 1973.

———. "Running with *Sweetback*." *Black Creation* (Fall 1971): 10–12.

Newton, Huey P. "He Won't Bleed Me: A Revolutionary Analysis of 'Sweet Sweetback's Baadasssss Song.' " *Black Panther* 6 (19 June 1971): A–L.

Peavy, Charles. "An Afro-American in Paris: The Films of Melvin Van Peebles." *Cineaste* 3 (Summer 1969): 2–3.

"Power to the Peebles." *Time* (16 August 1971): 47.

"*Sweet Sweetback's Baadasssss Song* and the Development of Contemporary Black Cinema: A Colloquy with Melvin Van Peebles, St. Claire Bourne, Haile Gerima, and Pearl Bowser." In *Black Cinema Aesthetics: Issues in Independent Black Filmmaking*, edited by Gladstone L. Yearwood. Athens, Ohio: Ohio University Center for Afro-American Studies, 1982.

Race and Genre

"The Black Movie Boom." *Newsweek* (6 September 1971): 66.

"Blacks vs. *Shaft*." *Newsweek* (28 August 1972): 88.

Bourne, St. Claire. "The Development of the Contemporary Black Film Movement." In *Black Cinema Aesthetics: Issues in Independent Black Filmmaking*, edited by Gladstone L. Yearwood. Athens, Ohio: Ohio University Center for Afro-American Studies, 1982.

Burton, Julianne. "Marginal Cinemas and Mainstream Critical Theory." *Screen* 26 (May–August 1985): 2–21.

Crusz, R. "Black Cinemas, Film Theory, and Dependent Knowledge." *Screen* 26 (May–August 1985): 152–56.

Diakite, Madubuko. *Film, Culture, and the Black Filmmaker: A Study of Functional Relationships and Parallel Developments*. New York: Arno, 1980.

Euvrard, Janine. "Warrington Hudlin: 'Je préfère le blues-réalisme au cinéma de victimisation.' " *CinémAction: Le cinéma noir américain*, no. 46 (1988): 164–67.

Goodwin, James. "Film Genre and Film Realism." *Quarterly Review of Film Studies* 8 (Fall 1982): 357–61.

Hall, Stuart. "Gramsci's Relevance for the Study of Race and Ethnicity." *Journal of Communication Inquiry* 10 (Summer 1986): 5–27.

Kael, Pauline. "Notes on Black Movies." In *Black Films and Filmmakers: A Comprehensive Anthology from Stereotype to Superhero*, compiled by Lindsay Patterson. New York: Dodd, 1975.

Michener, Charles. "Black Movies: Renaissance or Ripoff?" *Newsweek* (23 October 1972): 74–79.

Poussaint, Alvin. "Cheap Thrills That Degrade Blacks." *Psychology Today* 7 (February 1974).

Wander, Brandon. "Black Dreams: The Fantasy and Ritual of Black Films." *Film Quarterly* 29 (Fall 1975): 2–11.

Yearwood, Gladstone L. "The Hero in Black Film: An Analysis of the Film Industry and the Problems in Black Cinema." *Wide Angle* 5 (Spring 1982): 67–81.

———. "Towards a Theory of a Black Cinema Aesthetic." In *Black Cinema Aesthetics: Issues in Independent Black Filmmaking*. Edited by Gladstone L. Yearwood. Athens, Ohio: Ohio University Center for Afro-American Studies, 1982.

SWEET SWEETBACK'S BAADASSSS SONG

14

THE MASTER TEXT OF *BLOW-UP*

Robert T. Eberwein

Michelangelo Antonioni's film *Blow-Up* (1966) offers a challenging text for analysis. Although many of the other critical approaches represented in this anthology could be brought profitably to bear on the film, a perspective derived from psychoanalysis may permit one to incorporate some of the other methodologies. The following discussion attempts to demonstrate the usefulness of this perspective, to comment on relevant concerns raised by earlier commentary, and to present a *provisional* analysis. I believe that a psychoanalytic approach brings me closer to the text than other approaches can as I attempt to understand the film. But even though I privilege the psychoanalytic approach, I am aware that its language, at least what I can speak of it, is not fully adequate to the challenge posed by the work. Note, therefore, that this is not an "interpretation," for that word suggests that some sort of closure has been reached, that the text to be confronted has been mastered; you will see that Antonioni's text remains the master (text). I will not be looking at the film as a closed text, capable of complete explanation, but rather as a psyche, to use Elizabeth Wright's distinction (1984, 133–56). Like a psyche, it resists my attempts at analysis; part of it will be forever inaccessible to me.

Antonioni's introduction to the Italian edition of his screenplays, cited by Charles Thomas Samuels, offers us a pertinent comment: "We know that under the image revealed there is another which is truer to reality and under this image still another and yet again still another under this last one, right down to the true image of reality, absolute, mysterious, which no one will ever see or perhaps right down to the decomposition of any image, of any reality" (1972, 23). The condition he describes of multiple images of reality hidden under one another sounds strikingly similar to the construct that, following Sigmund Freud, we call the unconscious—which no one will ever know.

Blow-Up's key sequences depict the unnamed central character played by David Hemmings (called Thomas in the script) looking at images—photographs he took in some park—and discovering images that appear to reveal a reality underlying the reality he thought was there. His narrative path takes him from a position of mastery over images, as the successful photographer whose work includes taking "relevant" pictures in a doss house and creating appropriate moods and settings for high-fashion models, to a position of subservience to images, as the participant in a tennis game without visible equipment. In the final shot he appears/disappears as a decomposed image.

Thomas, a photographer producing a book that will convey a glimpse of contemporary society, first appears at work in his various activities. He has spent the night in a doss house secretly photographing bums and old men. This information appears in a cross-cutting pattern depicting the arrival of mimes in London. The next morning he photographs an attractive model, Verushka, and prompts her physical responses by engaging in mock intercourse, his camera serving as a surrogate for the penis. Next he has an unsuccessful photography session with five seemingly unresponsive models. Then he visits his neighbors Patricia and Bill (a painter), played by Sarah Miles and John Castle, checks out an antique shop he means to buy, and goes to a near-by park where he sees a girl, played by Vanessa Redgrave, and an older man apparently having a lyrical romantic interlude. He follows them and takes photographs but is stopped by the girl. She accuses him of invading her privacy and demands the pictures. He refuses and snaps some more as she leaves. He returns to the antique shop and then visits with his friend Ron at a restaurant; he learns he has been followed by a young man who looks like him. Back at his studio, he is confronted by the girl, who again demands the pictures. After he gives her a false roll of film, they smoke pot and are about to have sex when the delivery of a propeller, purchased earlier at the antique shop, interrupts them.

He develops the photographs after she leaves and through the process of blowing them up and arranging them in sequential order discovers that the idyll was in fact a murderous scene: a killer was lurking behind the bushes with a gun, ready to kill the older man. The photographer's intrusion prevented the murder. He calls his friend Ron with the news but is interrupted by two teeny-boppers who have come hoping to have their pictures taken. Casual playing leads to the apparent beginnings of an orgy in the studio; we see the stripping of the girls before the director cuts. After the orgy the photographer awakes and notices something previously unobserved in one picture. He investigates the photographs even more closely and learns that in fact he has not prevented a murder, for he sees the body of the older man lying beneath a tree.

The photographer returns to the park without his camera and finds the body. But when he returns home he learns that someone has rifled his studio: photographs and film are gone—except for one blow-up of the body. He visits his friends, intruding on their sexual intercourse, returns to his studio, and then speaks with Patricia, who has come to his apartment after making love with Bill. He leaves, hoping to engage Ron's help in photographing the body, sees the girl on the street, follows her, but loses her. He arrives at Ron's house to find everyone smoking pot. He cannot persuade Ron to go with him to photograph the body and stays at the party. The next morning he visits the park again, discovers the body is gone, and observes the mimes who opened the film now engaged in a mock tennis game. When the "ball" flies out of the court one mime beckons the photographer to assist them by retrieving the ball. He does so and we hear the sound of a tennis ball. The camera lingers on the photographer, pulls back, and then obliterates him, leaving only the landscape.

"Doesn't every text lead back to Oedipus?" asks Roland Barthes (1975, 47). The provisional answer to his query would seem to be yes if *Blow-Up* is considered, not only because of its narrative text but also because of the operation of the text as a signifying system.

The film has elicited excellent and informative criticism. Various commentaries consider it as an allegory about the nature of the artistic process; discuss its formal aspects, such as the balancing of beginning and ending with the appearance of the mimes; and point to the specifically psychoanalytic content figured in the narrative situation. The last strategy is of most interest here. For Jacob Arlow, Daniel Dervin and Melvin Goldstein, the hero is best approached in Oedipal terms. For them he is, with various degrees of difference, an Oedipal hero whose ultimate failure to act is a result of paralysis occasioned by an Oedipus complex complicated by primal scene trauma.

Arlow connects the experience of patients who have witnessed primal scenes to the photographer; they all feel excluded from the parental bond and take out their frustration by avenging themselves on the parents: "[Thomas] is a professional spy-voyeur who has lost faith in women. They may pursue him but he scorns them, for he judges them all as betrayers. . . . [T]he crime of murder in *Blow-Up* could represent a projection of the impulse to wreak vengeance on the oedipal father. . . . [T]he photographer hero . . . emerges almost as a universal symbol of the child traumatized by the primal scene. The photographer has witnessed and recorded a traumatic event. His life has been altered thereby, but out of the vast storehouse of his memory, that is, out of all his pictures, he cannot retrieve the one that contains the record of the trauma" (1980, 535–39).

Dervin sees the photographer's process of developing the pictures in psychoanalytic terms, as if he were discovering a dream within a dream or penetrating screen memories to discover the repressed memory of the primal scene:

> Reality has been yielding to the technology of the medium. The greater his blow-ups the narrower his field of vision. . . . The photograph . . . has latent content, like a screen memory or dream. Its surfaces must be peeled away. . . . [T]he photographer's voyeurism has carried him beyond himself. His cool mastery of surfaces is blown. Sexuality is disclosed as a dangerous situation, a fatal crossroad where life and death meet. And he is part of it. Like Oedipus, his own defensive maneuvers have brought him to this. All his sexual avoidances—retreating into the darkroom of his vocation, repudiating outer reality by making photos of photos, blow-ups of his blow-ups—have only brought him face to face with terrifying inner reality. He has penetrated beyond sublimated games to primitive instinct and beyond the scene in the park to its prototype—the primal scene. (1985, 76–78)

Goldstein stresses the connection between voyeurism and the Oedipus complex in Thomas:

> The typical voyeur, like all perverts, has organized his sexuality in such a way that genital orgasm is possible for him. His major problems are an unconscious Oedipus complex and an unconscious castration anxiety. . . . Regression to a level of infantile sexuality which once represented pleasure and security makes it possible for the pervert to obtain pleasure again, because simultaneously he has repressed feared aspects of his early childhood experiences. . . . Thomas's actions permit us to consider him a voyeur. . . . The avoidance of adult sexuality and repulsion by it is apparent in his teasing treatment of Verushka, his avoidance of sex with The Girl, his adolescent play

> with the teeny-boppers, and his rejection of Patricia's sexual overtures after he has seen her and her husband, Bill, making love. . . . His sadism toward women is flagrant, and his fear of homosexuality puts him in the classic bind of the voyeur. His latent homosexuality is exhibited in his hostile remarks about "queers" and French poodles moving into the neighborhood and in his selective views of the people he sees. . . . Thomas's need to avoid feelings of guilt and responsibility, characteristic of the voyeur, is equally characteristic of all persons who have not resolved their Oedipal complexes. . . . [Thomas in the park] is here the little boy peeping through the slats of his crib and just old enough to climb out and move to his parents' bedroom. . . . His need to deny his desire to kill an "older man" gets him to believe that his interference helped save the man's life. Once he knows this is not true, he sinks into a depression, one which keeps him from acting to find the murderer. Is it possible he wanted the older man dead so he might have the woman to himself? A glimpse at the possible murderer through the restaurant window tells us he is young and fair-haired, a physical double for Thomas. . . . Like Hamlet . . . he is too grateful to the murderer for having killed the "father" to kill him himself. Thus, Thomas does as little as possible to effectively inform those who could find the killer. (1975, 245–52)

I have quoted at length from Arlow, Dervin, and Goldstein because they illustrate clearly the operation of what we might call a traditional use of psychoanalytic criticism. Their interpretations rest on the assumption that Freudian analysis of character in terms of the master Oedipal text will yield viable information that explains behavior. Thus Thomas's cruelty to women, his inability to carry out a sexual act, and his refusal to pursue the killer(s) can be explained as results of his Oedipus complex and of the probable memory of a primal scene experience that has been triggered by his experience in the park. My synopsis in no way does justice to all the points made by these writers, but it does make sufficiently clear that their analyses are about Thomas and the text that he inhabits, not about the operations of the text in psychoanalytic terms.

Just as Jacques Lacan has rewritten Freud, so too has postmodern psychoanalytic criticism rewritten the kind of traditional Freudian criticism cited above. The same issues still engage one's critical attention—voyeurism, primal scene, the Oedipus complex—but in quite different ways. Although we can use the structure of the Oedipal plot as a point of entry, our confrontation with the master text will necessarily involve more than a consideration of the possibility that a character has an Oedipus complex. Instead, it demands examining the plot, narrative elements, and cinematic practice as well as our responses to them in much more complex terms.

The photographer can best be viewed in terms of the issue of language and discourse. When we first meet him he appears to be in complete control of the signifying practices at his command. He literally calls the shots, whether unacknowledged (as in the doss house) or known (as with Verushka). The one word he speaks consistently at the beginning of the film is "Yes"—to Verushka as he stimulates her response, to his assistant as he praises the doss house pictures, and to the female models when they assume a pose he likes (fig. 14–1). The affirmative signifier, "yes," is countered by

Figure 14-1. (Copyright 1966 by Metro-Goldwyn-Mayer, Inc.)

 his penultimate last word in the film, "Nothing," spoken in response to Ron's query as to what he saw in the park. He speaks affirmatively when he is caught up in an idealist view of his medium, when, that is, he thinks he can select aspects of his visual environment and make them represent what he wants them to, as demonstrated in his call to Verushka: "Give us a smile. Come on. That's it. Yes" (Script, 30).

His change from "Yes" to "Nothing" could conceivably be taken to signal a tragic fall from grace, but to view this change in terms of a classical rising and falling tragic narrative action is to miss the full complexity of what may be happening. The person who says "Yes" assigns meanings, determines signifieds for signifiers by his manipulation of reality (the women) or by his selective capturing of it (the doss house). His positioning of the idyllic pictures of the lovers at the end of his book will complete the book: "I've got something fab for the end. . . . It's very—peaceful. Very still . . ." (Script, 66). The last statement illustrates his naive assumption that the apparatus in fact registers what he sees and designates as meaning, an idealist's view of the medium.

The events in the park signal a change in this assured command over the discourse associated with the apparatus. To begin to understand the significance of this change, we must consider important hypotheses drawn from Lacan on the subject and from Christian Metz (following Lacan) on the nature of the cinematic signifier.

The most useful concepts extrapolated from Lacan's difficult writings concern the mirror phase; the view of the subject as constituted by language and signification exterior to it; and the privileging of the Phallus as the controlling signifier of all discourse. Any summary of these views is bound to be shallow and inadequate because of the complexity and interrelatedness of Lacan's concerns.

Briefly, the human subject can be considered with reference to three orders or phases: the *mirror*, the *symbolic*, and the *real*. The *mirror* refers to the experience of the pre-Oedipal infant, aged six to eighteen months, as it encounters its reflection in a mirror and assumes that the image of wholeness and completeness it sees there (sometimes with its mother), an image of the other, represents reality. The *symbolic* refers to that aspect of the subject's experience involving the acquisition of language, particularly as it passes through the Oedipus complex and comes to terms with the fact of sexual difference. Here desire for the mother must be repressed; this repression of desire occurs specifically in and through *language*. For the male this means acceding to the symbolic state Lacan refers to as the Name of the Father, where, safely removed from the threat of castration that follows from continuing to love the forbidden mother, the individual develops a social conscience, what Freud refers to as the super-ego. Henceforth, desire that cannot be spoken or named can only by signified through a series of linguistic displacements, an endless deferral of meaning achieved by means of metaphor and metonymy, tropes and contiguous associations that enter discourse as agents of repressive substitution for what is buried in the unconscious.

The *real* refers to that which exists for the individual functioning as a subject in language, as a signifier subject to the dominance of the Phallus as the mark of sexual difference and as the privileged signifier in discourse. As Lacan explains in "On a Question Preliminary to Any Possible Treatment of Psychosis," the individual engages in life as a signifier determined and "spoken" by the Other: all those elements constituting the complex signifying chain into which one has entered: "the condition of the subject . . . is dependent on what is being unfolded in the Other O. What is being unfolded there is articulated like a discourse (the unconscious is the discourse of the Other), whose syntax Freud first sought to define for those bits that come to us in privileged moments, in dreams, in slips of the tongue or pen, in flashes of wit" (1977, 193).

In "The Meaning of the Phallus," Lacan says the subject's relationship to the signifier "speaks in the Other . . . the very place called upon by a recourse to speech in any relation where it intervenes. If it speaks in the Other . . . it is because it is there that the subject, according to a logic prior to any awakening of the signified, finds his signifying place. . . . The phallus is the privileged signifier of that mark where the share of the logos is wedded to the advent of desire. . . . If the phallus is a signifier then it is in the place of the Other that the subject gains access to it" (1985, 79–83). In other words, learning to speak is, in effect, a learning how to be spoken as a sexed member of the signifying chain dominated by the signifier of the Phallus.

In *The Imaginary Signifier*, Metz draws on Lacanian theory to explain the nature of signification within cinema and the relationship of the spectator to the cinematic signifier. We are able to watch and understand films in part because we have passed through the mirror stage. Film itself is like a mirror in which we do not see ourselves, in contrast to the mirror phase in which "the child sees itself as an other, beside an other. . . . [W]hat *makes possible* the spectator's absence from the screen—or rather the intelligible unfolding of that film despite that absence—is the fact that the spectator has already known the experience of the mirror (of the true mirror), and is thus able to constitute a world of objects without having first to recognise himself within it. In this respect, the cinema is already on the side of the symbolic" (1982,

45–46). Absent to the object we watch, we observe an image that stands in for an absent object. The cinematic signifier is thus "imaginary": "What is characteristic of the cinema is not the imaginary that it may happen to represent, but the imaginary that it *is* from the start, the imaginary that constitutes it as a signifier" (44).

The act of watching a film appeals to our scopophilic drive, the desire to see, particularly the desire to watch unobserved, as voyeurs. This drive is linked, Metz argues, with primal scene experiences: "cinematic voyeurism, *unauthorised* scopophilia, is from the outset more strongly established than that of the theatre in direct line from the primal scene. . . . For its spectator the film unfolds in that simultaneously very close and definitely inaccessible 'elsewhere' in which the child *sees* the amorous play of the parental couple, who are similarly ignorant of it and leave it alone, a pure onlooker whose participation is inconceivable. In this respect the cinematic signifier is . . . more precisely Oedipal in type" (63–64).

We might consider *Blow-Up*'s earlier scene of photography—the session with Verushka—and Thomas's delight in the doss house pictures with reference to Lacan's mirror phase and the infant's fascination with the imaginary in the mirror that is seen to complete the infant and give it a sense of wholeness. That is, those scenes figure the photographer's apparent mastery over his environment and his ability to dominate the imaginary. The less satisfactory session with the five models may be a signal of the shift in control about to occur.

In the park and in the development scene, to continue the analogy, the photographer could be said to move into the next phase posited by Lacan. Here he engages in the symbolic. The entrance into the symbolic accompanies the formation of the Oedipus complex and hence of the institution of language as an agency of repression.

Observe the photographer as he watches the older man and younger woman (fig. 14–2). In addition to the obvious voyeuristic staging of the scene, there is an inevitable reverberation of the primal scene, as the critics cited earlier have noted. But I am more interested in the fact that during the voyeuristic picture-taking scene, the photographer leaps over the fence and squats close to where, we learn, the "killer" lurks. In other words, to extend this connection between the entrance simultaneously into the symbolic and the Oedipal configuration, the photographer literally and figuratively jumps into an Oedipal narrative of someone else's making: *another* younger man with a gun wants to shoot the older man; the photographer wants to "shoot" his picture. In other words, he enters a symbolic order having *in it* an essen-

Figure 14-2. (Copyright 1966 by Metro-Goldwyn-Mayer, Inc.)

tial Oedipal structure and occupies the place that awaits him in the narrative signifying chain.

He is caught up in various signifying structures: the narrative plot (written by Antonioni and Tonino Guerra); the plot within the narrative (the plan to kill the older man); and the *mise-en-scène*. The last positions him as a voyeur in a way to replicate the visual structure of a primal scene experience and imposes him on and within an Oedipal configuration. He has entered into the symbolic and as such is determined, signified, by a chain of signifiers and signifying practices over which he has no control. The similarity figured in the two kinds of "shooting," the physical similarity of the men, and their proximity in space all underscore the substitutive and metonymic relationship posited by the narrative and *mise-en-scène*. Unlike his experience in what I am calling analogously the mirror phase, the point at which he has mastery over the medium, he is no longer the master in the symbolic phase.

The fascinating scenes in which he develops the photographs invite consideration in terms of the analytical process, as Dervin notes. But interesting as that aspect might be, I think we must put the process in relation to the Oedipal structure we see emerging in the operation of the text and our relation to it. Thomas begins to develop the film after the girl leaves, their potential lovemaking having been interrupted by the arrival of the propeller. He scrutinizes the record of the encounter in various stages of its transformation from material in the roll to the actual blow-ups (figs. 14–3 and 14–4). As he hangs the pictures in his studio the *mise-en-scène* produces a remarkable effect. The interrelationship he was assigned as a signifier during the sequence in which he photographed the murder is here photographically fixed by positioning him in relationship to the photographs. The black-and-white photo of the couple embracing (fig. 14–5) precedes temporally the shot of the worried-looking girl (fig. 14–6). In the latter, Antonioni frames the photographer so as to include him in an eye-line match. Someone in a photograph in a photographed film (Redgrave) is looking off-screen, out-of-frame, at a photographed character in a film. A picture is looking at a picture. During the actual photographing sequence, Thomas was in fact at one point in an eye-line match relationship to the girl, unknown to her; the object of her gaze was the killer, unknown to Thomas. That is, at that point in the earlier scene we have a curious effect, understood retroactively, in which the older man sees nothing, only the girl; the girl looks at the killer she knows is there; and the photographer who observes the couple is unaware of the killer. Figure 14–6 captures this series of curiously relayed glances and reinscribes the photographer's previous lack of understanding or misunderstanding by positioning him as the object of a photograph's gaze.

Thomas's entrance into what I am calling a symbolic order thus is recorded and fixed after the fact by Antonioni in the photograph in which the object of the killer's desire looks at both the killer and at the photographer; he has literally taken the place in Antonioni's frame of the absent/present

Figure 14-3. (Copyright 1966 by Metro-Goldwyn-Mayer, Inc.)

Figure 14-4. (Copyright 1966 by Metro-Goldwyn-Mayer, Inc.)

Figure 14-5. (Copyright 1966 by Metro-Goldwyn-Mayer, Inc.)

Figure 14-6. (Copyright 1966 by Metro-Goldwyn-Mayer, Inc.)

killer. Whereas he thought he "saw" one reality with his eyes and camera, one in which his presence was unseen (he is absent from the photograph), the image of the other scene that was there now appears as he confronts the symbolic, an image that serves as a signifier for the absent and which now *includes* him as the object of a gaze and positions him in an Oedipal triangle. Significantly, during the scene in which the girl and the older man become aware of the *photographer*, who has now moved away from the fence where he and the killer are hiding, Antonioni shoots their recognition from the place where the *killer* still is—a curious break in the pattern of shots that we only understand later. Thomas's scrutiny of the photograph in which the girl looks at the killer sends him back to the darkroom for more developing and the discovery, finally, of the hand with the gun in the bushes, the sign of the killer from whose point of view the discovery of the *photographer* occurs.

Many critics remark on the similarity between montage and the developing, arranging, and blowing-up of the photographs. But from a psychoanalytic perspective more needs to be said. Following from the Oedipalized relationship between spectator and screen Metz describes is an analogous relationship that can be pointed out in relation to the photographer and his pictures that he assembles through a kind of montage into a filmic sequence. Antonioni uses *his* camera movements and framings to provide a sense of how the photographer reads and interprets the images before him. Thomas comes to a provisional interpretation of what the camera saw and what the figures in the photographs saw by scrutinizing as if he were filming and editing.

In so doing, the assumed point-of-view shots attributed to Thomas by Antonioni make of him a kind of camera/editing apparatus that reminds us of Metz's discussion of cinematic pleasure. Recall Metz's hypothesis that the pleasure of viewing the screen itself is understandable in terms of the primal scene, as a way of replaying one's earlier view of the forbidden. Thus the behavior of the camera, and obviously of editing itself, fits into a psychic structure of behavior involving *our* perception, a structure here mirrored in the Oedipal scene witnessed by *Thomas* and reexamined by him during the development sequence. Although it is not "erotic" in specific visual content, it is so in terms of the Oedipal triangle to which it points. Consider, then, Metz's connecting of camera movement and framing with the unveiling of events in the fiction film:

> Whether the form is static (framing) or dynamic (camera movements), the principle is the same. . . . The framing and its displacements . . . are in themselves forms of "suspense" and are extensively used in suspense films, though they retain this function in other cases. They have an inner affinity

> with the mechanisms of desire, its postponements, its new impetus, and they retain this affinity in other places than erotic sequences. . . . The way the cinema, with its wandering framings (wandering like the look, like the caress), finds the means to reveal space has something to do with a kind of permanent undressing, a generalised strip-tease, a less direct but more perfected strip-tease, since it also makes it possible to dress space again, to remove from view what was previously shown, to *take back* as well as retain (like the child at the moment of the birth of the fetish, the child who has already seen, but whose look beats a rapid retreat). (1982, 77)

His triumphant sense is that, as before in the doss house and with Verushka, he has called the shots or in this case effectively prevented a shot from occurring. At this point he phones his friend Ron to share the news with him, only to be interrupted by the teeny-boppers. Their arrival and the orgy create an apparent problem for analysis. In terms of narrative function, the orgy might be there to signal his immaturity; i.e., how could a serious artist interrupt a process of such importance. Or, to pursue on a superficial level for a moment the Oedipal suggestions made earlier, his dalliance with the teeny-boppers might be seen as a triumphant display of power as a result of his unconscious delight in having prevented the murder of an older man; that is, he is in the position of Oedipus before being informed of the truth. That seems an unsatisfactory explanation, though, because it has the effect of shifting interpretive attention away from the complex question raised by the (non)demonstration of Thomas engaged in sexual activity.

Instead, I propose we consider another aspect of the orgy sequence. Thomas fills in the narrative space previously occupied by the girl. John Freccero suggests a *narrative* parallel between Thomas and the girl: "the aspiring models . . . stand chronologically in relation to him as does the girl, Vanessa Redgrave, to the older man for whose death she is somehow responsible" (1971, 121). And Dervin observes: "The threatening triangle in the eloquently mute stills is briefly forgotten by a three-dimensional romp amid green body hose and purple crepe paper. The male-female-male configuration is made over into female-male-female, as simultaneously a full-color movie plays off against, and competes with a black-and-white still" (75).

Although one can agree that both the girl and Thomas are objects of desire, neither critic sees that the text is reinscribing the Oedipal configuration of triangulation involving older man, woman and younger man in a problematic form. Freccero argues that "with Vanessa Redgrave [Thomas] finds a kindred spirit whose past and identity are as mysterious as his own. Antonioni underscores their complementarity even by their dress, for in the scene that provided the publicity stills, the whiteness of her bare flesh and her blue skirt are the colors symmetrically reversed, in which he is dressed—blue shirt and white slacks—while both she and Thomas are wearing identical belts" (125).

The similar appearance of the two and Thomas's behavior with Verushka, the girl, and the teeny-boppers raise a question, unresolved in the text as far as I can see, of sexual identity *within* the configuration of the Oedipal triangle. The cinematic text shows the girl and Thomas shirtless in an aborted sexual encounter; but it reveals the pudendum of one of the teeny-boppers during a childish romp. It is not insignificant, I think, that the shot of female genitalia, the mark of sexual difference—the absence of a penis, the mark of castration—occurs in the apparently "innocent" infantile sexual play. On the one hand, that is, the text demonstrates the dominance of the Phallus by reminding the viewer of its absence, earlier in the sequence in which Thomas photographs Verushka and now in the shot of the teeny-bopper's pudendum. On the other hand, Thomas is himself feminized by the similarity to the girl and by his passive role as the object of desire—a state emphasized by the shot of him between the two girls after the orgy. By defining him sexually in a problematic manner through what it does and does not show in the *mise-en-scène* and in a sexually explicit shot, the text seems to be figuring its *own* uncertainty about the character it has manipulated.

Antonioni's comment on the scene raises more questions than it answers: "there is a scene in the photographer's studio in which two young girls, less than twenty years old, disport themselves in a way that is especially provocative. They are completely nude. But that scene was not constructed for ogling. I believe I filmed it in a way that no one would judge obscene. The sequence is not erotic, any more than it is vulgar. It is fresh, light—and I venture to hope—funny" (*Cahiers* 1971, 11).

I do not know how much more explicit the initial version of the orgy may have been, but nothing I am aware of suggests that the explicitness of the sequence included male frontal nudity. The *visual* treatment of Thomas, suggesting a physical similarity to the girl, connects to the *narrative* role he is made to play in the text. The narrative itself castrates Thomas by positioning him literally on Verushka with his clothes on (with the camera serving as a signifier for phallic power) and by cutting away from the orgy once the mark of sexual difference has been established. This visual and narrative castration is itself symptomatic of the manner in which the text has slotted him into the visual and narrative Oedipal structure called *Blow-Up*. In other words, Thomas's role as a character in an Oedipal drama about which he knows nothing is symptomatic of his status as a hero in a narrative that determines and speaks him as a signifier.

He goes to the park and encounters the body—but without his camera. There is no logical *narrative* reason why this should be so. Had he taken his camera, he could have had extra evidence that would then obviate the problem occasioned by the theft of the photographs occurring at the moment he is viewing the actual body. Moreover, had he taken a picture now he would not need to convince Ron to come with him later to do so. Why does he need Ron anyway to take the picture with him? Such a narrative impasse may be addressed in terms of the psychoanalytic concerns raised thus far.

Thomas's encounter with the body marks the superiority of the master text that he inhabits and that speaks him by positioning him within the Oedipal configuration. Confronting the dead body, the signifier of his impotence, he is without his camera, the apparatus that hitherto permitted him to master reality, or so he thought. The text has taken away his camera; his encounter with the reality rather than the appearance in the photographs is frightening, an example of what Freud and Lacan refer to as *Nachträglichkeit*, deferred action, in which the significance of an earlier event becomes clear. The removal of his camera is yet another castrating action of the text upon Thomas as an element absorbed in a signifying chain, a prelude to what will happen to him in the last scene of the film. Here he touches the body and then runs away when he hears a sound—a branch? a camera? a gun? In other words, Thomas's impotence here is not so much a narrative problem as it is a moment of revelation in which the text's manipulation of him appears even more clearly evident.

The apparently illogical scene—why doesn't he bring his camera?—should be combined with the final scene of the tennis match, for both work to the same end: they define him as a subject formed by the discourse of the Other. His cautious touching of the corpse that wasn't there, and now is, connects to his picking up of a tennis ball that isn't there but is heard as if it were.

Lacan's analysis of *Oedipus Rex* is pertinent here. As Shoshana Felman explains: " 'The unconscious,' says Lacan, 'is the discourse of the other.' *Oedipus Rex* could be viewed as nothing other than a spectacular dramatization, a calculated pedagogical demonstration, of this formula. For Oedipus' unconscious is quite literally embodied in the discourse of the Other—of the oracle. 'Oedipus' unconscious is nothing other than this fundamental discourse whereby, long since, for all time, Oedipus' history is out there—written, and we know it, but Oedipus is ignorant of it, even as he is played out by it since the beginning' " (1985, 1025).

Thomas's picking up of the tennis ball that isn't there marks the most overt point in the narrative demonstrating the manner in which he exists as an element in a signifying discourse over which he has no control. His encounter with the tennis ball figures his encounter with the *real*, the signifying determining discourses to which he lacks direct access. The blotting out of him at the end of the film is the last in a series of narrative moves by the text. All Thomas can do is cooperate with the mimes and engage in the play of the imaginary signifier. The tennis game works like a *mise en abyme* within the text of *Blow-Up* as a comment on its own operations. The universe Thomas inhabits is *all* imaginary signifiers: what is absent is or will be present; what is present is or will be absent. And presence and absence are elements in a narrative chain that sets the Oedipal text as its framework. Thomas—a figure in a narrative, in a landscape—is ultimately a mere signifier within the cinematic discourse called *Blow-Up*.

WORKS CITED

Antonioni, Michelangelo, and Tonino Guerra. 1971. *Blow-Up* (Script). New York: Simon and Schuster.

Arlow, Jacob. 1980. "The Revenge Motive in the Primal Scene." *Journal of the American Psychoanalytic Association* 28: 519–41.

Barthes, Roland. *The Pleasure of the Text*. 1975. Translated by Richard Miller. New York: Hill and Wang.

Cahiers du cinéma. 1971. "Antonioni in the English Style: A Day on the Set." In *Focus on Blow-Up*, edited by Roy Huss, 7–12. Englewood Cliffs, N.J.: Prentice-Hall.

Dervin, Daniel. 1985. *Through a Freudian Lens Deeply: A Psychoanalysis of Cinema*. Hillsdale, N.J.: Analytic Press.

Felman, Shoshana. 1985. "Beyond Oedipus: The Specimen Story of Psychoanalysis." In *Lacan and Narration: The Psychoanalytic Difference in Narrative Theory*, edited by Robert Con Davis. Baltimore: Johns Hopkins University Press.

Freccero, John. 1971. "*Blow-Up*: From the Word to the Image." In *Focus on Blow-Up*, edited by Roy Huss, 116–28. Englewood Cliffs, N.J.: Prentice-Hall.

Goldstein, Melvin. 1975. "Antonioni's *Blow-Up*: From Crib to Camera." *American Imago* 32: 240–63.

Lacan, Jacques. 1977. "On a Question Preliminary to Any Possible Treatment of Psychosis." In *Ecrits*, translated by Alan Sheridan, 179–225. New York: W. W. Norton and Company.

———. 1985. "The Meaning of the Phallus." In *Feminine Sexuality: Jacques Lacan and the école freudienne*, translated by Jacqueline Rose and edited by Juliet Mitchell and Jacqueline Rose, 74–85. New York: W. W. Norton and Company.

Metz, Christian. 1982. *The Imaginary Signifier: Psychoanalysis and the Cinema*. Translated by Celia Britton, Annwyl Williams, Ben Brewster, and Alfred Guzzetti. Bloomington: Indiana University Press.

Samuels, Charles Thomas. 1972. "Michelangelo Antonioni." In *Encountering Directors*, 15–32. New York: Capricorn Books.

Wright, Elizabeth, 1984. *Psychoanalytic Criticism: Theory in Practice*. London and New York, Methuen.

BIBLIOGRAPHY

Criticism of *Blow-Up*

Arlow, Jacob. "The Revenge Motive in the Primal Scene." *Journal of the American Psychoanalytic Association* 28 (1980): 519–41.

Cameron, Ian, and Robin Wood. *Antonioni*. Revised edition. New York: Praeger, 1975.

Chatman, Seymour. *Antonioni or The Surface of the World*. Berkeley: University of California Press, 1985.

Dervin, Daniel. *Through a Freudian Lens Deeply: A Psychoanalysis of Cinema*. Hillsdale, N.J.: Analytic Press, 1985.

D'Lugo, Marvin. "Signs and Meaning in *Blow Up*: From Cortazar to Antonioni." *Literature/Film Quarterly* 3 (1975): 23–29.

Eidsvik, Charles. *Cineliteracy Film Among the Arts*. New York: Random House, 1978.

Ferrua, Pietro. "*Blow-Up* from Cortazar to Antonioni." *Literature/Film Quarterly* 4 (1976): 68–75.

Francis, Richard Lee. "Transcending Metaphor: Antonioni's *Blow-Up*." *Literature/Film Quarterly* 13 (1985): 42–49.

Goldstein, Melvin. "Antonioni's *Blow-Up*: From Crib to Camera." *American Imago* 32 (1975): 240–63.

Huss, Roy, ed. *Focus on Blow-Up*. Englewood Cliffs, N.J.: Prentice-Hall, 1971.

Isaacs, Neil D. "The Triumph of Artifice: Antonioni's *Blow-Up* (1966)." In *Modern European Filmmakers and the Art of Adaptation*, edited by Andrew S. Horton and Joan Margretta. New York: Fredrick Ungar Publishing Co., 1981.

Palmer, William J. "*Blow-Up*: The Game with No Balls." *Literature/Film Quarterly* 7 (1979): 314–21.

Peavler, Terry J. "*Blow-Up*: A Reconsideration of Antonioni's Fidelity to Cortazar." *PMLA* 94 (1979): 887–93.

Prats, A. J. *The Autonomous Gaze: Cinematic Narration and Humanism*. Lexington: University of Kentucky Press, 1981.

Psychoanalytic Film Theory

Altman, Rick. "Psychoanalysis and Cinema: The Imaginary Discourse." *Quarterly Review of Film Studies* 2 (1977): 257–72.

Baudry, Jean-Louis. "The Apparatus." Translated by Jean Andrews and Bertrand Augst. *Camera Obscura* 1 (1976): 97–126.

———. "Ideological Effects of the Cinematic Apparatus." Translated by Alan Williams. *Film Quarterly* 28 (1974–75): 39–47.

Cha, Theresa Hak Kyung, ed. *Apparatus*. New York: Tanam Press, 1980.

Heath, Stephen. *Questions of Cinema*. Bloomington: Indiana University Press, 1981.

Kuntzel, Thierry. "The Film-Work." Translated by Lawrence Crawford, Kimball Lockhart, and Claudia Tysdale. *Enclitic* 2 (1978): 39–62.

———. "The Film-Work, 2." Translated by Nancy Houston. *Camera Obscura* 5 (1980): 7–69.

———. "A Note upon the Filmic Apparatus." *Quarterly Review of Film Studies* 1 (1976): 266–71.

Metz, Christian. *The Imaginary Signifier*. Translated by Celia Britton, Annwyl Williams, Ben Brewster, and Alfred Guzzetti. Bloomington: Indiana University Press, 1982.

Penley, Constance. "The Avant-Garde and Its Imaginary." *Camera Obscura* 2 (1978): 3–33.

Psychoanalytic Theory

Freud, Sigmund. *The Standard Edition of the Complete Psychological Works of Sigmund Freud*. 24 vols. Translated and edited by James Strachey. London: The Hogarth Press, 1953–74.

Lacan, Jacques. *Ecrits*. Translated by Alan Sheridan. New York: W. W. Norton and Co., Inc., 1977.

———. *The Four Fundamental Concepts of Psycho-Analysis*. Translated by Alan Sheridan. Edited by Jacques Alain-Miller. New York: W. W. Norton and Co., Inc., 1978.

I wanted the picture [Freud] *to be released as it was, but the reaction of the preview audience was against me. The studio executives prevailed upon me to cut one scene because it offended their moral concepts. The scene showed a girl under hypnosis telling, in the presence of her father, of his assault upon her. I should not have accepted this cut; the scene was very important to the story because it showed one of the false leads that put Freud onto a wrong line of country. The fact that this one incident was true led him to accept as true other similar testimonies regarding sexual assaults, whereas most of these other patients had merely imagined "relationships" with their father; their confessions were simply wish-fulfillments.*
—John Huston, *An Open Book*

15

JOHN HUSTON'S *FREUD* AND TEXTUAL REPRESSION: A PSYCHOANALYTIC FEMINIST READING

Janet Walker and Diane Waldman

The content of the missing scene Huston mentions—"a girl under hypnosis telling, in the presence of her father, of his assault upon her," and telling it to a credulous Freud—offers an entry point from which to evaluate psychoanalysis and psychoanalytic film criticism from a feminist perspective. The choice to use psychoanalytically informed feminist criticism to analyze a book or a film always raises the question of whether psychoanalysis and feminism are not mutually exclusive systems of thought. The question is all the more pressing for the fact that psychoanalytic methodology has been an important influence on film studies since the early 1970s. Pointing to the simultaneous development of the two institutions (psychoanalysis and cinema) in the late nineteenth century and to the emphasis on the visual ("scenarios") in the work of Sigmund Freud and Jacques Lacan, contemporary theorists have employed psychoanalytic models to explore both the relationship of the spectator to the text and, using the analogy of the dream, the operations of the "film work": repression, condensation, displacement, secondary re-vision, etc.[1] As film critics we may find such formulations useful and convincing, yet as feminists we believe that they are only useful to the extent that they address the masculine biases inherent in both the theory and its application to film analysis.[2]

Huston regrets the omission of a scene giving credence to a girl's tale of childhood sexual assault by her father. But his regret does not stem from the feminist insistence that child molestation be acknowledged as the pervasive social problem it is, a social problem the blame for which should not be attributed under any circumstances to the victim. Huston's regret stems instead from the concerns of the raconteur. The scene, writes Huston, would have enriched the story of Freud's eventual discovery of the truth of psychoanalysis by representing a "false lead." Thus Huston explicitly adopts the standard or orthodox view that psychoanalysis was born when Freud abandoned the seduction theory, i.e., when he stopped believing that his hysterical patients (most of whom were female) had actually been assaulted and started believing that their accounts of childhood seduction were based on fantasies stemming from the unconscious Oedipal desire of the little girl for her father.

This historical account of Freud's false start and final victory, a classical pattern of conflict and resolution that Huston would have preferred in his film fiction, has been accepted by some feminist scholars, particularly those interested in using psychoanalytic ideas for an analysis of patriarchy. Juliet Mitchell's work is central in this regard. She argues that it was exactly Freud's realization of the *irrelevance* of real events that allowed him to develop the concept of the unconscious and that of infantile sexuality. In Freud's eventual account, both the infant boy and the infant girl initially possess a sexual drive made up of various components but not differentiated into masculine or feminine sexuality. As the child develops, he or she gains awareness that the mother is the source of the satisfaction of the drives. Both male and female infants then share a "masculine" desire for the mother, expressed in fantasy as having the phallus the mother herself desires (the phallic phase). But the boy's desire for his mother is forbidden him by the rivalry

1. Important works here are Freud (*The Interpretation of Dreams*); Baudry (1976); and Metz (1981). For a summary of these developments see Andrew (1984, esp. 133–66) and Silverman (1983).

2. For discussions of the relationship between feminism and psychoanalytic film theory, see Bergstrom (1979); De Lauretis (1984, esp. 161–66); Doane (1987, esp. 1–22); Kaplan (1983, esp. 32–35); Kuhn (1982, esp. 59–83); and Mayne (1985, esp. 92–94).

of the father who, in the boy's eyes, both possesses the phallus and threatens his son's immature phallus (the castration complex). The girl's desire for the mother is also forbidden by the presence of the father who has the phallus the girl yearns to possess (penis envy). Disappointed in her mother, who lacks the phallus, the girl transfers her desire to her father.

What Mitchell finds particularly useful for feminism in Freud's work, then, is the notion that psychosexuality is not inborn but is rather derivative of the whole process of taking up a position in the family. It is a construction that *depends* on biology but may not be reduced to it. In other words, in Freud's work there is a gap or difference between biological femaleness and maleness and psychological femininity or masculinity. To suggest, as did Freud's neurologist colleagues, that a girl is "innocent" of sexual desire before puberty implies that sexuality is something that can be added to a person's already formed but asexual personality. This idea is problematic for Mitchell because it cannot explain why life experience renders males masculine or females feminine except by assuming preexisting biological differences according to which social experience is ultimately aligned. In other words, without Freud's ideas about the unconscious and infantile sexuality, thinking about gender and sexuality falls too easily into "biological determinism," the notion that "boys will be boys and girls will be girls" or that women can't do "X" because of their gender.

Other feminist scholars, notably Florence Rush and later Jeffrey Masson, consider psychoanalysis anathema to feminism. And a major objection is precisely the orthodox psychoanalytic view that the discipline was born when Freud stopped believing that his hysterical patients (most of whom were female) had actually been assaulted in childhood by their fathers. They object, in short, to what they regard as psychoanalysis's denial of women's accounts of their experience and of the significance or even existence of child molestation.

While we share the concerns of Rush and others that incest and child abuse not be denied, we would suggest that the existence of actual cases of incest does not necessarily preclude the possibility of incestuous desire and fantasy. Conversely, the recognition of the existence of fantasy does not necessarily preclude the importance of child molestation. The problem we see with these two positions, the one represented by Rush and that represented by Mitchell, is that they perpetuate a false dichotomy by failing to take adequate account of the *relationship between* women's social experience and psychic structure.

Both positions also downplay what we regard as an interesting tension in Freud's own work, a tension that functions to resist any such false dichotomy. While it is true that Freud's fundamental endeavor was to interpret the seduction scenarios recounted by patients as fantasies, he never actually denied the reality of incest and the sexual abuse of children. Furthermore, and much more significantly, he continued to seek a *relationship* between actual child abuse and unconscious Oedipal fantasies and desires. As late as 1933 he would refer to actual seduction, remarking that sexual trauma may play a part in the aetiology of neurosis, if not as great a part as he had once surmised.[3] Freud's work, then, is all the more interesting for its refusal to resolve the question by dismissing either the social reality of rape or the importance of fantasy construction—for its simultaneous insistence on both possibilities.

In its development from script to film and even in its final narrative version the film *Freud* bears the textual marks of this unresolved dilemma. As will be discussed, the resolution of the plot depends on the fictional Freud's discovery that actual incest did not really take place. In this respect the film falls in line with the ideology that denies seduction and reduces the complexity of the historical Freud's work on the subject. Yet by using a method informed by both psychoanalysis and feminism, we hope to demonstrate that the film's denial of incest is not complete, but rather operates as a repression, the symptoms of which can be read in the text itself.

THE DENIAL OF CHILDHOOD SEDUCTION

In 1958 John Huston asked Jean-Paul Sartre to write a script based upon Freud's life and work.[4] The resulting product, if filmed, would have been over five hours long. Huston sent it back for cutting and revision, and Sartre produced an even longer version. At this point, and after Huston had received the authorization from Universal to proceed with the project, he turned to a Hollywood screenwriter, Charles Kaufman, and his producer, Wolfgang Reinhardt, to prune and modify the script. Sartre refused to have anything to do with the result, and indeed his name does not appear in the final credits, although much of the conception, structure, and dialogue and

3. Examples can be found in Freud, *Introductory Lectures on Psychoanalysis* (1916) (S.E. 16, 370); a footnote written in 1924 to the 1896 "The Neuro-Psychoses of Defence" (S.E. 3, 168); the 1925 *Autobiographical Study* (S.E. 20, 33–34); the essay on "Female Sexuality" (1931) (S.E. 21, 238); and the essay on femininity in the 1933 *New Introductory Lectures* (S.E. 22, 120). These examples are cited in Masson (1984, 195–200), and the latter two are cited by Gallop (1982, 143–45).

4. See Huston (1980, 294–305), Pontalis (1986, vii–xviii), and the review of the Sartre script by Crinkley (1984) for descriptions of the film's production history.

 many of the ideas for the visual imagery of the film appear to be based on his two versions of the script. The first filmed version, starring Montgomery Clift as Freud and Susannah York as Cecily, ran about two hours and twenty minutes. After studio previews, however, the film was cut to just under two hours.[5] The film's name was changed to *Freud: The Secret Passion* in what was to be a futile and somewhat misleading attempt to generate additional interest in the film's sexual subject matter.

If the continual excisions that marked the project's development from script to film did not have the desired effect on box office receipts, they did have an effect on the film's depiction of childhood sexual assault, for one of the scenes excised was that to which Huston referred in the epigraph with which this essay begins. Thus while the Sartre script does present the orthodox view that traumatic sexual experiences are a "false lead" if one is trying to describe the aetiology of neurosis, at least it also acknowledges the occurrence of actual abuse. In eliminating the scene, however, the film attempts to do away altogether with any suggestion of actual abuse.

The film does have a major character, Cecily Kortner, who reports an incident of childhood molestation by her father, but this report is ultimately explained away as untrue. In fact, the film's resolution depends very specifically on the disavowal of this particular event. *Freud* focuses on a period of approximately twelve years, from 1885 to 1897, the period of Freud's transition from neurology to psychoanalysis.[6] Accordingly, the film represents Freud's interest in hysteria, his studies with the French neurologist Charcot, his adaptation of the latter's use of hypnosis, and his work with Breuer using the cathartic method on hysterical patients. It then goes on to depict Freud's gradual disillusionment with hypnosis, the development of the methods of free association and dream analysis, and the development of the seduction theory. The film culminates in Freud's abandonment of the seduction theory and the theorization of the Oedipus complex and infantile sexuality.

Freud's theories are represented as emanating from two sources: his patients and himself. His patients are condensed into two central figures: a male patient, Karl von Schlosser, and a female patient, Cecily Kortner.[7] The

5. We have seen what we assume to be both these filmed versions, and we base our analysis on these.

6. This periodization roughly coincides with Freud's own in "On the History of the Psychoanalytic Movement (1914)."

7. Freud did see a patient called Frau Cacile M., whom he describes in *Studies in Hysteria* as remarkable for the degree of symbolization in her conversion to hysterical symptoms. However, it is generally agreed that the film character Cecily is based largely on Breuer's patient, Anna O.

encounter with von Schlosser, which graphically depicts the latter's sexual desire for his mother and hostility toward his father, functions to illustrate Freud's early discomfort with these ideas. The subsequent dream sequence (in which von Schlosser and Freud enter a tunnel connected by a rope and von Schlosser embraces Freud's mother) further demonstrates that this discomfort derives in part from Freud's own unconscious desires. It is only after his work with Cecily and the crucial discovery that her report of a childhood assault by her father is a fantasy (a screen memory designed to mask her unconscious desire for her father) and after Freud's own self-analysis prompted by his ambivalent reaction to the death of his father that the notions of infantile sexuality and the Oedipus complex can be discovered and articulated.[8]

The film demonstrates this patriarchal logic through the following narrative sequence. Freud discusses with Breuer his theory that a traumatic sexual experience in childhood is at the root of neuroses. He refers to a half dozen cases but in particular to Cecily's and his own ("the memory of something I witnessed between my father and my sister"). In the following scene, Freud helps Cecily to uncover the painful memory of sexual molestation by her father. This is implied by the visual track that presents a repetition of a succession of images seen earlier in which Cecily's mother scolds the young child and strikes her for painting her face. This time, however, the story continues. Cecily's father enters, rescues the child, and takes her out of the room. The father and Cecily enter another room and Cecily's voice narrates over the image, confirming their status: "He carried me to his room and undressed me . . . he sang to comfort me." Freud asks, "Is that when he promised you the doll?" We return to a shot of the adult Cecily, who replies, "Yes . . . no . . . it was later in the night when I woke up and cried." After further interrogation by Freud as to why she was crying, Cecily replies, "He locked the door." This cues a return to the flashback on the visual track, as we see the father enter the room in the background of the shot. Cecily continues to narrate over the image: "Father came toward me in his red robe [at this point there is redundancy of sound and image]. Tall like a tower." The father turns off the light and the image fades to black. Cecily continues her narration over this blank image: "Strong like a god when he embraced me." In voiceover Freud asks: "And he promised you a doll if you wouldn't tell, is that right?" We return to the present, a shot of Freud and the adult Cecily.

8. In this particular interpretation, as Pontalis (1986) argues, Sartre's script and Huston's film follow Ernest Jones in his biography of Freud (1961) and Ernst Kris in his introduction to the Freud-Fliess correspondence (1954), both of which had been recently published when Sartre began to work on the script.

"Yes!" she replies and hesitantly begins to walk. "I can walk," she exclaims. "My father was a criminal." Freud: "I'm sure he suffered for what he did." The disappearance of Cecily's paralytic symptoms after this narration leads Freud (and the spectator) to conclude that we have uncovered the painful memory at the source of Cecily's hysteria. The disappearance confirms the idea that a traumatic sexual experience lies at the root of hysteria.

Yet Freud is still troubled by Cecily's fondness for the doll that should be the "evidence of her father's crime." "Perhaps the answer lies still farther back . . . as in my own case," he muses. At this point Freud turns to his mother to corroborate the intuition that he has repressed the memory of some incident concerning his father and sister. However, she supplies the information that his sister was not even born at the time of the incident in question. Therefore the film implies that Freud's father could not possibly have molested Freud's sister. This leads Freud to the discovery that Cecily's fondness for her doll is the symptom of her desire for her father and the expression of the wish to have a child by him. Cecily confirms this new interpretation when she confesses to Freud that she had lied about the incident with her father in order to please Freud.

These sequences build the case which is also made explicitly through the dialogue in the following scene where Freud, analyzing one of his own dreams, uncovers his desire for his mother and comes to the following conclusion:

> My theory has offended everyone and no wonder. It's false. I invented a theory to dishonor my father. . . . I desecrated his image and that of the fathers of my patients. . . . She [Cecily] claimed her father had seduced her. False. It wasn't he who desired his daughter, but she who wanted him. And it was not a memory which she had repressed. No. It was a fantasy. . . . Was she lying to me? No. To herself? No. The unconscious is pitch dark. . . . The truth has emerged upside down and it will walk on one premise alone. There must be sexuality in childhood.

The portentousness of this lengthy speech, Montgomery Clift's agitated pacing and delivery, and Martha's reaction (she opens the curtains to "let in the light," fulfilling the destiny of psychoanalysis promised in the film's introductory narration)[9] clearly mark this as the film's climactic moment.

Thus Cecily's report of molestation is untrue by virtue of having been a psychological fantasy mistakenly construed as actuality. But while the film

9. The opening narration concludes: "This is the story of Freud's descent into a region almost as black as hell itself—man's unconscious—and how he let in the light."

follows the letter of Freudian law in its identification of the fantasy construction, the whole trajectory of the film reduces the possibility of real molestation even further by simultaneously presenting Cecily's report as no more than a simple lie. To assign Cecily's original testimony this crude status the film must retreat from its initial liberal feminist position on female duplicity.

At the start of the film the fictional Freud is at great pains to show that women suffering from hysteria are not merely faking their symptoms. Their origin, Freud argues, is *psychic*. In the first diegetic scene of the film Dr. Meynert, head of neurology at a Vienna hospital, is incensed to discover that a woman suffering from hysterical blindness and paralysis has been given a bed in his ward. "Hysteria is another name for lying," he rages. The woman must be expelled from the hospital, and sent back to the duties she is shirking. "Her symptoms have been deliberately assumed with the purpose of attracting attention, gaining pity, and escaping the responsibilities of life," he claims. Freud, on the other hand, defends her contention that the blindness and paralysis are genuine. Sticking a tie pin through the skin of the woman's leg, he demonstrates that she doesn't flinch and cannot, therefore, be lying.

Just as important, the film offers a critique of the biological determinism so inimical to feminism by having Charcot refute the antiquated notion that hysterical symptoms may be adduced to organic causes in general and to one organic cause in particular: the diseased uterus. In the words of the fictional Charcot:

> The word hysteria is from the Greek word hysterum, meaning womb. To this day doctors believe the disease only exists in women . . . if, that is, they admit its existence at all. . . . Hysteria violated the medical tenet that all bodily symptoms must be of organic origin. . . . But facts do not cease to exist simply because they are in contradiction to a beloved theory. . . . hysteria is a purely mental malady.

Charcot's dialogue makes the link between disputing the organic cause of hysteria and disputing the notion that hysteria only affects women. In making this link the film, through Charcot, refutes the possibility that women's biological make-up is faulty or particularly prone to disease.

Hysteria is also emphasized as a human psychic rather than a female organic condition by the film's careful inclusion of male along with female patients: the male hysteric seen in Charcot's demonstration, von Schlosser, and another male patient who complains that his wife cast aspersions on his virility. The presentation of hysteria as symmetrically affecting male and female patients is actually a double-edged sword for feminism. On the one hand, as we are arguing, this symmetry discourages the view that psychic disorder results from feminine biology. On the other hand it masks the fact that the majority of Freud's hysterical patients were women and blocks the possibility of a nonbiological explanation for that fact. For example, some feminists have argued that hysteria is in part a refusal—a rejection of the narrow constraints of culturally constructed femininity. If we accept that view, then there is a certain core of truth in the contention that hysterics attempt (albeit unconsciously) to "escape the responsibilities of life," as the fictional Dr. Meynert claims. Nevertheless, in the opening scenes of the film Freud defends women against accusations of duplicity, but by the end of the film, as we have shown above, his own discoveries have been inextricably linked to the finding that women lie . . . and lie about one thing in particular: sexual molestation by their fathers.

That the little girl and not the adult male is the one with whom the blame for the seductive incestuous behavior rests in also made clear by the film's presentation of the relationship between Cecily and Breuer. And here too a comparison between Freud's work, Sartre's script, and the Huston film serves to highlight the film's ideological perspective. The character Cecily was based on Breuer's patient Anna O., whose treatment with Breuer ended rather abruptly. In Ernest Jones's biography of Freud he writes that Freud related to him "a fuller account that [sic] he described in his writings of the peculiar circumstances surrounding the end of the novel treatment." According to Jones, Breuer developed "what we should nowadays call a strong countertransference to his interesting patient," became totally engrossed in her case, talking of little else, making his wife, Mathilde, extremely jealous. When Breuer finally realized what was going on, "it provoked a violent reaction in him, perhaps compounded of love and guilt, and he decided to bring the treatment to an end."

> He announced this to Anna O., who was by now much better, and bade her good-bye. But that evening he was fetched back to find her in a greatly excited state, apparently as ill as ever. The patient, who according to him had appeared as an asexual being and had never made any allusions to such a forbidden topic throughout the treatment, was now in the throes of an hysterical childbirth . . . the logical termination of a phantom pregnancy that had been invisibly developing in response to Breuer's ministrations. Though profoundly shocked, he managed to calm her down by hypnotizing her, and then fled the house in a cold sweat. The next day he and his wife left for Venice, to spend a second honeymoon. (Jones 1961, 147–48)

Sartre's script emphasizes both sides of this transference-countertransference.[10] Not only does Cecily develop the hysterical pregnancy described above, but it is clear that Breuer is strongly attracted to her and engages in seductive behavior with her, something Freud notices and disapproves of. For example, in the scene where Freud first accompanies Breuer to Cecily's bedside, Sartre includes the following screen direction:

> *As they enter, Breuer whispers to Freud, with a kind of ecstasy that he barely attempts to conceal:*
> BREUER (*in a low whisper*): She's beautiful.

Further, when Breuer hypnotizes Cecily, we get the following:

> BREUER: Don't worry about a thing, Cacilie. Sleep.
>
> *She is still restless. He insists. Masterful, like a man who knows he is loved*:
>
> Do it *for me*.
>
> CACILIE: For you?
>
> *She closes her eyes and smiles. Freud has frowned. This over-intimate contact between the practitioner and his patient obviously displeases him, but without diminishing the rapt interest with which he follows the experiment*. (Sartre 1986, 145–47).

Yet in the film all traces of this "countertransference" have been removed. Here it is Cecily who sends Breuer flowers, asks for a good-bye kiss, gets erotic pleasure from the hypnosis. Breuer's attraction for Cecily is nonexistent. In this context, then, Mathilde's jealousy appears simply irrational, a product of the wife's ignorance of the mysteries of the therapeutic process. And, as in the case of the seduction of the father, the onus for seduction of the therapist is placed on the woman.

THE TEXTUAL ROLE OF REPRESSION

Yet this process we have been describing, the film's denial of the daughter's seduction, is far from complete. As in Freud's work, where the possibility that traumatic sexual assaults may play a role in the aetiology of neuroses continually reasserts itself, so in the film the spectre of childhood sexual assault is suggested at the same time it is denied. Freud used the term repression to describe an operation whereby a person turns away, or confines to the unconscious, thoughts, images, or memories that would provoke unpleasure if given conscious expression. And crucially, what has been repressed is

10. For a fuller discussion of the concepts of transference and countertransference and their representation in Hollywood films, see Walker (1987).

never completely abolished but rather tends to reappear in distorted form (Freud, "Repression"; Laplanche and Pontalis 1973, 390–94). We would theorize, then, that in the film *Freud* the daughter's seduction functions as a textual repression and is represented as the return of the repressed.

The central scene provided earlier as an example of the film's tendency to deny Cecily's testimony of childhood assault is actually an example of how the film *represses* rather than *erases* this traumatic memory. If father-daughter incest is unrepresentable *as such*, it is nevertheless representable in a covert manner. First, there is the odd disjunction between sound and image. When we hear "He carried me to his room and undressed me," we see Cecily's father carrying her into the room. The only subsequent "undressing" is Herr Kortner removing Cecily's socks. Second, the screen is completely blank as the actual embraces are described on the sound track. One might explain that these incidents remain unrepresented simply because Cecily's story is retrospectively revealed to be false. However, this practice is in marked contrast to an earlier sequence in which Cecily's screen memory (the death of her father in an Italian hospital) is graphically depicted although it too is subsequently revealed as false and corrected with a new version that is also depicted (the death of her father in a brothel). One might also argue that the scene couldn't be represented on the screen because, if Huston's account is accurate, it offended the morality of studio executives and audience. But that is precisely the point. Sexual molestation of daughters by fathers is repressed from film images in general and from this film in particular, and yet that very repression is also *represented*, in this case as the strange disjunction between sound and image and by the substitution of a blank, black screen for naturalistic images.

Repression is also evidenced in the way the film handles the daughter's seduction from the perspective of the father. On one hand the film *Freud* contains a curious omission that exonerates fathers from any culpability, going even further in this effort than either Freud's writing or Sartre's script. Yet even the banished notion of the guilt of the father returns in distorted form. Let's take the film's attempted omission first.

It has been argued that even when Freud admitted the reality of child abuse he was uncomfortable with the role of the father as seducer. For example, where Freud does speak of the reality of incest and the sexual abuse of children, the abuser is an uncle, an older child, or a servant. Or, where Freud argues that seduction *fantasies* "touch the ground of reality," it is the mother who is inadvertently responsible: "for it was really the *mother* who by her activities over the child's bodily hygiene inevitably stimulated, and perhaps even aroused for the first time, pleasurable sensations in her genitals."[11] Freud resisted the argument that the fantasy of seduction *by the father* "touches the ground of reality" either in actual sexual abuse, sexualizing behavior short of actual abuse,[12] or even in incestuous desire on the part of the father. For example, in a letter dated 31 May 1897, Freud described to Wilhelm Fliess a dream in which he was "feeling over-affectionately" toward Mathilde, his oldest daughter (*Origins*, 206). But rather than interpret this as evidence of his own incestuous desire, Freud writes that "the dream of course fulfills my wish to pin down a father as the originator of neurosis and put an end to my persistent doubts." As Charles Bernheimer argues, this allows Freud to "displac[e] his incestuous impulse into the realm of theory . . . the means through which Freud exonerates himself from a guilty complicity in male fantasies of seduction" (1985, 14).

Again we can trace the denial of the idea of father-daughter incest or more precisely paternal incestuous desire in the movement from script to film. Sartre's script includes a sequence based upon this biographical mate-

11. Rush (1980, 33), Masson (1984, 81–84, 197) and Poster (1986, 10) all refer to Freud's footnotes to the 1924 edition of the *Studies on Hysteria* in which he admits that he had altered two of the case studies to substitute an uncle for the father in the role of seducer. Rush (32), Masson (199–200), and Gallop (145–47) cite the passage from the 1933 lecture on femininity (S.E. 21, 238) about the mother's role in seduction fantasies. All note Freud's attempts to deny the role of the father.

12. Westkott uses the term "sexualization" to describe "girlhood sexual encounters ranging from incest to sexually suggestive, intrusive, or controlling treatment" (1986, 88), which she argues are part of the experience of females in a patriarchal culture. She further argues that "hysterical symptoms . . . can be interpreted as a psychological response to the more general exercise of eroticized power and not just the outcome of incest" (111). Similarly, Poster sees Freud's abandonment of the seduction theory as but one example of what he calls Freud's "ideology of parentism," a "recurrent systematic way in which Freud distorts the exchanges which occur in the family . . . masking the manner in which the parents constitute the child as their object by structuring an environment in which objects can be cathected and can be cathected only in certain ways" (1986, 4). In the case of the abandonment of the seduction theory, Poster argues that Freud ignores the role of the parents (and specifically the father) not only in actual rapes and incest but in *unconscious* sexual behavior that creates the ground for seduction fantasies (10–14). Both these writers, then, provide an alternate theoretical framework for explaining the prevalence of women's stories of seduction by the father, a framework that maintains the importance of fantasy but sees it as grounded in social reality.

rial, but the film eliminates it. Both the film and the script, then, overtly reject the suggestion that Freud (and by extension other fathers) may have sexually desired his own daughter: the script by including this dream but explaining it away theoretically; the film not only by eliminating this sequence but by simply refusing to represent Freud's daughter at all! This may in part explain psychoanalytically the curious omission of Freud's children from the final film.

Yet Freud went back to *Studies on Hysteria* over twenty-five years later and in a footnote admitted the role of the father as seducer, exposing the significance of having substituted "uncle" for "father" in the case history of Katharina:

> The girl fell ill, therefore, as a result of sexual attempts on the part of her own father. Distortions like the one which I introduced in the present instance should be altogether avoided in reporting a case history. (134)

To analyze Freud's own text from a psychoanalytic perspective, we could say that the uncle in the earlier version of the case history functions to mark the text's repression of the true fact of the father as seducer. Similarly in *Freud* the role of the father as seducer is not cleanly omitted but rather repressed, scheduled therefore to return in another form. Accordingly, the representation of father-daughter incest instigated by the father occurs through, and only through, a series of displacements or, to define this term introduced by Freud for dream analysis, through processes whereby a repressed idea's import and intensity are passed along to other ideas in a chain of associations (Freud, *Interpretation*, 340–44; Laplanche and Pontalis 1973, 121–24). Father-daughter incest (Herr Kortner and Cecily) is displaced onto *imagined* father-daughter incest (Freud's father and sister, and Freud's eventual interpretation of the true relationship between Herr Kortner and Cecily), and finally onto Oedipal desire (that of Freud for his mother). It is displaced further onto a textual omission readable in the comparison between the historical Freud and his fictional counterpart (the fictional Freud had no daughters). These displacements then are the textual traces of the narrative's inability to represent both childhood rape and psychic fantasy.

The film's concentration on Freud's own unconscious processes also gives weight to a symbolic register through which the film explores connections rejected at the level of the story. The three-shot sequence of Freud's departure for Paris, a sequence handled in a cinematic style at odds with the scenes of verbal exposition of supposed psychoanalytic truths, is crucial in this regard. In the first shot, Freud says good-bye to his fiancée, Martha, and then to his mother and father. As he gets on the train, his father hands him a watch that his father says was passed down to him by his father, Freud's grandfather. The first shot is also accompanied by some as yet unexplained female voices heard on the sound track, including one voice saying, "Sigi cried the whole way home." In the second shot of the sequence, the passing shadows of the train falling on Martha's face let us know that the train has begun to move. In the third shot, Freud is startled by the train whistle and drops the watch, which is framed in close-up as it is retrieved by an elderly gentleman who says, "Oh, what an unhappy accident."

If the watch is an heirloom that retraces patriarchal lineage in its passage from father to son, its breakage might be said to signify the breach between father and son or more specifically Freud's negative feelings toward his father.[13] This meaning is developed retrospectively in an evocative single shot when Freud recalls a childhood train journey that had been the scene of his father's sexual assault on his sister. In this shot we hear a shrill train whistle as the camera dollies in on the screaming boy Freud seated on his mother's lap, across from his father, in a train compartment. This traumatic memory is later discovered to have been a mere screen memory for the true Oedipal trauma—the child Freud's view of his mother undressing in a hotel near the train station and then leaving him to go into the next room to sleep with his father. According to the findings of the fictional Freud as an adult, there was no seduction of the daughter by the father but only Freud's own childhood desire for his mother, which, unrequited, caused him to "cry all the way home." What is significant, though, is that while the character Freud's conscious theoretical discoveries ultimately explain away father-daughter incest, the intensity with which the short departure scene is filmed asserts the presence of an alternative, nonexpository narrative logic that expresses fear of the father and anger at the sexual threat he poses. On its own terms this figural logic stands unrefuted. The sequence may also be regarded as an example of textual condensation, the process in which a single idea—in our example the cracked watch crystal—stands in for a number of associations—in our exam-

13. One might develop the argument that the departure scene and certain other shots and/or scenes in the film adopt the language of Hollywood melodrama by intensifying the meaning of everyday events and decor. (See Elsaesser [1987] for a seminal account of this characteristic representational strategy in Hollywood melodrama.) For example, the shot of Cecily's doll both symbolizes her Oedipal desire for her father and evokes prior uses of the doll in film melodrama: in *The Snake Pit*, the shot of a doll being smashed symbolizes a little girl's Oedipal conflict and the resulting traumatic memory she carries into adult life; in *Imitation of Life* (1959), the close-up of a discarded black doll represents a little girl's identity crisis in the context of racial tension.

 ple the father's role as seducer as well as the boy's Oedipal rivalry with his father (Freud, *Interpretation*, 312–39; Laplanche and Pontalis 1973, 82–83).

Another sequence designed to explore Freud's ambivalent feelings toward his father similarly intermingles "realistic" and "psychic" spaces and maintains a confusion between them. It is unclear whether the scene of Freud at his father's funeral is really supposed to have taken place or whether it is part of the scene that follows, a second funeral clearly demarcated as a dream by the fact that Freud is shown awakening from it. In some respects we are encouraged to believe that the first funeral scene really happened while the second is a dream: the first takes place in daylight, the second at night; the first depicts a horse-drawn hearse, mourners dressed in black, and the gates of a cemetery, whereas the second portrays a number of inappropriate images such as Freud dressed in his shirtsleeves, a train, and an enigmatic sign reading "the eyes shall be closed." Nevertheless, certain stylistic similarities between the scenes encourage the impression that both are dreams. The second funeral scene is accompanied by disturbing nondiegetic music such as accompanied Freud's earlier Oedipal dreams. But so is the first. Here more melodic but perhaps equally disturbing nondiegetic music drowns out the diegetic sounds of the funeral procession. The second funeral scene is shot with a distorting lens to give a surreal impression. But the first scene too gives such a distorting impression by beginning with a hand-held shot rendering Freud's disturbed psychological state as he marches in the procession behind his father's coffin. As the scene progresses an eyeline match establishes the cemetery gate as an entrance Freud inexplicably fears, and, after a shot-reverse shot series depicting Freud and the gate in turn, we see the gate "topple" from Freud's point of view as he faints and falls to the ground. When Freud awakens, ostensibly from the dream depicted in the second scene, the groggy and confused words he uses to recount the dream to Martha relate most clearly to the first scene: "I couldn't go through the gate."

As in the film's representation of Cecily's testimony as a fade to black and in its representation of Freud's memory of his sister's seduction as a startling train whistle and a cracked watch, the film represents Freud's desire *not* to honor his father at the funeral with non-naturalistic images. It is tempting to dismiss this stylistic choice as the film's way of cueing the spectator that the various fathers are not really guilty. Yet the daughter's seduction remains a possibility so threatening as to be unrepresentable in classical narrative terms, a possibility with which it is precisely the project of the narrative to grapple.

We are *not* claiming, then, that the film implies Freud's women patients really were molested in childhood by their fathers, as it would have to in order to conform to the position adopted by Masson and Rush. Nor are we saying that the film completely denies that childhood molestation is relevant to psychic structures of fantasy as it would have to in order to fall into line with Juliet Mitchell's delineation of concepts useful for feminism in Freud's work. What we are arguing is that the film represents, as the return of the repressed, the issue of childhood molestation in relation to ideas about fantasy and infantile sexuality and that the explanations the film's characters and narrative trajectory explicitly reject continually surface as textual disturbances, particularly at the level of sound and image. In this the film is consistent with what we see as an aspect of Freud's work crucial for feminism—the acknowledgment of *both* psychic and social reality and the exploration of the connections between these two determinations of individual psychosexuality.

WORKS CITED

Andrew, Dudley. 1984. *Concepts in Film Theory*. New York: Oxford University Press.

Baudry, Jean-Louis. 1976. "The Apparatus." *Camera Obscura* 2: 104–27.

Bergstrom, Janet. 1979. "Enunciation and Sexual Difference." Part 1. *Camera Obscura* 3–4: 33–69.

Bernheimer, Charles. 1985. Introduction: Part One. *In Dora's Case: Freud-Hysteria-Feminism*. Edited by Charles Bernheimer and Claire Kahane, 1–18. New York: Columbia University Press.

Breuer, Josef, and Sigmund Freud. 1957. *Studies on Hysteria*. Edited and translated by James Strachey. New York: Basic Books.

Crinkley, Richmond. 1984. "Metamorphoses: John and Jean-Paul." *Film Comment* 20 (November/December): 78–79.

De Lauretis, Teresa. 1984. *Alice Doesn't: Feminism, Semiotics, Cinema*. Bloomington: Indiana University Press.

Doane, Mary Ann. 1987. *The Desire to Desire*. Bloomington: Indiana University Press.

Elsaesser, Thomas. 1987. "Tales of Sound and Fury: Observations on the Family Melodrama." In *Home Is Where the Heart Is: Studies in Melodrama and the Woman's Film*, edited by Christine Gledhill, 43–69. London: British Film Institute.

Freud, Sigmund. 1963. "On the History of the Psychoanalytic Movement (1914)." In *The History of the Psychoanalytic Movement*, edited by Philip Rieff. New York: Collier.

———. *The Interpretation of Dreams*. 1965. Edited and translated by James Strachey. New York: Avon.

———. *The Origins of Psycho-Analysis: Letters to Wilhelm Fliess, Drafts and Notes:*

1887–1902. 1954. Edited by Marie Bonaparte, Anna Freud, and Ernst Kris. New York: Basic Books.

———. "Repression." 1963. In *General Psychological Theory*, edited by Philip Rieff, 104–15. New York: Collier.

———. *The Standard Edition of the Complete Psychological Works of Sigmund Freud*. 1953. Translated by James Strachey. London: Hogarth Press.

Gallop, Jane. 1982. *The Daughter's Seduction: Feminism and Psychoanalysis*. Ithaca: Cornell University Press.

Huston, John. 1980. *An Open Book*. New York: Alfred A. Knopf.

Jones, Ernest. 1961. *The Life and Work of Sigmund Freud*. Edited by Lionel Trilling and Steven Marcus. New York: Basic Books.

Kaplan, E. Ann. 1983. *Women and Film: Both Sides of the Camera*. New York: Methuen.

Kuhn, Annette. 1982. *Women's Pictures: Feminism and Cinema*. London: Routledge and Kegan Paul.

Laplanche, J., and J.-B. Pontalis. 1973. *The Language of Psycho-Analysis*. Translated by Donald Nicholson-Smith. New York: W. W. Norton.

Masson, Jeffrey. 1984. *The Assault on Truth: Freud's Suppression of the Seduction Theory*. New York: Penguin.

Mayne, Judith. 1985. "Feminist Film Theory and Criticism." *Signs* 11, no. 1 (Autumn): 81–100.

Metz, Christian. 1981. *The Imaginary Signifier*. Bloomington: Indiana University Press.

Mitchell, Juliet. 1975. *Psychoanalysis and Feminism: Freud, Reich, Laing and Women*. New York: Vintage.

———. 1985. Introduction to vol. 1, *Feminine Sexuality: Jacques Lacan and the école freudienne*, by Jacques Lacan, edited by Juliet Mitchell and Jacqueline Rose, and translated by Jacqueline Rose, 1–26. New York: W. W. Norton.

Pontalis, J.-B. 1986. Editor's preface to *The Freud Scenario*, by Jean-Paul Sartre, translated by Quintin Hoare, vii–xviii. Chicago: University of Chicago Press.

Poster, Mark. 1986. *Critical Theory of the Family*. New York: Seabury Press.

Rush, Florence. 1977. "The Freudian Cover-up: The Sexual Abuse of Children." *Chrysalis* 1.

———. 1980. *The Best Kept Secret: Sexual Abuse of Children*. Englewood Cliffs, N.J.: Prentice-Hall.

Sartre, Jean-Paul. 1986. *The Freud Scenario*. Edited by J.-B. Pontalis. Translated by Quintin Hoare. Chicago: University of Chicago Press.

Silverman, Kaja. 1983. *The Subject of Semiotics*. New York: Oxford University Press.

Walker, Janet. 1987. "Couching Resistance: Women, Film and Psychoanalytic Psychiatry From World War II Through the Mid 1960s." Ph.D. diss., UCLA.

Westkott, Marcia. 1986. *The Feminist Legacy of Karen Horney*. New Haven: Yale University Press.

On Feminism and Psychoanalysis

Chodorow, Nancy. *The Reproduction of Mothering*. Berkeley: University of California Press, 1978.

Doane, Mary Ann. "Film and the Masquerade: Theorising the Female Spectator." *Screen* 23, no. 3–4 (September-October 1982): 74–88.

Doane, Mary Ann, Patricia Mellencamp, and Linda Williams, eds. *Re-vision: Essays in Feminist Film Criticism*. Frederick, Md.: University Publications of America and The American Film Institute, 1984.

Eagleton, Terry. "Psychoanalysis." In *Literary Theory: An Introduction*. Minneapolis: University of Minnesota Press, 1983.

Gay, Peter. *Freud: A Life for Our Time*. New York: W. W. Norton, 1988.

Hunter, Dianne. "Hysteria, Psychoanalysis, and Feminism: The Case of Anna O." *Feminist Studies* 9, no. 3 (Fall 1983): 464–88.

Kaplan, E. Ann. "Feminist Film Criticism: Current Issues and Problems." *Studies in the Literary Imagination* 19, no. 1 (Spring 1986): 7–20.

Klein, Milton I. "Freud's Seduction Theory: Its Implications for Fantasy and Memory in Psychoanalytic Theory." *Bulletin of the Menninger Clinic* 45, no. 3 (May 1981): 185–208.

Moi, Toril, ed. *French Feminist Thought: A Reader*. Oxford and New York: Basil Blackwell, 1987.

Penley, Constance, ed. *Feminism and Film Theory*. New York: Routledge, 1988.

Silverman, Kaja. *The Acoustic Mirror*. Bloomington and Indianapolis: Indiana University Press, 1988.

Strouse, Jean, ed. *Women and Analysis: Dialogues on Psychoanalytic Views of Femininity*. New York: Dell, 1974.

On *Freud*

Cientot, M. "Freud: passion secrete." *Positif* 264 (February 1983): 83–84.

———. "Le scenario 'Freud' de Jean-Paul Sartre." *Positif* 283 (September 1984): 40–42.

Jameson, R. T. "John Huston." *Film Comment* 16 (May-June 1980): 25–56.

Shortland, Michael. "Screen Memories: Towards a History of Psychiatry and Psychoanalysis in the Movies." *British Journal for the History of Science* 20 (1987): 421–52.

16

MR. SMITH GOES TO WASHINGTON: DEMOCRATIC FORUMS AND REPRESENTATIONAL FORMS

Charles Wolfe

INSTITUTIONAL CONTEXT

At a rough average, about half a million words of political news and comment are telegraphed out of Washington daily. There is perhaps an equal volume of mailed material—daily and weekly "letters" and "columns," special feature articles, along with an oral flood of speeches, debates, and whatnot poured from local broadcasting stations directly into the Nation's homes. Finally, there is the presentation of political events, personalities, and interviews in the newsreels of at least four national motion-picture producers, and in the "stills" of many press photographers. . . . Probably no other city in the world is kept so prominently and continually in the public eye and the public mind.

As a result, most literate inhabitants of the United States are scarcely less familiar with Washington, its policies, personalities, and public buildings, than they are with their own communities; and sooner or later most of them come to the tangible city. They are thoroughly at home here in a historic and

> political atmosphere which they have breathed vicariously since childhood, and amid surroundings which they have seen pictured countless times.[1]

A 1937 Federal Writers' Project guidebook to Washington, D.C., thus describes political news coverage of the nation's capital in an age of media journalism. Notably absent from this description is any hint that the transmission of information from Washington was anything less than a neutral and natural process, that the system that ostensibly familiarized "literate inhabitants" with the central scene of national politics in America was itself an institutional structure with political force. Yet the passage tacitly acknowledges that what is made possible by the technological media is not simply the dissemination of an image of the "tangible city" of Washington but the forging of a national political identity, an audience's sense of belonging to a historical tradition and of inhabiting a political environment as familiar as home.

It is useful to keep the existence and impact of a mediating network of this kind in mind when attempting to place *Mr. Smith Goes to Washington* historically, for it reminds us that the system responsible for the production and circulation of this particular depiction of Washington—the motion picture industry—operated in relation to other image-making institutions with which it may have simultaneously competed and cooperated at different levels of activity.[2] Hollywood's domain, of course, was that of commercial en-

1. *The WPA Guide to Washington, D.C.* (New York: Random House, 1983), 7. Revised and condensed from *Washington: City and Capital* (Washington: Government Printing Office, 1937), first commercially published as *Washington, D.C.: A Guide to the Nation's Capital* (New York: Hastings House, 1942).

2. In contrast to the institutional analysis I am proposing here, historical assessments of *Mr. Smith Goes to Washington* to date have tended toward broad speculation concerning the possible relation of the film to American social values in the late 1930s. To the extent that questions concerning the production and reception of the film have been factored into these accounts they have tended to be circumscribed by a sole concern with the capacity of director Frank Capra to articulate a social vision for his audience. Analyses of the film based on this model can be traced back to Richard Griffith's review in *New Movies* in November 1939, in which he proposed that Capra and his audience were so attuned with one another that the film should be evaluated as "an index to the popular mind." Acknowledging the methodological pitfalls in proposing a relationship of this kind between artworks and society, Robert Sklar in "The Imagination of Stability" raises provocative questions concerning Hollywood's status as social institution, although Capra's capacity to communicate institutionalized values and beliefs remains Sklar's central concern. Nick Browne in "The

 tertainment. By the late 1930s the very term "Hollywood" had come to stand for both an economic system for the production and delivery of commercial motion pictures to theaters around the world and a particular way of organizing those pictures, a highly conventionalized system for the telling of stories and the display of spectacle and stars. In this sense Hollywood constituted a distinct sphere of activity, yet one bound to the world of media journalism by the industry's need for publicity and promotion and to federal, state, and local governments by the government's power to influence trade practices.

For the moviegoer perhaps the most visible connection between Hollywood's product and the work of media journalism occurred at the exhibition site itself, where the commercial newsreels to which the Federal Writers' Project guidebook alludes were shown as part of a package of motion picture entertainment. By way of these newsreels public officials entered into circulation as political performers—indeed they could become political stars—and political events were translated into news stories, mininarratives that on occasion included dramatic reenactment. Moreover, the escalation of political conflict in Europe at the close of the decade—and the growing popularity of celebrity radio commentators to narrate news about the outbreak of war—were met by increased attention to topical news material within the framework of the film exhibitor's program. In some cases the argument for such a move was economic in a local sense: broadcasting news in the theaters might lure the potential filmgoer away from the family radio. But a kind of civic argument—congruent with the long-term economic health of the industry to be sure—was articulated as well. Three days after the outbreak of war in Europe in September 1939, a columnist in *Variety*, John C. Flinn, proposed that in times of crisis film theaters should be thought of as "places of public assembly, meeting halls of democracy" where the "trend of national thought" was discernible, and that emphasis on this political function of the theater in the social life of a community could bring new prestige to the industry. Here Hollywood's trade press echoed concurrent efforts by the radio industry to promote the "service" it provided citizens by way of its coverage of political events. The chief distinction was the site of political engagement and debate:

Politics of Narrative Form: Capra's *Mr. Smith Goes to Washington*" likewise calls attention to Hollywood as a locus of media power, but primarily as a way of defining Capra's role as ritual storyteller and democratic martyr. Browne's "System of Production/System of Representation: Industry Context and Ideological Form in Capra's *Meet John Doe*," however, focuses on the history of Hollywood's relationship to media institutions in a particularly forceful way.

if radio had transformed domestic space into a new civic space, the commercial film theater, according to Flinn, provided a space for *public* assembly, a new American "town hall."[3]

The notion that public service was a product to be capitalized on at a time of social stress echoed the formal position articulated during the period by Will H. Hays, head of the Motion Picture Producers and Distributors Association. Well connected in Washington, Hays fended off federal censorship initiatives in the early thirties by overseeing the development of the Production Code Administration, the industry's self-censoring agency, headed after 1934 by Joseph Breen in Los Angeles. Following the passage of the New Deal's National Industrial Recovery Act in the summer of 1933, the Hays Office also assumed primary responsibility for drafting the Motion Picture Code of Fair Practice that granted tacit approval to the industry's oligopolistic structure and trade practices. But this code only remained in effect until the Supreme Court declared the NIRA unconstitutional in 1935, and even as one branch of the Roosevelt administration was catering to the demands of the MPPDA, the Justice Department was investigating the film industry for possible violation of antitrust laws. In the summer of 1938 Thurman Arnold, chief of the department's antitrust division, filed suit against the industry on these grounds, and efforts by the MPPDA to block this action by drafting a new trade practice code with the Commerce Department were derailed by Arnold in August 1939. Concurrently the U.S. Senate passed the Neely Bill, designed to ban Hollywood's practice of distributing films to theaters in blocks rather than selling them individually; scheduled to be voted on by the House in 1940, it was the object of extensive lobbying at the time of *Mr. Smith*'s release. Events in Europe only exacerbated the MPPDA's economic concerns: with the outbreak of war foreign markets began to close, an event lobbyists for the industry were quick to note when arguing against both the antitrust and Neely initiatives, and the threat of federal political censorship was raised anew in Congress.[4]

3. For the growth of radio news, see David Holbrook Culbert, *News for Everyman: Radio and Foreign Affairs in Thirties America* (Westport, Conn.: Greenwood Press, 1976), 4–6; Robert W. Desmond, *Tides of War: World News Reporting, 1931–1945* (Iowa City: Iowa University Press, 1984), 73–84. For radio broadcasts in film theaters, see *Variety*, 30 Aug. 1939, 1, 18; 13 Sept. 1939, 8, and 8 Nov. 1939, 2; John C. Flinn, "Film Showmanship," *Variety*, 6 Sept. 1939, 8. For an example of radio publicity, see RCA's *Listen*, no. 15, a five-page advertisement published in *Life*, 3 Oct. 1938, 35–39.

4. For the role of the Hays Office, see Garth Jowett, *Film: The Democratic Art* (Boston: Little, Brown & Co., 1976) 164–259, and J. Douglas Gomery, "Holly-

Hays's public response to these events was to seek out high moral ground, projecting an image of the industry as socially responsible and civic-minded. In his March 1939 address to the annual gathering of the MPPDA in New York, Hays argued that producers in Hollywood were increasingly selecting stories that emphasized "Americanism" and "mankind's struggle for freedom" and had discovered that these themes were not incompatible with "the best interest of the box-office." By distributing these films abroad, Hays proposed, the film industry also was countering the efforts of government-controlled media in foreign countries to portray American democracy as a failed political system. As for recent antitrust proceedings, Hays expressed hope that the federal government would recognize the "special significance and peculiarly difficult problems" of the film industry as an international leader in providing "good and necessary recreation at a moderate cost." In short, Hays was formulating precisely the kind of defense of the studio system that would allow the MPPDA to win the government's sanction as an "essential industry" during World War II, with economic profit inextricably linked to public policy at a time of national crisis.[5]

Given a political climate of this kind, it is perhaps not surprising that the Production Code Administration paid close attention to story material submitted to them that depicted the very governmental bodies with which the MPPDA had to deal. Thus when Lewis R. Foster's "The Gentleman from Montana" was submitted to the PCA for consideration as possible script material by both MGM and Paramount in January 1938, Joseph Breen

---

wood, the National Recovery Administration, and the Question of Monopoly Power," *Journal of the University Film Association* (Spring 1979): 47–52. Activity by the Justice and Commerce Departments was reported on in *The New York Times*, 8 June 1939, 30; 13 June 1939, 5; 16 August 1939, 12; 18 August 1939, 17. The progress of the Neely Bill was covered in *The New York Times*, 15 July 1939, 8; 18 July 1939, 14; and in *Variety*, 13 December 1939, 3; 20 December 1939, 4. For the impact of events in Europe, see *Variety*, 13 September 1939, 3; 4 October 1939, 4; 27 December 1939, 5; and *The New York Times*, 10 September 1939, 9:3; 17 September 1939, 10:3. Sen. Elmer Thomas (D-Okla.), for example, called for a complete prohibition on all war films, newsreels, and radio broadcasts on the grounds that spreading too much news of the conflict might endanger American neutrality. The press was to be exempt (*Variety*, 4 October 1939, 2).

5. Hays quoted in the *New York Times*, 28 March 1939, 25. Noting a shift in policy from previous reports in which Hays had emphasized entertainment over and against social comment, Frank S. Nugent interpreted the 1939 report as evidence that the "Americanism campaign" in recent Hollywood films was a planned development ("Will Hays, Movie Fan," *The New York Times*, 2 April 1939, 10:5).

quickly sent up a red flag, warning that its depiction of corruption in the Senate could be political dynamite both at home and abroad. In late February, when Columbia Pictures expressed interest in the material as well, Geoffrey Shurlock, Breen's assistant, met with three representatives from the studio to discuss the PCA's concerns about the material. Director Rouben Mamoulian visited PCA offices in June to discuss his interest in working on the project for Columbia; Shurlock similarly advised him of the PCA's misgivings.[6]

"The Gentleman from Montana," however, soon came to the attention of Columbia's premier director, Frank Capra, who announced in November that he saw in the story the possibility of making a more overtly political version of his successful 1936 film, *Mr. Deeds Goes to Town.*[7] After spending several weeks in Washington researching the production with writer Sidney Buchman and cinematographer Joe Walker, Capra had a draft of a screenplay ready for PCA inspection in January 1939. Breen's response was considerably milder: he proposed some minor deletions (primarily dialogue written for Smith's cynical secretary, Saunders) that toned down the implication that corruption was pervasive in Washington; but in deferring to Hays for a "policy" ruling on the material he advised his boss that the script's emphasis on the recovery of democratic traditions might prove very timely. Hays backed Breen's handling of the case but instructed him to advise Columbia

6. Breen letters to Louis B. Mayer (MGM) and John Hammell (Paramount), 19 January 1939; Breen report to Hays, 31 January 1938; Shurlock memos to Breen, 26 February 1938 and 10 June 1938; Production Code Administration case file for *Mr. Smith*, Academy of Motion Picture Arts and Sciences Library, Beverly Hills, Calif.

Foster's story reportedly was based on the early career of Burton K. Wheeler, who as a freshman senator in 1924 attacked corruption in the Harding administration, was indicted on trumped up charges, and was then exonerated as the Teapot Dome scandal unraveled. Postmaster General in the Harding administration prior to his acceptance of the MPPDA post in 1922, Hays was never tainted by the scandal but may have had personal reservations about a project focusing on Wheeler. Capra indicates in his autobiography that Wheeler was not amused by *Mr. Smith* at the premiere, but when the senator wrote his autobiography years later, his collaborator proudly noted that Wheeler's life was "the stuff of which melodramas [such as *Mr. Smith*] are made. (See Wheeler and Paul F. Healy, *Yankee from the West* [Garden City, N.Y.: Doubleday, 1962], ix.)

7. Capra interviewed by Frank Daugherty, *Christian Science Monitor Weekly Magazine*, 9 November 1938, 5. Joe Sistrom, one of Columbia's representatives at the February meeting with Shurlock, appears to have been the conduit to Capra (see *The Name Above the Title*, 254.)

of Hays's personal concern about the project and requested that the studio be especially careful to adhere to Senate protocol in any dramatic reenactments. Passing this message on to studio head Harry Cohn, Breen followed the script closely through its final revision in April. Upon seeing the finished film in September, he declared it a "magnificent picture" and recommended only a single deletion unrelated to political concerns.[8]

Breen's change of heart may have been motivated by alterations to the original material worked by Buchman's script (it is clear he read each version carefully), but it is also logical to assume that he was influenced by Capra's involvement on the project. By 1939 Capra had staked out a unique position as a director in Hollywood. The popular and critical success of his films had given him a platform to openly criticize industry practices, including censorship and block-booking, and to contemplate independent production.[9] At the same time respect for his work in Hollywood ran deep: he had received Academy Awards for his direction of *It Happened One Night* (1934) and *Mr. Deeds Goes to Town* (1936), and he would win a third for *You Can't Take It With You* (1938) while the PCA's review of *Mr. Smith*'s script was in progress. Moreover, by 1938 Capra had reached celebrity status in the national news media; featured on the cover of *Time* magazine in August and in a photo spread on the making of *You Can't Take It With You* in *Life* in No-

8. Breen to Cohn, 30 January 1939; Breen to Hays, 31 January 1939; Francis Harmon memo (for Hays) to Breen, 7 March 1939; Breen to Cohn, 8 March 1939, 24 March 1939, 17 April 1939, and 21 April 1939; Breen to Hays, 20 September 1939; PCA case file for *Mr. Smith*, Academy Library. Substantial revisions to the script were made after principal photography began, including the addition of the scene between Paine and Smith on the train (handwritten by Capra on his copy of the script), scenes between Smith and Saunders prior to the filibuster, and Vorkapich's montage of Taylor versus the Boy Rangers. Breen made no comments concerning these changes. (Capra's revised final script, dated 1 April 1939, is held in the Frank Capra Collection, Wesleyan Cinema Archive, Middletown, Conn.)

9. See, for example, Capra's "A Sick Dog Tells Where It Hurts," *Esquire* 5, no. 1 (January 1936): 87, 130. That *Mr. Smith* quickened interest in the Neely Bill is ironic in that all of Capra's films at Columbia between 1936 and 1939, including *Mr. Smith*, were sold individually rather than in blocks (Columbia sales manager report in *Mr. Smith* correspondence file no. 4, Wesleyan Cinema Archive). While *Mr. Smith* was in production, there was much discussion in the industry about efforts by Capra to establish his own production company. He announced its formation (with screenwriter Robert Riskin) three weeks before the film was released (*Variety*, 26 July 1939, 3; 2 August 1939, 2; and 18 October 1939, 4; *New York Times*, 4 October 1939, 31).

vember, he had acquired a reputation both for the control he exercised over his films and his willingness to tackle social themes.[10] His tendency to describe his work as motivated by a desire to both entertain and inspire—if far less gaseous than the pronouncements of Hays—nevertheless conformed to the ideal role the MPPDA chief laid out for the industry. Indeed, Capra's willingness to criticize the moguls of the MPPDA may have given this claim the kind of weight Hays's public statements lacked for many commentators on Hollywood during this period.[11]

Capra's name attached to the project also guaranteed that *Mr. Smith* attracted substantial publicity in advance of its release, and the subject matter of the film only amplified this media interest. Much of the publicity focused on Capra's effort to ensure the accuracy of the film's replication of the Senate chamber and the scripting of a typical Capra plot for this setting. In the popular press this combination of scrupulous documentation and Hollywood dramaturgy was a source of great interest.[12] Behind the scenes, however, the attempt to mix documentation and dramatization of the Washington political scene was not without practical difficulties. James B. Preston, an ex-superintendent of the Senate whose role as technical advisor on the film was much touted in the press, came into conflict with the crew and quit the project at a key moment in the production.[13] Capra also ran up against a

---

10. In 1938, for example, Capra was the subject of a *Time* cover story ("Columbia's Gem," 8 August 1938, 35–38), a *Life* photo-essay on the making of *You Can't Take It With You* (19 September 1938, 42–47), and profiles in *The Saturday Evening Post* (Alvah Johnston, "Capra Shoots as He Pleases," 4 May 1938) and *The Christian Science Monitor Weekly Magazine* (Frank Daugherty, "He Has the Common Touch," 9 November 1938, 5).

11. Frank S. Nugent, for example, ridiculed Hays's 1939 MPPDA report (see note 20 below) but praised Capra in several articles on *Mr. Smith* (see note 18 below). For a detailed discussion of the way in which Capra's public profile served as a cultural signpost marking the social circulation of his films, see my *Frank Capra: A Guide to References and Resources* (Boston: G. K. Hall, 1987), 10–35.

12. In the introduction to an eight-page photo-spread on *Mr. Smith, Life* magazine noted that Capra had "joined melodrama and background, Hollywood and Washington, fiction and fact, with spectacular success." The layout to follow was divided into two parts: one recounted the plot by way of a series of production stills; the other illustrated how the Senate chamber had been faithfully reconstructed ("Movie of the Week: *Mr. Smith Goes to Washington*," 16 October 1939, 67–74).

13. Capra's retrospective commentary in his autobiography suggests that Preston's contribution was rightly celebrated at the time, but his correspondence from the period indicates that he was disenchanted with Preston's condescending attitude on the set and angered by the fact that Preston quit the film just prior to the shoot-

 Department of the Interior ruling prohibiting the photographing of identifiable figures inside the Lincoln Memorial, thus jeopardizing his effort to dramatize and subjectify the space of the national monument.[14] And the national office of the Boy Scouts, upon reviewing the screenplay, refused permission for the name of their organization to be used in *Mr. Smith* in light of its depiction of the U.S. Senate.[15]

These incidents likely seemed minor at the time, but in retrospect they presaged a controversy that erupted in the nation's capital following the gala premiere of the film at Constitution Hall on 17 October. Sponsored by the National Press Club to honor Preston, the event attracted the Washington political establishment: an estimated four thousand congressmen, press correspondents, and invited guests crowded into the hall, while Capra and his wife shared a special box with the family of Burton K. Wheeler, the Montana senator on whose early career the original story for the film had presumably been based. But the planned celebration—a promotional event for moviemakers, politicians, and journalists alike—ended up an unhappy affair for all concerned. In his 1971 autobiography Capra describes in detail his memory

---

ing of the scene in the Senate press room (Capra to John Stuart, 20 July 1939; *Mr. Smith* correspondence file, Wesleyan Cinema Archive).

14. The restrictions on shooting an identifiable figure with the statue may explain why Smith and the statue appear together only in extreme long shot from behind interior columns. Closer shots (some of which were filmed at Columbia's studio) were later intercut so as to create a sense of spatial proximity. According to John Stuart, who handled the negotiations with Secretary of the Interior Harold Ickes (and arranged for some pick-up shots with James Stewart and Assistant Director Art Black in July), the local branch of the MPPDA in Washington registered concern about the sequence, and there was a good deal of suspense about whether or not the final version would be approved (Stuart to Capra, 12 July 1939; Capra to Stuart, 20 July 1939; Stuart to Capra, 24 July 1939; Capra telegram to Stuart, 5 August 1939; Stuart telegram to Capra, 15 August 1939; J. R. White telegram to Capra, 18 August 1939; *Mr. Smith* correspondence file, Wesleyan Cinema Archive). For an account of the problems this photographic regulation caused during shooting, see James Stewart's interview with Leonard Maltin in Jeanine Basinger's *It's a Wonderful Life Book* (New York: Knopf, 1986), 81–82.

15. Correspondence between Capra and chief scout executive James W. West suggests that West may also have been miffed that scout officials were not hired as consultants. In response to West's political critique of the script, Capra offered a spirited defense of the project, a warm-up for later debates (West to Capra, 29 March 1939; Capra telegram to West, 1 April 1939; West to Capra, 3 April 1939; *Mr. Smith* correspondence file, Wesleyan Cinema Archive).

of the film's cool reception by the audience that evening and the personal attack he endured at the hands of the Washington press corps at a party later that night. In the days to follow, moreover, reporters joined forces with irate senators (led by Majority Leader Alben W. Barkley of Kentucky) to make public their opposition to the film. Several congressmen let it be known that the Neely Bill hearings might be rushed through the house in retaliation. Legal counsel for the association of independent exhibitors (which favored the Neely Bill and was thus not reluctant to fan the flames of the controversy) advised all theaters showing the film to run a trailer disclaiming any intention to discredit Congress or the press. Criticism rapidly spread to the editorial pages of various newspapers around the country. Columbia closely monitored reactions in Washington in order to gauge the potential impact of the uproar, and industry leaders were rumored to be worried that the domestic release of the film had perhaps been a grave political blunder. Joseph P. Kennedy, U.S. Ambassador to England, personally urged Harry Cohn not to release the film overseas.[16]

A general theme of the attacks, as Breen had first warned, was that the film was unpatriotic for suggesting that corruption was deeply rooted in the American political system; more specific critiques from Washington focused on the film's depiction of senators and reporters and the staging of the filibuster. Those assembled at Constitution Hall, Richard L. Strout argued in *The Christian Science Monitor*, had learned how Hollywood viewed (and would have people see) Washington correspondents and politicians: the former were "cynical but lovable drunkards" and the latter "winked their eyes at political corruption." "It is a Senate," Strout went on to complain, "in which galleries freely cheer after speeches and spectators shout down instruc-

16. See Frank Capra, *The Name Above the Title*, 253–93; *New York Times*, 24 October 1939, 19; *Variety*, 25 October 1939, 1, 54; and 1 November 1939, 4; *Time*, 30 October 1939; Richard L. Strout, *Christian Science Monitor*, 19 October 1939, 1 and 27 Oct. 1939, 3; Harlan Kennedy, *Washington Post*, 20 October 1939; Nelson B. Bell, *Washington Post*, 21 October 1939, 16. Also see Capra to William Wilkerson, 20 October 1939; Nate Spingold to Capra, 30–31 October 1939; Joseph P. Kennedy to Cohn, 17 November 1939; *Mr. Smith* correspondence file, Wesleyan Cinema Archive. A report by James P. Cunningham in *Motion Picture Herald* (28 October 1939, 13) suggested that the campaign against the film was inaugurated by the Chicago Tribune Press Service rather than the Senate itself. Hollywood columnist Jimmie Fiedler also reported that other studios had made plans to buy *Mr. Smith* from Columbia and withdraw it from circulation so as to stave off federal action, but the MPPDA quickly squelched this rumor (*Motion Picture Herald*, 4 November 1939, 8).

 tions to favorite senators; it is a Senate in which members boo or applaud a colleague or shun him altogether." That the reproduction of the setting was so authentic, he and other critics noted, only made "distortions" of this kind more dangerous. Barkley angrily complained that outside of Washington—in "Queedunk and Podunk and Tracey Corners"—the film might be taken as true-to-life.[17]

Within a month, however, the furor had died down. Protests against the film had stimulated box office receipts during its opening run in Washington; further protest from congressmen and reporters thus may have appeared self-defeating. Moreover, harsh criticism from Washington soon engendered a backlash. Most critics in Los Angeles, who had previewed the film two weeks before, were on record as strong supporters; now they were joined by first-string critics for the major New York dailies who accused the Washington insiders of being exceptionally thin-skinned. Columbia abetted the campaign by circulating a press packet of reviews that emphasized the film's patriotic dimension; and the distribution of a *Photoplay* study guide, endorsed by National Education Association, to schools around the country likely enhanced the film's reputation as a civic-minded work.[18] In a sense the inter-

---

17. Strout, *Christian Science Monitor*, 19 October 1939, 1. Barkley quoted in *Variety*, 25 October 1939, 54. It is important to note that protests of this kind were bipartisan, and while it might have been possible to infer from Taylor's deceptive use of a deficiency bill an oblique critique of New Deal relief measures, such an interpretation of the film did not figure into congressional complaints. A topical political link Capra and Riskin could not have foreseen, however, was forged when in the very week that *Mr. Smith* went into national release, a filibuster to block passage of Roosevelt's arms-embargo repeal was led by Rush Holt of West Virginia, a thirty-four-year-old Democrat who had broken with the party leadership in the 1936 election and was an arch-foe of New Deal programs, especially the WPA. Two weeks after their photo-spread on Hollywood's "amazing reproduction of the Senate," *Life* magazine delighted in this coincidence, proposing that life imitated movies—and perhaps *Life* ("The U. S. Senate Winds Up Its 'Great Debate' on American Neutrality," 30 October 1939, 18–19). A shifting ground for political interpretation is also suggested by reports that *Mr. Smith* roused audiences to their feet as an antifascist work in Marseilles and Toulouse, France, just prior to the Vichy ban on American films in 1942, but also was received as an attack on American politics when shown (perhaps with an altered ending) in Moscow in 1950 (Georges Sadoul, "Capra ou la rénovation des mythes," *Les Lettres Françaises*, 24 Nov. 1945, 7; *Hollywood Reporter*, 20 December 1950, 2; *Variety*, 20 December 1950, 3, 19).

18. *Daily Variety*, 4 October 1939; *The Film Daily*, 6 October 1939, 8; *Variety*, 11 October 1939, 13; *Box Office*, 14 October 1939, 65; William R. Weaver, *Motion Picture Herald*, 7 October 1939; James P. Cunningham, *Motion Picture Herald*, 28

pretation of *Mr. Smith* offered by those who had attended the Washington preview came to be supplanted by an alternative one in which the film was understood, in Frank S. Nugent's phrase, as "a comic celebration of the spirit, rather than the form, of American government."[19] This second assessment, moreover, appears to have laid the groundwork for what has emerged over the years as a dominant cultural reading of the film in which *Mr. Smith* is understood to mark a transition in American popular thought as doubts raised by the Great Depression at home were superseded by anxieties concerning the outbreak of war overseas and to respond to those anxieties in a spirit of new nationalism with the invocation of an ideal political inheritance to be reclaimed. On this point Breen had been no less prescient.[20]

But the earlier reaction—shaped by the vested interests of the Washington political community—helps us place this reading in a critical perspective. First, it points to a certain contradiction in that particular American political myth that values the "spirit" of a national government over and against the constraints of its "form," as if the notion of government itself might somehow be wholly detached from those institutional structures and mechanisms by which it is constituted and sustained. Functional systems in this context are seen as a manifestation of a fallen world of real social practices. Second, it illuminates a structural tension produced by the growing power of Hollywood to intervene in the process by which activities in Washington were represented to the public at large. On the one hand, the motion picture industry

---

October 1939, 13; Edwin Schallert, *Los Angeles Times*, 4 October 1939, 2:32 and 25 October 1939, 2:15; Howard Barnes, New York *Herald Tribune*, 20 October 1939, 14; 22 October 1939; and 29 October 1939; William Boehnel, New York *World-Telegram*, 20 October 1939 and 28 October 1939; Frank S. Nugent, *New York Times*, 20 October 1939, 27; 22 October 1939, 9:5; 29 October 1939, 9: 5; Max J. Herzburg, ed., *Photoplay Studies* 5, no. 21 (1939). A copy of Columbia's press packet of favorable reviews is held in the *Mr. Smith* correspondence file, Wesleyan Cinema Archive.

19. Nugent, *New York Times*, 29 October 1939, 9:5.

20. At the next meeting of the MPPDA in New York, Hays was reported to be concerned about the controversy, but no official action was proposed (*Variety*, 1 Nov. 1939, 4). The question of the film's politics seems to have faded quickly; of the four letters of complaint retained in the PCA file, three are from journalists protesting the depiction of reporters in the film (one incredulous that the film had escaped "the tentative agreement" he understood to have been in effect against the misrepresentation of reporters on the screen). The fourth is a complaint from the Legion of Decency about intoxication scenes in this and other recent Hollywood films (PCA case file for *Mr. Smith*, Academy Library).

had the capacity to glamorize these activities, perhaps the very reason that the National Press Club sought to celebrate the making of the film in the first place. On the other hand, Hollywood could be considered a threat, a disrupting force with its own procedures for the dissemination of images and ideas from the seat of national politics. Thus while *Mr. Smith* can be logically considered part and parcel of Hollywood's contribution to the renewal of national political sentiment and in this respect to have helped build the kind of bridge between Hollywood and Washington that was to be crucial for wartime consensus, specific groups may have understood that with this interpenetration of systems of national representation they had something to lose; that by representing Washington on the screen, Hollywood was also modifying the terms by which the nation's capital was to be perceived in the popular imagination.

THE WORK OF THE TEXT

Thus far I have been concerned with the different institutional pressures—both competing and cooperative—that bore upon the making of *Mr. Smith Goes to Washington*, molding it as a social object at a particular historical moment. But it remains to be demonstrated how an understanding of this context helps us grasp *Mr. Smith* as a work of film fiction. To be aware of the varying responses to the project up through the time of its initial release is a step toward clarifying the social relations within which the work was deeply embedded in the late 1930s. But I am also interested here in identifying the work of this filmic text, the particular forms of coherence it mobilizes in constructing a fiction out of images, events, and political discourses drawn from the social field of which it is itself a part; in short, to specify how the film transforms the social material it engages.

Mr. Smith Goes to Washington, like the passage from the Federal Writers' guidebook quoted previously, offers a model for the relationship of national political institutions to a diffuse public as mediated by a news network. But where the guidebook describes a circular communication process operating in a state of perfect equilibrium, with the information transmitted out of Washington wholly commensurate with the "reality" of the city experienced by the visitor, *Mr. Smith* dramatizes imbalances and deceptions in a system that functions smoothly only to the extent that genuine political motives and machinations are masked. Under the terms of the guidebook's model, "informed" visitors, having absorbed in advance a stream of words and images flowing out of the city, are as at home in Washington as they would be in their local community and presumably can either return to that community with the reality of Washington reconfirmed by lived experience or stay to serve the ongoing reproduction of the image of that city in the "public mind." In *Mr. Smith*, however, the journey of the protagonist to Washington results in a divided conception of the capital city. For Smith, standing in front of the information counter at Union Station, his eye caught by a view of the distant Capitol dome (figs. 16–1, 16–2), it is the repository of a set of political ideals. For politicians and the press, however, it is a scene of compromise, chicanery, even corruption. The trajectory of the central character opens up the city to incompatible "readings"; Washington emerges as an unstable symbolic site.

Here we can isolate one aspect of the work of the text: its narrative construction, its plotting of a story. In simplest form this narrative is signaled by the film's title, itself an allusion (as the scoring of "Yankee Doodle [Went to Town]" under the credit sequence suggests) to a familiar narrative motif in American popular culture: the journey of an innocent protagonist from the country to the city where he or she is subject to mockery or exploitation. The premise of *Mr. Smith* thus can be said to activate a narrative founded on a binary motif that is at once culturally deep-rooted and topically charged. The spectator, fresh from a credit sequence printed on colonial signboards and overlayed with a colonial folk tune, is plunged at the outset into a world of contemporary political brokering, an inside view of the operation of a powerful political machine, set in motion (and at risk) by the death of a front man in the U.S. Senate. Deferred during the course of the opening passages is the debut of the film's title character, whose absence from and ignorance of any such scene of political intrigue is central to his value to Boss Taylor's machine, as well as to the fictional plotting of the film itself, which will exploit the gap between Smith's knowledge and that of the professional politicians to generate dramatic tension and irony.

Our introduction to Smith in the banquet sequence, however, inaugurates a countermovement in the narrative, one of retrospection, a power grounded in knowledge of and sentiment for the past. Thus against the machine's manufactured ballyhoo that opens the passage Smith invokes the memory of his socially committed father, and at the close of the sequence he exchanges tearful glances with his Boy Rangers as "Auld Lang Syne" swells up on the sound track. Then, his back to the forward motion of the train that propels him to a senatorial post in Washington at the behest of the political machine, Smith elicits from Joseph Paine a recollection of the senior senator's early crusades with Smith's father. Loss pervades the scene—a cause lost by a slain father, a father lost to his son, ideals lost by the partner that survives—but planted here by the plot (under the guise of a recollection of early story

Figure 16-1. (Copyright 1939, renewed 1967, by Columbia Pictures Corporation. All rights reserved. Courtesy of Columbia Pictures.)

Figure 16-2. (Copyright 1939, renewed 1967, by Columbia Pictures Corporation. All rights reserved. Courtesy of Columbia Pictures.)

material) is a model for political action (even if self-destructive) and a bond between two characters (established by their exchange of looks and the articulated memory they share) that will inform the film's climactic scene on the Senate floor. With Smith's arrival in Washington, this retrospective view then broadens to encompass a national political mythology. Smith's tour of the monuments and memorials of Washington weaves fragments of political icons, documents, and folk tunes into a kind of mythic reverie—Smith's reverie, the film suggests, but also a collective myth presumably shared by other visitors: an old man who assists his young companion in reciting the Gettysburg Address, for example, or a solitary black man who stands reverently before the statue of the "Great Emancipator."

A path through these conflicting views of federal politics is plotted by way of a narrative pattern of double exposure. Gradually exposed to the system he serves, Smith comes of age as an agent in the center of national political activity and (in a subordinate but interwoven story line) as romantic partner to Saunders, his secretary and tutor. Members of the political establishment in turn are exposed to Smith and to those "lost" values with which he is associated. In a series of metaphorical moves by the fiction Smith is figured as a contemporary Jefferson or Lincoln, and the "gaze" of the commemorative statue of Lincoln is explicitly interpreted by Saunders as a summons to Smith to accept the role of contemporary political hero. Arresting Taylor's machine just at the moment when its graft scheme is about to be unwittingly enacted by the Senate and sustaining that arrest through recourse to a filibuster, Smith brings to a halt the scripted proceedings of the Senate and substitutes for them a renewal of national political covenants within a Senate chamber where only a handful of representatives of a public constituency are licensed to speak and to act. Imagery first evoked during the young visitor's historical reverie—a montage designed by Slavko Vorkapich in which spatial and temporal limits seem temporarily suspended[21]—now

21. From one perspective, of course, this passage might be seen simply as one of economical temporal *compression*, after the fashion of the conventional Hollywood montage sequence, covering in three minutes and twenty-five seconds what the plot tells us is a five-hour period. But this tour is also something of a *de*tour from the main narrative up to this point, and the dense layering of images is only broadly chronological. A historical past is evoked through the animation of static icons, and a traveling shot past the Lincoln Memorial is edited so that the middle section of a spatially continuous, frontal shot of the columns is removed and placed after symmetrical, angled views from the left and right. The sequence is also graphically complicated by the superimposition of the waving lines of stripes on an American flag. The passage was greatly praised by critics of the time.

finds expression within a democratic forum for official political discourse and rule-governed public debate.

Here we can isolate a second way in which the film transforms social material: through performance. Performance figures, first of all, *within* narrative. The maturation of the hero and the conversion of cynics both hinge on a series of vocal performances by Smith, occasions for the protagonist to test his capacity to speak persuasively before skeptical auditors in contexts of increasing dramatic import.[22] "Character" becomes the locus point for the condensation of narrative tensions: having learned of his betrayal by Paine, Smith is forced to cope with those conflicting conceptions of the capital city that the film has dramatized. Silenced, on the verge of fleeing this scene of betrayal, he is then redirected by Saunders toward his heroic performance on the Senate floor. The central political question the film raises—what *is* Washington, a repository of political ideals or the scene of their inevitable compromise?—thus closes down around the question of character psychology and behavior: Smith fights back against disillusionment while Paine wrestles with guilt until public confession of the latter vindicates the former.

Performance, moreover, figures at the level of the production of this fiction. The very notion of a "Jefferson Smith" performing a heroic act depends on the real work of a film actor whose body and voice—recorded and synchronized by the machinery of cinema—provides a site of coherence for character construction. Through the vocalization and comportment of James Stewart, Smith's activity acquires a particular rhythm, tonality, and emotional investment. To transcribe the speeches Smith delivers up would be to undo precisely the work that Stewart performs, together with his companion actors (Claude Rains as Paine, Jean Arthur as Saunders, Edward Arnold as Taylor, et al.), who collectively provide a resonant backdrop of gestures and vocal inflections against which Stewart's idiosyncrasy as an actor—a simultaneous suggestion of eagerness and hesitancy—gains dramatic color.[23]

From this perspective the filibuster in *Mr. Smith* functions in part as a theatrical tour de force, at times a one-man show. But Stewart's performance

22. This aspect of the film has attracted a good deal of critical attention in recent years. For close analyses, see Nick Browne, "The Politics of Narrative Form"; Brian Gallagher, "Speech, Identity and Ideology in *Mr. Smith Goes to Washington*"; and Charles Affron, *Cinema and Sentiment*.

23. For critics in 1939 this performance was considered the one in which Stewart matured as an actor, displaying a capacity to render psychologically plausible wide swings of emotion—from comic embarrassment to fury, from youthful passion to bitterness. The New York Film Critics honored him for his labors with a best actor award.

never ruptures the fiction it serves; rather it doubles and deepens it. Its willful, searching aspect is interpreted within the fiction as a politically significant event, in the words of renowned radio news commentator H.V. Kaltenborn, as "the American privilege of free speech in its most dramatic form." Exploited here is a drama inherent in the Senate filibuster as a political tactic: the deliberations of a body of elected representatives operating under principles of majority rule are temporarily suspended so as to allow a single individual to hold the floor indefinitely and speak his piece without interruption. A loophole in the formal procedures of the Senate, the right to filibuster accommodates an eccentric act, the duration of which seems governed not by social limits but rather the physical capacity to sustain a performance. The legal text Smith seeks to enact is replaced as an item of narrative interest by his defense of his motives or, to be more precise, by the *performance* of that defense. For all the earlier emphasis placed on legislative procedure—with Saunders tutoring Smith in the encumbered process by which a bill is written and passes into law—focus shifts here to spectacle itself as a bearer of political meaning. The filibuster, Kaltenborn observes, is "democracy's finest *show*."

Yet if Stewart-as-Smith performs center stage through much of this passage, it is the particular conceit of this fiction that the character is persuasive precisely to the extent that he appears politically inadequate. As portrayed by Stewart, ordinary "Mr. Smith" is the kind of performer Roland Barthes has labeled the "imperfect orator," the speaker whose vocal patterns question his own authority and resist the restrictive discourse of any legal text. "Correcting, adding, wavering," notes Barthes, "the speaker . . . superimposes on the simple message that everyone expects of him a new message that ruins the very idea of a message and, through the shifting reflection of the blemishes and excesses with which he accompanies the line of the discourse, asks us to believe with him that language is not to be reduced to communication."[24] In this instance the "blemishes" and "excesses" of Smith's performance point toward an ideal truth, irreducible to oratory, never to be fully "said" if it is to remain equal to the enormity of the sentiment to be conveyed.[25] Thus, paradoxically, Smith exercises the greatest impact over his col-

---

24. Barthes, "Writers, Intellectuals, Teachers" in *Image-Music-Text*, edited and translated by Stephen Heath (New York: Hill and Wang, 1977), 191–92. Barthes places great stress on the fact that such a performance, no matter the degree to which it seeks to undermine its own authority, cannot escape a legality grounded in the very fact of speech making, the social premise that makes oration possible.

25. See Raymond Carney's chapter on *Mr. Smith*, "Speaking the Language of the Heart," in *American Vision: The Films of Frank Capra*, for a provocative discussion of

 leagues as his control of his performance erodes: it is the dissipation of his vocal and physical mastery that seems to rivet the attention of those who had turned their backs on him when he performed at full strength, and it is his physical collapse (fig. 16–3) that elicits a confession from Paine, which in turn motivates a dizzying reversal from melodramatic violence to comic celebration at the close.[26]

Reenacted here is a spectacle of martyrdom, a central component of the mythology of political heroism in America from Abraham Lincoln to Martin Luther King. What is perhaps most remarkable about Smith as a heroic figure of this kind, however, is the limits placed on the range of his knowledge at his moment of triumph, his lack of any sense of destiny (or premonition of personal doom), a mystical motif that runs through the legends of Lincoln and King. In contrast to the depiction of Lincoln in historical fictions of the late 1930s, for example, Smith never embodies History itself as a narrational force; he may know the past and may finally catch a glimpse of his present predicament, but he never has privileged access to the future.[27] The

---

this dimension of Smith's performance in terms of Capra's exploration of an American aesthetic of acting.

26. The first draft submitted to the PCA in January 1939 ends with Paine committing suicide but leaving behind a note that exonerates Smith. Smith then returns home with Saunders to be elected to serve a full term as senator. In the revised April script Paine's suicide attempt is blocked and his confession is voiced on the Senate floor. This script also called for a coda in which the windows of the *Jackson City Press* are smashed, Governor Hopper takes credit for Smith's appointment, and Smith and Saunders, while being treated to a hometown parade, discover Paine watching from the sidewalk and bring him home to Jeff's mother. In June 1939, Buchman scripted a slightly different ending in which Jeff arrives home to find that Paine has sent the Boy Rangers "a new press for new lost causes" and announces that he is married to Saunders. Production stills indicate that a scene in which Smith, Saunders, Paine and Mrs. Smith ride together in a hometown parade was shot, but it did not appear in the released version (PCA case file for *Mr. Smith*, Academy Library; Capra's revised final script, Wesleyan Cinema Archive).

27. See, for example, the endings to *Young Mr. Lincoln* (Ford, 1939) and *Abe Lincoln in Illinois* (Cromwell, 1940) or the Warner Brothers Vitaphone short, *Lincoln in the White House* (1939). The *locus classicus* of recent critical attention to this question is *Cahiers du cinéma*'s collectively authored "John Ford's *Young Mr. Lincoln*." Also see Nick Browne, "The Spectator of American Symbolic Forms: Re-reading John Ford's *Young Mr. Lincoln*," *Film Reader*, no. 4 (Northwestern University, 1979): 180–88; and Marsha Kinder, "The Image of Patriarchal Power in *Young Mr. Lincoln* (1939) and *Ivan the Terrible, Part 1* (1945)," *Film Quarterly* (Winter 1985–86): 29–49.

Figure 16-3. (Copyright 1939, renewed 1967, by Columbia Pictures Corporation. All rights reserved. Courtesy of Columbia Pictures.)

height of his power perhaps comes at that moment when he springs the idea of a filibuster on his colleagues (and to a certain extent on us), but what is underscored as the final drama unfolds is his remoteness from the true scene of battle and his ignorance of the full implications of his action, including a triumph born of defeat.

Behind his odd victory, then, we might discern an unresolved conflict between those ideals the film gives voice to through the figure of Smith and the institutional structures within which his vocal performance functions. Smith's original motive in staging the filibuster, it is important to keep in mind, is to use the Senate as a platform from which to speak to the people back home and so reclaim his political legitimacy and personal honor. But the very notion of a federal deliberative body—with diverse geographic regions represented at a national congress—denies the possibility of any immediate relationship between an elected spokesperson and his or her constituency. Free speech, that central tenet of democratic idealism, requires an open field of transmission, a free press, or, in light of the technological changes in the dissemination of political information since the days of Thomas Jefferson, free media, that neutral, natural system implied by the Federal Writers' guide to Washington.

From the very outset of *Mr. Smith Goes to Washington*, however, the news media have been presented as a parallel and to a certain extent as a rival social force to the political institutions they cover. In the opening expository move of the narrative, a Washington reporter phones his editor with news of Smith's predecessor's death, offering us the first glimpse of a media network with which the political machine must deal. As if in direct counterpoint to the public relations ballyhoo of the Taylor machine, moreover, an exploitative Washington press corps works to alter the image of Smith from small town folk hero to rural buffoon upon his arrival in the city. That it is Smith's knowledge of native American hand signals and animal calls that initially makes him an easy target for the journalists only serves to underscore the fact that—with his homing pigeons, his fumblings with the telephone—Smith is a technological primitive transplanted to the center of a vast media world. Radiating out from Washington to various regional constituencies, that network is heavily dependent on the technology of transcribing, amplifying, and transmitting the human voice.

The Senate chamber, however, is a theatrical preserve within this electronic environment. News service reporters "cover" proceedings but as gallery stenographers who must exit to an adjacent room to relay their reports to distant locations. In the conference room where the Committee on Privileges and Elections hears testimony that has been rigged against Smith by Taylor's machine, microphones are prominently displayed (as they were at Smith's send-off banquet early on), and voices reverberate tinnily (fig. 16–4). No such devices, however, are to be found on the Senate floor. Prompted by Saunders's hand signals, Smith speaks to the only audience he has: a gallery audience with a penchant for impulsive outbursts and a Senate president whose reign over the proceedings gradually loosens until in the final mo-

Figure 16-4. (Copyright 1939, renewed 1967, by Columbia Pictures Corporation. All rights reserved. Courtesy of Columbia Pictures.)

ments he sets gavel aside and the chamber is transformed into an arena for spontaneous cheering and dancing.

Between this public drama and a *national* audience, however, is a media system over which neither Smith nor the president has control. After the filibuster is launched Taylor swings into action, effectively controlling all channels of communication back to Smith's home state. When Saunders, newly converted to partisan journalism, attempts to establish an alternative network by the way of a telephone link to the Boy Rangers back home, the film dramatizes, in a series of blow-by-blow counterthrusts, how Smith's defenders are brutally silenced by their technologically superior counterparts. Paine then gains permission to import into the hermetic space of the Senate chamber for Smith's inspection thousands of hostile telegrams "wired" from constituents whose opinion has been made by the Taylor machine. In the end, then, the media seems either complicit with Taylor or ineffectual in opposing him.

In the two brief scenes in which H.V. Kaltenborn appears, however, the news media function thematically and textually in a different way. The film's inclusion of this famous radio news analyst—and the broadcasting equipment of the CBS and NBC radio networks—seems a gesture toward topical referentiality, in effect suspending the postcredit disclaimer that "the names, characters and incidents used herein are fictitious."[28] Kaltenborn's appearance in the fiction suggests that the filibuster the film plots is no less newsworthy an event than, say, the Munich Conference of August 1938, the coverage of which had vaulted him to national fame and helped to expand the market for network radio news, or the Senate neutrality debates, on which

---

28. By the fall of 1939 Kaltenborn was heard nightly in a fifteen-minute broadcast sponsored by Pure Oil and reportedly earned an income of $2,000 a week. War in Europe, an economic boon to radio news business in America, may also have whetted the appetite of movie audiences for behind-the-scenes glimpses of radio news personalities such as Kaltenborn. To satisfy the curiosity of tourists about radio reports on events in Europe, for example, NBC began allowing visitors to the RCA building in New York to observe news broadcasts through a window (*Variety*, 6 Sept. 1939, 23; 13 Sept. 1939, 1; 25 Oct. 1939, 1, 54). One reviewer of *Mr. Smith* observed that Kaltenborn's name was "almost as lively box-office as a film star's" and that his appearance, like the film's realistic settings, brought "the whole matter of government as it is achieved in the nation's capital smack into the audience's lap, unvarnished and unlibeled" (William R. Weaver, *Motion Picture Herald*, 7 Oct. 1939, 35, 38). The radio broadcast was topical in another sense as well: radio correspondents first obtained access to Senate gallery facilities in 1939 (see Edward W. Chester, *Radio, Television, and American Politics* [New York: Sheed and Ward, 1969], 62).

Kaltenborn reported in September and October 1939.[29] Concomitantly, a sequence such as this is a mechanism by which the film appears to address external events: social reality not only penetrates the fiction but the fiction is directed outward in relation to the daily news. The commentary scripted for Kaltenborn exploits this when he notes that envoys of two dictatorial powers in the galleries have come to witness "democracy in action." The viewer of 1939 is thus instructed in how to relate events in the fiction to political events overseas.

Yet having been interpolated into the text in this fashion, Kaltenborn also is transformed. His status as celebrity journalist outside the fiction may grant him a certain interpretive authority, but the framing of his performance by the fiction limits that authority as well. For "Kaltenborn" (the newscaster in the film whose role the real-life Kaltenborn plays) the meaning of the filibuster may be unambiguous, but events that transpire outside his purview may well lead the film spectator to question the notions that this "show" unequivocally signifies the power of free speech and that Kaltenborn fully speaks the truth of this scene for this text. After the film has contrasted the scene in the Senate with violent acts of repression perpetrated by Taylor's thugs, "Kaltenborn" in his second appearance simply calls attention to the heroic dimension of Smith's doomed performance before a packed house that has gathered "to be in on the kill." Foregrounding Smith's martrydom, this interpretation also neatly sidesteps the matter of institutional conflict and repression powerfully evoked by the text's intercutting of distant but related events.[30]

The inadequacy of Kaltenborn's radio commentary to account for the full

---

29. It is interesting to note that in his coverage of the neutrality debates Kaltenborn offered an interpretation of the congressional filibuster that contradicts the one scripted for "Kaltenborn" in the film. On 21 September, Kaltenborn quoted the warning of Sen. Arthur Vandenberg (R-Calif.) that "to filibuster on this issue would justify those who say that the democratic process will not work," and on 10 October he observed that isolationists in the Senate were agreed "there's little joy in talking for a lost cause" (Kaltenborn radio scripts, 1939, H. V. Kaltenborn Collection, Wisconsin Center for Film and Theater Research, Madison, Wis.).

30. Kaltenborn's commentary thus functions in a fashion similar to what Pierre Machery's has described as a "detachable utterance," a statement that appears to have been taken directly from ideology and inserted into the texture of a novel but that is also transformed by the new fictional context. "Detachable utterances are not detached utterances," Machery argues. "They are in the work not as real objects but as fictional objects. . . . They are in the text not as intruders, but effects" (Machery, *A Theory of Literary Production* [London: Routledge and Kegan Paul, 1978], 297).

panorama of events we witness is in part a matter of the text's distribution of narrative information, of the discrepancy between what this character tells us and what we have come to know. But we might also gauge its inadequacy in terms of a discrepancy in the stylistic richness of contrasting *means* of narration. *Mise-en-scène* in the two scenes in which Kaltenborn appears is relatively static and constricted: in shadow in the foreground right are radio equipment, an operator, and two NBC mikes; Kaltenborn stands in profile midground, facing his CBS mike to the left; beyond is a door to the Senate chamber. As if to punch up the scenes visually, the camera cuts in closer during his monologues—four times in the first instance, three in the second—ending on extreme, telephoto close-ups of his face in profile at the mike. But these close-ups only serve to emphasize what is most distinctive about the passage to begin with: the isolation and immobility of the newscaster, reading his script and cut off from the scene he intermittently describes, and a planar, uncontoured perspective on him (fig. 16–5).[31]

Contrast this with almost any other sequence in the film: the dynamic economy with which a series of phone calls links key political figures across the breadth of the country in the opening sequence, exemplifying the motor force of the political machine that the passage introduces; the graphic counterpoint and musical scoring of Vorkapich's montage tour of Washington; the carefully timed exchange of looks between Smith and Saunders in his office as the eager senator, in search of the proper words for his boys' camp bill, moves back and forth between two framed images: a western landscape painting and the lighted Capitol dome outside his window; the frontal reaction shots of Smith—wounded and silent—when Paine betrays him at the Senate hearing and again when he returns to the Lincoln Memorial to gaze up at his hero one last time. Above all, contrast the space of Kaltenborn's

31. Thomas Elsaesser proposes in "Film History as Social History" that what is often taken as the "ponderous" style of the Warner Brothers biopic cycle directed by William Dieterle in the late 1930s may be a function of the historically vanished intertext of live radio broadcasting and Roosevelt's fireside chats, with the film spectator positioned to identify with an audience as well as a protagonist. A similar stylistic logic may be at work in *Mr. Smith* but in such a fashion so as to emphasize a split between the radio commentary of Kaltenborn, with whom identification is never cued by the text, and the filibuster by Smith, who functions as both performer and optical relay in a dynamically edited sequence. That Capra's film served as an intertext for radio programming is suggested by the remark of a radio reviewer that the program "We the People" conveyed "a hint of brimming over with surprise. The tempo has to pick-up Capra-like, to convey the impression" (*Variety*, 20 December 1939, 28).

Figure 16-5. (Copyright 1939, renewed 1967, by Columbia Pictures Corporation. All rights reserved. Courtesy of Columbia Pictures.)

sideroom with the filmic construction of the Senate chamber itself. However faithful the decor to the original design of that chamber, the power of the drama played out in this space is less a matter of replicated ornamentation and statuary than of shot-by-shot articulation of a plastic space: aerial views of the amphitheater floor framed by tiered galleries (fig. 16–6); wide-angle shots of the senators' desks, alternately occupied and empty, defining a curvilinear arena (figs. 16–7, 16–8), and of the collapsing body of Smith in its

Figure 16-6. (Copyright 1939, renewed 1967, by Columbia Pictures Corporation. All rights reserved. Courtesy of Columbia Pictures.)

Figure 16-7. (Copyright 1939, renewed 1967, by Columbia Pictures Corporation. All rights reserved. Courtesy of Columbia Pictures.)

Figure 16-8. (Copyright 1939, renewed 1967, by Columbia Pictures Corporation. All rights reserved. Courtesy of Columbia Pictures.)

 inner ring; low-angle shots of Smith backed snugly by the converging diagonal lines of the cornice, or angled over Paine, with the Senate clock, press gallery, and paneled skylight beyond (figs. 16–9, 16–10). Perhaps most important, the film draws on a point-of-view editing structure through which classical film style subjectifies a fictional space, fixing Smith's performance within a network of facial and vocal reactions, most crucially those of Saunders, the Senate president, and Paine.[32]

Here, then, we might identify a third way in which *Mr. Smith Goes to Washington* transforms social material: by way of the "performance" of the film itself as an unfolding series of shifting views and modulating sounds. To conceptualize the film thusly is to approach the foundations of the text, to consider the range of filmic processes through which the fiction is made available to the spectator. From this perspective the problems of articulation that are explicitly raised by Smith in his late-night office session with Saunders—how does one put a lighted dome into a legislative text?—implicitly redound to the benefit of cinema, a medium of images and sound in time. If Smith's words are insufficient, the film has recourse to the image of the body of the actor; to a soft-focus lighting effect that seems to bathe Saunders, his auditor, in the very illumination (at the "end of the tunnel") that he describes; and to a subtle orchestration of familiar melodies on the sound track that carry with them connotations of the sentimental folk culture that he would revive. The film draws on a variety of cinematic effects, not the least of which is the optical trick by which a two-dimensional, painted image of the Capitol dome on the film set appears as an illuminated monument against a night sky on the screen (fig. 16–11). With this in mind, we might recast the notion of the Senate chamber as a *theatrical* space—in which the expressive hesitations and shifts in emotion of the performer and the spontaneous responses of his auditors transform a "staged" event into a seemingly "authentic" one—so as to account for the work of the host medium. The placement of characters within a particular *mise-en-scène*, the fragmentation

32. Capra shot the filibuster with multiple cameras and microphones placed at various vantage points around the set so that he could record performances simultaneously, thus anticipating the techniques of "live" television coverage of political events today. But contrast the flexible, volumetric space of this filmically constructed Senate chamber with the flat, constricted space defined by the telephoto lenses of immobile television cameras that have recently been allowed to enter the Senate chamber. The image of Kaltenborn poised outside the sideroom door now seems to presage the transformation of the chamber into a media space—but as a televisual backdrop for snippets of oratory by senators sporting eye-arresting red ties on the evening news.

Figure 16-9. (Copyright 1939, renewed 1967, by Columbia Pictures Corporation. All rights reserved. Courtesy of Columbia Pictures.)

Figure 16-10. (Copyright 1939, renewed 1967, by Columbia Pictures Corporation. All rights reserved. Courtesy of Columbia Pictures.)

Figure 16-11. (Copyright 1939, renewed 1967, by Columbia Pictures Corporation. All rights reserved. Courtesy of Columbia Pictures.)

and recombination of performances within a network of reaction shots and vocal overlays, and the restriction and revelation of narrative information are all part of the text's regulation, its government, of its own component parts.

We might say that *Mr. Smith*, as a text, *absorbs for cinema* a variety of means of addressing an audience: architecture and sculpture that guide a tourist's eye, the typographical and pictorial allure of a newspaper's front page or a billboard, theatrical performance within a politically charged arena, and the electronic amplification and transmission of the human voice. Whatever problems the fiction raises concerning the possibility of genuine political discourse in an age of technologically mediated relationships, it never calls into question this ground. If Taylor's exploitation of American folk culture for private profit and political gain is debunked within the fiction, the opening moment of this filmic text, in which the logo of Columbia Pictures is underscored with a musical phrase from "Columbia, the Gem of the Ocean," aligns patriotic folk culture with corporate self-promotion, seemingly without irony. The cinema of Hollywood emerges as an ideal medium for the revivification, authentication, and dissemination of political and cultural ideals; it is a guarantor of a compelling experience (a Capra film) yet itself not subject to the critique of machination and mediation the fiction otherwise provides.

Effaced in the Federal Writers' Project guidebook description of coverage of Washington is any notion of historical change in the representation of the nation's capital; before or after halftone printing, radio, or motion pictures, Washington remains the same imaginary place. The controversy in Washington after *Mr. Smith*'s premiere, in contrast, raised questions about the representation of Washington in the form of film fiction and about Hollywood's economic and political stake within a changing media environment. When Richard L. Strout worried that an "easy-going" viewer might find the film "pleasant and heart-warming in Mr. Capra's well-known manner," or when Nelson Bell of the *Washington Post* complained that Capra's sense of drama, humor, and melodramatic punch made a fraudulent filibuster appear rational and patriotic, they voiced concern about the manipulation of political material in the hands of a talented Hollywood director.[33] Similarly, Alben Barkley's condescending complaint about the wide-eyed acceptance of the film not as fiction but fact in cultural backwaters appears an anxious assessment of both the representational power of film and the systemic power of Hollywood to reach and consolidate a vast national audience. From this perspective, congressional saber-rattling about the passage of an anti–block booking bill does not seem quite as arbitrary a response to the controversy as one might first think.

By the fall of 1940, however, congressional sabers were stilled (and antitrust action temporarily suspended) as the major studios signed a consent decree with the Justice Department limiting blocks of films to five and placing a moratorium on the purchase of new theaters. Senate hearings on pro-Allied propaganda from Hollywood were undertaken by Wheeler and Gerald

33. Strout, *Christian Science Monitor*, 19 October 1939, 1; Bell, *Washington Post*, 20 October 1939, 16. Over the years, Capra has often suggested that *Mr. Smith* was singled out for attack because it was a film rather than a novel or a play and that the Washington press corps envied and feared the power of the culturally disreputable visitors from Hollywood. (See, for example, his first public response to the controversy in the *Christian Science Monitor*, 27 October 1939, 3, as well as his 1971 account in *The Name Above the Title*, 289–92.) In his autobiography Capra finesses the question of the support the film received from established critics and commentators *within* the news media by subsuming this response under the general category of "vox populi," but clearly these were voices—as Columbia's publicity department understood well—of a particularly potent kind in countering opposition to the film, and their verdict is an index to the degree to which Hollywood by the late 1930s could command a base of support within a civic and cultural sector.

 P. Nye (R–North Dakota) in the fall of 1941 but then were quietly abandoned in December as America went to war. The following February Hollywood was declared an "essential industry"; the popular media soon would be saturated with film stars making a pitch on behalf of the war effort, and theaters would become increasingly open to the circulation of government films.[34] The trajectory of Capra's career is no less instructive. On the day after Pearl Harbor, he was inducted into the army on a Warner Brothers set where he was directing *Arsenic and Old Lace*. Two months later he was in Washington organizing a military film unit of Hollywood personnel to produce propaganda films for recruits; four of these films were eventually distributed nationwide in the first-run theaters of the major studios.[35]

But this wartime alignment of institutions itself was short-lived. The consent decrees with the Justice Department never took hold, and renewed antitrust action culminated in a 1948 Supreme Court ruling that forced the major studios to divorce themselves of theater chains. Hollywood's vulnerability to congressional action was demonstrated in its capitulation to the Red Scare tactics of the House Un-American Activities Committee beginning in 1947.[36] Furthermore, the notion that the motion picture theater might be considered in some sense a "meeting hall of democracy," a spatial extension of the sphere of representational government in a media age, only briefly held sway. In the long run commercial broadcasting, not Hollywood, would cash in on the claim of public service to national governance by way of the televised network news.

Hollywood's relation to Washington and the news media during this period thus might best be thought of as one of ongoing negotiations among powerful institutions with overlapping but varied interests, marked by compacts and conflicts that were layered and shifting. Moments of disturbance and readjustment serve to illuminate the history of Hollywood's relation to a broader spectrum of social and political institutions, a history that today—when the collapse of entertainment, information, and politics (and the interchangeability of actors, anchormen, and politicians) has itself become a media cliche—should hold particular interest. The writing of this history, moreover, has much to gain from attention to specific films. If as a social ob-

34. See Jowett, *Film: The Democratic Art*, 277–78, 297–320.

35. For Capra's account of this period, see *The Name Above the Title*, 314–43.

36. For a subtle institutional analysis of the Supreme Court ruling, see Lea Jacobs, "The Paramount Case and the Role of the Distributor," *The Journal of the University Film and Video Association* 35, no. 1 (Winter 1983): 44–49. On the HUAC hearings, see Larry Ceplair and Steven Englund, *The Inquisition in Hollywood* (Berkeley: University of California, 1979).

ject *Mr. Smith* occasioned public debate and private discussion the record of which is partially available to us through existing documents, as a filmic text it translated cultural and political material of both a topical and mythic kind into the formal systems of the Hollywood cinema: narrational, specular, auditory. Offering a fictional model for social relations, *Mr. Smith* as a text addresses that fiction to a film spectator, and in the process it negotiates social relations of another order. A task of historical criticism is to make this work evident as well.

BIBLIOGRAPHY

Critical Method

Altman, Rick. "Representational Technologies and the History of Cinema." *Iris* 2, no. 2 (1984): 111–25.

Bordwell, David. "Lowering the Stakes: Prospects for a Historical Poetics of the Cinema" *Iris* 1, no. 1 (1983): 5–18.

Browne, Nick. "System of Production/System of Representation: Industry Context and Ideological Form in Capra's *Meet John Doe*." In *Meet John Doe*, edited by Charles Wolfe (New Brunswick, N.J.: Rutgers University Press, 1989).

Burch, Noël. "Film's Institutional Mode of Representation and the Soviet Response." *October*, no. 11 (Winter 1979): 77–96.

Buscombe, Edward. "Bread and Circuses: Economics and the Cinema." In *Cinema Histories, Cinema Practices*, edited by Patricia Mellencamp and Philip Rosen (Frederick, Md.: University Publications of America, 1984).

———. "Notes on Columbia Pictures Corporation, 1926–41." *Screen* 16, no 3 (August 1975): 65–82.

Cahiers du cinéma. "John Ford's *Young Mr. Lincoln*." *Cahiers du cinéma*, no. 223 (August 1970). English trans., *Screen* (Autumn 1972): 5–44.

Elsaesser, Thomas. "Film History as Social History: The Dieterle/Warner Brothers Biopic." *Wide Angle* 8, no. 2 (1986).

———. "Film History and Visual Pleasure: Weimar Cinema." In *Cinema Histories, Cinema Practices*, edited by Patricia Mellencamp and Philip Rosen (Frederick, Md.: University Publications of America, 1984).

Ferro, Marc. *Cinema and History*. Translated by Naomi Greene (Detroit: Wayne State University Press, 1988).

Isenberg, Michael T. "Toward a Historical Methodology for Film Scholarship." In *War on Film: The American Cinema and World War I, 1914–1941* (East Brunswick, N.J.: Associated University Press, 1981).

Kepley, Vance, Jr. "Griffith's *Broken Blossoms* and the Problem of Historical Specificity." *Quarterly Review of Film Studies* 3, no. 1 (Fall 1977): 37–48.

Lehman, Peter. "Style, Function and Ideology: A Problem in Film History." *Film Reader* 4 (1979): 72–80.

Rosen, Philip. "Securing the Historical: Historiography and the Classical Cinema." In *Cinema Histories, Cinema Practices*, edited by Patricia Mellencamp and Philip Rosen (Frederick, Md.: University Publications of America, 1984).

Thompson, Kristin. "Cinematic Specificity in Film Criticism and History." *Iris* 1, no. 1 (1983): 39–49.

Mr. Smith Goes to Washington

Affron, Charles. *Cinema and Sentiment* (Chicago: University of Chicago Press, 1982), 118–31.

Bergman, Andrew. *We're in the Money: Depression America and Its Films* (New York: New York University Press, 1971), 132–48.

Browne, Nick. "The Politics of Narrative Form: Capra's *Mr. Smith Goes to Washington*." *Wide Angle* 3, no. 4 (1979): 4–11.

Capra, Frank. *The Name Above the Title* (New York: Macmillan, 1971), 274–93.

Carney, Raymond. *American Vision: The Films of Frank Capra* (Cambridge: Cambridge University Press, 1986), 299–344.

Gallagher, Brian. "Speech, Identity and Ideology in *Mr. Smith Goes to Washington*." *Film Criticism* 5, no. 2 (Winter 1981): 12–22.

Handzo, Stephen. "Under Capracorn." *Film Comment* 8, no. 4 (November–December 1972): 8–14.

Maland, Charles J. *Frank Capra* (Boston: Twayne, 1980), 104–9.

Nelson, Joyce. "*Mr. Smith Goes to Washington*: Capra, Populism and Comic-Strip Art." *Journal of Popular Film* 3, no. 3 (Summer 1974): 245–55.

Poague, Leland. *The Cinema of Frank Capra* (Cranbury, N.J.: A.S. Barnes, 1975), 180–89.

Rose, Brian Geoffrey. *An Examination of Narrative Structure in Four Films of Frank Capra* (New York: Arno Press, 1980), 83–136.

Sklar, Robert. "The Imagination of Stability: The Depression Films of Frank Capra." In *Frank Capra: The Man and His Films*, edited by Richard Glatzer and John Raeburn (Ann Arbor: University of Michigan Press, 1975).

———. *Movie-Made America: A Cultural History of American Movies* (New York: Random House), 205–214.

Willis, Don C. *The Films of Frank Capra* (Metuchen, N.J.: Scarecrow Press, 1974), 23–37.

17

THE CABINET OF DOCTOR CALIGARI: PRODUCTION, RECEPTION, HISTORY

Mike Budd

Films, like other cultural products, are made and received within particular historical situations.[1] Thus close analyses of film texts will be most revealing when they demonstrate how textual operations and processes are implicated in larger historical processes. Rather than reified objects dissected by the critic, films are dynamic processes in which we as viewers make meaning and pleasure and knowledge—help make our own lives—but not under conditions of our own choosing. These conditions include the discourses and institutions that construct the complex matrix of alternatives within which we make history; they also often determine and disguise our choices. A truly democratic culture requires a critical history, which expands and clarifies present alternatives by reconstructing their bases in the past. This essay aims to contribute to such a critical history through an examination of the production, textual, and reception processes of *The Cabinet of Doctor Caligari* (1920).

Focused on alternatives, critical historical analysis begins with those

1. Thanks to Clay Steinman for useful comments on earlier drafts of this essay.

dominant institutions within and against which choices are generated and suppressed. Among these institutions are *discourses*, organized social processes of making and reproducing meaning (O'Sullivan et al. 1983, 72–75). Since the twenties, world cinema has been dominated by an institutional and discursive complex called classic realist cinema or classical Hollywood cinema (Kuhn 1982, 21–42; Bordwell, Staiger, and Thompson 1985). This mode has been most highly developed through the international hegemony of the Hollywood film industry and apparently has been adopted with modifications by virtually all other national cinemas. The institutional discourse of classic realist cinema limits the possible meanings of texts within this mode and marginalizes alternative modes. It is usually aligned with a specific set of institutions for producing and consuming those texts, including reading strategies by viewers. Produced within an industrial system of modified mass production, usually for private profit, films are consumed by spectators who have learned to "read" the realist discursive system.

The meanings and pleasures of classic realist cinema come through the telling and consuming of stories or narratives that seem to tell themselves. Stylistic techniques (cinematography, *mise en scène*, editing, sound) are designed to be transparent, self-effacingly subordinate to narration, the storytelling process. Rather than a criterion by which we can evaluate films as, say, good or bad imitations of reality, realism thus becomes a construct, an effect of a specific organization of film techniques. Most film viewers don't see the world on the screen as real, but they do learn to see the fictional narrative as natural, unmediated by discourse or narration. Diverting attention from the techniques that construct their narratives and characters, virtually all commercial films misrepresent themselves, covering their gaps and contradictions with often pleasurable effects of unity and continuity.

The Cabinet of Doctor Caligari[2] was made within a commercial studio system and shown initially in commercial theaters. But the production of such an unusual film only became possible through a special set of historical con-

2. One of the most famous films ever made, *Das Cabinett des Dr. Caligari* (*The Cabinet of Doctor Caligari*) was produced by Erich Pommer for the Decla studio in Berlin, Germany, in late 1919 and early 1920 and released there in February 1920. The tentative and unstable Weimar Republic, Germany's first democracy, had been established in early 1919, just after the end of World War I, and was destroyed with Hitler's rise to power in 1933. Written by Carl Mayer and Hans Janowitz, directed by Robert Wiene, the film starred Werner Krauss as Caligari, Conrad Veidt as Cesare, Lil Dagover as Jane, and Friedrich Feher as Francis. Original prints were tinted in several colors, and the German titles lettered in an expressionist graphic style consistent with the rest of the film.

ditions within the institutions of classic realist cinema in Germany. Dependent on exports, German film executives constantly looked for ways to sell in foreign markets (Kracauer 1947, 132). They were aided in this in the late teens and early twenties, when a period of inflation and currency devaluation followed Germany's defeat in World War I and further encouraged exports by making its products relatively cheap. But during the war Hollywood had become dominant internationally; in order to compete German films would have to be different (Thompson 1985, 104–5). An artistically oriented cadre of studio personnel made possible one kind of product differentiation: an artistic stylization that contrasted with the usual realism of U.S. films (Huaco 1965, 36; Elsaesser 1984, 70–71). "Artistic" films never constituted more than a small percentage of Germany's total output. Yet to bolster exports the German film industry for several years after the war was unusually open to experimentation labeled "artistic" and thus ordinarily excluded from the discourse of classic realism, with its rigid demands for the largest possible market.

In postwar Germany, "artistic" often meant expressionism, a movement in many arts that was part of the larger movement of cultural modernism. In the early decades of the twentieth century a revolution of international modernism took place in virtually all the arts. Cubism and surrealism in France, expressionism in Germany, futurism in Italy, and constructivism in the Soviet Union were all diverse and cross-cultural movements in themselves but part also of an international assault on traditional artistic processes and styles. Painting as a window on the world, poetry as a genteel mirror of cultural order, the well-made play with its plausible characters and naturalistic situations, the realist novel—these and other time-honored forms and conventions were attacked, ridiculed, and ignored by modernist artists. In quite divergent ways they often promoted disunity over unity, montage and collage over continuity, and shocking and subjective new styles over the conventional representation of an "objective" external world.

Yet as a modernist movement German expressionism was a profoundly contradictory, unstable, and transitional phenomenon. It was strongly influenced by the subjectivist traditions of nineteenth-century German romanticism, which glorified the unified vision of an isolated and rebellious artist. On the other hand, it developed the radical disjunction and abstraction of emergent modernist forms. Expressionism carried these contradictions within itself. It combined an intense desire to overthrow authority and change the world with a rejection of and retreat from the world into a grotesque realm of subjective expression. Many artists and writers hated the bourgeois forms of their political and cultural fathers, yet in their romantic idealism were often unable actively to support contemporary social (and socialist) movements for democratic change. Influenced by expressionism, many of them, including *Caligari*'s scriptwriters, Carl Mayer and Hans Janowitz, registered their political ambivalence in their work, often unintentionally.

The expressionist movement began in painting and poetry around 1910, spread first to literature and the theater, then to the most expensive arts—opera, architecture, and film. In the years immediately following World War I, wealthy art patrons, theater audiences and critics, government sponsors, and advertising and the mass media began to accept and promote expressionism. Yet at the precise moment of this acceptance, expressionism as an avant-garde phenomenon was dialectically transformed into its opposite and successor, the *Neue Sachlichkeit*, the new sobriety or sanity. The destruction and trauma of the war, cooptation by established institutions, and its own internal contradictions by 1924 transmogrified expressionism in the art world just as it found its public everywhere else. In the visual arts, for example, the

Figure 17-1. Product differentiation within a capitalist film industry: the artistic stylization of German expressionist settings in contrast to the realism of Hollywood films. (Film Stills Collection, George Eastman House.)

characteristic distorted and angular shapes and bright, almost deranged colors gave way to the cool, geometric forms and subdued colors of the new sobriety. More generally, expressionism's anguished protest against authority and its subjective expression of intense emotion became rationalized, calm, "objective." The tensions and contradictions of expressionism were the preconditions for its historical change; as an institutionalized discourse its gaps and stress points would appear especially in its intersection with other discourses.

One of these discourses was the classic realist cinema, and in *The Cabinet of Doctor Caligari* this dominant mode comes into incompatible juxtaposition with a carefully limited version of expressionism. We can specify *Caligari*'s relation to expressionism and explore the consequences of the film's uneasy place between dominant and oppositional discourses and institutions by locating three areas of differential influence by expressionism: theme, narrative form, and setting. Thematically, *Caligari* seems to be characteristic not only of expressionism but also of older and more popular German cultural traditions. Insanity, the grotesque and uncanny, the outcry against an older generation and against authority—expressionism, and *Caligari*, drew these themes largely from traditions of German romanticism in literature, theater, and the visual arts.[3]

But it is only when we leave these thematic generalities, these results of interpretation, and examine the bases for interpretation in the specificities of narrative and setting that we approach *Caligari* and expressionism concretely. In 1919 and 1920 literary expressionism was changing. The world war that lasted from 1914 to 1918 shocked many writers and others with its new scale of mindless technological barbarity. The abortive, compromised revolution in Germany that ended the war embittered many who had sought peace and social justice. Disillusioned, writers like Franz Werfel, Hanns Johst, and Paul Kornfeld rejected not only the socially activist themes of their earlier work but also their innovations (or imitations of innovations) in form. Late expressionism became antisubjective, antiromantic; following Goethe in rejecting modernism as sickness, all but a few writers by 1920 had either rediscovered the conservative forms of German literature or moved toward the sober style of the *Neue Sachlichkeit* (Sokel 1968, 221).

At the same time that the romantic rejection or political critique of society by the modernist artist was becoming untenable for many expressionist

3. My account of the history of expressionism is drawn primarily from the following sources: Stephen Eric Bronner and Douglas Kellner, eds. (1983); Peter Selz (1974); Walter H. Sokel (1968); John Willett (1970; 1978).

 writers, the movement was being accepted by the cultural establishment. At this moment expressionism began to find a carefully limited place in the commercial discourse of cinema. This acceptance was only possible because *Caligari*, like most other films influenced by expressionism, ignored the (largely antinarrative) avant-garde in favor of a conventional narrative form. In fact, *Caligari*'s unconventional aspects—the expressionist settings and plot reversal at the end—emerge from and are dependent on the largely conventional form of the film's classic realist narrative. Before it is anything else, *Caligari* is a story, told in the "invisible" discourse of classic realism for smooth consumption. Viewers may experience some disorientation because of the strange images, yet editing and cinematography help construct a reassuringly stable space and time where recognizable characters act out a story. (Indeed, when the film opened in New York in 1921, several reviewers noted how the initial sense of strangeness passed as one settled into the story ["Cabinet," *New York Times*, 1921; "Special" 1921; Reniers 1921].) Francis's tale, which comprises most of the film, is that most typical of realist narratives, the detective story. Thus it includes diversionary subplots (the attempted murderer imprisoned by the police—see figure 17–2), suspenseful chases (Francis following Caligari to the asylum), and the female character, Jane, used as token of exchange and power by the male characters. These strategies help subordinate style to narration and to produce what seems to have been for many exciting, largely commercial, and patriarchal cinema. But as narrative form, all this is very far from expressionist literature or drama, which was highly disjunctive, episodic, and modernist.

Whereas the narrative form of *Caligari* places it among the most advanced developments of the commercial realism of its time and seems virtually untouched by expressionism, the settings, derived from expressionist painting and theatrical set design, introduce the most disturbing and modernist elements. For whatever reason, the visual design of *Caligari* shows clearly the cubist influence on expressionism, specifically the styles of Robert Delaunay, Lyonel Feininger, and the painters associated with the *Brücke* (Bridge) group. In France the aesthetically radical principles of cubism would be applied to the overall formal design of a film in *Ballet Mécanique* (1924), for example. But from its inception the modernist qualities of *Caligari* were largely confined to its settings—to the angular, splintery shapes, the tilted houses, the distortions that can seem to infuse the world of the film with strangeness and dread. Disturbing, yet able to be coopted, *Caligari* exists in that anomalous cultural space between a modernist avant-garde and the capitalist institutions of mass-produced culture.

At the same time, *Caligari*'s visual style resembled what was appearing

Figure 17-2. A relatively conventional, consumable narrative form: the solution to the mysterious murders delayed by a diversionary subplot. (Film Stills Collection, George Eastman House.)

elsewhere in the German mass media. The film's designers—Hermann Warm, Walter Röhrig, and Walter Reimann—were part of the group around *Der Sturm*, Herwarth Walden's commercially successful Berlin magazine and publicity apparatus then riding the crest of the expressionist wave (Kracauer 1947, 68; Dube 1972, 159–61). How logical, then, for them to work for Erich Pommer, the film's producer, another businessman with an eye for exploiting a fashion. The capitalist corporation that Pommer supervised could exploit expressionism as international modernism, carefully containing its more radical dimensions. This was the corporation's way of differentiating its product as "artistic" though still (barely) within the relatively narrow parameters of a commercial cinema.[4]

As a part of making history, film viewing is an active and dynamic process in which people construct their experience and their relation to the text in

4. The material in this and preceding paragraphs on expressionism in *Caligari* appeared in an earlier version in Michael Budd (1981b).

 different ways. And as a model for and part of the historical process of generating (and closing down) emancipatory alternatives, film viewing is a reading, a working on and playing with a text that is nothing but the encoded traces, the mediations of the historical conditions and conflicts of its own production. Thus reading as making meaning and pleasure underlies usually unexamined processes of film viewing, and a crucial aspect of this activity is the revision of the narrative's past (what has been read) and predictions for the narrative's future (what will be read) in light of a changing present (what's being read); to read is to reread. Limited to being always at only one point in the temporal progression that is the phenomenal event of a film, viewers' minds nevertheless range constantly across their experience of the film so far and across expectations of what it will be. They compare, correct, specify, place, and predict, noting patterns of similarity and difference, of rhyming and progression. The classical narrative cinema attempts to rationalize and administer this process of consumption as it does the production of films. The management of such a closed system demands the projection of a semblance of continuity and coherence, so gaps and contradictions are for most viewers contained in a seemingly smooth production and consumption of narrative questions and answers. The rereading performed while viewing the film the first time can thus become a justification for not viewing it, not rereading it, again. In general, commercial films are made and presented as products that seem to be used up or consumed in the experience of "entertainment." For the film to become a commodity consumable in one viewing, rereading must be carefully contained, minimizing unsolved narrative or other puzzles that might prompt reflection or critical examination (Barthes 1974, 13).

What then of *The Cabinet of Doctor Caligari*, which near its end throws into question the status or truth-value of what has come before by revealing that its protagonist-narrator is mad? With its twist ending and expressionist settings the film virtually *demands* rereading. Although realist and commercial films, especially mysteries, commonly provide minor shocks of revelation that may prompt some more ambitious viewers to reread for narrational clues and deceptions, such rereadings usually seem to confirm and augment the managed pleasures of consumption. A film like *Caligari*, on the other hand, can radically *activate* rereading, can make it more than the tying up of loose narrative ends. One might try to explain, for example, the expressionist settings as the visions of the mad narrator, Francis. But the same settings are present in the frame story! Indeed, the more one tries to make everything fit, reconsidering the film retrospectively, the more difficult and

Figure 17-3. A classical narration juxtaposed with expressionist settings: realist and modernist features are intimately interrelated, generating gaps and contradictions. (Film Stills Collection, George Eastman House.)

problematic it becomes. These difficulties may prompt a more thorough, critical, and active rereading, even with the first viewing. Such an active re-reading would be a re-cognition, a radical problematization of the first, consumerist rereading.

A restrospective rereading of *Caligari* might take this radical path, or it might stay within the safe boundaries of the consumer of narrative. Insofar as it is a classical narrative, the film tries to guide us into the latter course. In order to do this it must accomplish two difficult things at the same time. It must fool us into believing that Francis is sane until the end of a first, "naive" reading. Yet it must also avoid any narrational inconsistencies or contradictions that might become apparent with the closer inspection of a retrospective rereading. The following analysis will show, however, that such contradictions are unavoidable in *Caligari* and thus can lead to a more radical rereading. Crucial aspects of the film are *necessary* in order to make both the first, "naive" reading and subsequent retrospective readings possible. Neither wholly conventional/classical nor simply transgressive/modernist, these aspects intimately intermingle the two.[5]

The contradictory demands of advancing and retrospective readings center on settings, since these are the most obviously modernist or transgressive aspects of a film that is primarily classical. These contradictory demands can be represented in a diagram (not "to scale") that presents the relations among the various segments of the film.

Diagram 17-1.

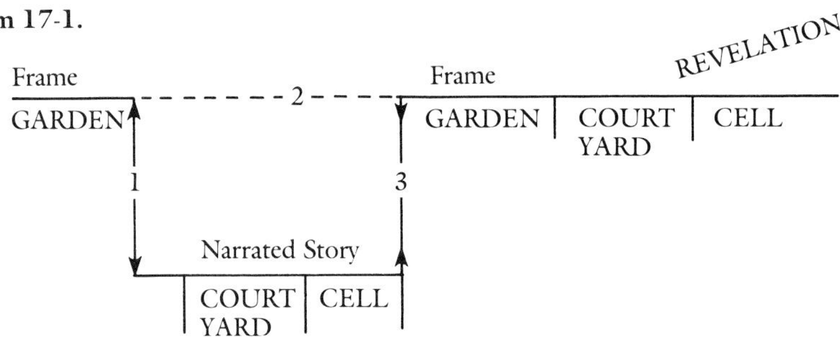

The film is not organized this way in itself. The structure here schematized and spatialized is actually a structuration, a temporal process through which the viewer as historical subject makes meaning and pleasure and across which she or he ranges, constructing and reconstructing. In classic realist cinema, dream sequences or stories told by the insane are usually clearly marked internally through stylistic elements such as setting, color, or acting in order to differentiate them from the naturalized, self-effacing discourse of realism. But the unexamined assumption that because setting functions to support

5. Few film "landmarks" have been so thoroughly associated with a single influential reading as has *The Cabinet of Doctor Caligari* with Siegfried Kracauer's *From Caligari to Hitler*. Supposedly added against the screenwriters' wishes, the frame story for Kracauer simply cancels out the attack on authority in Francis's story: "A revolutionary film was thus turned into a conformist one . . . by putting the original into a box, this version faithfully mirrored the general retreat into a shell" (67). Noting but failing to account for the continuation of expressionist settings in the frame story, Kracauer claims the hypnotic and tyrannical Caligari to be a premonition of Hitler.

In implicit opposition to Kracauer, Noël Burch and Jorge Dana propose a modernist reading of the film. For them, *Caligari* becomes "the first self-reflexive filmic work" (1975, 44) through a subversion of codes of illusionist representation that in 1919 were newly established. I propose to shift the terms of analysis in order to subsume these readings within a consideration of what processes and structures set the historical conditions of possibility for these and other readings and interpretations.

narrative, the setting's level of stylization should be consistent with the narrative's "degree of reality" is precisely what *Caligari* makes problematic. And it becomes so problematic because, unlike more radically modernist films like the surrealist *Un Chien Andalou* (1928), disturbing anomalies appear in what otherwise appears to be a relatively conventional narrational system. Keying the analysis to numbers in the diagram, we can identify stresses that prevent this system from attaining equilibrium and harmony.

1. In order to help explain Francis's story retrospectively as fantasy, the level of visual stylization of the frame and narrated segments must be as *different* as possible. This helps explain, for example, the relative bareness of the garden decor in which Francis tells his story. The garden contrasts with the deranged perspectives of Holstenwall that immediately follow it in opening the tale. The film begins again causally at this point to help create a "naive" first reading,[6] to induce forgetting of frame and telling; it seems also to start over *visually*, but in support of a retrospective reading.

2. Regardless of whether or not one sees the settings as motivated by Francis's madness, the implicit classical principle of consistency and homogeneity must keep the various settings of the frame story—garden, courtyard, and cell—on the *same* level of stylization, since they are proximate within the story space. This principle is even stronger in a reading that visually separates frame from framed, since that separation depends on the consistency of opposed parts.

3. Finally—and it is at this point that major stresses within the system of decor in *Caligari* emerge—a third contradictory stylistic pressure makes itself felt. The courtyard setting occurs in *both* frame and tale, thus holding those two levels *together* and working in diametrical opposition to attempts to keep them apart (1 above).

Architectonically, then, the system is unbalanced, out of true, a narrative and stylistic puzzle in which all the pieces don't fit. The film implicitly offers to explain one of its transgressions (the expressionist settings) with the other (the insane narrator), but only at the price of inconsistency. The attempted distinction between settings in (1), for example, is necessarily compromised and inconsistent, since to distinguish clearly between "normal" and "mad" worlds from the outset is to give the game away. In classical narrative most told stories are not stylistically different from their frames. Thus the min-

---

6. The "first" viewing may be a tenth viewing as long as it is at a point preceding the revelation, since viewers often play at not knowing the outcome during multiple viewings.

 imalism of the garden decor—a wall and bench, a few bushes and "branches"—wants to be read, relatively superficially the first time, as suggesting some continuity with the settings that follow while also retrospectively suggesting discontinuity. Of necessity both the same and different from the expressionist settings that follow, this minimalism ends up splitting the difference while trying to avoid salience. Attempting to accommodate two contradictory readings, the text produces a mild but functional heterogeneity, an inconsistency probably overlooked by most viewers in the realist effect of unity and continuity. The analysis here demonstrates that this inconsistency, this aporia of rereading, *is not a mistake but a necessary contradiction*. *Caligari* generally follows the realist subordination of style to narration while allowing one element of style, setting,[7] to get uppity; it also promotes an active rereading that may disrupt the positioning of the viewer as consumer.

We may restate the problem of *Caligari* by pointing to another, compounding contradiction. If the relation of garden setting to Holstenwall setting is, as argued, a kind of strategic compromise covering a contradiction, visually both similar and different, then we might expect that the courtyard in the frame story would appear different—but not too different—from its appearance in Francis's story, in order to support both advancing and retrospective readings. The difference would help suggest, retrospectively, that

7. Several commentators have pointed out the film's heterogeneity of acting styles, usually assuming it to be an error or inadequacy. The acting ranges from the expressionist stylization of Werner Krauss as Caligari and Conrad Veidt as Cesare, through the conventional silent film histrionics of Francis and Jane, to the restrained and relatively naturalistic portrayal of the white-coated doctors in the asylum. Yet this disjunction of acting styles is no accident, but like the settings a symptomatic contradiction produced by the conflicting projects of the film. On the one hand, there is the necessity for stylistic consistency between setting and character (as defined by acting, costume, and make-up). This consistency is limited to Caligari and Cesare, whose sharp, angular gestures, furtive lines, and stylized costumes and make-up mark them as one with their expressionist surroundings. On the other hand, there is the necessity for stylistic *in*consistency between setting and character. The text needs a stable reference point of sanity in a narration that suddenly reverses itself, shifting its ascription of madness from Caligari to Francis. With no stylistic relation to their surroundings, the asylum doctors, and especially the older one, constitute this reference point, since they are the only characters whose psychological traits are the same in both Francis's story and the frame that encloses it. Thus escaping from a reading of the film's expressionist aspects as motivated by the narrator's madness, these icons of objective science become virtually the last alibis for the invisible authority of classic realist narration itself; they become the stable ground that makes intelligible the sudden reverses of figures reread.

Figure 17-4. Illogical space, deranged perspective: a film so problematic that advertisers and exhibitors could not naturalize it. (Film Stills Collection, George Eastman House.)

Francis had constructed his mad tale by transforming his "real" environment. Why, then (asks your narrator), is the courtyard setting unchanged on its reappearance in the frame story?

The answer lies again in the difficult demands of a retrospective narration. Narratively, the final courtyard scene is a crucial one: the film's very intelligibility depends on the clear reversal and revelation that Francis has lied, that he is an inmate in the same asylum he virtually directs in his own tale. This point *prevents* any ascription of the setting to Francis's madness. But in order to ensure that the audience understands that this is the asylum, the courtyard must look the same in both frame and tale. The moment of shock in the realization of the narrator's unreliability, the temporary vertigo that may disturb the secure, knowing processing of the viewer as customer—this effect demands that the courtyard be *immediately recognizable*. Consider the alternative: if the courtyard *were* different, our difficulty would be increased intolerably; we would be genuinely puzzled as to the relative statuses of the parts; we might ask if Francis were right, the frame a lie; we might even begin to see the inadequacy of character as an explanation and move toward problems of how character is represented. But the film for most viewers probably contains these speculations, unless those viewers already have some theoretical and historical knowledge. It can still shock and disturb, not only in its relatively conventional elements of horror and the uncanny (as one of the links between the iconography of German romanticism and the Hollywood horror genre) but also in the stresses of an architectonic that must be traversed again, reconsidered, "where something past comes again, as though out of the future; something formerly accomplished as something to be completed" (Rilke, quoted in Howard, preface to Barthes, xi). That "something past" includes unexamined realist assumptions about narrational authority and neutrality, about a fixed and unchanging relation between segments designated "telling" and "tale," and about "the narrative's degree of reality" (Burch and Dana 1975, 44).[8]

Perhaps because of the heightened conflict of dominant and oppositional discourses that became the conditions of its production, *Caligari* condenses and mediates those conditions with unusual force and clarity. Yet production and text do not exhaust the moments in the history of a film; with *Caligari* the conflict of institutions is rearticulated in its conditions of reception, producing a fascinating reception history, only part of which we can sketch here.

As perhaps the most difficult and modernist of the German expressionist films of the twenties, *Caligari* was advertised and sold on the basis of its artistic innovations and prestige. In Paris it was an immediate and long-lasting success, playing for years there and even inspiring the term "Caligarisme" to designate "a postwar world seemingly all upside down" (Kracauer 1947, 71–72). In the United States the film was distributed by Samuel Goldwyn, opening at the Capitol Theatre in New York, one of the largest and most prestigious houses, on 3 April 1921 ("Cabinet," *Moving Picture World*, 1921). After breaking house records there for a week it played at a number of theaters in other cities, but it did not enjoy the general commercial success of the more conventional German imports of the time—Ernst Lubitsch's historical dramas *Madame DuBarry* (released in the United States as *Passion*) and *Anna Boleyn* (*Deception*).

Three aspects, three discourses of the publicity apparatus of the culture industries became important in the U.S. reception of *Caligari*: advertising, exhibition, and reviews. First, ads aggressively attempted to shape the film's reception in their own image, foregrounding characters and stars, making

8. In somewhat different form, the preceding analysis of *Caligari* appeared in Michael Budd (1979).

expressionism into a novelty, touting the suspenseful story, and trying to keep the whole thing dignified, as befitted a European art film. They also obsessively reproduced images of Cesare threatening Jane and tried to make *Caligari*'s expressionism into a continental clothing fashion with which to sell Goldwyn's new female stars to U.S. women; see fig. 17–5, from "Im-[p]ressionistic Photograph" (1921). These strategies took up the film's construction of Jane as object of desire for the male characters (and perhaps viewers), trying to assimilate it to the discourses of publicity.

Because of widespread anti-German prejudice, advertising called the film's origins "European," obscuring *Caligari*'s artistic as well as national context. Expressionism's extreme subjectivism attributed its representational distortion, abstraction, and fragmentation to the pure emotional expression of a transcendent artist. Thus it was of all styles in the modernist pantheon perhaps the most vulnerable to a naturalization and psychologization in which the transcendent artist becomes a character, whose pure expression becomes, in turn, madness. Mystification of the film's origins prepared it for insertion into the culture of commodities, but still word got out that it was a German film, a product of the diseased Hun mind, as some reviewers implied.[9] Thus, ironically, the naturalization of expressionism helped make possible the irrational attribution of madness to a whole nation.

But to make the film consumable, advertising was not enough. The text itself had to be changed in the exhibition situation. This was the age of the picture palace, the industry's attempt to attract more middle-class viewers and to make moviegoing itself a stable, profitable institution beyond the success or failure of any individual film. Fragments of high and mass culture were melded together in the larger theaters into presentations of which the feature film was only one part: selections from classical music played by a live orchestra, ballet or other dance numbers, newsreels and film shorts, and staged prologues and epilogues to the feature were all part of these presentations.

As organized by Sam "Roxy" Rothafel, who managed the Capitol Theatre and was one of the leading impresario-exhibitors in the country, the presentation for *The Cabinet of Doctor Caligari* was typically lavish but also somewhat unusual, with a live, *narrative* prologue and epilogue that essentially

9. "[*Caligari*] is one of those screen dissipations to be indulged in only once in a lifetime. The Germans, who seem still convinced that they won the war, are getting morbid over it. We've got more evidence on our side, but we want to get away from ghastliness as much as possible. Any second picture of this type would be like artistic slime" ("On the Screen in City Theatres" 1921).

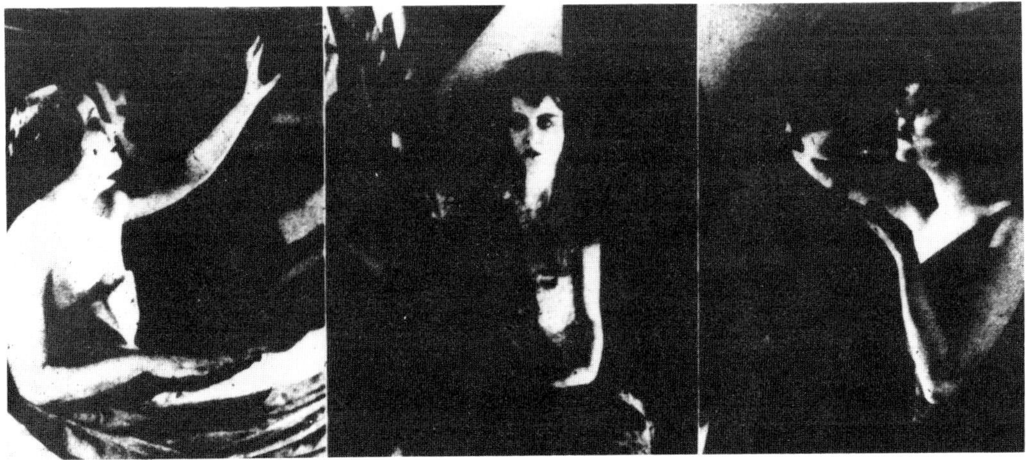

Figure 17-5. *Caligari*'s U.S. distributor, Samuel Goldwyn Pictures, tried to make the film's expressionism into a continental clothing fashion with which to sell its stars to women moviegoers. (Film Stills Collection, George Eastman House.)

placed a second frame onto Francis's story. The curtain opened on two characters, Cranford and Jane, sitting in front of a cozy fireplace. Cranford tells a story of walking through thick foliage into a garden where he encounters Francis ("like a man sleepwalking in a horrid nightmare" ["Rothafel" 1921]), who begins to tell him the story of "The Cabinet of Doctor Caligari." Then the curtains close, the lights fade, and this staged prologue slides seamlessly into the opening of the film. At the end, after the doctor has examined Francis and exclaimed in the final title, "I think I know how to cure him now," we return to the stage, where Cranford reassures (?) us that Francis, cured, today leads a happy, normal life, unable to remember his hallucination.

It's difficult to imagine a more blatant attempt to force a problematic text into conventional form, to contain its excesses in a frame of authoritarian and commodifying realism. The character who listens to Francis's story in the film is a potentially problematic one, since he seems to be an inmate of the asylum but must also serve as stand-in for the viewer at the crucial moment of the revelation of Francis's madness, when he recoils at the protagonist's ravings as a cue for our own response. The added second frame attempts to contain the sliding of this function, probably invisible to most viewers anyway, by making the listener a sane "anchor," an authoritative reference point outside the original text. The discourse of the film is attributed to a responsible source, since doubt is cast from the outset on Francis's sanity. With the problems and disturbances of the film not so much solved as enclosed, reframed, the limits of the culture industry's cooptation of *Caligari* were seemingly reached: the ruthless functionalism of this second frame tries to reestablish the hierarchy of discourses in realism, with style subordinate to (and dissolving into) narration, fantasies subordinate to (and demarcated from) a narrow, ideological concept of the real.[10]

Though the trade paper *Motion Picture News* claimed that the prologue and epilogue "were used by practically every exhibitor who has shown the picture" ("Rothafel" 1921), reviewers ignored the second frame and wrote about the film. Not that reviewers' comments were any more enlightening or less formulaic than they are today: in keeping with the pseudo-high culture milieu of the Capitol and other picture palaces, many reviewers and critics tried to spiritualize and mystify *Caligari*. Imitating the discourse of quasi-religious celebration used by reviewers of the higher arts, they posited a realm of gentility for this film, blessed by its separation from the material world of commodities and exchange. Yet as Herbert Marcuse has pointed out, this "affirmative culture" is not so far from the mundane world of capitalism:

> As in material practice the product separates itself from the producers and becomes independent as the universal reified form of the "commodity," so in cultural practice a work and its content congeal into universally valid "values." (1968, 94)

The ideas of the powerful are often the most powerful ideas. During this period the U.S. cultural establishment began to take a serious interest in the movies, and *Caligari*, like other German imports, became evidence for arguments by reviewers and others that film could be an art form, with all the prestige and mystification that nomination entails. In the stock exchange of cultural legitimation, *Caligari*'s deracinated expressionism and its limited modernist innovations became values that encouraged cultural "investment" in the new medium of film. Thus valued, such innovations also reciprocally added to the "cultural capital" (Bourdieu and Passeron 1977)—the power to *define* aesthetic value and status—of dominant social groups.[11]

---

10. Some of the preceding analysis of *Caligari*'s U.S. reception appeared in somewhat different form in Michael Budd (1981a).

11. Material in this paragraph on the mystification of *Caligari* as art summarizes arguments made in Michael Budd (1986).

Barthes, Roland. 1974. *S/Z*. Translated by Richard Miller. New York: Hill and Wang.

Bordwell, David, Janet Staiger, and Kristin Thompson. 1965. *The Classical Hollywood Cinema: Film Style and Mode of Production to 1960*. New York: Columbia University Press.

Bourdieu, Pierre, and Claude Passeron. 1977. *Reproduction in Education, Society and Culture*. Translated by Richard Nice. London: Sage Publications.

Bronner, Stephen Eric, and Douglas Kellner, eds. 1983. *Passion and Rebellion: The Expressionist Heritage*. South Hadley, Mass.: J.F. Bergin.

Budd, Michael. 1979. "Retrospective Narration in Film: Rereading 'The Cabinet of Doctor Caligari.' " *Film Criticism* 4, no. 1: 35–43.

———. 1981a. " 'The Cabinet of Doctor Caligari': Conditions of Reception." *Ciné-Tracts* 12: 41–49.

———. 1981b. "Contradictions of Expressionism in 'The Cabinet of Doctor Caligari.' " *Indiana Social Studies Quarterly* 34, no. 2: 19–25.

———. 1986. "The National Board of Review and the Early Art Cinema in New York: 'The Cabinet of Doctor Caligari' as Affirmative Culture." *Cinema Journal* 26, no. 1: 3–18.

Burch, Noël, and Jorge Dana. 1975. "Propositions." *Afterimage* 5: 40–66.

" 'The Cabinet of Doctor Caligari.' " 1921. *New York Times* (4 April): 18.

" 'The Cabinet of Doctor Caligari' Premiere at Capitol During Week of April 3." 1921. *Moving Picture World* 49, no. 5 (2 April): 481.

Dube, Wolf-Dieter. 1972. *Expressionism*. New York: Oxford University Press.

Elsaesser, Thomas. 1984. "Film History and Visual Pleasure: Weimar Cinema." In *Cinema Histories, Cinema Practices*, edited by Patricia Mellencamp and Philip Rosen. Frederick, Md: University Publications of America.

Huaco, George A. 1965. *The Sociology of Film Art*. New York: Basic Books.

"Im[p]ressionistic Photographs of Goldwyn Stars." 1921. *Moving Picture World* 50, no. 5 (4 June): 526.

Kracauer, Siegfried. 1947. *From Caligari to Hitler: A Psychological History of the German Film*. Princeton, N.J: Princeton University Press.

Kuhn, Annette. 1982. *Women's Pictures*. London: Routledge and Kegan Paul.

Marcuse, Herbert. 1968. "The Affirmative Character of Culture." In *Negations: Essays in Critical Theory*, translated by Jeremy J. Shapiro. Boston: Beacon Press.

"On the Screen in City Theatres." 1921. *New York Sun* (4 April): 11.

O'Sullivan, Tim, et al. 1983. *Key Concepts in Communication*. London: Methuen.

Reniers, P.F. 1921. "The Screen." *New York Evening Post* (4 April).

Rilke, Rainer Maria. 1974. Quoted in Richard Howard, preface to *S/Z*, by Roland Barthes, translated by Richard Miller. New York: Hill and Wang.

"Rothafel Prologue with Lines and Business." 1921. *Motion Picture News* 23, no. 26 (18 June): 3693.

Selz, Peter. 1974. *German Expressionist Painting*. Berkeley: University of California Press.

Sokel, Walter H. 1968. *The Writer in Extremis: Expressionism in Twentieth-Century German Literature*. Stanford, Conn.: Stanford University Press, 1968.

"Special Cast in 'The Cabinet of Dr. Caligari.' " 1921. *Exhibitor's Herald* (23 April): 64.

Thompson, Kristin. 1985. *Exporting Entertainment: America in the World Film Market, 1907–1934*. London: British Film Institute.

Willett, John. 1970. *Expressionism*. New York: McGraw-Hill.

———. 1978. *Art and Politics in the Weimar Period: The New Sobriety 1917–1933*. New York: Pantheon.

BIBLIOGRAPHY

The Cabinet of Doctor Caligari

Barlow, John D. *German Expressionist Film*. Boston: Twayne Publishers, 1982. 29–63.

Budd, Michael. "Authorship as a Commodity: The Art Cinema and 'The Cabinet of Doctor Caligari.' " *Wide Angle* 6, no. 1 (1984): 12–19.

———. " 'The Cabinet of Doctor Caligari': Conditions of Reception." *Ciné-Tracts* 12 (Winter 1981): 41–49.

———. "Contradictions of Expressionism in 'The Cabinet of Doctor Caligari.' " *Indiana Social Studies Quarterly* 34, no. 2 (Autumn 1981): 19–25.

———. "The National Board of Review and the Early Art Cinema in New York: 'The Cabinet of Doctor Caligari' as Affirmative Culture." *Cinema Journal* 26, no. 1 (Fall 1986): 3–18.

———. "Retrospective Narration in Film: Rereading 'The Cabinet of Doctor Caligari.' " *Film Criticism* 4, no. 1 (Fall 1979): 35–43.

———, ed. *'The Cabinet of Doctor Caligari': A Reader*. New Brunswick, N.J.: Rutgers University Press. Forthcoming.

Carroll, Noël. "The Cabinet of Dr. Kracauer." *Millennium Film Journal* 1, no. 2 (Spring-Summer 1978): 77–85.

Clément, Catherine. "Les Charlatans et Les Hysteriques." *Communications* 23 (1975): 213–22.

Eisner, Lotte H. *The Haunted Screen: Expressionism in the German Cinema and the Influence of Max Reinhardt*. Berkeley: University of California Press, 1968, 17–27.

Elsaesser, Thomas. "Social Mobility and the Fantastic: German Silent Cinema." *Wide Angle* 5, no. 2 (1982): 14–25.

Fischer, Robert, ed. *Das Cabinet des Dr. Caligari*. Stuttgart: Focus-Verlagsgemeinschaft, 1985.

Kaul, Walter, ed. *Caligari und Caligarismus*. Berlin: Deutsche Kinemathek, 1970.

Kracauer, Siegfried. "Caligari." In *From Caligari to Hitler: A Psychological History of the German Film*. Princeton, N.J.: Princeton University Press, 1947, 61–76.

Critical Method

Adorno, Theodor W. *Philosophy of Modern Music*. Translated by Anne G. Mitchell and Wesley V. Blomster. New York: Seabury Press, 1980.

Buck-Morss, Susan. *The Origin of Negative Dialectics: Theodor W. Adorno, Walter Benjamin, and the Frankfurt Institute*. New York: The Free Press, 1977.

Cahiers du cinéma, editors. "John Ford's 'Young Mr. Lincoln.' " *Screen* 13, no. 3 (Autumn 1972): 5–44 (reprinted in *Movies and Methods*, edited by Bill Nichols, 493–529 [Berkeley: University of California Press, 1976]); Wollen, Peter, "Afterword," *Screen* 13, no. 3 (Autumn 1972): 44–47; Brewster, Ben, "Notes on the Text, 'Young Mr. Lincoln,' by the Editors of 'Cahiers du Cinéma,' " *Screen* 14, no. 3 (Autumn 1973): 29–43.

Heath, Stephen. "Film and System: Terms of Analysis," Part 1, *Screen* 16, no. 1 (Spring 1975): 7–77; "Film and System: Terms of Analysis," Part 2, *Screen* 16, no. 2 (Summer 1975): 91–113.

Horkheimer, Max, and Theodor W. Adorno. *Dialectic of Enlightenment*. Translated by John Cumming. New York: Seabury Press, 1972.

White, Mimi. "Ideological Analysis and Television." In Robert C. Allen, ed., *Channels of Discourse*, 134–71. Chapel Hill: University of North Carolina Press, 1987.

18

FASSBINDER'S *ALI: FEAR EATS THE SOUL* AND SPECTATORSHIP

Judith Mayne

It is nearly impossible to imagine a discussion of film as an ideological medium that does not focus at some point on Hollywood cinema. Hollywood's domination of worldwide film production from approximately the post–World War I years through the 1940s firmly established the film industry within the laws of monopoly capitalism. Hollywood cinema has thus been central in understanding art in capitalist society as a kind of merchandise to be consumed. It is through Hollywood cinema as well that we understand the cinema in ideological terms as an apparatus, i.e., as a vast network of machinery that delivers and produces on the scale of commodity production.

Hollywood cinema, too, has defined what most of us expect from films and how we watch them. Such expectations and attitudes include terms like pleasure, fantasy, identification, enjoyment and, of course, the most common of all, entertainment. That these too are a part of the ideology of cinema is beyond question. What is questionable is whether they are ideological in the way that the conditions of Hollywood production and distribution imply. The model of a cinematic apparatus perhaps suggests that pleasure in watching a film is the simple result of manipulation, suggesting in turn the equation of cinema with a passive vehicle for bourgeois ideology at its hegemonic best. But if we focus on that "vast network" of the cinematic apparatus comprised of a series of relations between, for instance, industry and art, production and finished film, viewer and screen, then it is possible to speak of the ideology of cinema as a multidimensional process. The cinematic apparatus is an extensive business machine, an appendange of corporate power, as well as the complex technical, social, and psychic procedures that determine how spectators watch and enjoy films.

Rainer Fassbinder's 1974 film *Angst essen Seele auf (Ali: Fear Eats the Soul)* raises many crucial issues concerning the relationship between film and ideology, issues that focus precisely on the conditions of film viewing: the relationship between viewer and screen, the Hollywood legacy and the "entertainment factor," and the possibilities of radical social analysis within a conventional narrative framework. *Ali* tells the story of an unlikely romance between a German cleaning woman in her fifties and a Moroccan immigrant worker twenty years her junior. Such beginnings are reminiscent in a very general way of Hollywood melodramas of the 1950s. The two meet in a Munich bar, the Asphalt Pub, frequented by immigrant workers from North Africa. Emmi, the German woman, is clearly established as a outsider when she steps inside the bar to avoid the rain. As a joke, one of the women in the bar tells Moroccan Ali to ask the old woman to dance. This initial encounter sets the tone pursued through the entire film as Ali and Emmi discover a relationship based on common loneliness and isolation. In so doing they face the rejection of Emmi's children, her neighbors, and her coworkers.

The relationship between Emmi and Ali that we see is constantly defined by the constraints imposed by others. They dance together at the request of someone else and later decide to marry only when Emmi's landlord accuses her of violating her lease by taking in a lodger. Emmi and Ali's first meeting is characterized by a highly ritualistic quality. They literally march to the dance floor and exchange the clichés of small talk while they dance. This sense of stylized ritual dominates the entire film, accentuated by the way in which transitions are made from one scene to another, for each scene appears as a single, autonomous tableau rather than as part of a fluid dramatic development.

Throughout the initial Asphalt Pub scene our attention is drawn as spectators to the act of looking, relentlessly portrayed here as the interplay of objectifying gazes. The encounter of Emmi and Ali is initiated under and subjected to the stares of the other patrons and the bar owner, a pattern repeated in the film as the couple is portrayed most often being watched.

Emmi's relationship to Ali exists for the viewer through the disapproving gazes of her coworkers, neighbors, and children, as well as nameless figures in public places.

The exclusion of Emmi and Ali appears to reach such enormous proportions that Emmi, in exasperation, proposes a vacation where they can at least momentarily escape prejudice—or, as she sees it, jealousy. She describes the vacation as a way of escaping the "stares" and "horrible grins" of other people. As if to suggest that our "stares" as spectators of the film have something in common with those chilling looks of characters within the film, the vacation is never represented on the screen. Yet it marks the turning point of the film.

Upon the couple's return the tone of the film suddenly moves from the register of rejection to that of reacceptance, although the basic attitudes remain unchanged. The neighborhood grocer, who refused to serve Ali until he "learned to speak German properly," now unashamedly panders to Emmi to win her back as a customer. ("Everyone is shopping in the new supermarket now," he says. "Business must come before pleasure.") Emmi's grown children, who referred to her as a "filthy whore" when she introduced her new husband to them, are ready to make amends and conveniently so: one son wants to take advantage of Emmi's free afternoons for babysitting services. Her neighbors are all smiles as they ask Emmi for the use of her basement storage area.

As false as this reacceptance and reintegration is, it does not come cheaply. Emmi hovers in an uncomfortable space between her relationship to Ali—which makes her other, the object of vision—and her milieu, in which she is, like her neighbors and family, an onlooker. The distances between Emmi and Ali begin to grow, predictably so, and they climax almost farcically in Emmi's refusal to make couscous: "I don't know how. And besides, Germans don't eat couscous." Ali temporarily seeks shelter in the bed of Barbara, owner of the Asphalt Pub. This refuge is as tenuous as Emmi's so-called reacceptance by her children and neighbors. For just as Emmi must accept the terms of exclusion and objectification, so Ali's relationship to Barbara is first and foremost that of customer and proprietor.

Emmi and Ali, each in her/his turn, appear to have internalized the objectification that previously defined the reactions of other figures in the film to them. Emmi's coworkers come to her apartment, and she unwittingly joins them in making Ali into a circus sideshow. She shows off his muscles and his "good grip," proudly announcing that he takes a shower every day; and when he leaves the room somewhat abruptly, she says he has his "moods sometimes—that's his foreign mentality." Later in the film Emmi goes to the garage where Ali works. When one worker asks if "that's your grandmother from Morocco," Ali joins in the general laughter.

Ali drinks and gambles back at the Asphalt Pub until Emmi comes looking for him. In a repetition of the opening scene of the film they dance, this time clinging to each other and resolving not to part. Just when their difficulties seem to be resolved, Ali collapses. In an ambiguous final scene at the hospital, a doctor informs Emmi that Ali suffers from a perforated ulcer, common among immigrant workers because of the particular stress to which they are subjected. The film closes on an image of Ali, unconscious next to a blank window with a tearful Emmi at his side.

Like countless narrative films, *Ali* traces the history of a love story. Perhaps it is the unlikelihood of Emmi and Ali's romance in the first place, or the age and cultural differences between the two, or the cliché-ridden dialogue that makes viewing *Ali* an unsettling experience. For *Ali* is, certainly, a disturbing film. But I think this is due less to the more obvious features that violate our expectations of a love story than to its social dimensions. The relationship exists in the tenuous margins between public and private life, between social and personal existence. Put another way, the love story between Emmi and Ali occupies an ideological space where private and public exist in precarious balance. This space is ideological to the extent that people's lives within the culture depicted in *Ali* are divided between their places in the social division of labor and their personal lives of leisure, intimacy, friends, and home. In Marxist terms, the apparent divisions between production and consumption, work and leisure, and public life and private life mask the ways in which the development of capitalist society is marked by relentless and increased domination of the commodity form over all aspects of life. The context of Emmi and Ali's relationship is, in a word, that of reification.[1] Thus, Emmi's apartment is only briefly glimpsed as a refuge from the public

1. The concept of reification used in this essay comes from Lukács: "Neither objectively nor in his relation to his work does man appear as the authentic master of the process; on the contrary, he is a mechanical part incorporated into a mechanical system. He finds it already pre-existing and self-sufficient, it functions independently of him and he has to conform to its laws whether he likes it or not. As labour is progressively rationalized and mechanized his lack of will is reinforced by the way in which his activity becomes less and less active and more and more *contemplative*. The contemplative stance adopted towards a process mechanically conforming to fixed laws and enacted independently of man's consciousness and impervious to human intervention, i.e., a perfectly closed system, must likewise transform the basic categories of man's immediate attitude to the world; it reduces space and time to a common denominator and degrades time to the dimension of space" (1971, 89).

humiliation inflicted upon the couple; it becomes rather an arena for an acting out of the same factors of exclusion operative in the public realm.

The social history of the cinema reflects the extent to which the cinematic apparatus is an instrument of reification. When the first American films were shown in the late nineteenth and early twentieth centuries, they were popular with the urban working classes and immigrant populations. In a limited but nonetheless significant way the cinema brought technology into the lives of people whose participation in technological change had been limited to their roles in production.

> Five, ten, and fifteen cent prices brought theatrical entertainment to audiences that neither vaudeville nor the popular stage had ever touched. . . . Families went to the movies together, local merchants advertised on their screens, audiences sang together from song slides, people met and socialized—all for nickels and dimes. (Subtitles, of course, taught thousands of immigrants to speak English.) A city movie house could gross a thousand dollars a week with ease in 1908, and by that time every major city had a hundred or more of them. (Nye 1970, 364)

Movies responded to a genuine desire for collective entertainment and leisure, defining at the same time the conditions of that desire within the laws of commodity production.

The beginnings of moving pictures firmly situate the cinema as a mediation between private and public realms (Mayne 1988). Often metaphorized as either dreamlike or more real than life itself, the cinema delivered fantasies to satisfy personal desires and produced images of the world inviting collective participation. The cinematic apparatus that has evolved from those beginnings depends upon three interrelated mechanisms of containment, naturalization, and identification. Film genres contain what can be represented on the screen within certain boundaries: "It is clear that the optimal exploitation of the production apparatus, which ties up considerable amounts of capital, requires the containment of creative work within established frameworks and that genres, film kinds, even so-called studio styles, are crucial factors here" (Heath 1976, 256). The cinema's impression of reality, its apparently inherent realism, allows a transformation of reality to the screen in such a way that social and political realities can be obscured and contradiction dispelled since whatever passes on the screen is simply "there," as if it were an extension of the natural world. Just as cinema is a naturalizing force, so it assigns the spectator a specific place, an ideal vantage point from which the individual's perception is guided through the film.

Fassbinder's film works through these components of the cinematic apparatus. While *Ali* is not strictly a genre film, it relies heavily on conventions of the Hollywood melodrama perfected in the 1940s and 1950s. It is tempting to refer to Fassbinder's use of genre as a politicizing of the melodrama. Certainly *Ali* reflects and reflects upon the social reality of West German and modern industrial societies. Those political realities so often repressed in mainstream cinema appear to surface in this film, creating a confrontation between melodrama and politics. Yet there is little in Fassbinder's film that can be called political documentation. Even though nearly all the tensions generated in the film stem from Ali's position as an immigrant worker, there is little direct exploration of the political nature of that position. Rather, attention is focused on attitudes toward Ali as an outsider, attitudes conveyed primarily through a stunning interplay of gazes and exchanges of looks, nearly all of which possess an objectifying quality. The basic elements of cinematic continuity are replete with cultural and political significance in this film. The identification of the viewer with the film is mirrored by the use of shot/reverse shot to construct a series of spectacles within the film.

The ways in which *Ali* works through these components of the cinematic apparatus raise fundamental questions concerning both the ideology of cinema and its potential for radical critique. Fassbinder's use of the Hollywood melodrama invites a consideration of the social significance of popular culture and the extent to which the entertainment factor can function in a critical way. Melodrama is a term difficult to understand precisely because it is so widely used and often conveys negative judgment rather than description or analysis. In the strictest sense, melodrama refers to a type of drama developed in the eighteenth century in which spoken words and music were heard alternately. Music was a form of punctuation rather than simple accompaniment, and it served to orchestrate the emotional effects of the play.[2] The musical element in what was referred to as melodrama, especially on French and British stages of the nineteenth century, gradually dwindled, although the emotional principle it served did not. Melodrama came to mean a dramatic form characterized by at least three basic features: sensationalism, intense emotional appeal, and a happy ending. Frank Rahill's definition is helpful in defining the general parameters of melodrama:

> Melodrama is a form of dramatic composition in prose partaking of the nature of tragedy, comedy, pantomime, and spectacle, and intended for a popular audience. Primarily concerned with situation and plot, it calls upon mimed action extensively and employs a more or less fixed complement of stock

2. Sources for the discussion of melodrama are Elsaesser (1972), Rahill (1967), and Smith (1973).

> characters, the most important of which are a suffering heroine or hero, a persecuting villain, and a benevolent comic. It is conventionally moral and humanitarian in point of view and sentimental and optimistic in temper, concluding its fable happily with virtue rewarded after many trials and vice punished. Characteristically it offers elaborate scenic accessories and miscellaneous divertissements and introduces music freely, typically to underscore dramatic effect. (1967, xiv)

More often the term "melodrama" is used as a synonym for second-rate artistry, cheap sentimentalism, implausible plot and character development, and far-flung excesses. That many melodramas merit such judgment is beyond question, but of perhaps equal weight in this relegation of melodrama to the margins of official art is the fact that it is a popular art form par excellence.

However many definitions and forms of melodrama may exist, they share an emphasis on intense emotion. From this perspective *Ali* can be seen in direct connection to the tradition of melodrama. That melodrama relies so heavily on emotional trauma in its structure and invites strong emotional response from its audience has often been taken for granted as proof of a direct link between melodrama and pure escapism. Rahill points out, however, that along with the escapist trend, melodramas were used as vehicles for social commentary and outright calls to action:

> During the nineteenth century this instrument was pressed into the service of innumerable crusades: national patriotism, anticlericalism, abolition of slavery, prohibition, and even tax and prison reform, to name only a few. There was an avowedly Socialist school of melodrama in France during the period when the Communist Manifesto was proclaimed. (xvi)

Characters in the melodrama often exist as elements in an absolute typology of good and evil, and psychological complexity is downplayed for the sake of conflicts waged against external adversaries. The conflicts generated are extreme, as are their usually unambiguous resolutions. That sense of excess results not only from the intensity of conflict but also from an intensification of the rituals and banalities of everyday life to create a highly charged emotional atmosphere.

Ali is neither escapism nor a direct call to action; rather it hovers between those two functions that the melodrama has historically and traditionally served. Characters in the film are initially drawn as figures in a social, rather than universal, typology of good and evil. "Good" is equated in the characters of Emmi and Ali with the innocence and transcendence of social barriers, however unconscious. "Evil" is equated with crass economic motivation and transparent internalization of cultural conditioning. Symbolism emerges from a heightening of the commonplace. Thus a jukebox symbolizes the cultural parameters of Emmi and Ali's initial encounter and eventual relationship; the simple acts of eating in a restaurant or sitting in a park become intensely charged social acts; and the cultural connotations of food represent the differences that separate Emmi and Ali. *Ali* derives much of its strength from the melodramatic tradition that it taps, without completely defining itself within that tradition's boundaries. Much of the tension and conflict in *Ali* stems not directly from its melodramatic characteristics but from a refusal to take the conventions of melodrama to their logical conclusion. Rather, Fassbinder exploits the radical potential of the melodrama without giving us unequivocal resolution or continuous waves of high-pitched emotion. In short, Fassbinder exploits the radical potential of the melodrama, a potential that Thomas Elsaesser describes in the following terms:

> The melodrama, at its most accomplished, seems capable of reproducing more directly than other genres the patterns of domination and exploitation existing in a given society, especially the relation between psychology, morality, and class consciousness, by emphasizing so clearly an emotional dynamic whose social correlative is a network of external forces directed oppressingly inward, and with which the characters themselves unwittingly collide to become their agents. (1972, 14)

The specific contours of Fassbinder's use of melodrama are shaped by another filmmaker's experience with that form in Hollywood during the 1950s. German-born theater director and filmmaker Douglas Sirk emigrated to the United States in the late 1930s and worked under contract as a Hollywood film director. Sirk directed his most famous films—*Imitation of Life, All That Heaven Allows, Written on the Wind, Tarnished Angels, Magnificent Obsession*—for Universal Studios in the 1950s when it was under the control of Ross Hunter, known as master of the "weepie." Fassbinder's admiration for Sirk is well known. "I have seen six films by Douglas Sirk," Fassbinder wrote in 1971. "Among them were the most beautiful in the world" (1975, 96). In those films Fassbinder sees the possibility of working within a particular genre while simultaneously undercutting the social values that the genre is designed to perpetuate. "In other words," says Fassbinder, "use the emotions generated to a particular end. It's a preliminary stage in a kind of political presentation. The main thing to be learned from American films was the need to meet their entertainment factor halfway. The ideal is to make films as beautiful as America's, but which at the same time shift the content to other areas. I find the process beginning in Douglas Sirk's films" (Rayns 1974, 43).

Ali is a conscious homage to Sirk's 1955 melodrama *All That Heaven Allows*. In Sirk's film, a May-December romance joins a middle-class widow portrayed by Jane Wyman and her nature-loving gardener, portrayed by Rock Hudson. Predictably, Wyman's children and friends are horrified. She bows to their disapproval until tension, loneliness, and physical sickness mount to the point that she can no longer repress her desires. She drives to Hudson's home but hesitates at the last minute, while he, having spotted her, falls off a cliff. They are reunited at his sickbed. Beneath the polished, tear-jerker facade of this film lies a subtle, and sometimes not-so-subtle, critique of middle-class values. ("After seeing this film," Fassbinder writes, "small town America is the last place in the world I would want to go" [89].)

Certain melodramatic elements of *All That Heaven Allows* are so overdetermined as to function both within the boundaries of narrative configuration and as social commentary that bursts through the confines of that configuration. Jane Wyman makes an initial choice to abandon her love for Hudson in favor of her suburban home, her children, and her friends. The real choice the woman has made is revealed at Christmastime when her children, who had so emphatically invoked the authority of family tradition to dissuade her from marrying Hudson, announce their plans for independent lives. A salesman arrives to present their Christmas gift to their mother—a television set, "life's parade at your fingertips," in the salesman's words. The children leave, and in a close-up of the television screen we see the reflection of Wyman's face, isolated, lonely, and doomed, it would seem, to a future of passive contemplation. As spectators, we witness Wyman's confrontation with the futility of the life she has chosen; and yet that vision turns back onto itself, onto our own conception of family life equally dependent, although perhaps not quite so dramatically, on the banality and emptiness of a television screen.

I am not suggesting that Sirk openly subverts the conventions of the melodrama but rather that we are held within the sphere of narrative configuration in such a way that direct social commentary is possible. Fassbinder's film works on this model, shifting it so that our vision of the film is a constant movement between narrative intensity and social critique, never totally anchored in either one. In *Ali*, a scene similar to the one described above occurs. When Emmi calls her married children together to announce her marriage, Ali waits in the wings, as it were, for his cue to enter. Emmi's children look bored and anxious to leave. As Emmi introduces Ali, camera movement records the disgust on the faces of her children at this unexpected spectacle. One son actively expresses his disdain by kicking in Emmi's television set. As in Sirk's film, the television screen symbolizes the shallow middle-class morality unwittingly rejected by Emmi but unthinkingly embraced by Wyman. Yet in Fassbinder's film there is no ritual of gift giving, no pretense of devotion on the part of the children, no family holiday to enshroud the television with narrative complexity or density. Nor is there a figure comparable to the salesman to disrupt a family gathering with an ironic sales pitch. In Sirk's film social values are gradually revealed with the development of the narrative to be hollow and empty, whereas in Fassbinder's film there is no revelation but rather a constant exposure to human beings who look at each other as if at blank television screens. It is that act of vision that captures us in *Ali*; a vision that is one step removed from participation in dramatic action and not yet a vision turned against itself.

Sirk's film is a brilliant example of some of the strategies that in Hollywood cinema displace potentially subversive political considerations—in particular, those concerning social class. What is particularly interesting in Sirk is that while class conflict is averted, it remains beneath the surface of his films like an unconscious dynamic capable of surfacing any time. In *All That Heaven Allows*, Wyman and Hudson's first meeting is on the terms of employer and employee, for he is her gardener and has come to her house to prune trees. Quickly, however, Hudson is attributed with a certain amount of individual status, for he runs a nursery inherited from his father. In a later meeting Hudson admits that his true vocation is growing trees and that he plans to give up maintenance work. The differences between him and Wyman are gradually displaced into the realm of cultural rather than specifically economic factors. Hudson not only loves to grow trees but is also committed to a life style that draws him close to the earth, and he appropriately considers *Walden* his bible. His circle of friends covers a range of diversity lacking in Wyman's country club set, including first-generation Italians, a painter, a beekeeper and a birdwatcher. At Wyman's first introduction to them they dance to impromptu music in obvious contrast to the stilted atmosphere of the country club where Wyman's social life has been centered. Only briefly does the specific issue of class resurface through the web of Hudson's appealing life style, as when Wyman's best friend, upon learning of the romance, greets her with: "You can't be serious—your gardener?"

In a different way the use of chance accidents in Sirk's film attributes the success or failure of a relationship to fate or destiny rather than to the material conditions of class society. Thus Wyman wavers in her decision to leave her suburban life behind her and marry Hudson. She drives out to his home but changes her mind at the last minute; she decides to leave just as Hudson falls off the cliff and suffers a concussion. The accident seals the bond between the two and allows for the necessary happy ending. Yet, while the moment of the accident is, according to the laws of the genre, the turning point of the film, it is deliberately downplayed. The real turning point in the film is that Christmas scene described earlier, in which Wyman comes face to face with the terms of her choice—the social terms of that choice.

Some of the formal means of displacement are present in Fassbinder's film but pursued to different ends. For example, Fassbinder drains a convention of its depth. The potential is certainly there, in *Ali*, for the Moroccan to represent, if not an alternative life style, then at least a kind of exoticism. But the differences in culture are reduced to a jukebox and couscous, on the one hand, and to the racist clichés about sex-starved Arabs spoken by Emmi's coworkers, on the other. Fassbinder's alternative, having reduced cultural difference to a mere surface, is not to replenish the convention with a well-articulated class dynamic. Rather, Emmi and Ali's love story is told without the embellishment of conflicting "life styles" in such a way that the line between the demands of the story and an overtly expressed class dynamic is still drawn, but it is significantly thinner. Fassbinder also reinvests some of the conventions of melodrama with political substance. In the last scene at the Asphalt Pub, Ali's sudden collapse initially appears to be one of those chance events on the same order of Hudson's fall from the cliff. However, the final scene of the film reveals that it is not a deux ex machina device that caused Ali's collapse but rather the fact that he is an immigrant worker. Ali's situation is presented in a fatalistic way—the doctor promises little hope for recovery since the tension that produced the affliction will doubtless remain—and in that sense at least a minimum of melodramatic decorum is maintained. However, the roots of that "accident" are clearly the material conditions of Ali's existence.

Sirk's film is a special kind of melodrama that focuses on a love story and evokes tears, namely the "woman's film."[3] The only comparable genre that could be called the "man's film" is that of war movies and adventure stories that openly celebrate machismo values. Cinematic space is gendered, in other words, along the lines of the private and the public. In culture as in the movies, to women belong the tribulations of personal life, of love, and of the family. Yet while Sirk's film projects into that private space, it ostensibly

3. For discussions of the genre, see Doane (1987) and Haskell (1974).

 transcends it at the same time. Wyman falls in love with Hudson not primarily because she is a cliché of the frustrated housewife and he the available young stud but rather because he represents an alternative that puts the very basis of her own life into question. The love story here questions rather than maintains the boundaries between the personal and the social.

In a different way Fassbinder too turns around the expectations of his audience. Fassbinder's films are well known for their exposés, if not always critiques, of bourgeois values; they are films to which the label of "weepies," for example, does not adhere. That *Ali* works through the conventions of the melodrama suggests an affinity with many contemporary films that self-consciously and critically examine the nature of cinematic representation. Yet alongside of that examination *Ali* tells a straight love story, drawing us into the cinematic space traditionally defined as "women's" space and encouraging us to see—as Sirk does in reverse fashion—the tenuous boundaries between private and social experience.

There are other ways in which insights of a political nature inform the development of Fassbinder's film. The pattern of exclusion and pseudo-reacceptance that shapes the film reflects the prevalence of crass economic concerns. Social behavior is seen as the function of basic economic motivation. "Prejudice" is no longer indulged when child care service is necessary or when groceries have to be sold. Emmi and Ali themselves are working-class characters reflecting a particular phenomenon in capitalist society, the industrial reserve army that can be tapped at small cost when the need for cheap labor arises. Women in capitalist society have always been a part of this labor force, and more recently in Western Europe immigrant workers have been its primary component (Castles and Kosack 1974).

However, Emmi and Ali's exploitation as workers, at the workplace, is not a central concern in this film. More important is the specific form of alienation each character represents. Alienation is perceived in this film against the background, once again, of individuals divided between work and personal life. Emmi's job as a cleaner is "women's work," an extension of her position within the family. Similar to her are those widowed women in her apartment building whose social activity is limited to gossip and maintaining order in the "home," even though they are no longer responsible for family duties. Work, social life, public space: these are, for women, an endless magnification of the home, the private, the personal. Ali, on the other hand, has no real private life, given the ways in which all aspects of his life are governed by his visible otherness, his exclusion from German culture while being an integral part of the German economy. John Berger has described the phenomenon as follows:

> What has happened within him is not distinct from what happens within millions of others who are not migrant workers. It is simply more extreme. He experiences suddenly as an individual, as a man who believes he is choosing his own life, what the industrial consumer societies have experienced gradually through generations without the effort of choosing. He lives the content of our institutions: they transform him violently. They do not need to transform us. We are already within them. (1975, 197)

Emmi tells Ali early in the film that her husband was an immigrant worker from Poland, suggesting at the very least a shared situation. For Emmi and Ali share the impossible task of disentangling the tightly interwoven threads of public and private existence. Independently and together, their lives are an extreme crystallization of reification, of the permeation of capitalist values—exploitation, the false separation of home and work—into personal experience.

Ali does not fit the traditional conception of a "political film," since it neither analyzes social reality suggesting how it might be changed nor is at the service of a particular political line. Yet, that traditional conception of what is or is not political is itself grounded in the separation of the personal and the political. As Sheila Rowbotham points out, for example:

> The manifestations of the specific manner in which the dominant relations and values of capitalist society penetrate all the supposedly 'personal' areas of human life are still largely unexplored. The political expression of personal experience was traditionally confined to novels and poetry. Lenin told Inessa Armand that discussion of free love was out of place in a pamphlet. (1973, 55)

The scope of *Ali* includes emotions, everyday experience, and commonplace gestures, and this scope works to enlarge our vision of the political. Fiction film—and the melodrama in particular—may be in an ideal position to explore these areas because of its particular appeal to emotional response and its own tradition of turning personal experience into a commodity formula. The issue concerns what is political about film: film technique, style, and narrative structure.

Fassbinder draws heavily on the implications of cinematic form. Our perception of Emmi and Ali is directly formed by how they are looked at and how they relate to language. Neither character is in her/his element with verbal expression: Ali speaks broken German, and Emmi relies on cliché-ridden speech. Nor are they comfortable beneath the unrelenting stares of other people. The differences between public and private space are leveled by the ways in which scenes are filmed. From the beginning, Emmi's apartment is shot through slightly open doors with an emphasis on tight framing. Similarly, Emmi's workplace is depicted through a window or a staircase rail, and we see Ali and Emmi in the restaurant where they celebrate their marriage in a long shot through an archway. As Emmi and Ali are contained by image and sound, so the contexts in which they appear are marked by a series of formal constraints.

A majority of the tableaulike sequences in *Ali* are structured according to a principle of spectacle, where the basic continuity device of shot/reverse shot becomes an authoritative principle of objectifying gazes. The opening sequence of the film in the Asphalt Pub is characterized by a single continuous activity, that of looking. The effect is accentuated by an unrelenting duration of shots with minimal camera movement and by still bodies disinterestedly absorbed in the act of staring. Emmi is the object of vision when she enters the pub, and she and Ali become a literal spectacle when they dance, carefully watched by the bar owner and the other patrons. As in other scenes of the film, all activity is stripped down to the bare essentials of looking. When Emmi and Ali eat at the Osteria Italiana, they are the only patrons in the restaurant. Their discomfort at being in such luxurious surroundings is magnified by the waiter who stares at them unrelentingly. In another scene the couple is alone in a vast public garden of tables and chairs, except for a small group of people who also do nothing but stare at them. The individual and total effect of these looks conveys a reduction of human beings to the status of spectacle, objects existing solely in their capacity to be examined visually.

It is a critical commonplace that the basic continuity principles of the cinema—rules of editing and camera position, relations between sound and image, for instance—are designed to assign the spectator an ideal vantage point from which to witness the unfolding of the cinematic spectacle. One particularly privileged technique is shot/reverse shot, which constantly defines and redefines the viewer's place within the film narrative. Shot/reverse shot is the basis for the establishment of a spectator within the film, a device common to the classical Hollywood cinema and appearing in varying degrees in different types of films. The spectator within the film represents authoritative vision established along various possible axes, the most obvious such axis being a character who is the source and direction of the principal gaze of the film. Hence one particular point of view may be given more power than others as the representative of narrative truth or agency, as the organizing principle of vision. In some films, such as the 1933 *King Kong*, the spectator within the film—filmmaker Carl Denham—quite literally controls the spectacle. The universe of the film—and most emphatically, women—are apprehended as spectacle through his eyes (Mayne 1976). In other films, the principle of the spectator within the film cuts across several registers. In *Gentlemen Prefer Blondes* (1953), for instance, we see Marilyn Monroe and Jane Russell against stage backdrops, ourselves identified as the implicit spectators within the film. At the same time the figure of Malone, a private detective whose purpose is very literally to reestablish correct vision, functions in more narrow terms as a spectator within the film.

Many films display a fascination with the function of spectatorship, with the manipulation of spectators within the film to mirror the ways in which we as spectators in the audience identify with what occurs on-screen. A more limited number of films—one thinks immediately of Dziga Vertov's *Man with a Movie Camera*, Resnais and Duras's *Hiroshima mon amour*, and virtually all the films of Jean-Luc Godard—elevate these reflections upon spectatorship to a central narrative concern. Spectatorship is likewise a central concern in Fassbinder's film. The process of the film focuses on the nature of the gaze, on the objectifying look that transforms its field of vision into a stage, its object of vision into a spectacle. The permutations of these gazes mirror and reflect upon our situations as spectators. Fassbinder marks off emotionless spectators within the film whose major activity is simply looking, punctuated only by scenes in which frames within the frame and long shots are so prevalent that vision itself—its containment, its constraints—is remarked upon.

And yet if attention is focused upon the spectacle form in *Ali*, upon our roles as spectators, that attention is not limited to the space of the movie theater. What we see in the film is not simply vision mirrored as an objectifying act or the conditions of cinematic representation; rather we see spectacle as a social form through the basic elements of the cinema. Fassbinder has understood the extent to which the appeal of the cinema and its significance as a form of mass culture depend upon the effective means at its disposal to work upon and around and through the spectacle as social form. The spectacle is a guise through which the commodity form permeates social relationships; it is, in other words, a form of reification. The spectacle is a relation between observer and observed where the object of vision is rigidified, reduced to one-dimensionality. Yet the seeming power of the observer's gaze is illusory; like the observed, s/he is locked into the spectacle relationship and is defined as powerful only in relationship to the other's objectification.

In *Ali* the precarious boundaries between public and private life are apprehended and viewed through the spectacle form. Much of the appeal, the social function, and the mechanisms of spectator identification in the cinema can be illuminated by an understanding of film both as an instance of reification and as the projection of a reified form. In its turn cinema illuminates the extent to which reification pervades social life in the particular guise of the spectacle, precisely because of the extent to which the pleasure and the manipulation of cinema revolve around the organization of looks, gazes, and eye contact. Fassbinder's film indicates some directions that such an undertaking might pursue, for *Ali: Fear Eats the Soul* is a dialectical examination of spectatorship that, by stripping cinematic continuity down to its bare essentials of looking and vision, simultaneously lays bare spectacle as a social form.

WORKS CITED

Berger, John. 1975. *A Seventh Man*. New York: Viking.

Castles, Stephen, and Godula Kosack. 1974. "Immigrant Workers and Trade Unions in the German Federal Republic." *Radical America* 8: 55–76.

Doane, Mary Ann. 1987. *The Desire to Desire*. Bloomington: Indiana University Press.

Elsaesser, Thomas. 1972. "Tales of Sound and Fury: Observations on the Family Melodrama." *Monogram* 4: 2–15.

Fassbinder, Rainer. 1975. "Six Films by Douglas Sirk." Translated by Thomas Elsaesser. *New Left Review* 91: 94–97.

Haskell, Molly. 1974. *From Reverence to Rape*. New York: Holt, Rinehart & Winston.

Heath, Stephen. 1976. "On Screen, In Frame: Film and Ideology." *Quarterly Review of Film Studies* 1: 251–65.

Lukács, Georg. 1971. *History and Class Consciousness*. Translated by Rodney Livingstone. Cambridge: MIT University Press.

Mayne, Judith. 1976. "*King Kong* and the Ideology of Spectacle." *Quarterly Review of Film Studies* 1: 373–87.

———. 1988. *Private Novels, Public Films*. Athens: University of Georgia Press.

Nye, Russel. 1970. *The Unembarrassed Muse*. New York: Dial.

Rahill, Frank. 1967. *The World of Melodrama*. University Park: Pennsylvania State University Press.

Rayns, Tony. 1974. "Forms of Address: Tony Rayns Interviews Three German Filmmakers." *Sight and Sound* 44: 41–46.

Rowbotham, Sheila. 1973. *Women's Consciousness, Man's World*. Baltimore: Pelican.

Smith, James L. 1973. *Melodrama*. London: Methuen.

BIBLIOGRAPHY

Marxism and Film

Aristarco, Guido. "Marx, le cinéma et la critique du film." *Etudes cinématographiques* 88–92 (1972): 1–219.

Barrett, Michele, et al., eds. *Ideology and Cultural Production*. New York: St. Martin's Press, 1979.

Cahiers du cinéma, collective text. "John Ford's *Young Mr. Lincoln*." *Screen* 13 (1972): 12–25.

Comolli, Jean-Louis. "Technique and Ideology: Camera, Perspective, Depth of Field." *Film Reader* 2 (1977): 128–40.

Comolli, Jean-Louis, and Jean Narboni. "Cinema/Ideology/Criticism." In *Screen Reader I*, 2–12. London: Society for Education in Film & Television, 1977.

Grossberg, Lawrence. "Strategies of Marxist Cultural Interpretation." *Critical Studies in Mass Communication* 1 (1984): 392–421.

Hall, Stuart, et al., eds. *Culture, Media, Language*. London: Hutchinson, 1980.

Heath, Stephen. "Lessons from Brecht." *Screen* 15 (1974): 103–28.

Kuhn, Annette. "Ideology, Structure and Knowledge." *Screen Education* 28 (1978): 34–41.

Lebel, Jean-Patrick. *Cinéma et idéologie*. Paris: Editions Sociales, 1972.

Lovell, Terry. *Pictures of Reality: Aesthetics, Politics and Pleasure*. London: British Film Institute, 1980.

MacCabe, Colin. "The Discursive and the Ideological in Film: Notes on the Conditions of Political Intervention." *Screen* 19 (1978–79): 29–43.

Nelson, Cary, and Lawrence Grossberg. *Marxism and the Interpretation of Culture*. Urbana: University of Illinois Press, 1988.

Nichols, Bill. *Ideology and the Image*. Bloomington: Indiana University Press, 1981.

Rosen, Philip. "*Screen* and the Marxist Project in Film Criticism." *Quarterly Review of Film Studies* 2 (1977): 273–87.

Fassbinder and *Ali: Fear Eats the Soul*

Elsaesser, Thomas. "Primary Identification and the Historical Subject: Fassbinder and Germany." *Ciné-tracts* 11 (1980): 43–52.

Franklin, James. "Method and Message: Forms of Communication in Fassbinder's *Angst Essen Seele Auf*." *Literature-Film Quarterly* 7 (1979): 182–200.

Johnston, Sheila. "A Star Is Born: Fassbinder and the New German Cinema." *New German Critique* 24–25 (1981–82): 20–25.

McCormick, Ruth. "Fassbinder and the Politics of Everyday Life." *Cinéaste* 8 (1977): 22–30.

———, ed. *Fassbinder*. New York: Tanam, 1981.

Rayns, Tony, ed. *Fassbinder*. London: British Film Institute, 1979.

Ruppert, Peter. "Fassbinder, Spectatorship, and Utopian Desire." *Cinema Journal* 28 (1989): 28–47.

Sparrow, Norbert. " 'I Let the Audience Feel *and* Think'—An Interview with Rainer Werner Fassbinder." *Cinéaste* 8 (1977): 20–21.

19

THE SINGING FOOL

Douglas Gomery

Hollywood! No image stands more vividly in our minds: swimming pools, multimillion dollar deals, and crowded back lots. Capitalist America focuses on *Heaven's Gate* with its loss of millions of dollars and *Return of the Jedi*'s creation of much, much more. The dollars and cents of filmmaking and film exhibition raise an important set of questions for the study of film. How can we understand the business and economics of film? How does that industrial process affect the films we see? And what changes has the financial side of movies precipitated in the history of film? This essay takes up these important questions.

I

If one were to poll film fans, filmmakers, critics, and other interested parties and ask them what was the most significant American film made before 1940, one would undoubtedly get dozens of answers. Surely some would nominate the brilliant comedies of Charlie Chaplin and Buster Keaton. The stunning *mise-en-scène* of F. W. Murnau and Joseph von Sternberg would rank high. Other critics would push filmmakers who achieved a measure of social impact such as Frank Capra or D. W. Griffith. Simply put, each person would have certain criteria in mind for what makes for an influential film and then would search out and nominate the best within that category.

There is one criterion with which few would argue. We have a good idea of which films took in the most at the box office. Businesses, movie companies included, want to make as much in the way of profits as they can. That is, the enterprise seeks to make the difference between monies brought in (revenues) and monies spent (costs) as great as possible. Profit is the term for that difference.

Inflation and a new environment for release has created an ever-changing list of box office champs. Still, *the* film that stood as the most profitable through the 1940s, 1950s and 1960s, which with its profits corrected for inflation might still lead today, is *Gone With the Wind*. Usually forgotten, however, are the box office leaders before *Gone With the Wind*.

One such film that should not be forgotten stood as champion at the box office from 1928 to 1940. That was Warner Bros.' *The Singing Fool*, starring Al Jolson. *The Singing Fool*, a musical released in September 1928 during the coming of sound to the movies, cost an estimated $200,000 but drew a fabulous $5,000,000. The difference set a record surpassed only by *Gone With the Wind* (which earned more than $30,000,000 for initial runs in 1939–40 for a cost of an extraordinary $5,000,000, thus producing an unheard-of profit of approximately $25,000,000). *The Singing Fool* has been lost in the contours of film history.

Gone With the Wind held the box office record so long that it seems almost to have been forever. Moreover, a myth has built up that the first Jolson feature-length talkie, *The Jazz Singer*, was *the* box office champion. Industry insiders of the day knew better, and reliable figures ranked *The Singing Fool* one-third to one-half higher in box office take throughout the world.

If *The Singing Fool* stood as the most profitable film of the late 1920s and through most of the 1930s, how do we account for its success? Generally, industry pundits look to four variables to explain the box office take of a film: its stars, its story, its director and creative personnel, and its special effects. To gain the highest possible profits Hollywood seeks to combine a unique mixture of top stars, a gripping story, and breathtaking special effects, all put together by a first-rate production team. *The Singing Fool* certainly had all that.

The Singing Fool featured noted ingenue Betty Bronson and new child discovery Davey Lee, but to moviegoers of the day and historians today the

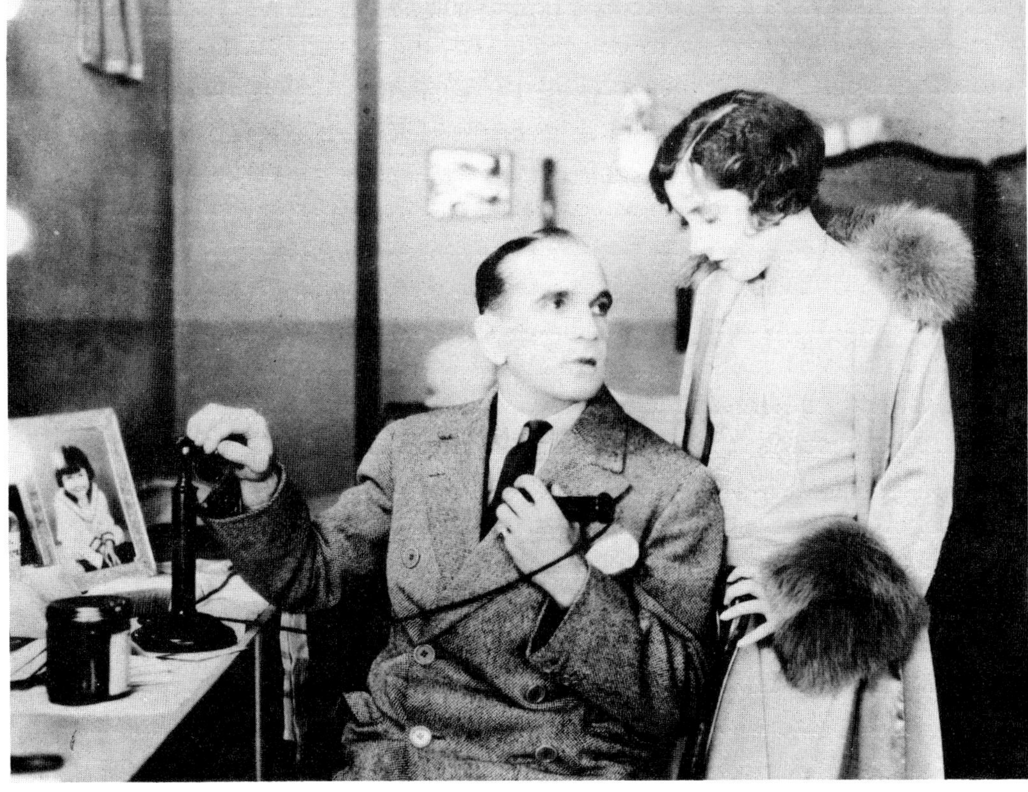

Figure 19-1. Al Stone (Al Jolson) and Grace (Betty Bronson) receive bad news about Sonny Boy (Davey Lee). (Courtesy of the Academy of Motion Picture Arts and Sciences.)

film really had only one draw above the title—Al Jolson. Jolson ranks as one of the great entertainers of the first half of the twentieth century. It is doubtful that any other performer introduced as many songs that have become true standards: "I'm Just Wild About Harry," "There's a Rainbow Round My Shoulder," "When the Red, Red Robin," and "April Showers." Al Jolson was more than just a singer or an actor—he was an *experience*, the entertainment king of the Roaring Twenties.

Jolson's success on the Broadway stage began nearly twenty years before the premiere of *The Singing Fool*. Few fans of the day did not know that Jolson's life story provided the model for the narratives of both *The Jazz Singer* and *The Singing Fool*. After *The Singing Fool* Jolson went on to become a major radio star of the 1930s, entertained the troops during World War II, and made a comeback after World War II with Columbia Pictures' hit film biographies *The Jolson Story* and its sequel, *Jolson Sings Again*. Larry Parks played Jolson in both films, but Jolson himself supplied the voice for the songs. *The Jolson Story* earned third place in 1947's run for the top grossing movies, while its sequel topped the movie money-making list for 1949.

Warner Bros. knew the Jolson persona represented the principal attraction for any film with sound and thus overtly formulated *The Singing Fool* around the trials and tribulations of the Jolsonesque Al Stone, a singing waiter who becomes a best-selling song writer. *The Singing Fool* may have offered a thin story, but it could tender the Jolson voice and mannerisms on film. The narrative provided Jolson endless opportunities to introduce new songs. In both *The Jazz Singer* and *The Singing Fool* the bulk of the story came in the form of a traditional silent film. Consequently, Jolson's songs (presented through the new Vitaphone recording process) titillated and thrilled the audience even more.

But *The Singing Fool* had much more going for it than the story of the life of one popular star. The production team who put together *The Singing Fool* was as professional as Hollywood could offer. Cinematographer Byron Haskin would go on to become a director in his own right. Editor Ralph Dawson would cut many a Warners' classic in the 1930s, winning the Academy Award in 1935 for *Anthony Adverse*.

Director Lloyd Bacon guided the creation of *The Singing Fool*. To film historians Bacon is well known for his credits for the Warner musicals *42nd Street* (1933) and *Footlight Parade* (1933). Yet he did much more. From the mid-1920s to the mid-1940s Hollywood insiders counted Bacon as one of the consummate professionals who could handle all genres. One cannot help but stand somewhat in awe of his directorial output during the 1930s when he cranked out a film every two months, year after year after year. Notoriously tight-fisted Warners rewarded this profitmaker by paying him $200,000 per year (equal to more than a million dollars per annum in 1989-inflation-adjusted dollars).

The apex of Lloyd Bacon's contribution to film history came early in his career during the coming of sound. He directed such significant early talkies as *The Lion and the Mouse* (1928) and *Moby Dick* (1930). *The Singing Fool* vaulted Bacon to the pantheon of Hollywood money-making craftsmen. Others may have produced "serious" films that conveyed the Hollywood studios' higher status in the minds of critics, but the Lloyd Bacons provided the "product" that generated the much sought after profits.

But in the end it was the novelty of the then special effect of sound which surely accounted for the special drawing power of *The Singing Fool*. "Silent" movies had always had live sound accompaniment with music and sound effects. Five-hundred-seat neighborhood theaters had to make do with a piano and violin. Four-thousand-seat picture palaces in urban centers such as New York and Chicago maintained resident orchestras of more than seventy members.

What the silent cinema lacked was prerecorded synchronized sound. Vaudeville shows and the legitimate theater thrived as long as the movies were silent. But within the space of five years during the 1920s the American film industry introduced sound recorded first on synchronized records, and then on the film alongside the images. It became possible to offer the equivalent of legitimate dramas plus the renderings of the most popular musical performers.

The coming of sound transformed filmmaking in its day as would the coming of color, wide-screen images, stereo sound, and other new technologies later in the history of film. To understand the drawing power of *The Singing Fool* it is important to understand how the coming of sound transformed the American film industry.

II

By the 1920s technological change in the motion picture industry functioned as part of a larger industrial process. The new ideas that led to the coming of sound did not emerge from the genius of one lone mind but rather were generated by corporate-sponsored research shops and then adopted by the major corporations of the film industry. When the giant motion picture industrial combines—the predecessors of today's Paramount, Twentieth-Century Fox, Universal, and Columbia—took up synchronized sound, this brand of special effects became part of standard film industry practice. If these corporations had wavered, the coming of sound would have been delayed until the chieftains of Paramount and its corporate competitors had approved.

What motivated these large corporations to take on sound? Money. They sought to use the new technology of sound to create higher profits. Corporate leaders reasoned that if Hollywood produced talkies, profits would rise. Technical change, in short, functioned as part of the matrix of economic decision making.

But how does a corporation decide to adopt any new system of knowledge, a new way of doing things? First, the appropriate knowledge must exist. That is, scientists must have created the necessary inventions. Usually this comes not as a single idea but as a system of concepts linked together. Certainly this has always been the case for the inventions that have most affected the movie industry in its short history—whether the change involved the nature of the image or adding sound.

Once the inventions are adopted for practical use, the industry's corporations enter a second phase—innovation. This aspect of technical change involves the reformulation of past modes of all aspects of the industry—in the case of movies: production, distribution, and exhibition. A corporation's owners and managers decide to innovate by developing a plan by which to use the new technology to increase profits. Many a technique has been delayed because (as with the coming of color) no one could find a satisfactory scheme for using the new knowledge to make more money.

Often the invention has been developed by scientists outside the industry that ultimately adopts it. Since the movie industry has done little of its own research and development, Hollywood leaders have always had to look elsewhere for inspiration. Indeed, for the coming of sound the necessary patents were molded in laboratories owned by the American Telephone and Telegraph Company (the fledgling Bell Labs) and the Radio Corporation of America (now RCA). The phone company developed sound recording to test its new long distance telephone circuits; RCA worked up parallel ideas for the testing of radio equipment.

The movie corporations, once offered new technology, have to devise a plan to make greater profits. Certainly sizable costs would be incurred—for example, hiring new talent, taking out substantial loans, and building new studios. The company that acts as the innovator has to formulate a scheme to generate more revenue at the box office. It seems obvious that patrons would want films with improved technology, but in what form and affecting what filmic parameters?

Warner Bros. pioneered the use of sound and thus functioned as the innovator of that important new film technique. The Fox Film Corporation (predecessor of the present Twentieth-Century Fox) came second. Then, once it was shown that talkies could make money—lots of money—the other major Hollywood movie corporations followed suit. Thus begun the third phase of any technical change in industrial America—diffusion.

Diffusion begins when the new technology begins to receive widespread use. This happened for the coming of sound during the fall of 1928. Many factors convinced the Paramounts, the MGMs, the Universals to follow Warner Bros.' lead. No one film could have ever convinced a skeptical Hollywood, but I argue that certainly the enormous success of *The Singing Fool* signaled the end of the innovation of sound and the beginning of the talkies era.

The preceding framework—invention, innovation, and diffusion—provides anyone studying film with a powerful methodology by which to analyze the introduction of any technology, whether it be a minor alternation of the camera or the introduction of color. The success of Warner Bros.' *The Sing-*

 ing Fool climaxed the pioneering innovation phase of the coming of sound and thus offers a case study of how to study the economics of technical change.

III

In 1924, just prior to the coming of sound, Warner Bros. (the official spelling, to cut costs of always printing "Brothers") stood as a prosperous, albeit small, corporation that produced movies. Lack of size and distribution exchanges and its owning no theaters (as did its larger rivals) made it difficult for Warner's to acquire needed financial backing at reasonable interest rates for its productions. Sometimes Harry Warner, eldest of the brothers and president of the corporation, had to pay interest rates exceeding 100 percent.

No wonder that in 1924 Warner approached the important Wall Street investment banking house of Goldman, Sachs for help. Goldman, Sachs, which had steered Sears onto the road to corporate success, agreed to help Warner's.

Warner Bros. moved quickly in 1925. With Goldman, Sachs' backing it purchased Vitagraph, a pioneer movie producer and distributor. In doing so Warner Bros. doubled production capacity and obtained a worldwide network to market its films. Warner's also purchased ten theaters, including a house on Broadway, to begin the makings of a chain of theaters. In 1925, before it ever considered the new sound technology, film industry watchers began to notice the rise of Warner Bros.

As part of this initial wave of expansion Warner's acquired a Los Angeles radio station in order to better publicize its films. Through this deal the brothers Warner learned of the new technology that the radio and telephone industries had developed to record sound. This new technology could be used for movies as well.

During the spring of 1925 the brothers devised a plan by which to use the new recording technology to help with the corporate expansion. Warner Bros. could record the most popular musical artists on film and then offer these short subjects as added attractions to theaters that booked Warner's features. So, for example, if Warner Bros. recorded Al Jolson doing his vaudeville act, it could book the short into thousands of theaters. (Jolson in person could obviously play only one theater at a time.) As a bonus, Warner Bros. could add recorded orchestral music to their feature films and offer it to those theaters without the means to provide live orchestral music.

Warner Bros. pushed this scheme for the innovation of sound simply as one part of a larger expansionary plan. The corporation began to produce important feature films (for example, it hired noted director Ernst Lubitsch) and to distribute them for the first time to theaters throughout the United States and to nearly all countries of the world. Even if the experiments with sound failed, Warner was moving slowly but steadily up the ranks using traditional means of silent filmmaking.

The innovation of sound did not come easily for Warner Bros. For example, it had to contract for equipment from AT&T. But the phone company would have preferred to deal with a more important Hollywood corporation (such as Paramount) rather than one "on the move." But Paramount (and the other major Hollywood companies of the day) did not want to risk their sizable profit positions by junking silent films for some version of films with sound. The giants of the film industry were doing just fine with what they had; they were not about to switch to something that had yet to be proven a winner.

Consequently AT&T harassed Warner Bros. unmercifully to move even faster into the ranks of the major movie corporations, to pay ever higher fees for equipment (despite the fact that the Warner corporation was taking a sizable risk), and to even sell the improvements Warner's had formulated to the Paramounts or MGMs if ever they decided to adopt sound. Warner Bros. had no choice but to cave in to AT&T's demands since RCA had not yet perfected its sound technology to the point that it could be used in day-to-day production and exhibition.

Warner's pressed on. On 6 August 1926 it premiered its new technology, which it labeled "Vitaphone." As planned, its first package consisted of a traditional silent film (*Don Juan*) with a recorded musical accompaniment plus six recordings of musical talent that were highlighted by the most famous opera tenor of the day, Giovanni Martinelli, doing his specialty from *I Pagliacci*.

During the fall of 1926 through the spring of 1927, the prime moviegoing season in those days before the air-conditioning of theaters, Warner's developed several packages of a silent film with recorded orchestral music plus a half-dozen shorts of noted musical talent. As this policy evolved, the shorts became more pop and less classical. Jolson, indeed, appeared before the Warner cameras and recorded two of his most famous hits. The trade paper *Variety* saw a bright future for the new technology, especially outside the larger urban environs in which Jolson regularly appeared on tour.

Warner Bros. concentrated on these so-called "vaudeville shorts." By April 1927 the company had recorded all the more popular stars of the day (who saw a Vitaphone recording as good publicity). Jolson and tenor Martinelli, the ranking pop and classical attractions of their day, drew the largest crowds and were paid the highest recording fees ($5,000 each or nearly $30,000 in 1989 inflation-adjusted dollars).

Warner Bros. soon ran out of stars. It had to devise something new. What the company did was add Vitaphone segments to feature films. That is, if Jolson was such a draw in a short subject, imagine what he could do in a feature film designed and written especially for him. The film would be silent as the necessary narrative moved along, but as soon as the Jolson character was required to break into song, the sound technology would be utilized. This strategy represented a merger of the new with the old and was designed not to offend dedicated silent filmgoers but to attract new patrons.

The first such Vitaphone feature was *The Jazz Singer*. It opened the 1927–28 movie season, premiering early in the fall of 1927. Over the summer months Warner's convinced enough theaters to install the required sound equipment to make the investment in the part-talkie feature film a financial success. During the down time of the summer of 1927 Warner salesmen performed a masterful job of selling skeptical exhibitors, and the Vitaphone projector equipment began to appear in picture palaces throughout the United States.

Slowly the brothers Warner and their financial advisors from Goldman, Sachs realized they were overseeing the creation of a new major movie company. The Warner corporation began to see the light at the end of the tunnel. If the innovation of sound worked as forecast, the company would begin to earn millions in profits before the end of the decade.

The plans worked, and the millions began to roll in—to a greater degree than anyone would have imagined.

The Jazz Singer premiered as scheduled in October 1927. From the opening it was a smash hit. *The Jazz Singer* package (including its accompanying shorts with sound) forced theaters in cities that rarely held over films for more than a single week to ask to have the package stay for two, three, and sometimes an extraordinary four straight weeks. (One week was considered normal in the late 1920s; two weeks usually set a house record.)

The Jazz Singer did well at the box office but failed to better records set by such silent film blockbusters as *Four Horsemen of the Apocalypse* (1921), *Ben Hur* (1926), and *The Big Parade* (1925). Skeptics questioned the staying power of talkies. If sound were so great, why didn't *The Jazz Singer* move to the top of the all-time box office list?

The boffo-socko blockbuster (to use *Variety*'s current terminology) that convinced all doubters was *The Singing Fool*. From opening day (20 September 1928) on, reviewers from the newspaper of record, *The New York*

Times, to the cynics writing for *Variety* correctly predicted an all-time hit. The premiere was held in a rented Broadway theater, the Winter Garden, and eleven-dollar first-night tickets (the equivalent of more than fifty dollars in 1989 inflation-adjusted dollars) were being sold at double the price by Broadway sharpies even before the doors of the Winter Garden opened.

By Thanksgiving day of 1928 Warners knew *The Singing Fool* was inexorably climbing toward becoming the new Hollywood box office champion. It had rung up some seventy box office records throughout the United States, and more premieres remained to be launched. In New York City *The Singing Fool* registered the heaviest business in Broadway history. The advance sales exceeded more than $100,000 (more than a half-million dollars in 1989 currency) before the film had played three full weeks. *The Singing Fool* had reached such proportions that every big ticket agency in Manhattan departed from a strict policy of not handling movie shows to broker blocks of seats.

Throughout the United States theaters owned by Warners' rivals (such as Paramount and Loew's, the parent company of MGM) scrambled to book the film. They ignored the fact that they were making business for a rival producer. Theaters by the dozens ordered sound equipment just to play *The Singing Fool*. Dozens more aped New York and added a midnight showing to handle interested crowds.

From around the United States records of unprecedented box office takes mounted. The manager of the Great Lakes Theatre in Buffalo, New York, reported nearly 170,000 saw *The Singing Fool* during the first two weeks it was booked. In Mansfield, Ohio, *The Singing Fool* played a solid two weeks when four days had been the town's previous record for a film. In Menominee, Michigan, the equivalent of one-and-one-half times the entire population of the town paid to see the attraction during its week run. In Albany, New York, *The Singing Fool* exceeded the record box office take of *The Big Parade* and *Ben Hur*.

The Singing Fool spilled over into other popular entertainment markets. It created the spin-offs we have come to expect in the contemporary film industry. Warner Bros., of course, created a sequel, *Say It with Songs*, which was released at the beginning of the 1929–30 movie season. Like many a follow-up, *Say It with Songs* failed to match the box office take of its predecessor.

Grossett and Dunlap issued a "novelized" version of the film complete with "illustrated scenes" (seven publicity production stills) from the "photoplay starring Al Jolson."

Two songs from the film, "Sonny Boy" and "There's a Rainbow 'Round My Shoulder," went on to comprise the first million-selling phonograph record of the talkie era. Both also sold a million copies in sheet music. When "Sonny Boy" was revived for *Jolson Sings Again*, it sold yet another million phonograph records, bringing the aggregate to more than three million. And this occurred in an era when a million seller came along at most once a year.

IV

The Singing Fool helped transform the American film industry in a way that can be claimed by few individual feature film titles. As a blockbuster—both as a film and a phonograph record—Jolson's vehicle assured that silent films would never return. The industrial transformation begun by Warner Bros. only three years before now moved from the innovation stage into the diffusion phase.

The economics of technical change help us understand the underlying forces that transformed the movie industry, although other important issues have not been explored here. For example, mention ought to made of the special ownership characteristics of the film industry that were created by the coming of sound and have remained with the film industry well into the 1980s. After 1930 there were only eight important movie companies, and those eight (save RKO, which dropped out in the 1950s, and MGM and United Artists, which merged) remain the dominant companies to this day.

This essay has attempted to illustrate the importance of film as a business. Hollywood is more than an image of glamour; it represents the production center of a billion-dollar business. To fully understand how film functions in American society we must completely explore the history and economic practices of the American film industry.

But the study of the economics of the film business can also tell us much about the textual features of individual films. During the late 1910s Hollywood film companies innovated a certain style of filmmaking we have come to call the classical Hollywood cinema. Such a style is centered around the use of popular stars in pleasurable stories that are made in the most efficient, cost-effective manner. *The Singing Fool* certainly illustrates how such a style was adapted to the use of sound.

The star of this classic text was drawn from another field—vaudeville—and was the most popular singer of his day, which ensured access to a large audience. The story was indeed drawn from the myth of how Jolson himself had broken into show business and how he overcame all obstacles to become a star. And Hollywood business and production apparatus had even this early begun to integrate the popular songs into the text. Warner's was able to do this by learning from the experience it had accumulated in producing vaudeville shorts during the prior two years.

Song, the star, a gripping story, and the attraction of sound, all enveloped within a continuous narrative form so familiar to movie fans, made *The Singing Fool* the biggest box office attraction of its day. The economics of the introduction of the new technology provided the framework in which the filmmakers could profitably operate over the long haul. Other essays in this book provide alternative systems for analysis that should further understanding of the precise workings of the sound, camera work, editing and *mise-en-scène* that make up the text of any sound film.

BIBLIOGRAPHY

The Singing Fool

Primary data on the production and distribution of *The Singing Fool* rests in the Warner Brothers corporate materials on file at the University of Southern California, Princeton University, and the University of Wisconsin.

Information on the exhibition of the film can be found in the trade press: *Motion Picture News, Motion Picture Herald*, and *Variety*.

Rankings of grosses come from *Motion Picture Almanacs*, which have been issued yearly by the Quigley corporation since 1929. Indeed, consider that the 1934–35 edition of the *Motion Picture Almanac* noted that although *The Jazz Singer* was the first all-talking feature film to be released and although it was a financial success—chalking up about $3,500,000 in world rentals—its successor, *The Singing Fool*, accrued not only one-third more in United States rentals alone but received even greater net profits throughout the world.

The novelization of the film can be found as Herbert Dahl, *The Singing Fool* (New York: Grossett & Dunlap, 1929). Information on the sales of the songs introduced in the movie is summarized in Joseph Murrells, comp., *The Book of Gold Discs* (London: Barrie and Jenkins, 1978).

Biographies of Al Jolson include Michael Freedland, *Jolson* (New York: Stein and Day, 1972), and Robert Oberfirst, *Al Jolson: You Ain't Heard Nothing Yet* (San Diego: A. S. Barnes, 1980). The career of Lloyd Bacon is treated in Christopher Lyon, ed., *The International Dictionary of Films and Filmmakers*, vol. 2 (Chicago: St. James Press, 1984).

For more on the Warner Bros. company see Douglas Gomery, *The Hollywood Studio System* (New York: St. Martin's, 1986), and Charles Higham, *Warner Brothers* (New York: Charles Scribner's Sons, 1975).

The Singing Fool is available for rental in 16mm from United Artists/16, 729 Seventh Avenue, New York, N.Y. 10019.

A convenient summary of the economic analysis of the motion picture industry can be found in Robert C. Allen and Douglas Gomery, *Film History: Theory and Practice* (New York: Alfred A. Knopf, 1985). See also Douglas Gomery, "The Economics of Film: What Is the Method?" in *Film/Culture: Explorations of Cinema and Its Social Context*, ed. Sari Thomas (Metuchen, N.J.: Scarecrow Press, 1982).

Douglas Gomery has written extensively on the coming of sound. For an overview see "The Coming of Sound: Technological Change in the American Film Industry," in *The American Film Industry*, ed. Tino Balio, rev. ed. (Madison: University of Wisconsin Press, 1985). Warner Bros.' pioneering efforts at innovation are analyzed in "Warner Bros. Innovates Sound: A Business History," in *The Movies In Our Midst*, ed. Gerald Mast (Chicago: University of Chicago Press, 1982). For further application read "Problems in Film History: How Fox Innovated Sound," in *Hollywood as Historian: American Film in a Cultural Context*, ed. Peter Rollins (Lexington: University of Kentucky Press, 1983), "Hollywood Converts to Sound: Chaos or Order," in *Sound and the Cinema*, ed. Evan William Cameron (Pleasantville, N.Y.: Redgrave, 1980), and "The Warner-Vitaphone Peril: The American Film Industry Reacts to the Innovation of Sound," in *American Film Industry: A Case Studies Approach*, ed. Gorham A. Kindem (Carbondale: Southern Illinois University Press, 1982).

The aforementioned Balio and Kindem anthologies contain extensive bibliographies for further reading in the economics of the American film industry.

Part 3

CONCLUSION

INTRODUCTION

Peter Lehman

In this concluding analysis I have used many of the forms of criticism illustrated in this book. It would, of course, take a book-length study to do that in a detailed, comprehensive fashion. I have therefore emphasized what seem to be the most significant formal and ideological features of a very complex film, John Ford's 1956 western, *The Searchers*. In keeping with the format of this book, the first part of my analysis deals with narrative structure, visual motifs, space, and sound; the second part analyzes the representation of women, American Indians, and economics.

My title, "Texas 1868/America 1956: *The Searchers*," indicates two important time frames and locations: the film's diegetic time and place and the historical time and place of its release. There is, of course, a third time and place—Academia 1990, that of this writing. The films represented in this collection and the analytical models applied to them are all part of this context. I mention in the following essay that many contemporary Hollywood filmmakers are obsessed with *The Searchers*; the same can be said of many current academicians—this one included. I started writing about the film in my doctoral dissertation in the mid-seventies, and I'm still writing about it more than a decade later. Not surprisingly, the work from different periods during that time (some of which is reformulated in the following chapter) poses different questions, explores different issues, and reveals entirely different assumptions about what is important in critical activity. Whether I am finally done writing about *The Searchers* I do not know nor do I care. In the spirit of theoretical inquiry that informs this entire book, what is important to me, and I hope to the readers of this anthology, is to always question the assumptions we have and to recognize that there are new areas to explore and perhaps old ones to return to and think over anew. If we ever stop questioning what films we write about, what features of those films we address and prioritize, or what questions we ask of those films, then a truly vital relationship between theory and criticism will be dead. In that spirit of critical inquiry and in the spirit of unanswered narrative questions that I analyze in *The Searchers*, I want to conclude with a question. Why *The Searchers*? So much has been written and said about it so often; do we need another essay on it? I hope the following chapter only partially answers that question, for it and questions like it should always occupy us. We should never think certain work safely completed any more than we should think that we can afford to stop developing challenging methods that jolt us out of our complacency. It has been the purpose of this book to show what an exciting activity that can be.

Postscript: Originally, the following chapter was to be illustrated with eleven frame enlargements from *The Searchers*. Warner Bros. granted permission for a maximum of six frames, contingent upon the permission of the John Wayne Estate for all frames in which Wayne appeared. Since we were unable to obtain this permission, we have chosen to use sketches for all eleven illustrations. While sketches are not an adequate substitute for frame enlargements, we hope they will help readers visualize the salient features of the images.

20

TEXAS 1868 / AMERICA 1956: *THE SEARCHERS*

Peter Lehman

"Ethan?" is the first word we hear spoken in *The Searchers*, and it follows the unanswered questions that comprise the song lyrics we hear over the credits.[1] It is fitting that the name is uttered as a question. Aaron stares into the desert and says the name in disbelief as his brother approaches the home. *The Searchers* is full of characters questioning names. As soon as he enters the home, Ethan mistakes his nieces. He lifts a little girl up in front of the fireplace and says, "Lucy, you ain't much bigger than when I last saw you." "I'm Deborah. There's Lucy over there," the little girl says. "Deborah? Debbie! And you're Lucy?" Ethan responds confusedly. In the next scene, Marty enters and Ethan stares at the young man uncomprehendingly. "Martin, Martin Pauley," Martha explains to Ethan with a strange, questioning tone in her voice. When Ethan returns to the destroyed homestead after the Indian attack, he yells "Martha? Martha?"—not knowing if she is still alive. After he

1. A shorter version of this analysis of names can be found in Lehman (1981, 41–42). Some of the points made in this chapter about the representation of women and about the use of off-screen space also appeared there and in my article, "An Absence Which Becomes a Legendary Presence" (1978a).

 discovers her body the same question arises about his nieces, and he yells, "Lucy? Debbie?"

When Marty returns from the search after years of absence, he and Laurie are reintroduced to each other in a manner that recalls Marty and Ethan's reintroduction. They stare at each other, once again almost uncomprehendingly. "Marty? Martin Pauley!" Laurie says to him, and her mother remarks, "And him probably forgetting all about you. Probably can't even call your name to mind." "Her name's Laurie," Marty replies. Earlier, when Laurie, reading a letter from Marty, comes across the name Scar, she pauses, looks up, and strangely repeats the name in a confused, questioning tone before continuing with the letter. When we see Marty first encountering the name, he similarly repeats, "Scar?"

This unusual emphasis on names and identification continues during the search and becomes part of a much larger issue in the film. When Ethan follows a lead to a trading post, he enters asking, "Futterman?" and when a man responds, "Yeah," Ethan orders, "Let's talk." When they first meet, Lieutenant Greenhill assumes Ethan to be Captain Clayton and when his error is pointed out he stupidly asks Clayton, "You're Captain Clayton?" Clayton then asks, "Who is this Colonel Greenhill you're talking about?" When he surmises that the messenger is the colonel's son, he gets the young man so confused that he calls his commanding officer "my pa" before correcting it to "Colonel Greenhill." Indeed, Clayton's very name and title, the Reverend Captain Clayton, epitomizes the confusion surrounding names in the film. He is both a minister and a military officer, two functions that we normally think of as quite disparate, and his full title yokes them together in a bewildering fashion; one hardly knows what he is or rather who he is at any given moment. Characters in *The Searchers* are constantly confusing, ascertaining, and questioning who people are. Bewilderment and disbelief predominate, and it affects the names of places as well as characters. At the film's climax Mose Harper reports to the cavalry that Debbie is at Seven Fingers. Everyone looks puzzled and Ethan repeats, "Seven Fingers?" Since the cavalry can't find the name on the map, they interpret it as being part of a crazy man's incoherent ramblings. Marty, however, immediately recognizes it as the Indian name for a place nearby.

This contagion of confusing names, people, and places relates to a much larger epistemological issue in the film: How is knowledge gained and what, indeed, is the status of knowledge? Somewhat unusually for a classical Hollywood film, this epistemological problem applies not only to the characters in the film but also to the audience of the film. It is a critical commonplace that the classical Hollywood film does not usually confuse or disorient its audience at any level. Motivation and psychology explain why characters behave the way they do; the 180 degree rule, eyeline matches, and the continuity editing system all create and maintain a coherent space; and the narrative eventually answers all the questions it raises. In short, when we watch a classical film we feel we understand what is happening, why it is happening, and where it is happening. Unlike in the European art cinema, ambiguity is minimized and disorientation is avoided.

Although *The Searchers* is a classical film and its director, John Ford, one of the acknowledged masters of that style, it creates some interesting problems within the form. What happens (or happened), where, and why, in the narrative is difficult at times to ascertain. Consider two examples involving Ethan Edwards. Following a mysterious absence of some years after the Civil War, he returns home with freshly minted money. What did he do during those years and where did he get the money? Has he been a bank robber? We never find the answers to the questions. At one point during the search Ethan separates from Marty and Brad. When they reunite Ethan acts feverishly distracted. He repeatedly stabs his knife into the ground, and when Brad asks him where his coat is he unconvincingly says he must have lost it in the canyon from which he has emerged. Although later in the film Ethan claims that he found Lucy's body and buried it with his coat, a number of unanswered questions remain. Did he find her alive after being raped by Indians and kill her himself? Is he cleaning blood from his knife?

In and of themselves such unanswered questions would be insignificant, little more than a game. Ford, however, weaves them into a complex set of related questions that undermine the fabric of knowledge that we as spectators have of characters and events in the film, and he explicitly links our spectatorial position to the dilemmas of the characters in the film.[2] When Marty and Ethan discover "Look" dead in an Indian village that has been attacked and destroyed by the cavalry, Marty speculates, "Whether she'd come to warn 'em or maybe find Debbie for me, there's no way of knowin'." We as spectators are similarly put in the position of having no way of knowing about this character and event or many of the others in the film we are watching, an unusual position for the viewer of a classical Hollywood film.

What exactly is the relationship between Ethan and Martha? Clearly they

2. This chapter extends and recontextualizes my previous work on the problem of knowledge in the film that I explored in my doctoral dissertation, *John Ford and the Auteur Theory* (1978b, 182–256). Some of the following formal analysis is also reworked from that dissertation. A version of the dissertation chapter appears in Luhr and Lehman (1977, 85–135).

have a secret and forbidden romantic bond. When Ethan arrives and he and the family prepare to enter the home, the music shifts to an ominous tone as he and Martha exchange glances. Once inside, Martha takes his coat into the bedroom, and we see Ethan staring after her as she fondly holds it. During the following dinner scene the two of them are seated in such a way that they are frequently seen together as a couple in a two-shot with Aaron excluded. Later that evening Aaron tells Ethan that he is puzzled as to why Ethan stayed around so long for no apparent reason before the war. Once again the framing links Martha and Ethan as the two exchange knowing glances that Aaron does not perceive; obviously his love for Martha was Ethan's reason. Before Ethan leaves with the Rangers, Captain Clayton sees Martha stroking Ethan's coat in the bedroom. Ford cuts from Clayton's point of view to a frontal shot of him with a troubled look on his face. Martha comes from the bedroom and meets Ethan behind Clayton. They exchange an intense look, she gives him his coat, and he kisses her and leaves. All the while Clayton's troubled look confirms that he has discovered the bond between Ethan and Martha and that he is disturbed by the knowledge. Finally, when Ethan returns to the burned home after the Indian attack, he frantically yells, "Martha? Martha?", showing primary concern for her rather than his brother and nieces. Nevertheless, the film never confirms for us the nature of the past relationship between Ethan and Martha. Were they lovers before she married Aaron? Did Ethan have a sexual relationship with his sister-in-law? Or were they bound together by an unfulfilled passion that neither has forgotten?

Even the relationship between Ethan and Marty involves an element of mystery. When Martha reminds Marty that it was Ethan who found him as a child after his mother had been killed by Indians, Ethan insists, "Just happened to be me." He also insults Marty by telling him, "Fella could mistake you for a half-breed," though Marty says he is only one-eighth Cherokee. What accounts for Ethan's disavowal of his rescue of Marty? Why is he so contemptuous of Marty's racial appearance? He seems to have too much emotion invested in the entire affair. Indeed, his paradoxically intense disclaimer prevents us from accepting it at face value. Perhaps it didn't "just happen" to be him? At one point Ethan begins to confide to Marty by saying, "Marty, there's something I want you to know." Marty angrily cuts him off by saying, "Yeah, I know what you want me to know . . . so shut your mouth." Ethan never finishes with what he was going to say, and we are left wondering as to what it may have been. Later Ethan recognizes Marty's mother's scalp in Scar's tent. Why, if she had been just a casual acquaintance, does he immediately recognize it after all these years? Is Ethan Marty's father? This would of course explain his reaction to Marty's Indian-like appearance.

I am not seriously proposing that Ethan is a bank robber who had an affair with his sister-in-law, killed his niece, and fathered Marty but rather that all those things are suggested as possibilities. The film abounds in oddly indeterminable character relationships and actions. In fact, this becomes one of the film's themes. In one scene Ford complexly intercuts between Mr. and Mrs. Jorgenson, Laurie, and Charlie McCorry, who read a letter from Marty about the progress of the search. The cutting pattern indicates how tenuous the knowledge is which the characters think they possess about the events related in the letter. First we see a scene in which Marty, thinking that he is bargaining for a blanket, actually bargains for a wife. After he learns what he has done, Ford cuts back to the Jorgenson home and Laurie reads, "There is one thing I got to tell you before you hear it from Ethan. How I got myself a wife." Everyone immediately reacts to the information in a different way. Charlie, who sees Marty as a rival for Laurie's affections, is pleased; Laurie is hurt; Mr. Jorgenson, totally oblivious of the impact this has on his daughter, indicates his approval by saying it is good for a man to marry young; and Mrs. Jorgenson, in polar opposition to her husband, is attuned to the import this news has for her daughter. Four characters react in four different ways to the same piece of information that has just been narrated to them. But this, of course, is not a simple piece of neutral information; the narrational style of Marty's letter determines what each of the characters think has happened. They have not seen it; they have only read about it. Marty has unwittingly constructed a plot and it is not a good one for furthering his prospects with Laurie.

When the letter reading resumes this process of narrative misinformation continues, for the very next line is "A little Comanche squaw." Predictably, the reactions are strong again. Laurie repeats "squaw" with disgust and even tries to destroy the letter. This latest piece of narrative information has not "corrected" the previous notion the listeners had of the event; rather the entire process has just slid to the next narrative segment. Laurie presumes that the insult to her is all the greater since she lost Marty to a "squaw" rather than to another white woman. But once again she is misinformed by this new piece of information, since Marty has not narrated how the event came to pass. Just as Marty does not know what it is that he does when he trades for Look, Laurie does not know how it is that Marty ended up marrying an Indian.

When the letter reading resumes again, several of the events encountered by Marty and Ethan continue this theme of knowledge. When Look leaves them, Marty narrates, "Maybe she left other signs to follow but . . ." and Ford cuts to Laurie who reads, "we'll never know 'cause it snowed that day and all the next week." Laurie's attempt here to gain knowledge of what happened is explicitly linked to Marty's attempt to do the same thing, something that he concedes is hopeless. Marty returns to this idea again when he remarks of an episode, "Something happened that I ain't got straight in my own mind yet," and finally when he concludes of Look's behavior, "there's no way of ever knowing."

For a final example of the problem that characters in the film have of establishing knowledge of events that they have not directly witnessed, consider the scene where Ethan and Marty return home from the search only to learn of a warrant out for Ethan's arrest. He is charged with killing Jerem Futterman, the trader, who is found with his men lying dead near Ethan's camp. They have been shot in the back, and gold coins that Futterman possessed are missing. Furthermore, Ethan carries coins like those Futterman had. Virtually anyone would conclude his guilt from those circumstances. We, however, have witnessed the events and know that Futterman and his men are the guilty ones; they attempted to ambush Ethan and Marty. Ethan, after successfully foiling their plan, merely takes back the money that he had earlier paid the trader for information on Scar's whereabouts. Thus he had shot the men in self-defense rather than murdered them, and he has reclaimed his money rather than robbed Futterman.

Just as Marty can never be sure of Look's motives and what it is that she has done, Captain Clayton and the law cannot be sure of Ethan's motives and what he has done in regard to Futterman, and Aaron cannot be sure of his brother's motives in staying around so long before the war and what it is that he has done since. Remarkably, we can be no more sure of many things in the film than those characters. If Laurie and the group gathered around her as she reads the letter are dependent upon Marty's narrational style to make sense out of events that they have not witnessed, so are we, the audience of the film, dependent upon Ford—and he is frequently not much more helpful than Marty, though unlike Marty, he cleverly controls this process.

Ford's use of off-screen space, primarily developed around the use of glances, relates to the film's concern with knowledge and how it is gathered. Characters constantly look off and stare out of the frame in ways that emphasize their attempt to understand who or what is out there and what is happening. The opening scene of the film establishes this pattern. The first shot shows Martha looking out into the wilderness, and that shot is followed by a whole series of shots showing all the family members staring off into the distance as Aaron questions what he sees.

Throughout the film these stares are associated with potentially disruptive forces. The family members interrupt their normal work to stare off at the man who threatens to disrupt their harmonious family structure. Captain Clayton stares off-screen when he initially perceives these destructive possibilities and continues to stare away while Ethan kisses Martha good-bye.

More direct forces of power and physical destruction are also associated with off-screen space. After guessing that the Rangers were tricked by Indians into venturing away from their homes, Ethan stares off-screen over his horse realizing that his brother's homestead is in danger of attack. Little Debbie stares off as Scar's shadow passes over her from off-screen before he signals the attack on the Edwards's home. When Brad rushes to his death, Ethan and Marty both stare after him, the echoing gunshots further developing the off-screen space and action we never see. When Laurie encounters Scar's name while reading a letter, she looks up, stares off, and mysteriously repeats his name before continuing. Later, when Marty leaves the disrupted wedding to pursue Scar, his shadow passes over Laurie's white wedding dress. Marty is off-screen just as Scar was when his shadow passed over Debbie, and the connection is an ominous foreboding of what Marty's powerful commitment to the search could do to his desires to marry and settle down.

As were events and character motivations, space too is confusing both to characters within the diegesis and to the audience of the film. A simple example illustrates the former. After the Indian raid on the Edwards's home, a search party led by Captain Clayton moves through a swamp at night. They hear a whistle and all turn in one direction and stare off; only moments later they hear another whistle and stare in the opposite direction. They are totally disoriented since they do not know if the sounds they hear are a signal, and if so where the signaler or signalers are. Are they surrounded or are they alone?

Later in the film during the course of their search, Ethan and Marty encounter a herd of buffalo. Ethan, for no reason apparent to Marty, starts to slaughter them. As Marty desperately tries to stop Ethan from this senseless destruction they hear the distant sounds of a cavalry bugle. Both men immediately stop what they are doing and stare off-screen left in the direction from which the sound comes. Ford cuts to several shots of the cavalry crossing an icy river surrounded by snow. Then he cuts to Marty and Ethan riding down a snowy hill. They move right to left, and by every convention of Hollywood cutting patterns based upon off-screen sound, eyeline matches, directional screen movement and spatio-temporal continuity we expect Ethan and

 Marty to approach the cavalry. Instead, a panning shot brings dead bodies and burned teepees into the foreground of the frame. We soon realize they are in a village the cavalry has just destroyed and not by the river we have seen the cavalry crossing.

The scene is baffling on many levels. When the bugle is first heard, its associations of law and order and restraint are so strong that they even stop Ethan's brutal slaughter of the buffalo. Furthermore, the sound of a cavalry bugle in the distance has strong positive generic connotations, frequently heralding a last-minute rescue. Indeed, Ford himself used the cavalry in precisely this way in *Stagecoach* (1939). We have many reasons to expect that they will arrive on the scene and restore order. It is shocking, therefore, to be faced with the evidence of their brutal and seemingly senseless destruction of an Indian village—women, children, and all. But we are equally disoriented by Ford's handling of space and time. Even in retrospect we cannot situate the relationship between the spaces we have just seen. How close is the stream the cavalry crosses to the site of the buffalo slaughter? Where is the Indian village in relationship to both of these other places? If these places are close together, why is there no trace of the cavalry by the time Ethan and Marty get to the village? All of these questions are intensified by Ford's abandonment of the editing conventions cited earlier. If he had faded out on Marty and Ethan and then shown them in the village, all of our confusion would vanish. The fade would indicate the passage of time and a new locale. Indeed, it is hard to imagine in any conventional cutting scenario why Ford would include the shots of the cavalry crossing the stream, since Marty and Ethan do not meet or even pass them and they do not figure in the following scene of Marty and Ethan discovering the ruined village.

Even the central action of the film is not exempt from confusion and ambiguity. Simply stated, why does Ethan launch a vengeful, five-year search for his niece Debbie with the intent of killing her when he finds her? Why does he suddenly change his mind when he finally does find her? Unlike many of the unanswerable questions outlined above, these crucial questions have answers, but in them lies yet another unusual variation on classical Hollywood film form.

Like all classical texts, *The Searchers* has a hermeneutic structure that poses a central narrative question near the beginning of the film and answers it near the end. As defined by Roland Barthes, this structure involves delays and snares before the "truth" is known, and once it is known the text is "used up" and ends. There is nothing left to tell or maintain our interest. In this film the central hermeneutic might be formulated as: Will Ethan find Debbie and if he does will he carry out his desire to kill her? True to form, the answer to this question comes in the climactic scene of the film and is followed only by a brief denouement. Before the film formally announces that it is over, members of an audience frequently leave the theater during the final scene in which the search party arrives home. They intuitively know that the film is almost over and, since the burning question in their minds has been answered, they do not care about the details of the resolution; Ethan has succeeded, Scar is dead, and Debbie is safely returned to a white family. The end.

As with the main hermeneutic, many of the film's other narrative questions are resolved in conventional fashion. A romantic subplot turns on whether Laurie and Marty will get married, and after a delay (due to the search) and a snare (Charlie McCorry plans to marry her) they are reunited. In Mose Harper the film follows yet another common practice—having a comic subplot with a minor character whose situation in some ways parallels and comments on that of the main character. Like Ethan, Mose has no home and seeks a rocking chair by the fireplace. Although Ethan will occupy that position only momentarily, Mose seems to have found a place for himself by the film's end.

As a final example, consider the hermeneutic structure surrounding Futterman's death. This is a classic snare since we wonder whether Ethan will be arrested for the crime with which he is charged. Captain Clayton places him under arrest but then returns his gun to him so that Ethan can accompany the Rangers as they prepare to attack Scar's village. By the conclusion, however, we know that Clayton has not followed through on the charges (though we don't know why), since Ethan is allowed to return home with the group and the law is nowhere in sight. Although this question seems to have been more forgotten than answered, it certainly is not an open ending in which we do not know whether Ethan will be convicted of the crime with which he is charged. As he turns to go back into the desert from which he came, we simply presume that the issue has been resolved, perhaps due to his role in rescuing Debbie. Nor are we overly preoccupied with his loner status at the end, since it is a commonplace of the western genre that the hero, after fulfilling his function, leaves the community rather than integrate himself into it (e.g., *Shane* [1953]).

But if we return to our earlier questions about Ethan's motivation, we discover something unusual. To many spectators the end of the film may very well seem to be a silly Hollywood "happy ending." In a related vein, Robert Ardrey remarked of the film in a discussion of Hollywood's decline to mediocrity—which he attributed to the industry desire to "achieve an audience made up exclusively of children"—that "the same John Ford who once gave adults 'The Informer' must now give children 'The Searcher[s]'." (quoted in Macgowan 1965, 3). Whatever else can be said of *The Searchers*, it is not for children, since the film deals centrally with illicit sexual desire that threatens the family, with miscegenation, and with racism. In fact, the film might more accurately be characterized as one of an emergent group of mid-fifties westerns that have been dubbed "adult" westerns precisely because their subject matter and themes introduced new, disturbing material into the genre. How is it that a critic could pick such a film to be the crowning example of an argument that Hollywood was aiming movies only at children? The answer to this question returns us to our earlier question about the film's ending.

All the material surrounding Ethan's sexual desire for Martha, his initial desire to kill Debbie, and his later impulse to save her is developed exclusively in visual terms; it is never spoken of or even hinted at in the dialogue, though we have seen earlier that the music cues the observant spectator to some of the visual information. It is primarily through glances, gestures, actions and framing that Ford establishes the bond between Martha and Ethan. No character ever says a word about it, including Captain Clayton once he discovers it.

Similarly, Ethan's actions at the conclusion of the film can only be understood with reference to intricately developed visual motifs. The opening shot of the film is totally dark until Martha (whom we do not yet see) opens a door onto the bright desert. She stands in the doorway looking out at Ethan who approaches the home. In a rhyme that typifies classical filmmaking, the closing shot answers to the opening shot in bookend fashion. The camera is inside the Jorgenson home as we see the members of the search party returning home with Debbie. Once again it is totally dark within. All the characters except Ethan enter, and as he turns to go back into the desert the door is pushed closed and the entire screen is dark as it was at the beginning. Thus the film begins with Ethan approaching a home with a complete family and it ends with him leaving a home after restoring Debbie to it.

We repeatedly see Ethan Edwards framed through doorways and related compositions. After he returns to his brother's home to find it ruined by Indians, we see him framed through a dark doorway moments before he discovers Martha's body within. When he and Marty return from the first leg of their search, we see them framed from within the Jorgenson home. In a manner that recalls Martha at the beginning of the film, Mrs. Jorgenson stands on the porch looking out at the approaching men. After the search is continued, we see Ethan framed through the opening of a teepee before he goes inside to discover Look's body. Later we see Ethan and Marty, attempting to escape attacking Indians, framed by the opening of a cave they ride toward seeking shelter. Once again the opening is surrounded by total darkness. Then, during the film's climax, as Ethan chases Debbie and she flees fearing for her life, Ford cuts so that we see the action framed through the mouth of another dark cave.

At the simplest level, these recurring compositions that frame Ethan mark our progress through the film. There is a constant tension in the film between Ethan and interior spaces; he does not fit in anywhere. He arrives initially at a family home to which he poses a threat. When Scar literally enacts the destruction that Ethan symbolically poses, Ethan displaces his inner feelings onto this "other" and begins his obsessive quest. In the process he contributes to the partial destruction of yet another family through Brad's death. He then journeys to another culture, and finally he regresses to a state of retreat from any culture before attempting to reintegrate himself within his own culture. Thus the teepees and caves compare and contrast with the doorways of his own culture; they remind us of how far Ethan has traveled from his brother's home and the community to which it belongs. But the doorway/teepee/cave motif also serves a much more complex function in its interaction with another motif that helps explain the enigma surrounding Ethan's actions at the end of the film.

When Ethan enters his brother's home, he lifts Debbie up in front of the fireplace (fig. 20–1). When he finally catches up with Debbie at the end of the film by the mouth of the cave, he repeats the gesture (fig. 20–2). This recurrence combined with the contrast between the settings of the cave and the home suggest a powerful explanation for his inability to carry through his plans of killing her. Earlier, when Ethan and Marty seek refuge in a cave,

Figure 20-1.

Figure 20-2.

their relationship degenerates to near barbarism. Ethan speaks brutally about Debbie, whom he no longer considers a kin of his, and Marty almost loses control of himself by picking up a knife and threatening to kill Ethan. Away from both white and Indian civilizations they become atavistic. The shot through the mouth of the cave at the end of the film (fig. 20–3) triggers a complex set of associations that reminds us of the full extent of Ethan's journey from the loving gesture he performs in front of the hearth in his brother's home (the symbolic center of the family and the place that Mose constantly reminds us he wishes to occupy) to his nearly animalistic behavior in the wilderness. The way in which he lifts Debbie shows us that at some, probably unconscious, level, he remembers having similarly lifted the little

Figure 20-3.

girl in a context far removed from the brutal act he now consciously seeks to enact.[3]

At this point in the film a central question of knowledge comes together for both the spectator of the film and the central character in the film. Ethan finds himself unable to kill Debbie because he remembers having lovingly held her in his brother's home and because he is aware of the startling contrast between that moment before the fireplace and this moment before the cave. And the spectators who have paid careful attention to the film's visual motifs are also aware of these profound dynamics, but only if they have seen the intricate development of the motifs, for this is never spoken of anywhere in the film. The thematic development of visual motifs is not uncommon in the classical cinema. However, it is unusual that something as central to a film as the comprehension of the main character's motivations at critical moments in the film (e.g., Ethan's reasons for searching for Debbie and for not killing her when he finds her) are explained solely in visual terms and never spoken about.

Christian Metz has characterized the distinction between theater and cinema in the following way: "the theater play has a text while the film does not—at least if we take the notion of text in its strict and most simple sense as a continuous verbal tissue, a tight contexture which forms a totality sufficient onto itself. . . . *The true text in the cinema is the image-strip*" (1973, 52). Put another way, in the classical theater the dialogue speaks of what is "fundamentally at issue and creates the diegesis" (Lehman 1978c, 200). It is for this reason that we can read *Hamlet*, for example, and understand what the play is about even if we have never seen a production of it. It is also for this reason that different productions are staged quite differently with regard to sets, blocking, and gesturing. Shakespeare's stage directions can be changed or even ignored and the costuming can be done in modern dress. Since a complete fictional world is created by the spoken dialogue, this totality that is complete unto itself and cannot be changed without altering the integrity of the work can sustain many different interpretations. One actor reportedly performed Hamlet differently every night of the run of a production in which he appeared. Thus, for example, perhaps one night he raised his left arm in a dramatic gesture when he spoke a line and the next night he raised neither arm. Perhaps one night he jumped on a table during a monologue but the next night delivered it from the floor. Indeed, the continuous

3. Joseph McBride and Michael Wilmington also make this point (1975, 162). Their frequently perceptive discussion of *The Searchers* contains several other observations that are similar or related to my analysis of the film.

 verbal tissue of a play's text is so complete unto itself that it is not uncommon to have staged readings. The actors simply deliver the dialogue while remaining seated; no sets, movements, or lighting changes are used.

Imagine now such a staged reading of *The Searchers*. It would be incoherent. Even if we read the screenplay without seeing the film, it would be banal. This is not due to some flaw in Frank Nugent's excellent script but rather to the status of what a script is within the classical cinema. It is not a dense, rich, aesthetic text; it does not create the diegesis but is a part of it. Think of what would happen if, for example, John Wayne had decided to play Ethan Edwards in the manner in which our actor played Hamlet. What if he decided not to lift Debbie up in front of the fireplace or changed the gesture outside the cave? What if he told Ford that he was tired of standing in doorways, preferring instead to come inside? The aesthetic text would crumble. The spoken words do not create a totality sufficient to support such variations; rather they are a part of the totality and—as the climax of *The Searchers* demonstrates—not always an important part. As Ethan picks up Debbie in front of the cave he says to her, "Let's go home, Debbie." He might just as well have said, "C'mon Debbie, let's go home," or just "Let's go home," or he might even have said nothing! The meaning of the scene would remain essentially intact. Yet without the shot through the mouth of the dark cave followed by the lifting gesture, it would collapse and we would indeed have a mindless happy ending.

This is not to argue that neither scripts nor the spoken word are important in classical cinema; that would be folly. Rather, the extraordinary beginning and conclusion of *The Searchers* push an element of the distinction between classical theater and cinema to an extreme. Although much of the film remains enigmatic, if we pay careful attention to Ford's camera positioning, visual motifs, and direction of actors we can grasp something of the dynamics that explain why Ethan launches and pursues his monomaniacal search in the first place and why, at the moment of its conclusion, he suddenly reverses his intended actions and saves Debbie rather than kills her.

II

During the opening credit sequence of *The Searchers*, we hear an all-male singing group asking:

> What makes a man to wander?
> What makes a man to roam?
> What makes a man to leave bed and board
> And turn his back on home?

After the credit sequence raises these questions, the very first shot of the film, before we see the live action begin as Martha opens the door and looks out, is inscribed "Texas 1868." After listening to the song lyrics dwell romantically on male wanderlust, we may very well wonder, what must a woman do? The answer comes in the first shot of the film: A woman must wait for a man to get done searching.

The opening shot of the film is curious since it begins in mid-action. Nothing has been established (the entire screen is black); a door opens and we see a woman frozen in the doorway looking out. It is as if her function were to wait and open the door at the right moment. We see her open the door, but we do not see her engaged in activity from which she is interrupted or even distracted. She seems to exist waiting, immobile, looking out. Thus the credit sequence with the male group singing about masculine concerns excludes any place for the woman, and the first shot of the film gives her the only place possible: If men must search their whole lives through, women must wait at home for them to return. When Ethan and Marty return to the Jorgenson homestead after the first unsuccessful portion of their search, Mrs. Jorgenson stands waiting for them in a manner that recalls Martha. Marty just presumes that Laurie will wait for him until the search is completed. Her rebellion points to how extreme and confining waiting can be. And in this oddly indeterminable film, we may even speculate that the Marty/Laurie/Charlie relationship parallels what the Ethan/Martha/Aaron relationship may have been years earlier; perhaps Martha got tired of waiting for Ethan and married Aaron as Laurie is about to marry Charlie.

I mention the inscription of time and place in the opening shot since it helps to create a context that naturalizes what we are about to see. Many viewers will respond to an analysis of the place of women in the film by saying, "But that's the way things were in the West and it's wrong to judge them by contemporary standards." This response is naively inadequate in two ways. First of all, that is not the way things were in the West in 1868. Women and Indians, for example, all lived twenty-four hours each day then as now, and we can explain nothing about their place within the narrative structure of the film with reference to actual conditions. A story about Texas in 1868 could just as well centralize women and Indians and peripheralize white men as do the reverse.

John Ford himself at least implicitly recognized this when late in his career he made *Cheyenne Autumn* (1964) and *Seven Women* (1966). The titles of both indicate the remarkable shift in emphasis in both of the films: the former tells an Indian/cavalry story from the point of view of the Indians, and the latter centers its numerous women characters and relegates its few male characters to secondary status. Whereas both of those films remain problematic in their representation of Indians and women, they point to how superficial is the defense of *The Searchers* referred to above. Nothing in any representational system can be adequately explained with reference to how things are or how they were. Whatever occurred historically can be shown and narrated from innumerable perspectives. What we see and what we don't see, what is emphasized and what is de-emphasized can be explained only with reference to the representational system since such things are not properties of events that happened but rather choices of representation. Ford could have, for example, filmed *The Searchers* from the point of view of the women waiting at home. We would then see a great deal of the activities they engage in and only get brief glimpses of the searchers at those times that they return home.

This points to the other inadequacy with our hypothetical naturalized response to the film (actually not so hypothetical, since it has been expressed by many of my students over the years). Although the film marks itself as taking place in 1868, there is another time frame that it represses: America 1956, the year the film was released. In this regard *The Searchers* is once again a conventional classical film, since classical cinema masks the signs of its production rather than refers to them. Traditional Hollywood cinema presents us with a seemingly authorless, unified, self-contained world that somehow magically unfolds; we are not asked to notice or think about how it was made or even that it was made. In this section of my discussion of *The Searchers*, however, I wish to consider the film as a product made in a capitalist, patriarchal society and, more specifically, as one made in America in 1956. For even if one naively believes that we can explain the place of women in the film with reference to the West of 1868, we are still left with the thorny problem of explaining why such a story and many others like it were told in America in 1956 and are still being told today. Indeed, *The Searchers* continues to have a strong appeal in 1990. It is often cited as the most influential movie by a whole generation of filmmakers including Martin Scorsese, Steven Spielberg, and George Lucas; they and other directors frequently refer to it in their own films.

Part 1 of this essay outlined the formal complexity of *The Searchers*; now I want to similarly analyze three areas of ideological concern in the film—the representation of women, Indians, and capitalism. From a feminist perspective, Teresa de Lauretis has analyzed the Oedipal structure of the classical cinema and the ways in which it centers and privileges male concerns. Referring to Jurij Lotman's work on narrative structure, she notes, "Lotman finds a simple chain of two functions, open at both ends and thus endlessly repeatable: 'entry into a closed space, and emergence from it. . . . Inasmuch as closed space *can be interpreted as* 'a cave', 'the grave', 'a house', 'woman' (and correspondingly, be allotted the features of darkness, warmth, dampness) entry into it *is interpreted* on various levels as 'death', 'conception', 'return home' and so on" (De Lauretis 1984, 118). De Lauretis notes that given this structure the hero of the narrative must be male (regardless of gender representation), since the narrative obstacle is morphologically female, specifically the womb.

The Searchers not only conforms to this pattern in general, but Lotman's specific listing of caves, graves, houses, and women along with the attributes of darkness, warmth, and dampness fit the film with an eerie specificity. Indeed, at a strictly formal level it is difficult to account for the darkness surrounding the doorways in the film. The shots even violate realist lighting assumptions. Since it is broad daylight outside, Martha, for example, would not be in total darkness inside at the beginning of the film. The same is true of the Jorgenson home at the film's conclusion. Only the dark mouths of the caves seem lit within the codes of Hollywood realism. The lighting, however, unites all these spaces with womblike connotations.

The womb imagery in *The Searchers* also relates to the function of rape in the film. Several literal rapes occur or are implied: Scar presumably rapes Martha before killing her, and Indian "bucks" presumably rape Lucy before killing (or abandoning) her. At a more symbolic level Ethan's "entry" into his brother's house is a similar violation paralleling Scar's literal forced entry, rape, and murder of Martha. Rape also holds a particular dread for the white men in the film. Again, at the most explicit level Ethan's mania is fueled by the knowledge that after being kidnapped, Debbie would have been subjected to sex with Indians. Brad, upon hearing that Lucy had been raped before being killed, loses all control and rushes wildly to his death. Although distraught by the news of her death, his awareness that she was first raped is too much for him. The film thus literally and symbolically plays out the male's entry and departure from the female space as at times being a violent rape. The entire narrative is set in motion by Scar's literal penetration of the womblike space and his rape of Martha.

This then is a film about men who actively move between and into womblike spaces, at times forcing their way in. (At the end of the film, Ethan actually rides his horse into Scar's teepee in a powerful, animalistic image of spatial violation and penetration.) If the women within such an Oedipal narrative structure are relegated to peripheral positions in general, it is instructive to analyze the specific positioning of Look within this film. To do so, however, we must also turn our attention to racial issues.

The Searchers deals centrally with racism, and its main character is a racist. This does not mean, however, that the film should be simply characterized as racist. Much of the film critiques racism, and this is accomplished in part through a structure of narrative counterpoint. Ethan's racism manifests itself throughout the film. He is contemptuous of Marty's Indian-like appearance and obsessed with the fact that Debbie has had sex with Indians, something which in his view disqualifies her as being white and a blood kin. It is for the latter reason that he develops the obsessive need to kill her. As we have seen, however, the film explains this behavior as pathological; Ethan displaces onto Scar the threat that he himself poses to the family.

In addition, Ethan's bizarre behavior is continually counterpointed by other characters. The Jorgensons, for example, lovingly accept Marty into their home and have no problem with either his appearance or his racial composition. Reverend Clayton comments on Ethan's brutal, seemingly senseless gesture of shooting the eyes out of an Indian corpse. Most significantly, Marty supplies a rational foil to Ethan's lunatic ravings throughout the film. He explicitly notes Ethan's "crazy" behavior and announces his intention to be present to stop him from carrying out his goals. Since Marty is a sympathetic, attractive character he becomes a point of identification for the audience. Furthermore, Ethan's behavior is linked to Mose's overt lunacy; both are "crazy" homeless wanderers who seek a place within the community and, paradoxically, both are marked by and possess knowledge of Indian culture.

The way in which the plot orders the story events also contributes to a critique of racism. It may initially seem that the Indians in this film are represented as cliché savages, but we later learn that Scar's behavior is motivated by his personal losses to the whites; far from simply being barbaric, he has been treated barbarically by whites. The previously described sequence of the cavalry's introduction into the film makes this graphically clear; we see the ruins of their destruction of an entire Indian village.

Despite all these critiques of racism, the fact remains that the film contains disturbing moments of racism. In the letter reading scene discussed above, Laurie's anger at Marty for getting married is heightened when she learns he has married a "squaw," as if that made the insult greater. Nothing in the film distances the audience from her response. Similarly, near the end of the film Scar throws a stone at a barking dog and we hear an off-screen whine when it hits the target. The moment serves no purpose other than to characterize Scar as a villain who brutally tortures pets. These isolated moments of racism, however, are compounded by the fact that the film's racist protagonist is powerfully and charismatically played by John Wayne. The star system is important here since Wayne was an immensely popular actor at the time as well as the one most associated with the western hero. This combined with his place in the narrative structure makes him a strong point of emotional identification for the audience; even as we may distance ourselves from his crazed racism, we are drawn toward him. Ethan, however, is not just the hero of a patriarchal narrative; he is the hero of a *white* patriarchal narrative. The full impact of this can be seen in the scenes with Look.

Look gets her name because Marty speaks to her by saying such things as "Aw, look," and "Hey, look." Once, desperately trying to communicate with her, he repeats, "Aw, look." She responds in her native language, and Ethan, overhearing the exchange, translates for Marty, "She says her name is Wild Goose Flying in the Night Sky, but she'll answer to 'Luke' if that pleases you." Ethan pronounces the name as that commonly spelled L-u-k-e, but that is his pronunciation; it is not what Marty calls her.

In a film that deals with epistemological questions relating to language and perception, this is of obvious importance. Direct visual perception is contrasted with mediated accounts of events—what the eye sees is contrasted with what one hears or reads about—and the phonetic alphabet is contrasted with other kinds of signs such as an arrow shape constructed on the ground out of rocks. Look's place in the film is thematized in this and other ways. In a scene that comments on intercultural knowledge, Marty acquires her in a trade without awareness of what he is doing. But what interests me here is something other than this thematization of Look's place in the film; it is the specific way in which she is spatially represented in the scene where Marty kicks her down the hill.

The moment in question comes in the scene where Look acquires her name. The scene begins with an unusually long-held establishing shot (fig. 20–4) during which the characters talk. The length of the shot gives us a very clear understanding of the space within the scene: Ethan sits by the campfire drinking a cup of coffee in the lower left part of the frame, and Marty and Look stand talking to him; in the upper right rear of the frame we see sleeping bags on top of a hill. Marty, despairing of being able to make Look understand what has happened, goes off to sleep on the top of the hill, and she follows and lies down next to him. In a two-shot we see Marty sit up and kick her down the hill. She rolls out of the frame, and Ford cuts to a shot of Ethan laughing heartily at the spectacle. Suddenly Marty runs up to Ethan and exchanges words with him. Each time that I have seen the film, there is wild laughter when Marty kicks Look. In fact, the laughter is always so uproarious that it drowns out the ensuing dialogue between Marty and Ethan.

Figure 20-4.

One might be tempted to write the laughter off to audience insensitivity since the moment is so brutal, but throughout the film and in this particular scene Look is treated as a comic character. The part is cast with a woman (Beulah Archuletta) whose body type and face are, within the codes of the star system, meant to suggest an undesirable, silly chubbiness. The character has her own musical theme on the sound track that is lighthearted and comic. All of these things position the audience to respond lightly to Look; she is part of a comic subplot in the film.

The subplot has a formally complex place within the film since it supplies a variation on Ethan's search that is motivated by his racist fear of miscegenation between a white woman and an Indian man. Yet when faced with the sexual reversal of an Indian woman with a white man (Marty, technically one-eighth Cherokee, is fully a member of white society), Ethan finds the whole thing funny. He makes no connection between the two and sees no contradiction. He laughs when he first realizes that Marty has married Look. Thus the apparent motivation of the cut to him after Marty kicks her is that everything to do with Look is nothing but a joke to Ethan. The scene is also part of a larger formal context that contrasts courtship rituals between cultures: while Laurie reads about the event we see the ludicrous spectacle of Charlie McCorry's courtship of her. Suddenly the Indian custom whereby Marty ended up with Look doesn't seem so strange.

It is not, however, at the level of narrative or formal thematic relationships that the disturbing problem in the scene lies; rather it is in the way Ford spatially and temporally structures it. He shoots and edits the scene in such a way that we never see the consequences of Look being kicked down the hill.

This is accomplished by a slight spatio-temporal discontinuity at the heart of the moment.

The conventional way of structuring the scene would be to follow the action. Thus, for example, there could be a reverse shot showing Look roll down the hill, or a pan shot could follow her movement. This, in fact, is precisely what happens in a later moment in the film that rhymes with this one. After returning home during the search, Marty is having breakfast with Laurie. When he makes clear his plans to leave again with Ethan to continue the search, she becomes angry at his insensitivity to her needs and accidentally pushes him over. We see the action in a two-shot, and the camera pans with Marty's movement. Although he sits embarrassedly, we see immediately that he has not been hurt. Furthermore, Laurie has not viciously planned to knock Marty over, and even though angry with him she clearly cares about him after having done it. But when Marty kicks Look, she does not get the same kind of spatial attention that Marty does, since instead of showing a reverse shot or panning with the action, Ford follows another convention—the cut to a reaction shot. He never returns, however, to the action involving Look.

The shot sequence is as follows. In a frontal view long shot (fig. 20–5) we see Marty kick Look down the hill and she rolls out of the frame (fig. 20–6). Cut to a frontal view medium shot (fig. 20–7) of Ethan laughing and then cut back to the previous shot (fig. 20–8) with Marty getting up and rushing out of the frame. Cut, just as Marty exits the frame, to a long shot side view of Ethan as Marty enters frame right (fig. 20–9). Thus, once Look rolls out of the frame in the first shot of this sequence, we don't see her again until the action of the fall is completed.

But what has happened to Look? Where is she? How can Marty cross over to Ethan in such a way that we don't even glimpse her in the background of the frame? The problem is that she lies between the two men, and the establishing shot that begins the scene has made this clear. The answer to these questions lies with figures 20–8 and 20–9.

The cut in figure 20–8 occurs precisely as Marty exits the frame in a diagonal movement from the lower left-hand corner, and figure 20–9 begins with him almost immediately entering the frame at the right center. But something is wrong—a moment in space and time is missing, and it's not just the innocent Hollywood elision of insignificant moments. Marty reaches Ethan too quickly considering the space to be crossed. The cut between figures 20–8 and 20–9 suggests a continuity that is not there. The reason that Marty arrives too quickly is that there is a bit of space that he doesn't cross—precisely that space where Look lies. Not only doesn't Ford follow Look's

Figure 20-5.

Figure 20-6.

Figure 20-7.

Figure 20-8.

Figure 20-9.

Figure 20-10.

movement in the fall, he can't even allow a glimpse of it in the rear of the frame.

After Marty and Ethan talk, Ethan gets concerned that Look has overheard them and walks out frame right, followed by Marty. Ford cuts to an empty frame (only a bit of Look's head is barely visible in the lower right-hand corner), which Ethan and Marty then enter. They reach down and pull Look up into the frame (fig. 20–10). This odd shot poses yet another spatial problem. We last saw Look rolling rapidly out of a long shot. Given the establishing shot of the scene, we have some idea of where she would be, but she is nowhere near there. In fact, she is close to where she was when we last saw her roll out of figure 20–6. And why the empty space for a moment at the beginning of this shot? Ford doesn't want us to see Look lying on the ground, so she suddenly reappears and the narrative continues.

To complete an analysis of this scene, we must pay careful attention to the scene in which Ethan and Marty discover the attacked Indian village. Ethan enters a teepee and looks intensely off-screen. He calls for Marty, and then Ford cuts to a shot of Look lying dead on the ground (fig. 20–11). Ethan approaches her body, kneels down, and reverently covers her with a blanket.

Figure 20-11.

When I first wrote about this scene, I concluded that in a profound sense this is the missing reverse shot, displaced into another scene, for here Look is taken seriously and we are allowed to see her (Lehman 1981, 67–68). It now seems to me that although this is true, there is yet another displacement operative in the shot. At the beginning of the film, when Ethan discovers Martha's body, he refuses to let Marty go in and see it. Later Ethan tells Brad that when he found Lucy's body, he covered it with his own coat. We do not see either Martha's or Lucy's bodies, though these are white women with whom Ethan has strong emotional bonds, but here we see him with an Indian woman for whom, until this moment, he has shown no genuine feeling.

How may we account for what has happened to Look in this film? As we have seen, *The Searchers* deals with a number of highly charged sexual and racial themes such as incest and miscegenation. It is important here to remember that America in 1956 was fraught with serious racial tension between whites and blacks. Furthermore, these tensions were highly sexualized and included the stereotype of the well-endowed black stud and the dread of mixed couples, particularly black men and white women. American Indians were neither highly visible to nor feared by the average white American in 1956. The conventions of the western allowed Ford to displace present-day racial tensions into the past and onto another race. He handles these subjects with surprising maturity and formal complexity throughout the film with a major exception in his treatment of Look.[4]

It is as if for one moment the "great artist" has to behave like a schoolboy, as if the almost unbearable tensions raised by the subjects of incest, racism, and miscegenation need an outlet. Ford's momentarily vicious and brutal treatment of Look is that outlet. He, more than Marty, needs to kick Look down the hill, and he, more than Ethan, needs to laugh at it. Then, by not looking, he does not acknowledge what he has done. Indeed, if we saw what happened to Look after she is kicked, it would be difficult for an audience to respond to the moment as comic. Finally, in an attempt to recuperate and reinscribe Look into the film with some dignity, we see her body found and covered and thus linked with Lucy's and Martha's bodies.

The subplot involving Look begins when Marty unknowingly acquires her in a trade, and it relates to ways in which the film represents economic value and exchange. Marty even mentions in his letter that Laurie would be

4. Ford did in fact make a western, *Sergeant Rutledge* (1960), about a black man accused of raping a white woman. It is interesting to note that to this day the film is seldom televised, presumably due to its touchy subject matter.

surprised by the things the Indians most value. We then see him holding up blue ribbons with the word "lard" written on them. Even though in this trade the ribbons are rejected, in a sense neither the Indians who value worthless trinkets nor Marty know what they are trading for. As with almost everything else in this formally complex film, Marty's trade has an echo later in the film when he and Ethan visit Futterman, the trader. Ethan goes with the explicit intention of gathering information about Debbie's whereabouts and ends up trading for it. Futterman drives a hard bargain and forces Ethan to give him gold as reimbursement for his trouble, expenses, and time in sending him a letter with the information he has come upon. After that is completed, Futterman tries to get Ethan to stay the night so that he can spend some more of his money. He offers cards and a jug and seems about to mention women when Ethan brusquely cuts him off and leaves. As Ethan leaves, Futtermen greedily reminds him, "Don't forget my $1,000." When Futterman follows Ethan and Marty and attempts to rob them, he and his men are killed in the scene previously discussed.

When Ethan pays Futterman for his information with gold coins, it is, of course, not the first or the last time that we will see and hear about Ethan's money. The first night after Ethan returns home he sits in a rocking chair in front of the fireplace, talking with his brother. For one brief moment Ethan occupies the position Mose always longs for. When Aaron expresses his puzzlement at Ethan's past behavior of staying on at their home long past any reason, Ethan gets out of the chair, says, "I expect to pay my way," and throws his brother a bag of money. Aaron examines the money and is further puzzled by the fact that it is newly minted. The coins reappear in two other scenes. After Ethan kills Futterman he takes back the coins he paid the trader for the information. Finally, he flips one of the coins in front of Clayton before being told that he is under arrest for the murder and robbery of Futterman.

In all of these scenes money is suspect and treacherous. The origin of Ethan's money remains a mystery, and it also implicates him in bank robbery. The music turns ominous when Aaron discovers the money to be freshly minted, and later Clayton mentions that Ethan may fit descriptions on wanted posters. Ironically, the money implicates Ethan in guilt once again when it appears to be the motive for Futterman's murder. If money cannot be trusted, it is not surprising that neither can the trader. Futterman is represented as being a totally undesirable type; he looks sleazy and behaves vulgarly (his letter mentions that Ethan should bring the "reward," and he greedily grabs the money that he extracts from Ethan) even before we learn that he plans to murder Ethan and Marty in order to rob them.

If money and trading circulate throughout the film as mysterious and treacherous, land owning and homesteading appear nearly opposite. In his analysis of Balzac's *Sarrazine*, Roland Barthes distinguishes between money-based capitalism (a "sign") and a feudal system centered on land-ownership (an "index") (1974, 39–40). Since money is of unknown origin it is suspicious, and it upsets the orderly patriarchal control of land in which property is passed on from generation to generation. Not only do we know where such wealth comes from, but also the mark of the wealth and its actual value are closely linked through the indexical relationship of the two. A hundred acres with cattle and crops, for example, don't just arbitrarily indicate wealth but produce the food we eat. Money, on the other hand, is an empty signifier of wealth. In and of itself it is worth little or nothing; its worth comes from representing exchange value. Not only, in other words, do we not know where it comes from, but it is in some sense false and valueless. This distinction is helpful in understanding the representation of capitalism in *The Searchers*.

The film valorizes ownership of the land and its attendant family lifestyle. It is no coincidence that Futterman is unmarried. The Jorgensons are the family par excellence, even extending themselves to include Marty. When Ethan and Marty return home after Brad has been killed (and Ethan again momentarily occupies a rocking chair), the conversation turns to the land. Lars, Brad's father, blames "this country" for his son's death, but Mrs. Jorgenson says the country is not evil. She sees their circumstances as part of a developing historical process: "Now, Lars, we just happen to be Texicans. Texican is nothing but a human *man* way out on a limb, this year and next, maybe for a hundred more, but I don't think it'll be forever. Someday this country's going to be a fine, good place to be. Maybe it needs our bones in the ground before that time can come" (my emphasis). Even the image of their bones in the ground binds them to the land.

We see two families in detail in *The Searchers*; both are idealized. Each is comprised of loving, hard-working parents and obedient children. The decency of these family members stands in stark contrast to Futterman's greedy, shady, and ultimately depraved behavior. Ownership of the land for the purpose of farming is thus associated with virtue and family values, and trading and money with greedy individualism and immorality.

Homesteading the land is of course also associated with danger as we see at the beginning of the film when the Edwards family is destroyed in an Indian attack. But this is danger of a different kind from that which comes with the circulation of money. The dangers associated with the land do not corrupt; they strengthen and ennoble the spirit and bind people together within a community. For urban Americans living in a money-based economy in 1956 such a land/money opposition creates a nostalgic longing for a mythic western past.

Not surprisingly, money and traders are represented in other Ford films in related ways. In *Fort Apache* (1947) a trader named Mecham lives alone and, in an image that links him to animals, in a structure built into the ground. He is totally unscrupulous in his dealings with Indians: his scales are rigged, and he sells them illegal rot-gut whiskey. In *She Wore a Yellow Ribbon* (1949) the fort sutler is a gunrunner who sells rifles to the Indians. In both of these films the trader is contrasted not with homesteading families but with the cavalry. The opposition, however, functions similarly since the cavalry is itself a sort of idealized family. In *Young Mister Lincoln* (1939) the situation is slightly more complex. Lincoln himself is a storeowner at the beginning of the film, but he is marked immediately as an inept businessman since he is willing to give goods on credit to total strangers, telling them that this is his common practice for dealing with his other customers. When they are unwilling to accept that, he trades with them. His trade, however, is not motivated by his desire for profit. He seems to function as a businessman without touching money. When he becomes a lawyer, he settles his first case by minimizing his fee as a way of resolving a lawsuit. When one of his clients pays him, he picks up the coin and bites it, and when he suspects it is counterfeit a disturbing powerful look comes over his face. The main plot of the film deals with Lincoln offering his services to a homesteading family who cannot afford to pay for it. He is a noble figure untainted by and suspicious of money.

I mention these other films not to make a case for yet another auteurist theme in Ford's work. The films are, rather, symptomatic of a deeply troubling ideology of money. All of them, including *The Searchers*, want to simultaneously affirm fundamental American values (cavalry life, the Lincoln myth, the family homestead) and yet repress and disavow the central economic fact of American capitalism (both then and now)—money, profit, and trading.

Ethan is an outsider in more ways than one; in a sense, he doesn't pose just a sexual threat to the family but also an economic one. The money of mysterious origin that he brings with him strikes the same discordant note within the Edwards home as does his tense exchange of glances with Martha. His coins are as out of place as his desires for Martha, and indeed he uses the former to seemingly buy the latter when he throws his money to Aaron as payment for staying around too long. In some ways Ethan even resembles the despicable Futterman. Like the trader he is not tied to land or family but rather to money and crime. Like his coins circulating through society, he wanders endlessly through the desert. Both are mysterious and enigmatic; where they came from and where they are going are unknowable. One thing is certain—they can never come to rest like the families that occupy the land.

WORKS CITED

Barthes, Roland. 1974. *S/Z*. Translated by Richard Miller. New York: Hill and Wang.

De Lauretis, Teresa. 1984. *Alice Doesn't: Feminism, Semiotics, Cinema*. Bloomington: Indiana University Press.

Lehman, Peter. 1978a. "An Absence Which Becomes a Legendary Presence: John Ford's Structured Use of Off-Screen Space." *Wide Angle* 2, no. 4: 36–42.

———. *John Ford and the Auteur Theory*. 1978b. Ph.D. dissertation, University of Wisconsin, Madison.

———. 1978c. "Script/Performance/Text: Performance Theory and Auteur Theory." *Film Reader* 3: 197–206.

———. 1981. "Looking at Look's Missing Reverse Shot: Psychoanalysis and Style in John Ford's *The Searchers*." *Wide Angle* 4, no. 4: 65–70.

Luhr, William, and Peter Lehman. 1977. *Authorship and Narrative in the Cinema: Issues in Contemporary Aesthetics and Criticism*. New York: G. P. Putnam's Sons.

Macgowan, Kenneth. *Behind the Screen*. 1965. New York: Delta.

McBride, Joseph, and Michael Wilmington. 1975. *John Ford*. New York: Da Capo Press.

Metz, Christian. 1973. "Current Problems of Film Theory." Translated by Diana Matias. *Screen* 14, no. 1–2: 40–87.

BIBLIOGRAPHY

Baxter, John. *The Cinema of John Ford*. New York: A. S. Barnes & Co., 1971.

Henderson, Brian. "*The Searchers*: An American Dilemma." In *Movies and Methods*, vol. 2, edited by Bill Nichols, 429–49. Berkeley: University of California Press, 1985.

Place, J. A. *The Western Films of John Ford*. Secaucus: Citadel Press, 1974.

Sarris, Andrew. *The John Ford Movie Mystery*. Bloomington: Indiana University Press, 1975.

"*The Searchers*: Materials and Approaches." *Screen Education*, 17 (Winter 1975–76).

INDEX